THE FLAME
OF FREEDOM

KU-592-334

THE FLAME OF FREEDOM

THE GREEK WAR OF INDEPENDENCE
1821–1833

David Brewer

Rise like Lions after slumber
In unvanquishable number –
Shake your chains to earth like dew
Which in sleep have fallen on you.
    Shelley, *The Mask of Anarchy*

JOHN MURRAY
Albemarle Street, London

LYIT
LIBRARY
40023044
LETTERKENNY

© David Brewer 2001

First published in 2001
by John Murray (Publishers) Ltd,
50 Albemarle Street, London W1S 4BD

The moral right of the author has been asserted

All rights reserved. No part of this publication may be reproduced in any material
form (including photocopying or storing it in any medium by electronic means and
whether or not transiently or incidentally to some other use of this publication)
without the written permission of the copyright owner, except in accordance with
the provisions of the Copyright, Designs and Patents Act 1988 or under the terms of
a licence issued by the Copyright Licensing Agency, 90 Tottenham Court Road,
London W1P 9HE. Applications for the copyright owner's written permission to
reproduce any part of this publication should be addressed to the publisher.

A catalogue record for this book is available from the British Library

ISBN 0-7195-5447-0

Typeset in Adobe Garamond by Servis Filmsetting Ltd
Printed and bound in Great Britain by St Edmundsbury Press Ltd
Bury St Edmunds, Suffolk

For Elisabeth

Contents

Contents

Illustrations

(between pages 172 and 173)

ix

23. Iánnis Kapodhístrias, by Am. Bouvier
24. The assassination of Kapodhístrias, by Dhionísios Tsókos

The author and publisher would like to thank the following for permission to reproduce illustrations: Plate 1, © Rouen, Musée des Beaux-Arts, photograph Didier Tragin/Catherine Lancien; 2 and 6, National Historical Museum, Athens; 3, 7 and 21, Gennadius Library, American School of Classical Studies, Athens; 4, 9 above left, above right, 10, 11, 14, 15 and 23, John Murray Archive; 12, Musée du Louvre, Paris; 16, National Portrait Gallery, London; 18, © Musée des Beaux-Arts, Bordeaux, photograph Lysiane Gauthier; 20, Mesolongi Museum; 22, Private Collection; and 24, Benaki Museum, Athens.

Acknowledgements

My sincere thanks, not just formal ones, to my agent Bruce Hunter of David Higham Associates, who backed this book from his first sight of the text; to all at John Murray and especially my editor Grant McIntyre, whose perceptive advice gave this book its shape; and to my daughter Sophie and my nephew Nick McDowell who pointed the way through the, to me, uncharted seas of publishing to such congenial havens.

The book has been greatly improved by the meticulous and thoughtful copy-editing of Peter James. Any remaining errors are, of course, my responsibility.

My thanks also to the unfailingly helpful staff of a number of libraries and museums: in London, the British Library, King's College Library and the London Library; in Athens, the Gennadios Library and the National Historical Museum; and elsewhere in Greece the Koraís library in Chios, the Mesolongi museum, the Navplion public library, the René Puaux gallery and library in Pílos, and the Centre for Hellenic Studies in Thessalonika. Quotations from Richard Clogg, ed., *The Movement for Greek Independence 1770–1821*, Macmillan, 1976, are reproduced with permission of Palgrave.

Many people have read part or all of the text and their comments have been most valuable. Thank you to Geoffrey Chandler, Irene Chapman, Penry Evans, Anne Fleming, Olga Hill, John Laughland, Geoffrey Lewis, Ethel Martin, Christopher and Sue McDowell, Diana Owen, Michael Ward and Bill White. I am particularly indebted to two friends who have read the whole text: to Nikos Kokantzis, not least for pointing out ways in which I may unwittingly have offended Greek susceptibilities, and to Jerry Schneewind for his unerring advice on accuracy, clarity and proper presentation of the wider picture. Special thanks also to James and Poppet Codrington for access to and guidance through the Codrington papers, and their hospitality while I studied this rich archive.

A writer's family is always part of the making of a book, and my own family has been involved in the fortunes of this one for a long time. Thank you to my daughters, who have given it their interest and backing for as long as they can remember, and to my stepchildren who have joined that chorus of generous encouragement. My biggest thank-you goes to my wife Elisabeth. Her patience and persistence in turning jumbled manuscript into a presentable text, and her forthright comments on it, were invaluable. But her greatest contribution was her love and support throughout the pains and pleasures of the book's emergence from the chrysalis of an idea to fly off fully formed into the sunlight. It is her book too, and I am delighted to dedicate it to her.

A Note on Pronunciation

The large number of Greek names which inevitably appear in this story can be an irritant or even a barrier to a reader who is not sure how to pronounce them. Stress often falls in unexpected places, so has been marked, but pronunciation of Greek is relatively straightforward because unlike in English each letter or combination of letters is always pronounced the same. In the transliteration of Greek used here, the vowel sounds are:

a   as in basket
e   as in bed
i   as the first i in blini
o   as in box – even at the end of a word
ou   as in boot

The only unusual consonant sounds are:

ch   as in loch
dh   a soft th as in then – but
th   a hard th as in thin

Anglicised versions have been used for the better-known place names – Athens, Corinth, Hydra (not Ídhra) – and personal names – Alexander and, a bit of a hybrid, Georgios rather than Yeóryios or George. Odysseus, always a problem for the transliterator, has not been changed to the strange-looking Ódhissefs but left in its familiar form.

All translations are by the author unless otherwise attributed.

A Note on Currencies and Prices

Throughout the 1820s the major currencies were fairly stable against each other. The pound sterling was worth about 5 dollars (American or Spanish), 25 francs and just over 100 Russian roubles.

The Turkish piastre however, which was also the Greek currency, was in sharp decline during this period. A few years before 1821 there were 20 piastres to the pound, in 1824 when Byron was in Greece the rate was 50/£, and by 1832 it had fallen to 86½. So the piastre had lost three-quarters of its international value in a couple of decades.

What would currencies of that time be worth today? Precision is impossible, not least because relative prices have changed. For example, in Greece at that time housing was cheap and transport expensive: you could rent a good house for a year for the price of three horses. Also labour was cheap and livestock expensive: a turkey would cost a labourer four days' wages. However, it is safe to say that the pound sterling in Greece then – a strong currency in an impoverished country – had the buying power of at least £100 today.

Maps

(*drawn by Martin Collins*)

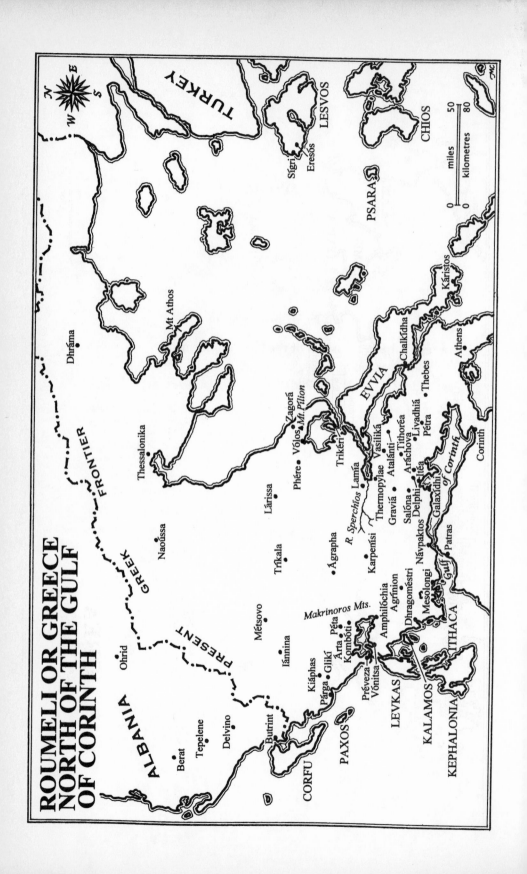

ROUMELI OR GREECE
NORTH OF THE GULF
OF CORINTH

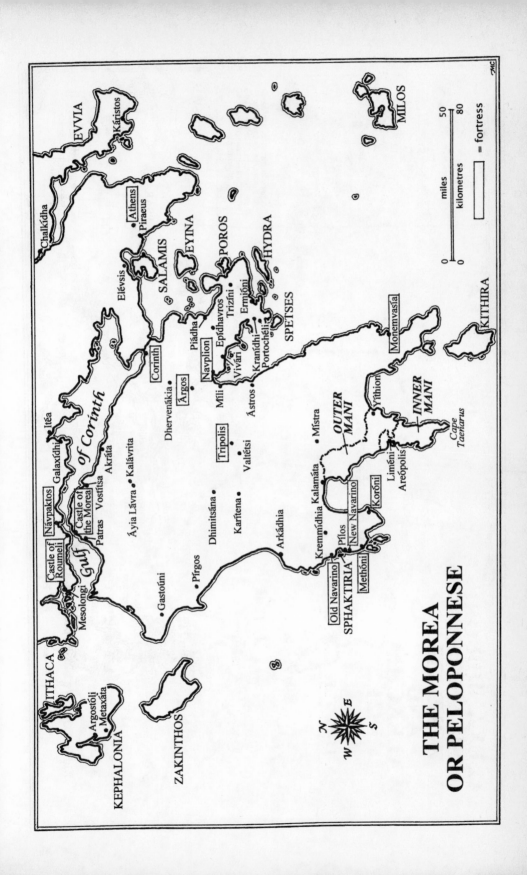

THE MOREA
OR PELOPONNESE

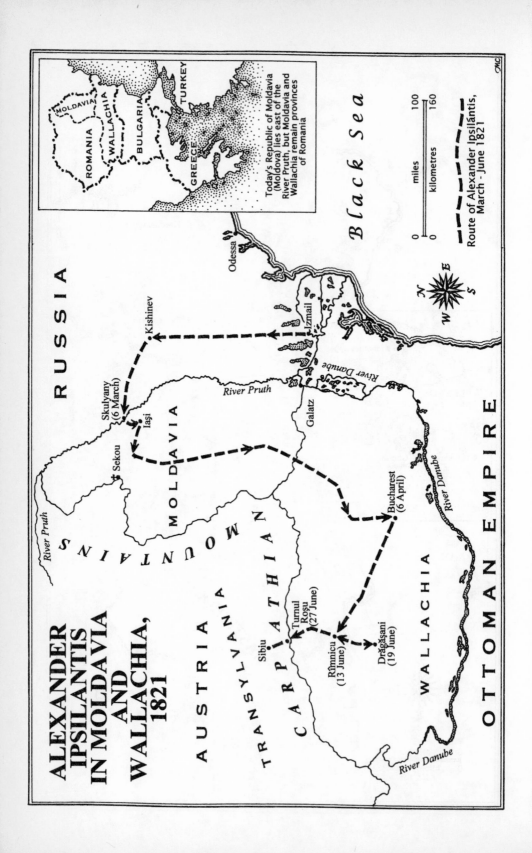

ALEXANDER IPSILANTIS IN MOLDAVIA AND WALLACHIA, 1821

RUSSIA

Black Sea

Odessa

Kishinev

Skulyany
(6 March)

Iași

Sekou

River Pruth

MOLDAVIA

River Pruth

Izmail

River Danube

Galatz

MOUNTAINS

CARPATHIAN

AUSTRIA

TRANSYLVANIA

Sibiu

Turnul
Roşu
(27 June)

Rîmnicu
(13 June)

Drăgăşani
(19 June)

Bucharest
(6 April)

River Danube

WALLACHIA

River Danube

OTTOMAN EMPIRE

Today's Republic of Moldavia
(Moldova) lies east of the
River Pruth, but Moldavia and
Wallachia remain provinces
of Romania

MOLDAVIA

ROMANIA

WALLACHIA

BULGARIA

GREECE

TURKEY

miles   100
kilometres   160

0
0

Route of Alexander Ipsilāntis,
March – June 1821

N
E
W
S

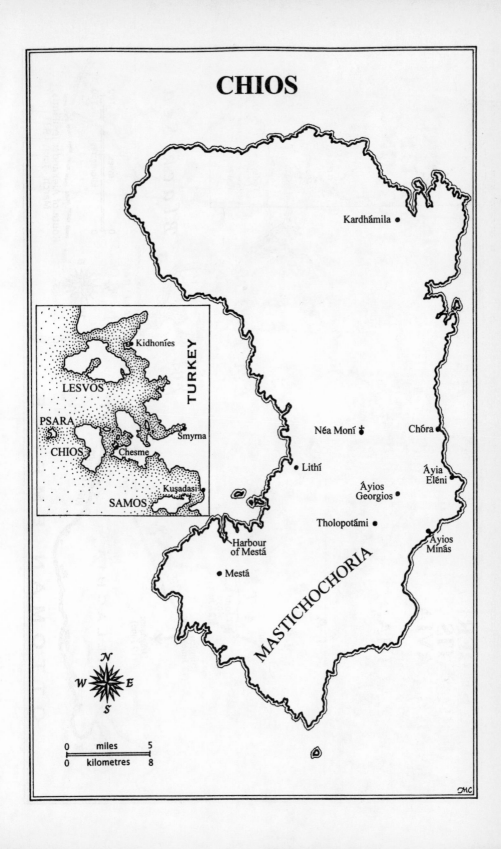

CHIOS

Kardhámila •

Kidhoníes •

TURKEY

LESVOS

PSARA

Smyrna

CHIOS   Chesme

Kuşadasi •

SAMOS

Néa Moní ⚓   Chóra •

Lithí •   Áyia
Eléni •

Áyios
Georgios •

Tholopotámi •

Áyios
Mínás •

Harbour
of Mestá

MASTICHOCHORIA

• Mestá

N
W   E
S

0   miles   5
0   kilometres   8

JMC

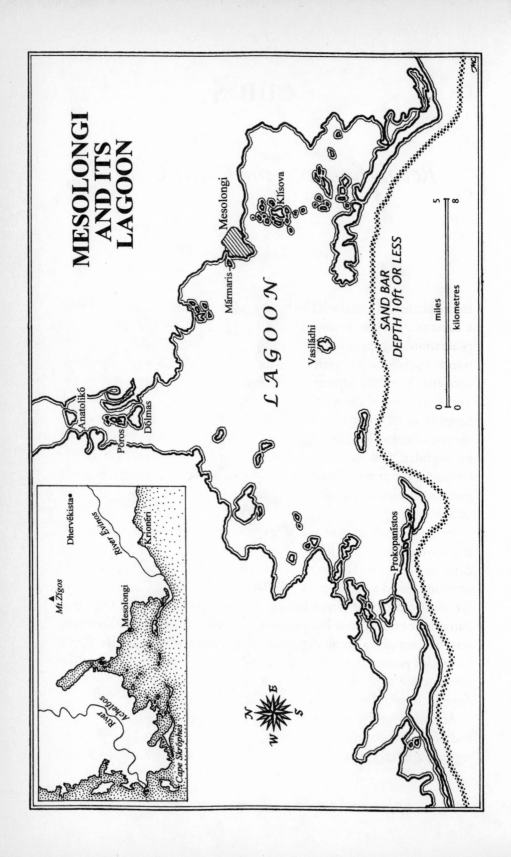

MESOLONGI AND ITS LAGOON

Mesolongi

Mármaris

Klísova

Vasiládhi

L A G O O N

Anatolikó

Póros

Dólmas

Prokopanístos

SAND BAR
DEPTH 10ft OR LESS

miles
0   5
kilometres
0   8

Mt. Zígos

Dhervékista●

River Évinos

Mesolongi

Krionéri

River Achelóös

Cape Skróphes

N
W — E
S

I

Revolution and the Great Church

In the history of a nation's hour of triumph a myth is often embedded, a romantic story of heroic action or noble gesture which passes from generation to generation even though nobody really believes it. The Greeks cherish such a myth about the outbreak of their war to win independence from the Ottoman empire. This empire, dominated by the Turks, was one of the most impressive that the world has ever seen. It lasted from its foundation by Osman I in the fourteenth century until the end of the 1914–18 war. At its greatest extent it stretched from Algiers to Baghdad and from Cairo to Budapest. From the time of the Ottoman capture of Constantinople in 1453 Greece became a small, poor and backward part of this great empire, and remained so for nearly 400 years.

In the early months of 1821 Greece showed all the signs of impending revolution against her Turkish rulers. Plans for it were debated, dates for its outbreak were discussed, and widespread purchase of weapons led to a shortage of powder and shot in the bazaars. One of the most prominent Greek leaders was Georgios Yermanós, bishop of Patras in the north-west Peloponnese for the last fifteen years. Yermanós was not simply a local dignitary. A personal friend of the Greek Orthodox patriarch, his reputation and influence extended beyond the Peloponnese to the rest of mainland Greece and to the islands of the Aegean. It is on Bishop Yermanós that the myth centres.

According to the story Yermanós was summoned from Patras at the end of March 1821 to Tripolis in the central Peloponnese for one of the regular meetings of Greek leaders with the Turkish authorities. His route took him to Kalávrita, high in the hills above the Gulf of Corinth, and there he declared that he would go no further. After spending a night in prayer at a convent, he proceeded on 25 March to the nearby monastery of Áyia Lávra, where 1,500 armed peasants were assembled. He promised them a miracle: that when the Turks came to seize him, the Greeks needed only to shout the Old Testament slogan 'Thine, O Lord, is the victory.' So it turned out: when sixty Turkish cavalry appeared, the united roar echoed from the surrounding mountains and the Turks scattered and fled pell-mell back to Kalávrita.

As the story continues, a Te Deum was sung, and Yermanós, now regarded as a supernatural being, celebrated mass, and then addressed the assembled throng. There will be no help, he said, from the Christian powers. What benefit, he asked the military leader and former mercenary Kolokotrónis, did you ever get for shedding your blood under the Russian flag? France, always the friend of the Greeks, could provide only distant and indirect help. As for Britain, the governor of the British-held Ionian islands and the English consuls in Greece were so hostile that one could count them as on the Turkish side.

Nevertheless, Yermanós went on, we can no longer remain subjects of the Sultan, and he pointed out that the die was now cast. The whole of Greece was compromised by action already taken against the Turks, which he described as 'a spark which will produce a general conflagration'. The attempted revolution now in progress among the weak-spirited people of Moldavia and Wallachia would fail, but both that venture and the rebellion in Iánnina of Ali Pasha, the 'criminal', would helpfully divert Turkish forces. He claimed for Greece the islands of the Aegean, and districts and cities as far north as Ali Pasha's domain, a boundary not in fact achieved until nearly a century later. The supreme principle of our policy, he said, must be to conquer or to die, and he concluded: 'I will go back into the Lord's house and will repeat to you from the pulpit of truth what I have told you today: that our whole history, and our whole future, are enshrined in the words religion, freedom and fatherland.'

His speech ended, Yermanós allocated tasks to each leader, and with other priests received confessions. Then he mounted a knoll and gave a general absolution to the crowd, which had now grown to 5,000, the same number as those to whom Christ preached in the desert. After distributing to each, by his own hand, the consecrated bread, he released the faithful from their Lenten fast, publicly doing so himself and declaring that, since the life and religion of all were under threat, they must have strength to defend the people and the altar.[1]

So ends the legend-creating account. The Greek revolution did in fact begin in the spring of 1821, but this whole incident was pure invention. Neither Yermanós nor Kolokotrónis, whom he is supposed to have addressed, were at Áyia Lávra on 25 March, Kolokotrónis being miles away in the southern Peloponnese. Contemporary historians, Greek and foreign, dismissed the episode as only assumed to be historical or as simply false. The story comes from the pen of François Pouqueville, French consul in Greece and author of a four-volume history of the Greek rising rushed out in 1824. Pouqueville is not to be trusted. He invents incidents, and plucks convenient facts and figures from the air. He does so either to enhance a story or to express his animus against any country but his own, as he did in Yermanós' supposed references to Russia and Britain and in his own calumnies against some of his fellow consuls. If Chauvin had not given his name to bellicose and exaggerated nationalism, Pouqueville might have done so.

Nevertheless Áyia Lávra has become for Greeks the defining venue for the outbreak of their revolution, and 25 March is still a day of national celebration. The appeal of Pouqueville's story is that it links the Greeks' revolution in every possible way to the Bible, to religious faith and to the Orthodox church: the setting at a monastery, the Biblical slogan which scattered the Turkish cavalry, the gathering of a Biblical 5,000, the date which coincided with the religious Feast of the Annunciation, the emphasis on religion ahead even of freedom and fatherland. In this the myth reflects reality. The church had indeed been the main preserver of Greek national identity throughout nearly 400 years of Turkish rule.

As Sultan Mehmed II launched his Ottoman forces in a final attack on Byzantium's capital Constantinople in the early hours of Tuesday 29 May 1453 it was the churches whose bells rang the alarm throughout the city, and whose buildings were sought as asylum by the terrified inhabitants. Constantinople fell that day. Churches were pillaged, and the refugees still sheltering there either slaughtered or led away for ransom

3

or to slavery. In the late afternoon of that cataclysmic Tuesday the Sultan entered Áyia Sophía, the greatest church in the city and indeed in the whole of Byzantium. From the pulpit a Muslim cleric proclaimed that there was no God but Allah, and the Sultan himself mounted the altar slab and made obeisance to the God of his faith.

The triumph of the Ottomans might have been expected to mark the end of the Greek Orthodox church, but this did not happen. Many of the churches of Constantinople were saved from destruction on the grounds, sometimes rather artificial, that they had surrendered rather than been captured. The Sultan, still only 21, had Greek blood, a beloved Greek stepmother and a profound admiration for the Byzantine achievement. He was therefore sympathetic to his new Greek subjects, and his policy towards them was from the beginning pragmatic rather than destructive. The Greeks were to form a separate community within the Ottoman empire, subject to its laws and taxes but otherwise largely self-governing. The ultimate responsibility for their good behaviour was to lie with the patriarch of the Orthodox church who would, as in Byzantine times, reside in the city which was now named Istanbul, though for the Greeks it would always remain Constantinople.

The office of patriarch was at that moment vacant, and the Sultan could make his own choice. This fell on the eminent and widely respected scholar Georgios Yennádhios. There was an excellent political reason for appointing Yennádhios, in that he was the leading opponent of the union of the Eastern and Western churches, that is of the Orthodox and the Catholics. This union was the subject that the two sides had met to discuss at the Council of Florence fourteen years earlier. There the Orthodox, under pressure from the Byzantine Emperor John VIII Palaeologos, who wanted Western political and military support against Ottoman invasion, had reluctantly signed an act of union with the Catholics which was widely unpopular with the Greeks. A later historian described the strength of anti-union feeling on the eve of Constantinople's fall: 'If, at this ultimate hour, an angel had appeared to the Byzantines and had told them: "Admit the union of the two Churches and I will scatter your enemies," the Greeks would not have listened and would have preferred the yoke of the Ottomans; such deep traces had the schism left.'[2]

The Sultan had no wish to see the western European powers giving to their fellow Christians the support against Islam which John VIII had tried to secure at Florence. Thus the anti-union Yennádhios was a highly suitable candidate for patriarch, but at first he could not be found. Eventually it was learnt that he had been captured at the fall of Constantinople and was now the house slave of a wealthy Turk in Adrianople, modern Edirne. He was brought back to Constantinople and in January 1454 was enthroned as patriarch in the Church of the Holy Apostles. The formal enthronement was a link with the past. A secure future was promised in the words of the Sultan as he handed Yennádhios the robes, staff and pectoral cross of office: 'Be Patriarch, with good fortune, and be assured of our friendship, keeping all the privileges that the Patriarchs before you enjoyed.'[3]

The terms on which Yennádhios accepted the patriarchate laid down the framework of semi-autonomy for the Christians in the Ottoman empire. The patriarch himself, and his successors, were guaranteed personal inviolability, freedom of movement and exemption from taxes. No more churches were to be converted to mosques. Patriarchal rather than Turkish courts were to deal with all cases where only the Orthodox were involved. The patriarch could tax the Orthodox to raise money for the church. In return for these privileges the patriarch was responsible to the Ottoman authorities for the good behaviour of his flock and for ensuring that they paid their taxes to the state. These patriarchal powers and responsibilities were not limited to the Greek members of his flock. They extended in principle to all the Orthodox churches which then or later were part of the Ottoman empire: the patriarchates of Alexandria, Jerusalem and Antioch, the Slav Orthodox churches and even nominally the Russian.

All this promised well. The patriarchate was under the protection of the state, its powers were consolidated and in some respects extended, and the rights as well as duties of the Christian community were formally established. But the weaknesses of the arrangement soon became evident. The promise not to convert churches to mosques was overridden by later sultans. Church leaders were now involved in the politics of the Sultan's court and skill in intrigue became as important an attribute as spirituality. Finally, there was the question of money. Though the patriarch was personally exempt from taxes, the patriarchate as an office was not, and taxes on it steadily rose. Furthermore, since under the Yennádhios agreement a patriarch, though elected by the Holy Synod, needed confirmation by the state, the practice developed of making a payment to the state on election. These payments increased not only in amount but also in frequency, as Turkish intrigues brought about repeated changes of patriarch: a total of sixty-one elections in the hundred years 1595–1695. Thus by the eve of the Greek war of independence the patriarchate was hugely in debt.

Chronically short of funds, the church neglected the clergy in the towns and villages. Little was done for the clergy's own education, or to enable them to provide schooling for their parishioners. In fact, with the Turkish conquest, Greece entered a dark age of education. The university at Constantinople and the academies at Thessalonika, Místra and Trebizond all disappeared. A century after the fall of Constantinople a professor from Tübingen, Martin Crusius, on a visit to Greece lamented: 'In all Greece studies nowhere flourish. They have no public academies or professors, except for the most trivial schools in which the boys are taught to read the Horologion, the Octoëchon, the Psalter, and other books which are used in the liturgy. But amongst the priests and monks those who really understand these books are very few indeed.'[4] By the beginning of the nineteenth century a disgruntled traveller could maintain that Orthodoxy was no more than 'a leprous composition of ignorance, superstition and fanaticism'.[5]

Nevertheless, the church remained in close touch with the people. The village priest was chosen from among the villagers, and lived as they did. If the community wanted to protest against acts of aggression or extortion by the state, it was often through the local *pappás* and his superiors that this could be done. While the nation's Muslim occupiers attended the mosque, a sense of Greek national identity was maintained by the church services in the Greek language. It is still widely believed in Greece that the local churches were also used as secret schools. Greeks of today still remember the children's rhyme beginning 'Phengaráki mou lambró':

> Little moon, so bright and cool,
> Light me on my way to school,
> Where to study I am free,
> And God's word is taught to me.

Why, the mystified child would ask, should it be the moon which lights the way to school, and would be told that because of Turkish oppression children had to creep from their homes at night to learn their language and religion secretly from the local *pappás*. But the Turks did not suppress education, secular or religious: they left it in the hands of the Orthodox patriarch. Probably many children did go to a makeshift school, often in a church and with a priest as teacher, but went at night simply because they were working in the fields all day.

By the end of the eighteenth century the patriarch was faced with an increasingly difficult dilemma. On the one hand, the church was, for the Greek people, the trustee of their continuity with the past, and many saw it as the guarantor of their eventual liberation. On the other hand, the patriarch had sworn an oath of loyalty to the Sultan on taking office, and had accepted the agreement made by Yennádhios at the very beginning of Turkish rule. Was it not therefore the patriarch's duty to render unto Caesar the things that are Caesar's? The church was thus at the head of both collaboration and resistance and was, as it were, cast simultaneously in the roles of Pétain and de Gaulle. The collaborationist role was the dominant one, in public at least. A Paternal Exhortation was published in 1798, over the signature of the patriarch of Jerusalem but perhaps composed by Grigórios V, then patriarch of Constantinople as he was again in 1821. The document could hardly have been more obsequious: the author thanked God for the establishment of the Ottoman empire, which had preserved Orthodoxy and saved it from the incipient heresies of Byzantium, and he ordered the faithful to obey and respect the Sultan whom God had set in authority over them.[6]

As revolution approached, the patriarchal line hardened even further, and at the first outbreak of revolt in March 1821 an encyclical was circulated, over the signatures of the patriarch Grigórios and twenty-two other prominent churchmen, excommunicating any who took part in a revolution against their lawful sovereign the Sultan. But the dilemma of the church could not be resolved in this or any other way. Grigórios was arrested for supposed complicity in the revolt, hanged at the gate of his own palace and his body dragged through the city and thrown into the Bosphorus. The Great Church still had a significant contribution to make in the fight for independence, but the patriarchate now had none.

2

Resentment and Regeneration

Of all the issues which incensed the Greek subjects of the Ottoman empire against their overlords, the way they were taxed was one of the most inflammatory. Foreigners visiting Greece in the years before the revolution heard constant bitter complaints about the burden of taxation, particularly the harach or poll tax. There was a constitutional basis to the tax system, and indeed to all relations between the Ottoman empire and its non-Muslim population, including Greeks: the theory that, on the incorporation of their country into the empire, a contract was deemed to have been made between the Sultan and his new non-Muslim subjects. Under this contract, the Sultan guaranteed to his subjects their lives, and to some extent their liberties and their property, and allowed them to follow their own religion; in return the subjects suffered certain restrictions of their rights and were taxed. But in practice of course this theory did not make paying any more palatable, and the annual collection of taxes from the whole community was felt as a chastisement with scorpions.

During the centuries of Turkish rule the Greek peasants, who formed the bulk of the population, found themselves trapped in a web of increasingly complex, arbitrary and oppressive taxes. They commonly worked as tenants on land owned by an individual landlord or the state, and could be liable for the sheep-pen due, payable when the sheep were penned for breeding; the sheep custom levied at lambing; dues for using the pasturage owned by the landlord; tithes (not always a tenth – sometimes as much as half) on grain, honey and grape products; and fixed dues on most vineyards, orchards and vegetable gardens, as well as on mills (related to the time the mill was in use) and on the peasant's privately owned house and sheds. In addition all Greeks had to pay to the central government the harach or poll tax, at three different levels according to the individual's wealth.

The situation worsened for the tax-paying Greek when, in the course of the sixteenth century, tax collection was increasingly put out to tax farmers. The tax farmer paid the bid price over to the treasury, and kept for himself all the taxes he collected. Alternatively, he might sell on the tax-farming rights at a profit to sub-contractors, who then needed to be even more rapacious. Not surprisingly, tax farmers were unscrupulous in wringing the maximum, legally or otherwise, from their victims in order to realise their profit. Also the system became increasingly oppressive. Once it was known that a particular area was profitable, the tax-farming rights were sold for ever higher sums, requiring ever harsher exactions from the peasants. The spread of tax farming, it has been said, 'accounted more than any other cause for the disruption of the order that had formerly ruled in the provinces'.[1]

There was a minor change for the better around 1700. From then on tax-farming rights were sold not for a few years at a time but for the lifetime of the tax farmer, thus giving him an interest in the long-term prosperity of the peasants. But by the end of the eighteenth century matters had deteriorated further, for two main reasons. Dues paid to landowners increased because previously independent communities were turned into private estates, or chiftliks; and taxes paid to the government fell increasingly heavily on regions where the population was declining, because the required total remained constant however few people remained to pay it.

In the years preceding the revolution, Ali Pasha of Iánnina in northwest Greece was the most glaring example of a local potentate who increased his private estates at the expense of the long-suffering peasants. His method was to establish a foothold in a village by acquiring some land there, sometimes simply by claiming it as his right. The next step was to put pressure on other villagers to sell to him by driving them into debt at high interest rates through extraordinary exactions, and sometimes also by quartering his Albanian soldiers in their houses. When the peasants could no longer pay their debts, Ali made the village his chiftlik and the villagers in effect his tithe-paying serfs. Ali Pasha and his sons eventually controlled, by one count, 915 chiftliks, and 'great terror of such a disaster' was how one contemporary traveller described the villagers' feelings at this prospect.[2]

The total tax due from a district took no account of changes in its population, and by the early nineteenth century there were flagrant examples of this inequity. Some areas were favoured because their populations were rising, but Místra in the Peloponnese, with a population of 3,000, had to pay the poll tax for 8,500, and on the Cycladic island of Mílos between 2,000 and 3,000 had to pay for 16,000, an injustice so glaring that the Turkish governor felt obliged to contribute. Peasants fled when they could to a more favoured area, or took to brigandage, creating a vicious spiral in Ottoman administration: as a community's numbers fell, the tax burden on those remaining increased, driving away yet more of them. By the end of the eighteenth century deserted villages were a common sight, in Greece as well as in other parts of the Ottoman empire. The process has been concisely described: 'The classes that lived on . . . dues and taxes were engaged during the seventeenth and eighteenth centuries on a long-drawn-out strangling of the unfortunate geese that laid their golden eggs.'[3]

Another burden, memory of which still smoulders in the Greek national consciousness, was the Turkish system of devshirme: the forcible conscription of young men and their removal to Istanbul to join the imperial service, especially in a military role as janissaries. This practice, however, had been virtually abandoned by about 1700 and, oppressive as it was, nevertheless gave these young men an opportunity to win advancement and wealth which many exploited to the full.

From the early days of the Ottoman empire its army had been boosted by slave recruits, non-Muslim captives from wars of expansion, but as the empire's expansion slowed this source of troops dried up. To make up the shortfall the Ottomans introduced compulsory conscription, called devshirme by the Turks and *pedhomázoma*, or child-collection, by the Greeks. Under this system non-Muslim youths were forcibly taken as recruits for the so-called new troops, the janissaries, or for other offices in which they owed allegiance to no Turkish faction but only to the sultan himself.

The decrees of the sultans show how the system worked. In 1601 Mehmed III called for a devshirme in Roumeli, northern Greece, ordering the governor-general to ensure that 'the most good-looking, well-bodied and spirited youths of the infidels between fifteen and twenty years of age be drafted and sent to the janissary units'. The officers in charge were to be totally ruthless: 'The infidel parents or anybody else who resists the surrender of their janissary sons are to be hanged at once in front of their house-gate, their blood being considered of no importance whatsoever.'[4] A later decree dated 1666 from Mehmed IV was concerned, as it says, with the first devshirme in Roumeli for a long time. The age range was now wider: 10 to 20 instead of 15 to 20. Only sons were excluded, and, where there was more than one son, only one might be taken unless another volunteered. The man in charge was no longer the provincial governor but an official sent from Istanbul, since local Turkish authorities were becoming unwilling to lose some of their best manpower and were likely to frustrate the devshirme. As for the treatment of the local population, the tone, belying the brutal facts, was now emollient: 'No-one is to be wronged or coerced of the villagers during my reign.'[5] By the turn of the century resistance to the devshirme had become open and violent. In 1705 the official sent to the northern Greek town of Naoússa to draft fifty new janissaries was murdered, while the crowd shouted their resistance to giving up their sons. The leaders of this resistance took to the hills, but were captured and their severed heads were displayed in Naoússa before being sent on to the governor of Thessalonika.

By this time the practice of the devshirme, though still brutally enforced when it was called for, was becoming extinct and it had been dead for a century when the war of independence began. Though it provided a unique opportunity for some of the conscripts to achieve fame and fortune at the sultan's court – the path to glory, it has been called – it was the capricious inhumanity of the system that was forever associated in Greek minds with the centuries of Turkish rule. The harsh memory of it has survived to our own day. In the Greek civil war of the late 1940s the Communist-backed rebels removed whole families of children for indoctrination behind the Iron Curtain, and were denounced in an impassioned article by Georgios Vláchos in his respected paper *Kathimeriní*. Even the Sultan, he commented bitterly, took only one son, and Ottoman oppression was immediately recalled in the article's title: 'To Pedhomázoma'.[6]

*

At the end of the eighteenth century most of Greece had been subject to the Ottoman empire for over 300 years, but the Greeks still fiercely resented the Turks as interlopers whose occupation of the country would one day be ended. At the same time ideas from abroad, especially the ideas of the French Enlightenment, began to circulate in Greece.

From the 1750s onwards books by French authors, including Voltaire, Montesquieu and Rousseau, were translated into Greek for the first time, though since many of the translations were only circulated in manuscript, not published, their influence was limited. Some works by Enlightenment authors directly addressed the Greeks' situation. Voltaire's *Épitre à l'Imperatrice de Russie* of 1770 urged Catherine the Great to liberate Greece (which through the Greek revolt led by Count Orlov she tried but failed to do), and in his *Tocsin des rois aux souverains de l'Europe* he called on the European rulers to drive the Turks from Europe and thus give Greece her freedom. Other works reminded the Greeks of their great classical past: for example, Charles Rollin's *Histoire ancienne*, translated into Greek as early as 1750, and in lighter vein Jean-Jacques Barthélemy's *Voyage du jeune Anacharsis*, the story of the Scythian prince Anacharsis who goes to classical Greece to be civilised. Even more popular, and with even stronger resonances for the Greeks, was the play *Harmodius and Aristogeiton*, which told the story of the two ancient Greek heroes who lost their lives in the attempt to overthrow Hippias, the sixth-century BC tyrant of Athens.

The most comprehensive statement in Greek of the Greek situation and of the path to liberation was the *Elliniki Nomarchía*, or 'The Rule of Law for Greece'. Subtitled 'A Discourse on Freedom', it was published anonymously in Italy in 1806. It contains some wild invective against those seen as enemies of freedom, but in its sober passages its debt to Enlightenment thinkers is obvious. It begins, following Rousseau, by describing man's original state as one of primitive happiness where men had 'all the virtues without a single fault'; this ended when man in society became dependent on his fellows and so 'abandoned true happiness and became a slave'. All was not lost, however, because as Condorcet had maintained 'man is endowed by nature with reason' and 'has a proclivity for the better which always motivates him to seek improvement in whatever condition he may be'. But improvement requires the cultivation of virtue, defined in terms reminiscent of

Montesquieu as living for the sake of the many and always giving priority to the common good. The *Elliniki Nomarchía* then returns to Rousseau's thought and states that a constitution must be pleasing to the majority; that before a satisfactory constitution can be established there must be a progression from original freedom through anarchy, monarchy and tyranny to *nomarchía*, the rule of law; and that each of these stages, even *nomarchía* the best of them, goes through a natural cycle of birth and death. Finally the *Elliniki Nomarchía* applies this philosophy to the present situation of the Greeks. The tyranny of the Turks is dying, it claims: 'The Ottoman state finds itself today in its death throes, and can be compared to a human body, gripped by apoplexy . . . which little by little weakens and finally dies.' Only two groups, it says, stand in the way of Greek liberation: the merchants of the diaspora, who enjoy an easy life abroad instead of returning to serve their country, and the corrupt and subservient clergy.[7]

The church reacted vigorously to this onslaught of Enlightenment ideas. The Paternal Exhortation issued by the patriarchate in 1798 rejected Rousseau's theory of man's primitive state of nature, and reasserted the view that man was expelled by God from the Biblical paradise because of sin, and would be readmitted to it in the next life only after enduring the tribulations and resisting the temptations of this one. The devil, responsible for all temptations, had 'devised in the present century another artifice and pre-eminent deception, namely the much vaunted system of liberty', but the only true liberty was 'to live according to divine and human laws'. Therefore the Christian flock was enjoined to 'guard steadfastly your ancestral faith and, as followers of Jesus Christ, resolutely give your obedience to the civil government'.[8] An even more explicit attack on the Enlightenment came in 1819, with the encyclical of Patriarch Grigórios entitled *Enlightenment as the Handmaid of Irreligion*. What is the point, asked the patriarch, of the young learning about 'numbers, and algebra, and cubes and cube roots . . . and atoms and vacuums and whirlpools . . . and optical and acoustic matters and a myriad of the same kind and other monstrous things . . . if as a consequence they are . . . ignorant in the things of religion, injurious to the state, false patriots and unworthy of their ancestral calling?' Therefore the patriarch commanded his flock to 'hate the profane mouthings, the manifestly ungodly teachings, of the aforementioned'.[9]

There was a pungent sexual content in this debate between conservatives and progressives. The patriarch in his 1819 encyclical spoke of the young becoming 'degenerate and frenzied in morals'. Another conservative asked why people followed Voltaire, and answered his own question: 'Because his philosophy is profitable to the indulgence of the belly and those parts under the belly.' Voltaire himself was accused of being 'a man of violent passions and thoroughly lascivious'. A further writer of the same persuasion broadened the scope of the sexual theme and described Europe as a whole as 'the great prostitute'.[10] The progressives replied in the same coin. The writer of the *Elliniki Nomarchía* castigates the Greeks living abroad because they find beautiful 'the painted and most impudent faces of the most immoral foreigners' and 'try as far as they can to flatter, without resistance, some whore', while he denounces the clergy for worshipping 'two or three noblewomen, with the greatest shamelessness', and states flatly that 'the present bishop of Iánnina is an adulterer and a sodomite'. Perhaps this style of invective was natural in a culture where the Turk was regularly depicted as both a ravisher of women and a homosexual predator, and Greece was portrayed as a desolate maiden awaiting rescue.

The ideas of the Enlightenment now began to seep into Greek education. The church-dominated curriculum had hitherto been deeply conservative. Theology was supreme, next came study of logic, rhetoric and metaphysics, and mathematics and the sciences were barely touched. Science teaching was in any case archaic. As late as 1797 a conservative professor published a work dismissing the ideas of Copernicus and Newton, and the physics taught was based on Aristotle until well into the nineteenth century. The nature of phlogiston, the substance supposed to embody heat, was still being debated in 1813, though the phlogiston theory had been exploded by Lavoisier over twenty years earlier. In the non-scientific subjects teaching was bogged down by being conducted in ancient Greek. Gradually however the educational darkness was illuminated. In 1766 a textbook on physics was published in Greek which for the first time introduced up-to-date science into Greece. Its author wrote: 'The characters of the book of nature are not letters but triangles, parallelograms, circles . . . pyramids, cones, cubes, cylinders and spheres and all the rest. How can one read the book of nature if he does not know the characters in which it is written?'[11] In

1791 the first book on geography was published in Greek, with accurate contemporary maps and observations on the cultures of different peoples. The first book in Greek on algebra was published in 1793 and on chemistry in 1802, both being translations from French and published in Venice. French influence was also dominant in the Chios school founded in 1817, which had expensive laboratory equipment brought from Paris and where the language teacher was Jules David, son of the famous French artist.

The ideas to invigorate Greek education thus came from abroad, and so did most of the money, from prosperous Greek merchants in the major cities of Europe. Schools fell into three categories: primary, where pupils simply learnt to read, with emphasis on church texts; secondary, where ancient Greek was studied; and a few academies, which extended the range to philosophy and the sciences. The local community could often afford a primary or secondary school and these had become widespread by the early nineteenth century; in 1814 the English traveller William Leake claimed that 'at present there is not a Greek community in a moderate state of opulence . . . that does not support a school for teaching their children the ancient Greek, and in many instances the other principal branches of polite education'.[12] But it was the academies which carried the greatest prestige, and it was these which rich merchants endowed. They were naturally concentrated in places where these merchants operated: around the Aegean, with its seafaring wealth, as at the Greek communities of Smyrna and Kidhoníes (modern Ayvalık) on the Turkish coast, at Patmos and Chios on the islands, and at Athens and Zagorá on the Greek coast, or centred on Iánnina, enriched by the overland trade route from Europe. Only one was built in the heartland of Greece, the academy at Dhimitsána in the central Peloponnese. Unhappily neither the Dhimitsána school nor its magnificent library survived the revolution.

The merchants, not the church, were now paying the piper and were calling an increasingly secular tune. When the Rev. William Jowett visited the Greek academy at Kidhoníes in 1818 he found a well-stocked library and a collection of astronomical and other scientific instruments, while the only vestigial remnant of the church's influence was a music master to teach church chanting. But secular education still had some way to go. Jowett attended a class in which a master who had studied in Paris and Pisa was lecturing to thirty students on astronomy as part of a three-year course. 'His audience, however,' said Jowett, 'could not all understand him. I liked their practice of putting questions to him though some asked very absurd ones,' and he concluded that 'the scientific part of education in Greece is evidently in its infancy'.[13]

Some saw education, and enlightenment in its broadest sense, as the key to Greece's liberation: let new ideas enter, and in time the old ideas will wither away and a new society will emerge. Iánnis Kapodhístrias, later Greece's first president, held this view strongly. His *Observations sur les moyens d'améliorer le sort des Grecs*, written in 1819, maintained that education, in the hands of a reformed and better-funded church, was the only route to the regeneration of the nation: 'Nous le repétons, c'est de l'éducation morale et littéraire de la Grèce que les Grecs doivent s'occuper uniquement et exclusivement: tout autre objet est vain, tout autre travail est dangereux.'[14] But this gradualist approach was not enough for most Greeks. Even for the unschooled Kolokotrónis the message of the new ideas emanating from France was already clear. As he succinctly put it, 'The French Revolution and the doings of Napoleon opened the eyes of the world. The nations knew nothing before, and the people thought that kings were gods upon earth, and that they were bound to say that whatever they did was well done.'[15] What the Greeks now needed was voices to speak specifically to their country of the steps which would lead to a Greece reborn, and ultimately they needed a call to arms.

3

Two Prophets of Revolution

The names of two men are most often associated with the first stirrings of Greek ideas of independence: Adhamántios Koraís and Rígas Pheréos. A lithograph of the time shows the two men on either side of a maiden representing suffering Greece who is in an attitude of extreme dejection, half crouched on one knee and dressed in rags. A gaunt-looking Koraís on the left is dressed in the frock coat of an academic, and on the right is the more solidly built Rígas, in a long gown that might have been worn by a Turkish official. Each man holds an out-stretched hand of the unhappy girl. What reality does this touching allegory represent?

Rígas was born in 1757 in the Thessalian village of Velestíno, the ancient Phére; hence his two toponymics, Velestinlís or, more commonly, Pheréos. After an impressive scholastic career Rígas went at the age of 23 to Wallachia in today's Romania, where he became secretary first to the principality's governor and then to an Austrian baron who brought him to Vienna for the first time in June 1790. Vienna, where Rígas spent much of the following years, provided both the stimulus and the opportunity for the expression of his revolutionary ideas. There was a considerable Greek community in Vienna, mainly merchants and students of science, who would meet at the city's Tavérna ton Éllinon. Also in Vienna were the brothers Markídhis-Poúlios, natives of Macedonia, who published works in Greek. The brothers were able to publish openly the works which provided Rígas' income, innocuous translations into Greek of physics texts from French and German and of recent French fiction, but under the repressive regime of the Austrian government anything subversive, such as the Greek newspaper *Ephimerís* and Rígas' revolutionary writings, had to be printed secretly at night.

It is for two works that Rígas is best remembered, both dating from 1797: a revolutionary hymn including an oath against tyranny, in rhyming couplets to be sung to a well-known tune, and in more philosophical vein a statement of the rights of man, combined with a proposed constitution for a new Greek republic.

The hymn with its oath is vigorous stuff, in the thumping, galloping metre of traditional Greek klephtic ballads which this translation of the opening of the hymn reproduces:

> Shall we live in the mountain passes, like warriors of old?
> Shall we live alone like lions, on the top of the mountain ridge?
> Shall we live in caves in darkness, shall slavery drive us away?
> Shall we say farewell to our family and to our beloved land?
> No! Better an hour of freedom, than forty years as a slave.

Similarly, the oath begins:

> O Lord of all creation, I solemnly swear to Thee
> Never to act as tyrants do and never be slave to them

and concludes:

> And if this oath is broken, may lightning strike me down,
> And may I be burnt to nothing, and vanish like smoke on the wind.[1]

But the revolutionary hymn was not simply rhetoric, or something to be sung late in the evening at the Tavérna ton Éllinon; it embodied important elements of Rígas' philosophy, some unexpected. First, the revolution is to be not against the Turks as such, but against tyranny. Turks, he says, are oppressed equally with Greeks, equally with Christians:

> We who suffer under the yoke, let us kill the ravening wolves
> Who keep us in harsh subjection, Christian and Turk alike.

Thus Turks are summoned to join in the coming struggle and not only the Turks: in the course of some twenty lines Rígas calls for support from Bulgarians, Albanians, Armenians and Arabs, and from the people of Malta, Egypt and Aleppo.[2] Although the appeal was to Muslims as well as Christians, Rígas somewhat naively proposed that the symbol of the united movement against tyranny should be the cross. Turks would also have been unsympathetic to his call to the islanders of Spétses, Psará and Hydra to burn the Turkish armada and reoccupy Constantinople and the church of Áyia Sophía.

Rígas' thoroughly ecumenical vision was also based on the idea of the supremacy of the law: 'So let the law be paramount, our country's only guide.' This leads to Rígas' declaration of the rights of man, and his proposed constitution. Rígas' rights follow closely those proclaimed a few years earlier in America and in France: equality, liberty, security of life and security of property. To these are added later in the document freedom of speech, of religion and of petition to authority. But Rígas makes it clear that the overriding right is the right to resist and if necessary overthrow an unjust government: 'When the Government harasses, breaches, disdains the rights of the people and does not heed its complaints, then for the people or each part of the people to make a revolution, take up arms and punish their tyrants is the most sacred of all their rights and the most compelling of all their obligations.'[3]

The other rights which Rígas maintains all hinge on the law. Only the law can restrict a man's freedom, not the whim of a judge; law is for the fault, so punishment is the same for all, and must fit the fault; legislation cannot be retrospective; a man is innocent until proved guilty. On the question of how actual laws are to be derived from the general law, Rígas is not clear; but then nor were many of his predecessors of the Enlightenment. He suggests that laws spring naturally from something like Rousseau's general will: 'The law is that free decision, that has come about with the consent of all people; for example, we all wish that the murderer be executed. And to take another law which is protecting us, we all wish to have authority over our property, no one therefore has permission to take anything from us by force. This is a law, because singly we accept it and we wish it.'[4] And even more imprecise is a later article stating that 'every citizen has an equal right with other citizens to combine to enact a law'.[5]

A number of Rígas' specific proposals are very far-sighted. There must be civilian control of the military. The government must be open, so the public should have access to all details of taxation. The law should be known to all, so Rígas' constitution must be inscribed on copper tablets and set up in every town and village. Rígas even proposes

LYIT
LIBRARY
40023094
LETTERKENNY

a form of welfare state to help 'unfortunate inhabitants both in supplying them with the wherewithal to work, as well as giving the means of subsistence to those who can no longer work'.[6]

The value of Rígas' contribution to the Greek cause was that he took the principles underlying the American and French revolutionary declarations and adapted them for Greece. His message was that Greece too could enjoy a constitution, and here is what its articles would actually say. With the help of his compatriots in Vienna, he was able to print and distribute his calls for revolt. Three thousand copies of the revolutionary declaration, constitution and hymn were produced in October 1797, and the hymn was sung over the next two decades throughout the Greek Orthodox world, even it was said in the Turkish capital.

While Rígas remained in Vienna he had been able to escape the attention of the autocratic and anti-revolutionary Austrian authorities. That he eventually fell into their hands was a matter of mischance and betrayal. In December 1797 Rígas with his faithful companion and biographer Perrevós set out for Trieste, sending ahead to a friend a letter and boxes containing copies of all his writings, the subversive ones at the bottom. The friend was away, but his business partner opened the letter and boxes and handed them over to the Austrian authorities.

When Rígas arrived in Trieste he was arrested. Perrevós, on Rígas' instructions, sought the help of the French consul, who was prepared to say that Perrevós was a French citizen, and thus he escaped. Seventeen others were arrested with Rígas as members of a conspiratorial brotherhood and sent to Vienna for interrogation. Those with Austrian or Russian nationality were expelled from Austria. Rígas, after a failed suicide attempt, was handed over with the seven other Turkish nationals to the Turkish authorities at Belgrade, where on the night of 24 June 1798 all were murdered on orders from Istanbul and their bodies thrown into the river Sava; drowned while trying to escape, said their captors. In a story that can only have come from his executioners, an improbable source, it is reported that just before he died Rígas said: 'This is how brave men die. I have sown; the time will soon come when my country will gather the harvest.'[7]

Rígas quickly became revered. When in 1809 Byron met the young Andréas Lóndos, later a revolutionary leader, the poet mentioned Rígas' name, at which Lóndos immediately jumped up and 'clasping his hands repeated the name of the patriot with a thousand passionate exclamations, the tears streaming down his cheeks'.[8] In the next century Rígas' portrait was appropriated by the Communist resistance to German wartime occupation, and his name was used by the secret society of students opposed to Greece's military dictatorship of 1967–74. Rígas' dying words may well have been apocryphal, but his name is still alive today as both prophet and proto-martyr of the Greek revolution.

Adhamántios Koraís was born in Smyrna, modern İzmir, in 1748, so was some ten years older than Rígas, but far outlived him. His youth, he tells us in his autobiography, was spent in efforts to get an education in a city where at that time it was almost unobtainable. The Greek school in Smyrna, only recently established, had a single teacher who provided 'very poor teaching, accompanied by frequent beating'. Languages were Koraís' passion. He found for himself teachers of Italian and French, but they differed from his Greek teacher, he says, only in that they taught him without beatings. Latin could not be learnt because the only teachers were the Jesuits, hated for their proselytising. Learning Arabic would mean a Turkish teacher, a prospect he could not stomach. When Koraís' family silk business sent him to Amsterdam for six years in his twenties he continued his education there. After an unhappy return to Smyrna, devastated not long before by an earthquake and fire in which the family house was destroyed, he went in 1782 to Montpellier in southern France for six years' study of medicine, and reached Paris in 1788 at the age of 40, his period of self-education at last completed.

Apart from his passion for learning, two other factors dominated Koraís' youth: ill-health and hatred of the Turks. Of his health he says: 'After my thirteenth year I began to spit blood, and I spat it incessantly until my twentieth year. From that time I did not cease spitting blood, but at long intervals, however, until my sixtieth year. For all this neither my unhealthy condition, nor the fear of worsening it, stood in the way of my thirst for knowledge.'[9] Of his hatred of the Turks he says that it had been nourished in his soul since birth and that the devastation of Smyrna 'transformed my abhorrence of living together with Turks into such a melancholy that I was in danger of falling into genuine madness'.[10] For Rígas some Turks were potential allies; for Koraís all Turks were obsessively loathed.

Koraís arrived in Paris in May 1788, and fell immediately in love with the city, its cosmopolitan bustle, its learned men, its academies and libraries. This, he wrote wistfully to a friend the following September, was what ancient Athens must have been like. To earn his living Koraís turned, like Rígas, to translations, mainly from the ancient or the later Hellenistic Greek into French. He was also keen to alert the French to the situation in Greece, as he did in his *Mémoire sur l'état actuel de la civilisation en Grèce*, delivered to an attentive human rights society in 1803.

Koraís did not translate, as one might have expected, any of the books of the French Enlightenment into Greek, though he was well versed in their ideas and spoke in glowing terms of the compendium of their theories, *L'Encyclopédie*. His main effort was the production of his 'Greek Library', translations of ancient Greek authors into a form of modern Greek, which eventually reached some thirty volumes, each preceded by an introduction. These introductions, which he called 'Impromptu Thoughts', were not simply scholarly essays, but were used by Koraís to make rousing personal appeals to his fellow countrymen. The introduction, written in September 1821, to Aristotle's *Politics* gives the flavour:

> I can write no more, beloved fatherland, prevented as I am by the turmoil in my heart, which paralyses my hand and darkens my eyes with tears. I was a willing exile from your bosom, unable to bear the sight of your daily torments from the lawless acts of the barbarians. In these last days of my painful life I have learnt, beyond all my hopes, that your liberty, which had withered under the tyrants, has blossomed again. I shall not see or learn of its fruits, as I shall soon depart this life, but I pray that they may be abundant and beautiful for all your children, my own brothers.[11]

Such a statement was intended, of course, for a far wider audience than the learned, and here Koraís faced a difficulty: in what form of Greek should he write? The written and the spoken language had begun to diverge from around 300 BC. The archaic written form, the only one considered suitable for serious works, had remained very close to its ancient classical ancestor, while the demotic spoken form had developed along paths of its own, generally simplifying grammar and syntax and incorporating foreign words, especially from Turkish and Italian.

The spoken form was understood by all, the written form only by the educated. By the time of Koraís, there were two opposed schools of thought about the language to be used to enlighten and educate the Greeks: those who believed that only a form close to ancient Greek would properly reflect the nation's heritage, and those arguing that to spread the message widely it was essential to write in the language of the people. It was as if a serious writer in English was constrained to choose between writing in Anglo-Saxon or writing in the Dorset dialect of, say, William Barnes.

However, more numerous than either of the opposed groups were the compromisers, including Koraís, who favoured for his works a language that was largely based on the structure of the spoken variety, but retained many ancient features and rejected foreign importations. This last element gave Koraís' form of Greek its name, *katharévousa* or purged. Koraís was not an innovator but was certainly a trail-blazer in the development of a new, more accessible Greek. What, in his publications and copious worldwide correspondence, did he use it to say?

Koraís' main preoccupation was with education. It had been the basis of the French Revolution, he believed: 'I had learned that the increase and spread of education in the French nation gave birth to the love of liberty.'[12] He also attributed military success to education: 'the amazing French victories were the result of learning'.[13] He encouraged rich Greeks to 'multiply throughout Greece schools and libraries; at common expense send promising youths to Europe, that they may bring her benefits back to you; and entrust to them the education of our people'.[14] When in 1802 the people of Soúli in north-west Greece were in the last stages of their resistance to the attacks of Ali Pasha, he advised them, as Albanian speakers: 'When you have a little peace, bring to your country a teacher to instruct your dear children in the Greek tongue. When the warriors of Soúli learn from what ancestors they have sprung, nobody will be able to defeat them, either by guile or by force.'[15]

The results of education were, in Koraís' view, almost guaranteed: in his metaphor, if the seed was planted in the right conditions, the plant would inevitably bear fruit. Education would ensure not only the achievement of independence but also the establishment of a proper constitution for the new state. But if education was essential to the success of a revolution, and the process of reviving and reinvigorating Greek education was only beginning in the first years of the nineteenth century, it followed for Koraís that revolution must wait, in his view till 1850 or later. He held this opinion consistently, expressing it well before the revolution (1807: 'our people need at least fifty years of education'), during the revolution (end of 1821: 'the event has come too soon for our people, who have not yet enough learning to understand their true interest; if it had come twenty years later . . . '), and after independence (1831: 'the Greek rising was fully justified, but inopportune; the right time would have been 1850').[16]

The two revolutions which he saw as models were the French and the American. Koraís was guarded in his comments on the later brutal developments of the French Revolution, but whatever the rulers of France did the French people retained Koraís' esteem. The United States, of course, had no interests to defend in Greece, and Koraís warmly approved of the Americans, corresponding with President Jefferson and with the ardent philhellene Edward Everett.

We have come to the end of causes and people of whom Koraís approved, and must now turn to his hates, which were many and fierce. First on his list of antipathies were, of course, the Turks, 'that race of sodomites'. The other European powers, always excepting France, fared little better. He suspected Russia of 'pushing us forward to tame the wild beast so that they can then strike the final blow',[17] leading to a Greece occupied by Cossacks. The English, 'uncircumcised Turks', were to be distrusted because they too were simply pursuing their own interests. Special ire was reserved for the church, though Koraís himself was devout. He blamed it for the neglect of education, and for preaching obedience to the Turkish government: the Paternal Exhortation of 1798, enjoining submission, drew a forceful reply from Koraís, which he entitled the Brotherly Exhortation, and in which he proclaimed 'the inalienable right of the oppressed to seek every means to throw off the yoke of tyranny'. In a telling contrast he pointed out that just as the Paternal Exhortation was being written Rígas and his followers were being martyred: 'Perhaps at that very moment the knife of the executioner was descending on their sacred heads, their noble Greek blood was flowing from their veins, and their spirits were rising up to join the blessed souls of all who had died for freedom.'[18]

What then are we to make of Koraís' contribution to the Greek movement for independence? He insisted on the importance of education, and his urging of rich merchants to spend their money promoting education was a sensible practical step. To Koraís too can be attributed the promotion and diffusion, if not the invention, of a form of Greek, *katharévousa*, which as well as helping to disseminate education would provide the linguistic bond of the new state. 'Language is the nation,' he wrote. On the other hand, though, Koraís' insistence on education came to smack of single-issue fanaticism. To tell the starving war-weary Souliots to go home and learn Greek showed little appreciation of the realities. A similar myopia affected him in international matters. He blamed the powers of Europe, particularly Russia and England, for pursuing their own interests. It does not seem to have occurred to him that all nations, including the Greeks, pursued their own interests, and that salvation lay in finding ways to make the interests of other nations coincide with those of Greece.

Some of the ideas of both Rígas and Koraís were impractical if not daft. Even their practical proposals were in some ways tangential to the revolution which actually happened: Rígas wanted a different struggle, involving all who suffered from Ottoman rule, and Koraís wanted liberation to come much later. But each was a force for change by disseminating Enlightenment ideas, by articulating a commitment to a regenerated nation, and by the passionate rhetoric each used to advocate it. It is that commitment which is symbolised by their supportive hands ready to raise to her feet the suffering maiden Greece.

4

The Philikí Etería

In September 1814 three expatriate Greeks in the Russian Black Sea port of Odessa set up a secret society whose aim was both simple and visionary: the liberation of Greece. The names of the three founders were Skoúphas, Tsákalov and Xánthos, and the society was given the bland name of Philikí Etería or Friendly Association. The idea was far from being a new one. The Masonic lodges of the eighteenth century had been the model for secret revolutionary societies which had sprung up in many European countries under innocuous-seeming names: the Carbonari in Italy, the Tugendbund (League of Virtue) in Germany, the Philomathians in Poland. There were also Greek precedents. Rígas was said to have founded an Etería of this sort in Vienna in the 1790s, but no details have ever come to light. In 1809 Greeks in Paris set up a mutual-help group for Greeks in France, and its members were rich enough for the badge of membership to be a gold ring engraved with the society's symbol. Tsákalov, one of the co-founders of the Philikí Etería, joined this association while briefly in Paris as a student.

The three founders of the Philikí Etería were of a very different stamp from the prosperous Parisian expatriates. All three had been born in Greece, but had left to seek their fortunes in the Greek trading communities abroad, none with much success, and were now in lowly commercial jobs as secretaries or sales representatives. Nikólaos Skoúphas, regarded as first among equals of the trio, was born in 1779 in a village near Árta, and had worked at various times as an apothecary, a commercial secretary and a hatter. Emmanuel Xánthos, the eldest of the three, was born in 1772 in Patmos, and by 1810, at the age of 38, had

26

risen no higher than clerk to a merchant in Odessa. Two years later he set up in Constantinople, with three merchants from Iánnina, a company to trade in olive oil, but the company failed. While visiting Lévkas, Xánthos had been initiated into the Freemasons, as a result of which, he says in his memoirs, he 'immediately lighted upon the idea that it would be possible to found a secret society on the lines of that of the Freemasons, having as a basis the union of all the *kapetanioi* of the *armatoloi*, and other leaders of all classes of Greeks, whether in Greece or in other parts, with the object of bringing about, in time, the liberation of the fatherland (*patrídha*)'.[1] Athanásios Tsákalov, born in Iánnina in 1788, was the youngest and perhaps best educated of the three, and brought to the society his knowledge of the Paris group. At 26 he had as yet no settled career. A hatter, a bankrupt and a recent ex-student: an improbable triumvirate to launch a national movement.

There were five levels in the society. In the lowest category, for the illiterate, were the Brothers. Next came the Associates (literally, the recommended ones), for the literate. Above them were the Priests, who could recruit to their own or a lower grade. Next were the Shepherds, men of exceptional ability or wealth, and at the highest level of all was the Supreme Council, referred to as the Aórati Archí, the Invisible Directorate. Membership of the Council was kept a close secret. Initially it consisted of the three founders, to whom were added in the course of time other Greeks, most of whom were scarcely better known than themselves. But the society did nothing to discourage the idea that a great man – the Tsar's foreign minister Kapodhístrias, or even Tsar Alexander himself – was at the head of the movement. This was to be the most important dividend from the Council's invisibility.

The first aim of the Philikí Etería had to be survival, and the betrayal and death of Rígas made it clear that this meant keeping the society secret. The founders therefore developed a number of codes. One of these, which was used on the membership certificates, was a simple substitution code, in which numbers and other symbols were used for the letters of the Greek alphabet: 2 for theta, 8 for omega or omicron, 9 for pi and so on. This code would probably not defeat an intelligent schoolboy, but others were more complicated, and some have still not been cracked. As well as letter substitution, word substitution was used. Individual members had a variety of noms de guerre: some were martial (such as captains Iánnis, Dhimítris and so on, or the good hunter), some complimentary (the beloved, the noble), some less so (the fool, the lazy, the playboy). Some of the most important members had numbers not names: Kolokotrónis for example was simply 118. Surprisingly, none of the great names from the classical past appears on the list of aliases. Other word equivalents were colourful: a large ship was an elephant, a small one a horse, and a merchant ship a camel. Bands of warriors were dancers, and a spy a cyclops. The word for murder was adultery, a term which the society's ruling body was going to need in its instructions to members. The substitutions for individual and collective names were often revealing. Thus Kapodhístrias was the man of good deeds, and the Tsar the philanthropist; Sir Thomas Maitland, the distrusted British governor of the Ionian islands, was the old man (nothing worse), and Ali Pasha the father-in-law. In the list of nations, the English were, in free translation, the hard men, the Italians the sweeties, the Turks the squatters and the Greeks the valiant.[2]

To develop their society the founders needed two things: members and money. The key to both was mystery going well beyond the practical need for secrecy: with no specific aims, only the general objective of one day liberating their country, and with as yet no influential backers, the society had to use the packaging of mystery to make the organisation seem larger and more alluring than it really was. Mystery accordingly shrouded the rituals of initiation into the society, which varied according to the grade of the recruiter and the recruit. The higher the rank the more complex the initiation ceremony, and each included a sworn promise to serve the society, culminating in the so-called Great Oath. Initiation also carried an obligation to contribute money. A new Associate had to hand over his subscription to the initiator for passing on to the society with a letter purporting, in case it was seized by the authorities, to contain some money for a long-absent friend: 'I am sorry I have not been able to send you anything before, but now that my luck has changed . . . ' At the higher level of Priest the new member's letter was supposed to be from a long-time exile in a distant town, who had always cherished his birthplace in his heart, and now wished to contribute substantial funds to support the local school.

In spite of the elaborate preparations for recruiting members, the Philikí Etería made little progress in the first few years. The founders soon discovered that their business affairs took them away from Odessa and in different directions: Skoúphas and Tsákalov in September 1814 to Moscow, where they remained for about two years, Xánthos in December to Constantinople. The Moscow pair had some successes; within a month of arriving they had enrolled Georgios Sekéris, whose rich brother Panayiótis was later to become a major contributor of money to the society. Skoúphas, back in Odessa in 1816, met four Greek military captains from the Peloponnese who had served in the Russian army during Russia's occupation of the Ionian islands and were on their way to St Petersburg to try to secure their arrears of pay through Kapodhístrias. Skoúphas initiated them into the society, and the ex-soldiers vigorously promoted it, no doubt using the recruiting sergeant's methods of persuasion. One of these captains, Anagnostarás, became the society's most successful recruiter, with forty-nine new members to his credit by the time the revolution began. However, Skoúphas made other less successful initiations. It was he who recruited the flashy and unreliable Nikólaos Galátis, a young man from Ithaca who was to cause the society a great deal of trouble until he was removed from the scene. By the end of the society's first few years of activity, the overall picture was bleak. By 1816, after two years of operation, the three founders had enrolled no more than twenty members, and in 1817 the number reached only forty-two. Contributions from initiates were far below expectations, and the society's total income for the first three years was a mere trickle.

The basic reason for this early lack of success was that the founders could not break into Greek society on Greek soil since they were themselves expatriates, and could not break into Greek society abroad since they were of a lower class than the prosperous Greek merchants of the diaspora. Those limited numbers who joined the Etería early were, like its founders, part of the most recent wave of financially insecure émigrés. In the established Greek communities abroad, the society was able to recruit only a handful of members in Italy, one in Vienna, and none at all in London, Paris, Marseilles or Amsterdam. Indeed when Skoúphas tried in the early days to enlist some of the rich merchants of Moscow, they sent him packing 'with rude and barbaric jeering' and called him an uncouth oik. Kapodhístrias called the Eterists 'miserable merchants' clerks', and the contemporary historian George Finlay, in a typically acerbic comment, dismissed the founders as 'counting-house Catilines'.[3]

It is thus not surprising that by the end of 1817 the Etería was in a desperate state: far too few members, and far too little money. During the winter and spring of 1817–18 in Constantinople the three founders discussed what to do next. Tsákalov was at first in favour of giving up the plan and disbanding the Etería, but by the end of their discussions the leaders had worked out a programme that was a good deal more realistic and practical than any they had devised before.

First, they recognised the need for an established headquarters for the society. According to Xánthos' account, in the years since late 1814 when Skoúphas and Tsákalov left Odessa for Moscow and Xánthos left for Constantinople, the three founders had never been together in the same place at the same time until they were reunited in Constantinople nearly three years later. They now chose as their centre Xánthos' house in that city. This was, of course, the capital of the empire they were trying to subvert, but it was thronged with Greeks of all classes, among whom it was easy to mingle unobserved, and it had a much less efficient surveillance system than Metternich's in Vienna. Finlay even claimed that the Turks employed no spies at all.

Hitherto the society's activity had been concentrated in Russia and neighbouring countries. The leaders now decided that they must send emissaries to Greece proper, both to gauge the degree of popular support and to determine where the planned revolution should begin. The four ex-soldiers whose proselytising had been so successful were therefore despatched as apostles of the society. Anagnostarás, the most successful of the recruiters, went to Hydra, Spétses and the Peloponnese, another to Macedonia and Thessaly in north-east Greece, and the remaining two to the Mani in the southern Peloponnese, where their principal target was the Maniot leader Pétrobey Mavromichális. The society was already short of money, and this new proselytising effort was going to need yet more. Skoúphas was entrusted with fund-raising, and in May 1818 Panayiótis Sekéris, elder brother of the very first initiate Georgios Sekéris, contributed 10,000 piastres, more than double the whole amount raised by the society since its inception, and was rewarded with membership of the Supreme Council. By August the first Sekéris donation had been spent and Sekéris was approached again, this time contributing 25,000 piastres with promises of more. 'I commit to you', he is reported as saying, 'my whole wealth and my very life-blood.'[4] Others followed Sekéris' lead. Finally, the Council decided that they could no longer pretend that some unnamed great man, and behind him great power, was at the head of the society. The time had come to make a formal and explicit offer of the leadership to a Greek of distinction who had the backing of a major nation.

Thus the leaders of the Philikí Etería, for all their air of shoestring amateurism, had carried out a reorganisation which could hardly have been bettered by a twenty-first-century management consultant. They had set up a permanent headquarters, they had identified a new market and taken steps to exploit it, and they had a reliable source of funds. Finally, they were now starting the search for, as it were, a new chairman and chief executive. This approach was entrusted to Xánthos.

The obvious candidate to lead the Philikí Etería was the Tsar's foreign minister Iánnis Kapodhístrias. Kapodhístrias was a Greek born in Corfu in 1776, into a distinguished family whose forebears had come to the Ionian islands from Italy in the fourteenth century: hence the Italianate form of his name, Capo d'Istria. As a young man Kapodhístrias was prominent in the politics of the Ionian islands, and won the respect of the Russians during their occupation. In 1808 he was invited to St Petersburg to become one of the many non-Russians in the Tsar's foreign ministry, and rose rapidly. In 1815 the Tsar appointed Kapodhístrias as foreign minister jointly with the German Count Nesselrode.

Xánthos' mission was not in fact the first to offer the leadership of the Etería to Kapodhístrias. Some two years earlier in 1816 the maverick Galátis had been enrolled into the society by Skoúphas, who was impressed by his claims to be a count and a relation of Kapodhístrias. Galátis reached St Petersburg in January 1817, with, he said, an important message for Kapodhístrias 'concerning our nation'. Galátis' behaviour in St Petersburg was wildly indiscreet. He lived extravagantly on borrowed money, he consorted with known conspirators, and he boasted that he had a thousand men under his command and would assassinate the Tsar himself if ordered to do so. When Galátis offered Kapodhístrias the leadership of the Etería, he was immediately dismissed, in biting words which Kapodhístrias later recorded in his autobiography:

> You must be out of your senses, Sir, to dream of such a project. No one could dare communicate such a thing to me in this house, where I have

the honour to serve a great and powerful sovereign, except a young man like you, straight from the rocks of Ithaka and carried away by some sort of blind passion. I can no longer continue this discussion of the objects of your mission, and I assure you that I shall never take note of your papers. The only advice I can give you is to tell nobody about them, to return immediately where you have come from, and to tell those who sent you that unless they want to destroy themselves, and their innocent and unhappy nation with them, they must abandon their revolutionary course and continue to live as before under their present governments, until Providence decrees otherwise.[5]

After this rebuff Galátis departed for the principalities of Moldavia and Wallachia, where he recruited indiscriminately to the Etería. He eventually returned to Constantinople, where he added to his iniquities by demanding money from fellow members under threat of denunciation. The society had had enough. Tsákalov the co-founder and another senior Eterist persuaded Galátis to accompany them to the Mani. In January 1819 they stopped en route at Ermióni, the little port opposite Hydra, and there, on the pretext of visiting some ruins, they lured him to a secluded spot and killed him.

Another mission to Kapodhístrias immediately preceded Xánthos' visit. Kamárinos, an emissary of Pétrobey Mavromichális the Maniot leader, arrived in St Petersburg in late 1819 with letters from Pétrobey asking, innocently enough, for funds to support a school in the Mani, but also with an oral message in which it was clearly assumed that Kapodhístrias was the leader of the Etería. Kapodhístrias wrote a long and careful letter to Pétrobey disabusing him of this assumption. Kamárinos was shocked to learn the truth, and on his return to Constantinople caused so much trouble by revealing what he knew that he too, like Galátis, was killed.

Why did the axe fall on these two particular members? Both were a nuisance, especially Galátis, but there were often dissensions in the society, as Xánthos' autobiography shows. What appears to distinguish Galátis and Kamárinos from other unruly members is that they, and perhaps they alone, knew from Kapodhístrias' own lips that he was not the leader of the Etería nor in any way involved with it. The society had been mightily helped hitherto by the opposite assumption, and two murders were a price worth paying to keep the truth concealed. But rumour is a hydra whose heads cannot be chopped off indefinitely; the society could not forever pretend that Kapodhístrias was its leader and assassinate anyone who knew and said otherwise. Thus when Xánthos came to St Petersburg in a final attempt to persuade Kapodhístrias to accept the leadership, it is highly probable that he had an alternative plan for securing a leader from Russia, with implicit Russian support, in case Kapodhístrias again refused.

Xánthos was the best emissary the Etería could have sent. Of the two remaining co-founders, Skoúphas having died in July 1818, Xánthos was the elder – 48 to Tsákalov's 32. He had been a member of the Council from the beginning, and he had a further card to play in the shape of a letter of introduction from Kapodhístrias' old friend Ánthimos Gázis, a member of the Etería's Council, now running a school in the Mount Pílion area. Xánthos arrived in the Russian capital in January 1820. His mission was delicate. The best outcome would be for Kapodhístrias to agree after all to lead the society. This would achieve in fact what had hitherto only been hopefully hinted. But it was important not to alienate Kapodhístrias, and if he refused he should be given the impression that he was still the society's first choice as leader, but should be encouraged, if possible, to suggest an alternative choice himself.

The progress of Xánthos' discussions with Kapodhístrias confirms this view of his tactics. At a first meeting, two days after his arrival, Xánthos threw everything into the effort to persuade Kapodhístrias to accept the leadership.

> He revealed the whole organisation of the Society, its *arkhigoi*, the multiplication of its members, its extent and everything else he considered necessary, and finally that [the society] besought [Kapodhístrias] to direct, as *arkhigos*, the movement of the nation, either directly or through some suitable plan, and that he should inform the most important of his fellow countrymen who had been enrolled about the most suitable means of beginning the war. But Kapodhístrias did not accept, saying that he, being a minister of the Emperor, could not do so, and many other such things.[6]

So far, a disappointing outcome, though not unexpected. But Xánthos had still not won from Kapodhístrias the clear lead that he wanted for the society to look elsewhere for its leader. A second meeting, which to Kapodhístrias must have seemed totally unnecessary, was therefore arranged through the good offices of a Greek secretary to Kapodhístrias who was himself a member of the Etería. At this second meeting, as Xánthos records it, he repeated to Kapodhístrias 'that it was impossible for the Greeks in the future to remain under tyranny, that the revolution was inevitable, and that because they had need of a leader it was not right for him, as a Greek held in high esteem by them and many others, to remain indifferent, and so on. But the latter repeated that he could not become involved for the above reasons and that if the *arkhigoi* knew of other means to carry out their object, let them use them.'[7] The final sentence about 'other means', even if vague, was what Xánthos had been angling for. At last he had got it.

The obvious alternative candidate was Alexander Ipsilántis, a gallant soldier who had lost an arm in Russian service, who was an aide-de-camp of the Tsar and whose two brothers were already members of the Etería. At a first meeting with him, Xánthos spoke generally of the wretched condition of the Greeks, which prompted Ipsilántis to exclaim: 'If I knew that my compatriots had need of me, and thought that I could contribute to their well-being, I say to you honestly that I would gladly make any sacrifice, even of my wealth and of myself for them.'[8] Xánthos did not immediately offer him the leadership, but left Ipsilántis a night for reflection: a premature offer, and its rejection by a second distinguished Greek, would have been a catastrophe. However, at a second meeting next day the offer was made, Ipsilántis enthusiastically accepted it, and his position was confirmed in a document that he and Xánthos signed on 24 April 1820. Significantly, this paper referred to the leadership not of the Philikí Etería but of the Ellinikí Etería – the Greek Association. From its parochial beginnings the society was at last within sight of becoming a national movement.

Nevertheless the Philikí Etería was still far from being representative of Greek society as a whole. By the time the revolution began in 1821 the society's known membership was 1,093. Three-quarters of all the members were recruited abroad, over half of those in Russia and the neighbouring principalities of Moldavia and Wallachia. Of the 910 in the total membership whose occupations are known, over half were merchants, including a few commercial secretaries and ships' captains – not surprisingly given the commercial background of the founders.

The professions (teachers, doctors and so on) and prominent civilian leaders, the so-called primates or notables, each comprised a little over 10 per cent, and the clergy and the military each made up a little under 10 per cent. By far the largest stratum of Greek society, the peasants, were represented by a mere six members; obviously not much use had been made of the procedure for enrolling the illiterate. But, despite these limitations, the society had achieved a great deal. Largely thanks to the new plan of action initiated in 1818, they now had as members many men of power and position – notables such as Pétrobey Mavromichális in the Mani, soldiers such as Kolokotrónis, intellectuals such as Ánthimos Gázis. The society may have had relatively few not-ables, soldiers and intellectuals, but those they had were big names, and most were not in exile but in Greece proper. There was thus a network for passing information and orders for action, and now to activate it a battle-hardened leader whose adopted country could be expected to support him.

The Philikí Etería had also significantly begun to change the meaning of the word *patrídha*. For most Greeks its meaning was closer to 'home town' or 'birthplace' than to 'fatherland'. The problem for the Etería had been how to create a national body within a highly tradi-tional and rural society; in other words, how to extend the concept of *patrídha*. The Philikí Etería had gone some way to solving this problem, despite its improbable beginnings, uncertain start and stumbles or worse along the way. It had also succeeded in bringing together many of the elements needed for the revolution to begin. One further thing was needed: some diversion of the Turkish armed forces, which would otherwise be able to snuff out the flames of revolt before they took hold. This element was now provided by the rebellion of the Turks' nominal viceroy in Iánnina, Ali Pasha.

5

Ali Pasha

Byron visited Ali Pasha at Tepelene in 1809, and wrote a lively description of his host: 'His Highness is 60 years old, very fat and not tall, but with a fine face, light blue eyes & a white beard, his manner is very kind & at the same time he possesses that dignity which I find universal amongst the Turks. – – He has the appearance of any thing but his real character, for he is a remorseless tyrant, guilty of the most horrible cruelties, very brave & so good a general, that they call him the Mohametan Buonaparte.' After the publication of *Childe Harold's Pilgrimage* in 1812 Byron awoke to find himself famous, and Ali shared some of the fame from his cameo appearance in the work:

> 'I talk not of mercy, I talk not of fear;
> He neither must know who would serve the Vizier:
> Since the days of our prophet the Crescent ne'er saw
> A chief ever glorious like Ali Pashaw.'

Victor Hugo also compared Ali with Napoleon, but with reservations: Ali, he said, was 'the only colossus of this century who can be compared to Bonaparte . . . and is to Napoleon as the tiger to the lion, or the vulture to the eagle.'[1] Ali was visited by diplomats and soldiers, scholars and writers, tourists and adventurers, and was the inspiration for a host of more or less fanciful books, articles and dramas, becoming in western Europe the best-known figure of the Ottoman empire. His satrapy, which with those of his sons eventually covered most of Greece and some of its adjoining territory, became for a time a force with which the great powers of the day had to reckon.

The story of a girl called Euphrosyne added to Ali's reputation by making him an ogre of myth. Euphrosyne, accused of a liaison with Ali's son Mukhtar, was snatched from her house by Ali's guards and imprisoned for a day with sixteen other women, many of them prostitutes. The following night all were taken out in a boat into the middle of the Iánnina lake, and drowned in sacks. There was a storm that night, which added to the horror of the scene. The sacks were not tied, contrary to Muslim ritual, so that the women's arms were free to cling to the side of the boat, and one of the executioners in the boat never forgot the screams as the victims' desperate fingers were pried loose. The story is full of ambivalences. Was Euphrosyne, the niece of a bishop, guilty of the offence, or was she a chaste martyr? Was Ali's motive revenge for a disgrace brought on his family, or anger that his own advances to Euphrosyne had been spurned, or simply the hope of extracting bribes from the women's husbands or protectors? Whatever the answers, Ali came to be seen as a Bluebeard, striking against women as well as men, the assassin in the boudoir, a figure even more sinister than the killer on the battlefield.

Ali's grandfather, a brigand in south-west Albania, had first fought against the Turks and then switched allegiance and joined them, dying in Ottoman service. His father had killed his own brother and taken over his position as local governor. Ali was born probably in 1750, and the background of his childhood was thus the struggle for power, the necessity to change sides when opportune, and the ruthless elimination of opponents within the family as well as outside it. The family's seat of power was Tepelene, a southern Albanian town perched high on a bluff above the confluence of two rivers, and at the junction of two trade routes. Byron's Childe Harold spoke of 'the glittering minarets of Tepalen, whose walls o'erlook the stream', and the British soldier–diplomat William Leake also admired it: 'The palace is one of the most romantic and delightful country-houses that can be imagined.'[2] Today the town is wholly unremarkable, and no trace remains of the impressive buildings of Ali Pasha's time.

Ali's opportunity to begin building a power base came in 1778 when he was in his late twenties, and was appointed the derbend aga, guardian of the passes, for the whole of Roumeli, that is Greece north of the Gulf of Corinth. Ali held the post for only five winter months, but in that time he established a network of control over local officials and armed bands, and, since his autocratic rule however harsh was preferable to the lawless anarchy that had gone before, he acquired a reputation as a peacemaker. He also acquired, through protection rackets and other illegal exactions, a substantial amount of money, estimated at 150,000 piastres.

In the following years Ali led his Albanian warriors on campaigns of widespread pillaging and extortion, demonstrating that he was more than a match for any government forces sent against him. Eventually the Ottoman authorities accepted the futility of trying to crush Ali and the inevitability of accepting him into the imperial structure. In 1784, five years after losing his position as derbend aga, he was appointed governor of Delvino, in 1786 governor of Tríkala and in 1787 governor of Iánnina, the place with which he was henceforward always associated. From this base he expanded his domain to the point when by 1807 he or his sons were rulers of the Peloponnese, of virtually all Roumeli except Athens and Attica, and of much of Albania.

One small area, however, remained for a long time outside Ali's control: the Soúli region. This lies some thirty miles south-west of Iánnina, and is one of the most precipitous and romantic areas in the whole of Greece. Mountains surround it in the shape of an elongated north–south horseshoe, and even today the southern end offers the only reasonable access, where the river Acheron of classical legend, emerging from a deep and gloomy glen, flows past the village of Glikí towards the sea. Within the area of Soúli stony tracks wind round the sides of deep ravines, a few villages huddle round the small areas of cultivable land, and passes are overlooked by fortresses perched on steep rocky outcrops. It is, and always has been, a natural centre of resistance: successive pashas of Iánnina had failed to subdue the Souliots, and in the 1940s the Greek resistance and their British advisers set up a base in the Soúli area which was able to operate for many months almost undisturbed by the surrounding Germans.

The Souliots were of Albanian origin and like other warrior Albanians lived by plunder and extortion practised on their neighbours. 'Depredation they honoured with the name of war,' wrote Finlay, 'and war they considered to be the only honourable occupation for a true Suliot.'[3] It was impossible for Ali Pasha to ignore the threat of Soúli. Here within a day or two's march of his seat of power in Iánnina was a nest of rebels who could raid at will the surrounding country. The task of subduing Soúli did not look too difficult: the area was a tiny part of Ali's domains, and the population amounted to no more than 450 families divided into nineteen clans, with a fighting force of only 1,500 men.

Ali attacked Soúli without success in 1790, and again in 1792. It was a further seven years before he launched his final assault on Soúli in 1799. In the interval some of the alliances on both sides had begun to shift. A number of Ali Pasha's supporters began to see his total domination of the region as a threat to themselves, and so dragged their feet in Ali's support or even actively helped the Souliots with forewarnings of attack. On the Souliot side, cracks in the solidarity of the clans had begun to appear, prised open by Ali's offers of money, office or both. As direct assaults on the Souliots had failed, Ali now set about blockading them, building a ring of twelve fortresses on the edge of the mountains around Soúli, including one at Glikí to close off the southern and only easy road into and out of the region. Building these fortresses was slow and dangerous work: many of the masons were killed, sitting targets for Souliot sharpshooters, and during the construction an estimated one-third of Ali's troops deserted. But eventually his policy of strangulation began to take effect. By the autumn of 1803 the main body of Souliots, starving and exhausted, were assembled in the stronghold of Kúngi, just above the village of Soúli. At the eventual capitulation of Kúngi the leader of the Souliot forces, a strange nomadic monk named Last Judgement Samuel, waited with five companions until Ali's troops came to take over the arsenal, and then put a match to it, blowing himself to glory and the others to oblivion. The defeated Souliot soldiers took service wherever they could: with their old foe Ali Pasha, with the Russians or French in the Ionian islands, or with the Turkish army. A number of Souliots fought on the Greek side in the war of independence, leaders such as Márkos Bótsaris and footsoldiers such as those whose courage and élan captivated Byron and whose duplicity infuriated him.

Iánnina under Ali was one of the finest towns in all Greece. As well as its beautiful situation on the lake, overlooked by a dramatic ring of mountains, Iánnina's commerce was unrivalled. Roads ran north–south and east–west, which Ali improved. He built a canal to bring ships part of the way from Árta to Iánnina. He encouraged the building of *khans*, or *caravanserais*, inns which were often primitive and filthy but still offered the traveller some shelter and security. Also Ali regularly took what might be called commercial hostages. When Henry Holland visited Iánnina in 1812 during his extensive travels in Greece he commented on 'the system of Ali Pasha, never to allow a family to quit his territory, unless leaving behind some principal members of it, and their property also, to be responsible for their final return'.[4]

The commercial results of Ali's measures were obvious. A series of fairs was held in different towns of northern Greece during the summer, and only in Iánnina were there two fairs a year. For permanent trading, Iánnina had a large covered market, and an extensive bazaar, a string of wooden booths stretching through a number of intersecting streets, where the bustle of business there was comparable only with Constantinople's. Wages in Iánnina were among the highest in Greece and prices were correspondingly high. Iánnina had two academies, one run by the abrasive Athanásios Psalídhas who regularly castigated foreign visitors for their countries' part in the Fourth Crusade which sacked Byzantium, their current practice of removing Greek antiquities, and their failure to help Greece to her proper status in the world. Even after Ali's death and the destruction that accompanied his downfall, a visitor in 1833 declared that Iánnina was the Manchester and Paris of Roumeli.

Ali himself lived in a resplendently grand style which much impressed his visitors. He received guests in a magnificent room which was adorned by a Gobelin tapestry bearing the cypher of the King of France, the largest Gobelin ever made which had originally hung in Versailles. When Byron and his friend Hobhouse visited Iánnina in 1809, they found Ali absent in Tepelene, from where he was conducting military operations against a rival in Berat. On Ali's instructions they were royally treated in Iánnina and shown round the palace of Ali's eldest son Mukhtar by Mukhtar's son, 'a little fellow ten years old, with large black eyes as big as pigeon's eggs, and all the gravity of sixty'.[5] Byron and Hobhouse then followed Ali to Tepelene, a seventy-five-mile journey in constant torrential rain which took them nine days (the return took only four). 'I shall never forget', Byron wrote to his mother,

> the singular scene on entering Tepaleen at five in the afternoon as the Sun was going down. . . . The Albanians in their dresses (the most magnificent in the world, consisting of a long white kilt, gold worked cloak, crimson velvet gold laced jacket and waistcoat, silver mounted pistols &

daggers,) the Tartars with their high caps, the Turks in their vast pelisses & turbans, the soldiers & black slaves with the horses, the former stretched in groups in an immense open gallery in front of the palace, the latter placed in a kind of cloister below it, two hundred steeds ready caparisoned to move in a moment, couriers entering or passing out with dispatches, the kettle drums beating. . . .[6]

Tepelene the military base was as impressive as Iánnina the commercial centre.

During the long course of the Napoleonic wars, the powers from whom Ali was most anxious to gain advantage were France, Russia, Britain and of course his nominal suzerain, Turkey. Obtaining their favour was made extremely complicated by the fact that these powers were sometimes at war with other members of the group and sometimes at peace: a kaleidoscope whose pattern changed at each tap from events on the battlefield or in Europe's chancelleries. The shifting alliances and the victories or reverses of one nation or another immediately affected Ali's neighbouring territory, the Ionian islands. These comprised, as now, six islands off the west coat of Greece – Corfu, Páxos, Lévkas, Ithaca, Kephaloniá and Zákinthos – and Kíthira off the southern Peloponnese. The islands were Venetian until seized by Napoleon in 1797; captured progressively by a Russo-Turkish alliance between 1797 and 1799; under joint Russian and Turkish (but mainly Russian) control until 1807, when Russia handed them back to France as part of the Treaty of Tilsit; taken, apart from Corfu, by the British in a series of annexations from 1809 onwards, and in the end formally ceded to Britain at the Congress of Vienna in 1814, the start of fifty years of British possession of the islands during which Britain was inevitably involved in the affairs of Greece. Ali took care to maintain good relations with both France and Britain, and secured representatives of both nations at his court. France's emissary was François Pouqueville, whose unreliable history of the revolution included the myth of the revolution's beginning at Áyia Lávra. Britain was represented first by J. P. Morier, formerly Lord Elgin's secretary and so well versed in the politics of the Ottoman Balkans, and subsequently by the energetic young soldier Captain William Leake.

Ali's immediate concern was with outposts of the Ionian islands in his territory. Under the Venetians possession of the islands also included control of four coastal towns on the mainland: Butrint, a few miles across the water from the northern end of Corfu; Párga, opposite Páxos; and Préveza and Vónitsa on either side of the entrance to the Gulf of Árta. Párga was the smallest and least important but the most attractive, a little harbour with houses clustered round a half-enclosed bay, in which lies a small wooded island with a tiny white cube of a church. When the French acquired the Ionian islands from Russia by treaty in 1807, Ali seized Butrint, Préveza and Vónitsa, but the Russians garrisoned Párga against him and handed it over to the French as agreed. As the Napoleonic wars drew to an end the Pargiots sought help from Britain against their French occupiers and it was agreed that, if the inhabitants seized the town themselves and raised the British flag, the British forces would support them. The Pargiots also believed that they had been offered British protection in the future, an offer which the British said had never been made. A Union Jack was duly smuggled in, the garrison was overpowered, and British troops took possession of Párga on 22 March 1814. At the Congress of Vienna in the following year a British protectorate was imposed on the Ionian islands, but excluding the coastal towns, which were placed under direct Turkish rule. But it was also stipulated at the Congress of Vienna that any inhabitant of Párga who wished to cross to the islands could do so, and would be compensated by the Turkish government for property left behind. Not surprisingly, every single Pargiot chose to leave, and the Turkish government, unwilling to pay the obviously substantial compensation, offered Párga to Ali Pasha if he would himself undertake the compensation payments.

How much was the compensation to be? The first estimate by the Pargiots themselves was, naturally, very high, at £500,000. When British and Turkish commissioners made separate assessments of the compensation, the British estimate was £276,075, about half the Pargiots' claim, while the Turkish estimate at £56,756 was barely a tenth of it. Sir Thomas Maitland, govenor of the Ionian islands, was finally authorised to settle the amount of compensation directly with Ali, Párga not to be handed over until the pasha had paid. The sum agreed was £150,000.

On Good Friday of 1819 the people of Párga prepared to leave the homes for which they had fought so long. The bones of their ancestors were disinterred so that they would not be left behind in Ali Pasha's domain, and were burnt, thrown into the sea or carried away into exile, as were the images of saints from the churches. Three thousand Pargiots crossed to Corfu, where they were housed, and the poorest provided with food. In May the payment from Ali arrived, giving him access at last to Párga, and commissioners in Corfu distributed the money to the exiles, though not before Maitland had made some niggling deductions from the original sum. But the Pargiots were not to be consoled, and the exiles would sit on the Corfu shore gazing towards their home with tears in their eyes.

What then were the rights and wrongs of this unhappy episode? Kapodhístrias made his views clear: 'The sacrifice of Párga was carried out before my eyes. I had the sadness of seeing the population arrive on the shores of Corfu, uprooted by the bad faith and false calculations of British agents, obliged to deliver their old homes to Ali Pasha for a modest sum of money and carrying away with them only the exhumed bones of their fathers.'[7] Greek historians to this day ignore the fact that Ali's money was distributed to the exiled Pargiots and not kept by Maitland, and maintain that Britain sold Párga to Ali.[8]

It is indeed a terrible thing, at any time and place, for people to be forced to leave their settled homes, and the plight of the Pargiots roused widespread sympathy and indignation. What else could or should Britain have done for them? It would have been unrealistic for Britain to insist on the old definition of the Ionian islands, which included four towns in the territory of another power. Maitland could perhaps have extracted more in compensation for the Pargiots from Ali Pasha, but the amount agreed, at about a third of the Pargiots' own obviously inflated estimate but three times the Turkish valuation, was not unreasonable. Baggally suggests in his 1938 book, perhaps with League of Nations ideals in mind, that the status of Párga could have been decided by the wishes of the inhabitants; but territorial adjustments were not so made at the time, nor regrettably are they usually so made now. Nevertheless, the distressing representations of Párga's sufferings were widely published, especially of the Pargiots' departure by moonlight on Good Friday 1819, typically showing a majestic priest carrying the holy relics, women distraught and men with looks of stern determination. For much of Europe three sets of images came to define the sufferings of the Greeks: paintings of the massacres on Chios, of the fall of Mesolongi and, earliest of the three, of the flight from Párga.

The acquisition of Párga in 1819 was Ali's last important success, but it came well after the high tide of his fortunes. For the previous ten years the Ottoman government, under the new Sultan Mahmud II, had been taking steps to cut back Ali's excessive powers. The Sultan, proceeding carefully, made his first moves against Ali's son Veli rather than Ali himself. Veli first took over his father's pashalik of Tríkala, and in 1807 in a major addition to the power of Ali and his family he was appointed governor of the Morea, that is the whole of the Peloponnese except the Mani. The Sultan transferred Veli in 1812 to the less important pashalik of Lárissa, and in 1819 to the wholly insignificant one of Návpaktos.

So far the Porte had not used force against Ali, but an incident now occurred which raised the stakes. A relation of Ali's, Ismael Pasha, had served under Ali but had incurred his enmity and fled, arriving eventually in Constantinople, where he achieved a position of some influence and importance with the Ottoman authorities. In February 1820 an attempt was made on the life of Ismael in the streets of Constantinople; three Albanians were arrested, declared that they had been sent by Ali Pasha on their assassination mission, and were immediately executed. Ismael was appointed pasha of Iánnina in Ali's place, and ordered to lead an army against him. Things thus fell out very conveniently, and suspiciously so, for the Sultan, who now had justification for using force against his turbulent viceroy, and for Ismael, who now had the promise of a coveted pashalik and a body of troops with which to attack his old enemy.

In the summer of 1820 Ismael assembled his forces to attack Iánnina, having under his nominal command a number of other pashas and their troops. This combined force was chaotic. As Finlay put it:

> The Othoman army was slowly collected, and it formed a motley assembly, without order and without artillery. Each pasha moved forward as he mustered his followers, with a separate commissariat and a separate military chest. The daily rations and daily pay of the soldier differed in different divisions of the army. Ismael was really only the nominal commander-in-chief. He was not a soldier, and had he been an experienced officer, he could have done little to enforce order in the forces he commanded.[9]

Ali, on the other hand, appeared much better prepared for defence. An attack from the east would have to cross the Píndos range over the pass of Métsovo, one of the highest in Greece, which was defended by the Albanian chieftain Omer Vrionis with 15,000 men. To the far south-east Odysseus Andhroútsos held Livadhiá for Ali. To the north Ali's son Mukhtar, pasha of Berat, was responsible for repelling any attack from Ali's enemy the pasha of Shkoder. To the south, Préveza was the key to preventing the overland advance of an army or the landing of Ottoman troops from the sea; the defence of Préveza was entrusted to Ali's other son Veli.

Ali had, for the present at least, sufficient military resources, but he also needed the support of one of the major powers. In April 1820 at Préveza Ali met Maitland's representative Sir Frederick Hankey. Ali, while declaring that he wanted only a reconciliation with the Porte, asked the British to prevent a Turkish fleet from entering the Ionian Sea, his exposed western flank, and at the same time offered to seize the Peloponnese with the help of a few British ships and hand the territory over to Britain. This confusing and self-contradictory set of proposals worried Maitland extremely – 'I have been thinking over this unpleas-ant business all night' – especially as he foresaw Ali turning to Russia if Britain disappointed him. But instructions from the colonial secretary, Lord Bathurst, were unequivocal: as there was no treaty barring Turkish warships from the Ionian Sea, His Majesty had no right, even if he wished, to prevent any naval operations by the Ottoman Porte against the coast of the pasha.

Ali had not waited for Britain's response before turning to Russia through Paparigópoulos, the Greek secretary at the Russian consulate in Patras. Ali offered Russia even more than he offered Britain: if Russia would recognise his autonomy under the Tsar, he would raise all his subjects in revolt against the Sultan and help Russia to conquer the whole of European Turkey. These proposals of Ali's were grandiose in the extreme, and Paparigópoulos felt that he must go to St Petersburg to sound out the reactions of Russia and of the Philikí Etería to them; this took up the summer of 1820. Meanwhile Ali courted the Greeks, regarded as Russia's natural protégés because of their shared Orthodox faith: if Ali favoured the Greeks, Russia might favour him. The common people thus found their taxes reduced, debts cancelled and forced labour on Ali's projects abolished. There was even talk of Ali converting to Christianity. Moreover, as the winter of 1820 approached and the discipline and supplies of the Ottoman army, already haphazard, deteriorated further, the country round Iánnina was mercilessly ravaged. A Greek eyewitness spoke of 'troops raiding cities, townships and villages without the slightest restraint and stealing the last morsel of food from the mouths of the poor Greeks'.[10] It was not surprising that many Greeks longed to be under Ali's rule once again.

The Greeks wavered over backing Ali, and the only new allies to commit themselves to Ali's cause were, in a surprising turnaround, his old enemies the Souliots. Many had escaped to Corfu after Ali's destruction of Soúli in 1804, and had there lived on charity or on what employment they could find as mercenaries of Corfu's successive occupiers. In the conflict between the Turks and Ali the Souliots first accepted a Turkish offer: fight for us against Ali and you may return to your homeland. However, the Souliots were expected to retake Soúli by their own efforts against Ali's forces, and they proved unable to capture the central fort of Kiáphas which Ali had built after his conquest of Soúli and which, a home today only for saplings, tall grass and butterflies, still dominates the skyline. The Souliots, having failed to take Kiáphas, were withdrawn to the main body of Turkish troops outside Iánnina, where they found themselves stationed in the most exposed positions and given little support when attacked. They therefore opened negotiations with Ali, and in the middle of a December night in 1820 left the Turkish camp for Soúli, where Ali's commander handed over to them the castle of Kiáphas. The Souliots had at last returned to their barren, spectacular and beloved homeland.

Ali had gained allies in the Souliots, but had lost more important supporters. Omer Vrionis, who was deputed to hold the Métsovo pass, deserted to the Ottoman side and his army of 15,000 men dispersed. Odysseus Andhroútsos was driven out of Livadhiá. Ali's sons served him no better: in return for promises of their own safe conduct, and of pashaliks elsewhere, Mukhtar abandoned his Albanian fortresses, and Veli handed over the crucial town of Préveza. Moreover, there was no help for Ali from the powers.

As Ismael and his forces closed in on Iánnina in October 1820 Ali burnt the town and retreated to the citadel, which stood on a promontory projecting into the lake and was separated from the town by a moat. A winter of stalemate followed, with Ali and his forces isolated except for passage by boat across the lake, and Ismael unable to make any impression on the walls of the Iánnina citadel with guns brought up from Préveza. But at the beginning of January 1821 a change occurred that was of the greatest significance for the Greeks and their revolution: the Sultan dismissed Ismael as commander of the forces against Ali, and appointed in his place Khurshid Pasha, Veli's successor as governor of the Morea. Khurshid Pasha was energetic and capable, and the Sultan's natural choice to crush Ali. He at once set about reorganising Ismael's army, which was scarcely more coherent now than when it was first assembled; and the risk of defections was still so great that Khurshid, in Finlay's view, felt unable to leave the Ottoman camp for a single day. It took Khurshid almost a year to bring Ali down, a year in which Khurshid could spare only parts of his forces to fight the Greeks, and was unable to direct operations in person in the crucial area of the Peloponnese. Had he been left at his post with an intact army, the Greek rising in the Peloponnese might well have been stifled at birth.

It was not until January 1822 that Khurshid's troops finally forced their way into Ali's citadel, in which only about a hundred defenders were left. Ali offered to surrender if granted a formal pardon by the Sultan, and was persuaded to go to the little monastery of Áyios Pantelímon, a two-storey wooden building on the island in the lake, while the Sultan's decision was awaited. No such pardon was of course forthcoming. There are many accounts of the end of Ali. One story is that an officer sent by Khurshid, at the end of a meeting with Ali in the monastery, turned and stabbed him, another that the officer arrived with a document but accompanied by troops, which showed Ali that the document was not a pardon, whereupon both sides opened fire and Ali was wounded. The final shot came, it was said, when Ali after a confused struggle took refuge in a room on the upper floor of the monastery, and his attackers fired up through the floorboards, fatally wounding him in the groin. However, Finlay had not heard this version until he visited the monastery thirty years later, and it is just the sort of story that an inventive guide would spin when showing a visitor a hole in the floor. Whatever the details, Ali's death was confirmed when his severed head was exhibited first in Iánnina and then in Constantinople, where it was joined soon afterwards by those of his sons.

Was Ali Pasha, then, worthy of comparison with Napoleon? Both came from nothing and founded an empire – in Ali's case, an empire within an empire. Both set up dynasties, making members of their families governors of lands they had conquered or otherwise acquired, but neither family dynasty survived its founder. It can also be said that Ali destabilised the Ottoman empire in somewhat the same way as Napoleon destabilised Europe, releasing forces for profound change, in Ali's case the forces of Greek aspirations to independence. But Ali, even on his small stage, was no Bonaparte. His motives were at best his own security, at worst cupidity and vengeance. His understanding of the people and clans that he governed was used only in attempts to manipulate them for his short-term advantage. He was unable to get support from any outside power. His distinguished visitors usually saw him as a colourful rogue rather than a great man. Victor Hugo was therefore right to imply that Ali was to Napoleon as no more than the vulture to the eagle.

6

Revolt along the Danube

In April 1820 the Philikí Etería had at last found a leader in Alexander Ipsilántis, the dashing soldier not yet 30 with impressive credentials both as a staff officer – he had been ADC to the Tsar – and on the battlefield, where he had lost his right arm. However, Ipsilántis' mandate was only the very general one that he should 'supervise and command [the society] in every respect'.[1] He had to decide what to make of his new position.

The first step was to discover what support he might expect from Russia, that is from Kapodhístrias and from the Tsar. Ipsilántis was later to claim that Kapodhístrias had encouraged him, and Kapodhístrias to deny it. Kapodhístrias by his own account urged extreme caution, saying, 'Those drawing up such plans are most guilty and it is they who are driving Greece to calamity. They are wretched hucksters destroyed by their own evil conduct and now taking money from simple souls in the name of the fatherland they do not possess. They want you in their conspiracy to inspire trust in their operations. I repeat: be on your guard against these men.'[2] Kapodhístrias also refused to allow Ipsilántis an interview with the Tsar, and Ipsilántis had to contrive the meeting himself, coming across the Tsar as if by chance while he was walking in the garden of the summer palace at Tsarskoe Selo. Ipsilántis tried to talk to him about the plight of the Greeks, but the Tsar would go no further than to say: 'You are young and eager, as always, my friend, but you can see that Europe is at peace.'[3] The tone was genial, but the message was clear: do nothing to disturb the peace of Europe.

For the next year of preparation Ipsilántis, unrestrained it seems by

the cautions of Kapodhístrias and the Tsar, embarked on a hectic programme of travel, mainly in the company of Xánthos, the man who had
brought him to the leadership of the Philikí Etería. He went for a few
days to Moscow, from there to Kiev, Ipsilántis' family home, in early
August to Odessa and finally to the town of Izmail, no more than
twenty-five miles from the Wallachian border, where many leaders of the
society were now assembled. From Izmail on 8 October Ipsilántis issued
a proclamation calling on all Greeks to prepare for the coming struggle,
in words which betrayed a dangerous incoherence in his thinking. He
first dismissed the idea that the Greeks needed foreign help to achieve
their independence, claiming that they still had the military prowess of
their classical ancestors: 'Cast your eyes toward the seas, which are
covered by our seafaring cousins, ready to follow the example of Salamis.
Look to the land, and everywhere you will see Leonidas at the head of
patriotic Spartans.' By contrast, he said, the Turks were flabby, weak and
disunited, so the Greeks could easily defeat them alone. Moreover,
foreigners always exacted a price for their aid. Let the Greeks therefore
first shake off the tyrants' yoke by their own efforts, and then the great
powers would be forced to make alliances with them.[4] But the reality
was that foreign support was vital to the success of a Greek revolution,
and Ipsilántis knew it. Indeed his whole strategy was based on the
assumption that his venture would have Russian support.

Ipsilántis had from the first envisaged a revolt beginning in the
Danubian principalities of Moldavia and Wallachia, but by October
1820, at the time of the Izmail proclamation, he had changed his mind
and announced that the revolution should be launched in the
Peloponnese before the end of the year. However, his contacts in the
Peloponnese told him that the Peloponnese was not yet ready, information which Ipsilántis should have sought before publicising his plan
rather than after. Ipsilántis therefore reverted to the original idea of
beginning the revolt in Moldavia and Wallachia, a decision for which
there had always been a number of compelling reasons.

Ipsilántis knew the region, as his father had been governor of
Wallachia until deposed in 1806. More importantly, Ipsilántis' forces, if
gathered in south-west Russia, were only the width of a river from
Moldavia, but would need complex and risky transport to reach the
Peloponnese. Ipsilántis also hoped that the immediate neighbours of

the principalities, the Serbs and the Bulgarians, would join the rising – hopes which came to nothing. Another factor, cynically suggested at the time, was that Ipsilántis wanted his campaign near a frontier across which he could escape if things went wrong: either the Russian frontier on the east of the principalities or, if necessary, the less welcoming Austrian frontier to the north. Furthermore, Russia had a basis for intervention in the principalities which she did not have elsewhere in Ottoman territory. Moldavia and Wallachia were technically only vassal states of Turkey, not part of the empire, and the Sultan was forbidden by treaty to send troops into the area without Russian agreement. Thus Russia might, it was hoped, prevent by her veto the use of Turkish forces against Ipsilántis, or, if the veto was disregarded, drive the Turks back, or, at worst, occupy the principalities jointly with Turkey, which could be regarded as a step towards their freedom. Crucial to all these calculations, of course, was the assumption that once Ipsilántis crossed the border and raised the banner of freedom the people of the principalities would flock to it and help him to establish their independence.

Moldavia comprised the eastern part of present-day Romania, and Wallachia the southern, both being separated by the Carpathian mountains from Transylvania, then part of Austria's empire. The river Pruth marked Moldavia's eastern frontier with Russia, and the Danube Wallachia's southern border with present-day Bulgaria. The plains of the principalities formed one of the most fertile and productive parts of the Ottoman domains and were Constantinople's main providers of food. Since 1716 the principalities had been governed by phanariot Greeks, that is Greeks from the prosperous Phanar district of Constantinople who formed the upper ranks of the Ottoman civil service, and it was thanks to their initiatives in agriculture that the region had become Constantinople's main granary. They also introduced schools, printing presses and a theatre in Bucharest which put on tragedies and comedies in French and plays translated into Greek. With wealth and culture came decadence. Neroúlos, first minister to the governor of Moldavia when Ipsilántis invaded, wrote: 'On remarquait dans ces provinces la frivolité à côté de la politesse, et le relâchement des moeurs à côté de l'urbanité.'[5] The principalities were thus ripe for exploitation by a succession of Turkish-appointed hospodars or governors. 'As the fiscal agent of the sultan,' wrote Finlay, '[the hospodar] was terrible to his subjects, and as an extortioner, for his own profit, he was hateful. The hospodars themselves amassed large fortunes in a few years, and every new hospodar came attended by a crowd of hungry and rapacious Greeks, who usually arrived loaded with debts, but who expected, like their master, to enrich themselves during a short tenure of office.' Thus the inhabitants of the principalities 'were the wretched slaves of a race of rapacious oppressors, who were also themselves slaves'.[6]

It was therefore unlikely, on any realistic view, that Ipsilántis would receive support for the Greek cause from the people of the principalities; the poor had every reason to hate their Greek overlords and the rich had no inclination to change their comfortable and cultivated lives. He could however expect support from some of the leaders, at least so long as he was useful to them in their own pursuit of increased power. One supporter was the governor of Moldavia, Michael Soútsos, ruling from the capital Iaşi. He seemed an enthusiastic member of the Philikí Etería and offered the society substantial sums of money, but he may not have been as committed to Ipsilántis' cause as he appeared. Neroúlos, his first minister, recorded that Soútsos warned the Turkish foreign minister of Ipsilántis' imminent entry into Moldavia and asked for instructions. This was a prudent move, since if Ipsilántis succeeded Soútsos could ignore the instructions, and if Ipsilántis failed Soútsos could claim to have been a loyal servant of the Porte throughout.

In Wallachia intrigue was rife. The governor, Alexander Soútsos (no relation of the Moldavian governor), was gravely ill, some said poisoned by agents of the Etería, and in January 1821 on his deathbed set up a caretaker government of native nobles or boyars. These saw this interregnum as an opportunity to establish Wallachian rights, in particular the right to be governed by a native prince rather than a phanariot Greek. To this end they sent at the end of January one of the government's military commanders, Theodore Vladimirescu, into western Wallachia, ostensibly to put down disturbances there, but in fact with instructions to create a disturbance of his own, aimed at inciting the local inhabitants and boyars against the phanariot Greeks. Vladimirescu's private motive, however, was to make himself prince of an independent Wallachia. His game was thus a double one from the start, and its increasing deceptions finally undid him. Of a different stamp was another of the Bucharest commanders, Iorgáki Olimpiótis. Thomas Gordon, historian of the Greek revolution and participant in it, described Iorgáki as 'distinguished for prudence, valour, and patriotism, and enthusiastically wedded to the principles of the Hetoeria [Etería]. He would have been the most proper man to take the direction of the war beyond the Danube, but . . . Ypsilanti reserved that task to himself.'[7] Initially Vladimirescu and Iorgáki were on the same side, both apparently devoted to the Philikí Etería, and they had even signed an agreement to support each other in its cause. Vladimirescu was a political animal, Iorgáki quite the opposite: Neroúlos wrote that 'le capitaine Georgaky, intrépide en face des armées ennemies, montrait de la timidité devant les prétendus politiques, qui fourmillaient dans le camp d'Ypsilanty'.[8] The co-operation between Iorgáki and Vladimirescu was not to last.

We left Ipsilántis at the Russian town of Izmail on the Danube in October 1820, having decided that the rising should after all begin in Moldavia and Wallachia, not in the Peloponnese. In December 1820 he moved his headquarters north to Kishinev, the Russian town closest to the Moldavian capital Iaşi, and on 6 March 1821 crossed the river Pruth at the border settlement of Skulyany. He was accompanied only by two of his younger brothers, by Georgios Kantakouzinós, a Russian colonel from an old Wallachian family who was shortly to be appointed Ipsilántis' chief of staff, and a handful of others including servants, about ten people in all; but 70,000 Russian troops, he claimed, would soon follow. On the same day that they crossed the Pruth Ipsilántis and his party, with a troop of 200 cavalry sent out from Iaşi to escort them, entered the city half an hour after sunset.

Ipsilántis' first proclamation from Iaşi expressed no doubts about the success of his venture. Running to well over a thousand words, it recalled again the heroes of antiquity and claimed that the descendants of Athens' ancient enemy Persia, the barbarous and inhuman Turks, 'we today, with very little effort, are about to annihilate completely'. Perhaps no effort at all would be needed: if the Greeks united, they would 'see those old giants of despotism fall of their own accord'. Ipsilántis no longer spurned foreign assistance, as in his proclamation of the previous October, but now looked to the enlightened peoples of Europe and hoped that 'we will achieve their support and help'. In a clear reference to Russia, he said: 'Move, O friends, and you will see a mighty Empire defend our rights.'[9] But however confident Ipsilántis appeared in his public pronouncements, privately he nursed doubts. On the same day that he issued the proclamation from Iaşi he sent a letter to the Tsar in a final attempt to turn his hopes of Russian support into reality: 'Will you, Sire, abandon the Greeks to their fate, when a single word from you can deliver them from the most monstrous tyranny and save them from the horrors of a long and terrible struggle?'[10] He was proclaiming that aid from the 'mighty Empire' was certain, but he knew that it was far from being guaranteed.

The confident tone of the proclamation was soon belied, since Ipsilántis' campaign could hardly have got off to a worse start. At Galatz, some 120 miles south of Iaşi, supporters of Ipsilántis, led by Vasílios Karaviás, killed the local Turkish commander and his men, and murdered the Turkish merchants in the town. Karaviás was rewarded with appointment as one of Ipsilántis' two battalion commanders, and was to prove nothing but trouble throughout the campaign. A second massacre took place at Iaşi, where the governor Michael Soútsos persuaded the Turkish guard of about fifty men to disarm, promising them security of life and property. When the news of the Galatz slaughter arrived, the promise was disregarded and these Turks too were killed, without either Soútsos or Ipsilántis intervening at the time or condemning the action afterwards. Furthermore Ipsilántis found far less money available to him in Iaşi than he had expected. He tried to remedy this by extortion from the rich, extracting large sums from one Greek banker on the ground that he had concealed Etería funds. Because there was not enough money to pay the troops which Ipsilántis was beginning to assemble, they took to plundering the region. Thus within days of Ipsilántis' arrival he or his subordinates had provoked the Turks to retaliation, had alienated potential supporters among the rich and had shown the inhabitants of Moldavia that they could expect nothing but disorder from his expedition.

What strategies were now open to Ipsilántis? The most aggressive would have been to seize the three Turkish fortresses on the southern side of the Danube, the approach favoured with hindsight by Finlay, who was ever ready to revise the strategy of past campaigns from his study. A less aggressive but more realistic approach would have been to move quickly to Bucharest, thus becoming master of the capital of

Wallachia as well as of Moldavia. Ipsilántis did move towards Bucharest but not quickly enough, and it was a full month before he reached the outskirts of the city in early April. He was accompanied by a force of about 2,000, including 800 horsemen and a body of 500 young Greeks from outside the principalities, designated the Sacred Battalion in memory of the picked troops of fourth-century BC Thebes. These young men, with their black uniforms and death's-head cap badges, formed a spectacular but wholly inexperienced part of Ipsilántis' forces, the greater part of them, said Gordon, having just quitted colleges or counting-houses in Russia, Germany and Italy. It was during Ipsilántis' leisurely progress to Bucharest that the Greeks of the Peloponnese rose against the Turks, though it was some time before Ipsilántis had news of it. When he reached Bucharest he found that Vladimirescu had seized control of the city ahead of him.

It was by now clear that Vladimirescu was not going to play the part simply of a servant of the Philikí Etería and a subordinate of Ipsilántis. He had left Bucharest at the end of January, ostensibly to restore order in the west of Wallachia. Before he had gone far he learnt that the ailing governor, Alexander Soútsos, had died, which emboldened him to issue a proclamation to all Wallachians. This called on them to assemble, at a place to be announced, with whatever weapons they had, and stated that his movement was against the government of the phanariot Greeks ('the dragons who swallow us alive') and not against the Turks. A petition that he sent to Constantinople at the same time, assuring the Sultan of his loyalty and asking only for a commissioner to investigate complaints, made his conciliatory attitude to the Turks even clearer. A break with Ipsilántis was becoming inevitable.

At the beginning of March Vladimirescu began his march on Bucharest, sending ahead among others Iorgáki Olympiótis, who was still at this stage his ally. A panic-stricken exodus from the city began, and by 23 March the Prussian consul reported that everyone who could leave had fled and that the lower classes were left without work. By the end of the month Vladimirescu was installed in a monastery on the edge of the city, of which he was effectively in control. Thus when Ipsilántis arrived a week later a British despatch reported: 'Theodore has succeeded in preventing the entry of the army of Ypsilandi into Buccarest (*his* capital), but treats Ypsilandi himself with great respect, has given him a superb house for his residence, and offered him all necessary supplies, upon payment of ready money.'[11] However, the manoeuvres for power within the principalities were now to be disrupted by two almost simultaneous interventions from outside.

One intervention was the announcement of the Orthodox church's anathema against Ipsilántis' revolt, signed by the patriarch and twenty-two other bishops. The anathema specifically named Ipsilántis and Michael Soútsos, and was in savage terms. The powers that be were ordained by God, it declared, and whoever objected to this empire, which was vouchsafed to them by God, rebelled against God's command. Ipsilántis and Soútsos were therefore guilty of 'a foul, impious and foolish work', which had provoked 'the exasperation of our benevolent powerful Empire against our compatriots and fellow subjects, hastening to bring common and general ruin on the whole nation'. All church and secular leaders were to shun the rebels and do all they could to undermine the rebellion. As for the rebels themselves, 'may they be excommunicated and be cursed and be not forgiven and be anathematised after death and suffer for all eternity'.[12]

The patriarch's anathema predictably followed the lines of the Paternal Exhortation of 1798. The other intervention, which preceded it by a few days, was wholly unexpected. The previous year had seen an outbreak of revolutionary activity in several different parts of Europe. There had been a military insurrection in Spain, followed by a rising in Portugal, and an army mutiny in Naples prompted by the Carbonari, and there were fears of similar risings in Germany and France. Some, including Tsar Alexander, believed that all these movements were controlled by a directing committee in Paris. Towards the end of 1820 therefore the Tsar called a conference of the Quintuple Alliance – Russia, Austria, Prussia, Britain and France – which met first at Troppau (modern Opava, in the Czech Republic) and in early 1821 moved to Laibach (modern Ljubljana, in Slovenia). The conference, in both locations on Austrian territory, was dominated by the Austrian chancellor Metternich, whose determination to suppress revolt and refuse demands for reform finally swayed the Tsar against his previously held liberal convictions. These had long been weakening and had received a further blow when news reached the conference in November 1820 of the mutiny of the elite Semeonovsky Regiment in St Petersburg. By

February 1821 Metternich was able to write of the Tsar: 'His innermost thoughts have undergone a profound change, and I believe I have contributed a good deal to it.'[13] Metternich's antagonist in the struggle for the Tsar's soul was Kapodhístrias, still Russia's joint foreign minister, who although firmly for the restoration of order ('there is no doubt that what exists in Naples must be destroyed') continued to press for mediation in disputes and readiness to grant constitutional rights. 'One cannot', he wrote, 'reform the mind with bayonets.'[14]

When news of Ipsilántis' rising reached the conference Kapodhístrias was said to have been 'like a man struck by a thunderbolt', probably because he realised that the Tsar would now disown Ipsilántis' rising explicitly and publicly, and that he as foreign minister would have to help the Tsar to do so. Thus it fell to Kapodhístrias to draft the Tsar's severe response. This expressed the Tsar's sorrow at Ipsilántis' abandonment of 'the precepts of religion and morality', condemned Ipsilántis' 'obscure devices and shady plots', especially his implication of Russian support, and ordered him to withdraw at once from the principalities, where the Tsar would give him no support and would in no circumstances intervene. Ipsilántis himself was dismissed from the Tsar's army, and would never be allowed to return to Russia.[15] The Tsar's denunciation was published by the Russian consuls and vice-consuls throughout the principalities.

Ipsilántis' venture was now doomed; and, as well as the blows inflicted by denunciations from the church and the Tsar, the Turks were preparing to move against him from their fortresses on the southern bank of the Danube. Michael Soútsos was under pressure both from his subjects, now thoroughly disillusioned about Ipsilántis' enterprise, and from the threat of Turkish invasion, and fled with his family across the Pruth into Bessarabia. It is hard to see him as anything more than a fairweather friend of the Etería. A further problem was the questionable conduct of Vladimirescu, who, as Ipsilántis learnt from intercepted despatches, was now negotiating with the Turks, offering them military help in return for the coveted governorship of Wallachia. Ipsilántis, now banned from Russian soil, could escape only northwards to the hardly more welcoming territory of Austria, and feared that Vladimirescu's forces would cut off his northern route while the Turks pressed him from the south.

Vladimirescu's harsh discipline had made him increasingly unpopular with his officers and men alike. Some of these officers, sympathetic to the Etería and outraged by their commander's execution of one of their own number, engineered a public confrontation between Vladimirescu and Iorgáki Olimpiótis, who was now firmly in Ipsilántis' camp and intent on preventing Vladimirescu blocking the route to the north. At this meeting Iorgáki produced and read out to the assembled company both the original agreement between the two men, in which Vladimirescu promised support for the Etería, and Vladimirescu's later compromising letters to the Turks. Vladimirescu was seized and taken to Ipsilántis' camp, and two nights later was butchered by the sabres of two of Ipsilántis' officers, one of them Karaviás, who had in the first days of the rising demonstrated his brutality at Galatz.

Ipsilántis' escape route to the north was now open and by mid-June he had reached Rîmnicu, about twenty miles south of the pass of Turnul Roşu, the only significant gap in the western Carpathians. His forces, now augmented by Vladimirescu's disaffected men, were considerable: about 2,500 cavalry, and an infantry of some 3,000 to 4,000 local militia plus the 500 youths of the Sacred Battalion. There now seemed an opportunity for some military success at last against the advancing Turks. On 19 June a force under the command of Iorgáki, and including the Sacred Battalion under Ipsilántis' younger brother Nicholas and a body of 500 cavalry under Karaviás, moved south from Rîmnicu and trapped 800 Turkish soldiers in the village of Drăgăşani. Rain had been incessant that day, and as Iorgáki's men were exhausted by a long march over sodden ground he postponed the attack on the heavily outnumbered Turks until next day. Karaviás however, eager to secure glory for himself, and reportedly drunk at the time, persuaded Nicholas Ipsilántis to lead the Sacred Battalion into battle at once, promising support from his cavalry. The young men of the Battalion, exhausted by their march, stiff from a short rest and totally inexperienced in battle, stumbled forward and the Turkish cavalry, charging out from their cover in the buildings of Drăgăşani, fell upon them before they had time to form squares. Karaviás and his cavalry turned and fled. Iorgáki led a counter-attack in the course of which his horse was shot from under him, and rescued the standard of the Sacred Battalion and a hundred of their number. The remaining 400 lay dead in a muddy field, cut to pieces in a few minutes, and the single direct engagement of Ipsilántis' forces with the Turks had ended in a crushing defeat. Among the dead was Tsákalov, one of the founders of the Philikí Etería. The whole army was thrown into confusion, as a contemporary recorded: 'In vain did Ipsilántis rush into the middle of the road in an attempt to block further flight, reform his forces and renew the battle. Officers and men, seized by a great terror, fled helter-skelter, deaf to all commands, exhortations, entreaties and supplications. The army had fallen apart.'[16]

Ipsilántis was now concerned solely with his own escape into Austrian territory, fearing not only capture by the Turks but the possibility of arrest by some of his followers, who would then use him as a bargaining counter in negotiation for their own safety. Most of his companions left him, some to carry on the fight as best they could in the principalities, some to escape to friendly territory. Ipsilántis, after a three-day wait within half an hour's march of the frontier for permission to cross into Austria, finally made his way through the pass of Turnul Roşu to Sibiu with his two brothers, four other officers, and seven of his closest friends disguised as servants.

There he issued a final proclamation, antedated to before his flight so that it could be read as if he was still in command of his troops and prepared to fight and die with them. Ipsilántis praised the dead of the Sacred Battalion, and 'those friends who have shown me loyalty and honesty to the last'. On the other hand he consigned six of his commanders to 'the hatred of humanity, the justice of the laws and the curses of their countrymen'. A seventh commander, the infamous Karaviás, he stripped of his rank. The most searing condemnation, however, was for his troops:

> Soldiers! No! I will no longer pollute that sacred and honourable name by applying it to you. You are a cowardly rabble. . . . You have broken your oaths, you have betrayed God and your country, you have betrayed me too at the moment when I hoped either to conquer or to die with honour among you. . . . Run off to the Turks, who alone are worthy of your support . . . run off to the Turks, and kiss their hands from which still drips the blood of those they have inhumanly slaughtered. Yes! Run off to them, buy slavery with your lives and with the honour of your wives and children.[17]

It was a disgraceful outburst by a failed commander against the men he had undertaken to lead.

Ipsilántis was arrested on crossing the frontier and imprisoned by the Austrians at Mohács, then reputedly one of the unhealthiest places in Hungary. He remained in prison until 1827, when he was released with his health broken, and he died in the following year. For the rest of the summer of 1821 Ipsilántis' former troops, now dispersed under individual commanders, were harried by the Turkish forces. Kantakouzinós escaped to Russia across the river Pruth at Skulyany, where the ill-fated venture had begun. Iorgáki was eventually cornered at the monastery of Sekou in the north-west corner of Moldavia, with about a hundred companions. The belfry where his ammunition was stored caught fire, possibly ignited by Iorgáki himself, and he died in the explosion. Thus in a few months between the spring and autumn of 1821 Ipsilántis' venture was launched, sputtered uncertainly into life, and came to a bloody end.

Ipsilántis and his expedition are usually given a place of honour in Greek histories, Ipsilántis as one of the first martyrs in the cause of independence and his expedition as the first step towards achieving it. Other commentators view the matter very differently. Gordon speaks of Ipsilántis' mistaken ideas and want of sound judgement, his dilatory and vacillating movements, his indulgence in vain pomp and frivolous amusements; and, after recounting the quarrels between Ipsilántis' commanders, asks in exasperation: 'What could be expected from an army so constituted and so commanded?'[18] Neroúlos comments: 'Tout était désordre dans le conseil d'Ypsilanty: point de plan systématique, point d'organisation, ni prévoyance ni mesure efficace.'[19] George Finlay, who described himself as alternately English traveller and volunteer in the Greek war, is even more forthright and crushingly concludes that 'the public career of Prince Alexander Hypsilantes offers not one single virtuous or courageous deed on which the historian can dwell with satisfaction. He was a contemptible leader, and a worthless man.'[20]

In Ipsilántis' defence it must be said that the Philikí Etería, in its desperate search for a leader, had settled on a man both too young and too inexperienced for the task. He was quite unfitted to deal with the multiple manoeuvres of supposed supporters of the Etería, the slippery allegiances of his captains and the uncertain adherence of his allies. His empty right sleeve was a mark of his courage in battle, but was no guarantee of his grasp as a commander. It must also be said that Ipsilántis' gamble on support from Russia was not totally naive. The Tsar's actions were profoundly influenced by his devout religious beliefs and his sympathy for fellow Orthodox Greeks, and in the battle for his soul Metternich was far from winning the complete victory which he claimed. It was Ipsilántis' tragedy that, at the moment when he most needed the Tsar's support, the Tsar was under the combined pressures of fear of widespread revolt in Europe, alarm at mutiny in his own army, and the influence of Metternich rather than Kapodhístrias.

All that Ipsilántis' expedition had achieved was proof of certain uncomfortable facts: that there would be no pan-Balkan rising against the Ottoman empire, as Rígas had dreamed; that to win independence the Greeks were going to need the help of outside powers; and that this help would not easily be forthcoming. These were very small gains for all the blood and treasure expended. But when all the expedition's bunglings and disasters have been listed, its story yet reveals gleams of the heroic idealism that was to attract so many foreign philhellenes to the cause. There is no better example than the letter written by a young officer of the Sacred Battalion a few days before it was destroyed at Drăgăşani:

> I no longer have any boots, and my feet are cut to pieces. I sleep in the middle of dangerous swamps. I live on wild fruit, and can scarcely find a broken crust of bread. But these privations are sweet to me, and my life is a delight. From a child I have dreamt of nothing else but the day of our uprising. I now find myself for the first time at the head of free men, who do not load me with empty titles but give me the sweet name of brother. . . . When and where are we to see each other again? Only God can know.[21]

7

Doubts and Deliberations in the South

In the Peloponnese, during the winter of 1820–1, both Greeks and Turks lived in an uneasy atmosphere compounded of expectation and apprehension. It was said to be like calm before a storm, or dry tinder awaiting a spark, or perhaps most aptly in Finlay's words, 'Each party seemed to be waiting for a signal from a distance, and the winter was passed in anxiety and hope.'[1]

The landscape of the Peloponnese is largely mountainous, with limited fertile plains, and communication and transport easier by sea than by land. Well-established harbours had therefore become the main centres of population, and were the sites of a chain of major fortresses built or extended by the Venetians, possession of which was seen by both Greeks and Turks as the key to control of the Peloponnese. These were at Patras and the nearby Castle of the Morea, modern Río, with its twin the Castle of Roumeli, modern Antírio, just across the Gulf of Corinth; and, reading clockwise, the Akrokórinthos above the town of Corinth; the fortress of Palamídhi at Navplion overlooking one of the best harbours in the Peloponnese, and its near neighbour at Árgos; the great fortified rock at Monemvasía in the south-east; Koróni and Methóni on the tip of the south-western promontory of the Peloponnese; and two castles at Navarino by the modern town of Pílos, Old Navarino on a cliff top away from the town and New Navarino immediately above the town itself. A further stronghold was the walled town of Tripolis in the centre of the Peloponnese, which was the seat of Ottoman government.

There were only two routes by which a Turkish overland army could enter the Peloponnese. One was in the north-east across the Corinth isthmus, an unbroken land bridge, and from there the road south led through a narrow pass, the Dhervenákia, which was later the scene of a crushing defeat of the Turks by the Greeks. The other route into the Peloponnese was in the north-west at the narrowest part of the Gulf of Corinth. This involved a short sea crossing some twenty miles east of Mesolongi from the Castle of Roumeli to the Castle of the Morea, with a landfall about five miles east of Patras.

The government of the Peloponnese was unusual in the autonomy it allowed to one of its provinces, the Mani. The inner Mani comprises the last twenty miles or so of the central promontory of the Peloponnese, while the outer Mani extends to Yíthion on the east side and almost to Kalamáta on the west. The inner Mani especially is rocky, barren and spectacular; 'No prospect', says Gordon, 'can be more dismal than that of the Laconian coast about Cape Taenarus (or Matapan); stormy waves chafing against huge masses of rock, bare and pointed mountains separated by deep chasms, rudely constructed towers surrounded by miserable hamlets, and a squalid and half-naked population.'[2] The modern traveller still finds the landscape dotted with the forbidding towers in which feuding Maniots would take shelter from their enemies, sometimes for years. The inhabitants had always been ferociously warlike. In 1600 a French visitor, Castella, reported that 'These mountain dwellers are so laden with weapons that they look like hedgehogs,' and a century later the Venetian governor of the area commented that 'their past successes make them disposed to uprisings and they want to keep their privileges immutable'.[3]

These privileges were increased as a result of the revolt of 1770, inspired by Russia through Count Gregory Orlov and centred on the Mani. The Greeks were abandoned by their Russian instigators, and the Turks used Albanian mercenaries, many of whom later settled in the region, in a ferocious suppression of the rising. Six years later jurisdiction over the Mani was transferred from the pasha of the Morea, governor till now of the whole Peloponnese, to the kapitan pasha, head of the Turkish army as well as the navy and overlord of the islands of the Aegean, one of which the Mani was now in a sense deemed to be. The kapitan pasha delegated his responsibility for order and for tax collection in the Mani to a representative of one of the leading local families as bey of the Mani, following the regular Ottoman practice of devolving power, especially in difficult areas, to the local level. Under their local beys the Mani began to enjoy increased prosperity in an era characterised as the golden age of Mani. The eighth bey since 1776, appointed in 1815, was Pétrobey Mavromichális.

Pétrobey was in some ways an unlikely figure to find among the leaders of the rising in 1821. There are contemporary descriptions which portray him as an avuncular patriarch. Finlay writes of 'his frank, joyous disposition', and Gordon describes him as 'a very handsome man, dignified in his deportment, mild in his manners, fond of the pleasures of the table, lavish in his expenditure, and therefore always pinched for money . . . fitted by nature rather to indulge in opulent ease than to take part in a revolutionary tempest'. But Finlay also presents another side to Pétrobey, as 'restless, vain, bold, and ambitious . . . more prompt to form courageous resolutions than most of his countrymen in high station',[4] and enjoying great personal influence through his extended family, of whom no fewer than forty-nine fell in battle during the revolution. In its first years Pétrobey was one of the main figures to be reckoned with by the Ottoman government and by his Greek colleagues.

The turn of the year from 1820 to 1821 saw one significant departure from the Peloponnese and two important arrivals. The departure was that of Khurshid, pasha of the Morea, who was transferred to Iánnina to take command of operations against Ali Pasha, and left the Peloponnese in mid-January 1821. Appointed only in the previous November, Khurshid had not had time to establish a policy or even fully to assess the situation in his area of command, which despatches from his superiors told him was potentially explosive and the Greeks assured him was calm apart from a few troublemaking agents of Ali Pasha. Khurshid left behind as acting governor of the Peloponnese his deputy Mehmed Salik, characterised by Finlay as 'a young man of an arrogant disposition and no military experience'.[5] It was not until late April that Mustafa Bey arrived as lieutenant-governer of the Morea. There was thus a slackening of the reins of Ottoman control of the Peloponnese in the crucial months before and just after rebellion broke out.

The arrivals in the Peloponnese during the winter of 1820–1 were of two Greeks: Theódhoros Kolokotrónis and Grigórios Dhikéos, commonly called Papaphléssas, both members of the Philikí Etería since

1818. Kolokotrónis above all others personifies the revolution for Greece. Statues of him mark his victories and ballads commemorate his achievements. An Athens street – unfortunately now one of the seedier ones – bears his name. His face, from the lithograph by Hanfstaengl, gazes sombrely from the 5,000 drachma banknote. He was 50 years old in 1821 when he came to the Peloponnese, where his youth had been spent in brigand warfare, and to which he was returning after years of service as a mercenary in the Ionian islands under the successive Russian, French and British occupiers. 'It would be impossible', wrote Gordon, 'for a painter or a novelist to trace a more romantic delineation of a robber chieftain, than the figure of Colocotroni presented; tall and athletic, with a profusion of black hair and expressive features, alternately lighted up with boisterous gaiety, or darkened by bursts of passion: among his soldiers, he seemed born to command, having just the manners and bearing calculated to gain their confidence.'[6] Kolokotrónis had no doubt of his own abilities: 'If Wellington had given me an army of forty thousand,' he wrote, 'I could have governed it, but if five hundred Greeks had been given to him to lead, he could not have governed them for an hour.'[7]

In mid-January 1821, within a day or two of Khurshid's departure from the Peloponnese, Kolokotrónis arrived there from Zákinthos. According to his own memoirs, he came to the Peloponnese with a clear plan of action in mind which he immediately set about putting into effect. He wrote to the various and often antagonistic families of the Mani; he sent messages to the common people throughout central and southern Peloponnese to be ready to rise in revolt; he instructed that all the fortresses should be besieged simultaneously; and he fixed the day of the rising as 25 March (Old Style), the feast of the Evangelismós or Annunciation, thus linking the revolutionary with the Biblical announcement.

Kolokotrónis came to the struggle as a warrior, whereas the contribution of the other arrival in the Peloponnese, Papaphléssas, was that of a firebrand orator. He was in his early thirties and was the youngest of his father's twenty-eight children, thus offering an interesting case-study to those who link aggressive characteristics to intense sibling rivalry. After an education at the famous school in Dhimitsána, he became a monk and later an archimandrite (roughly equivalent to a dean). In October 1820 Papaphléssas was a member of the gathering at Izmail near the Wallachian border, from which Alexander Ipsilántis issued his first revolutionary proclamation. Moving on to Kidhoníes, on the west coast of Turkey, he organised a shipment of powder, lead and other war materials for the Mani. Crossing the Aegean he tried to inspire the leading families of Hydra and Spétses to revolt, but met opposition from the cautious and conservative elements. When, to counter the Hydriots' fear of the Turkish fleet, he told them that he would sink it in its harbour at Constantinople, they asked him drily to let them know when he had done so. It is not surprising that his preaching did not appeal to the unconverted. His style was threatening and insistent rather than persuasive, and a letter from him to Xánthos is typical: 'We need action! Talk is not work, and you do not become a man by sitting in clubs or by warming yourself at a stove. I say these things emphatically, since so much time has been wasted. The fault is yours. Finally, if the skies are dark now, they may be darker still in the future.'[8] Breathing such fiery and hectoring oratory, and following Kolokotrónis in naming the Feast of the Annunciation as the date of the rising, Papaphléssas reached the Peloponnese in December 1820.

There was now a clear and urgent need for some co-ordination of all these various initiatives. It was no longer sufficient to rely on individual attempts by captains such as Kolokotrónis to unify the armed bands, on personal arrangements like those of Papaphléssas for assembling war supplies, and on the generalised preaching of revolt by members of the Etería. In particular, the political and church leaders in the Peloponnese needed to establish how far they could trust Papaphléssas and his grandiose proposals. In late January 1821 therefore they assembled for a meeting to discuss what was to be done. Four bishops attended, of whom the most influential was Bishop Yermanós of Old Patras, along with other clerics. Among the political leaders were Andréas Lóndos and the brothers Asimákis and Andréas Zaímis, and the two Andréases later played a significant part in the war of independence. Photákos, adjutant to Kolokotrónis and future biographer of Papaphléssas, was there, as was Papaphléssas himself, who brought with him two supporters, one of them his brother Nikítas, all three of them carrying weapons.

The place chosen for the meeting was Vostítsa, ancient Aegeum and modern Éyio, some twenty miles east of Patras on the southern shore of the Gulf of Corinth, and the pretext for it was the resolution of a long-standing boundary dispute between two local monasteries. The dominant figure at the meeting was Bishop Yermanós. Born fifty years before in Dhimitsána, and educated there, he had risen rapidly in the church hierarchy and was a personal friend of the current patriarch Grigórios. Appointed to the see of Old Patras in 1806, he had influence, it was said, throughout the Peloponnese, Roumeli and the islands, and had been an important figure in the Philikí Etería since 1818. He regarded Papaphléssas as an unmitigated rogue and charlatan, describing him in his memoirs as 'a cheat and rotten through and through, thinking of nothing else but how to stir up trouble among the people so as to enrich himself by plunder'.[9] No wonder that Papaphléssas and his companions carried weapons.

The meeting spread over four days and Yermanós took immediate control of the agenda by posing a string of highly pertinent questions:

— Is the whole Greek nation willing to rise in revolt, and will it follow our lead?
— What are the absolute necessities for the struggle? What do we need, what have we got, and where is the rest to come from?
— How and when should the rising begin? Should our attacks be simultaneous or one after another?
— Is a foreign power [meaning Russia] ready to help us? What form will any promised support take, and how firm is the promise?
— If any foreign power opposes us, what do we do?
— Who will lead the revolution in other parts of Greece?
— Should Greeks in Europe, especially the educated ones, join the struggle?
— If we fail to seize power, what then?
— If the Turks learn of our plans in advance, what action do we take?

Faced with these searching questions, Papaphléssas blustered, threatening to start the revolution himself with a band of a thousand men from the Mani and another thousand from elsewhere, and warning that the Turks would then kill anyone who was not armed. He had some success only in answering a question not on Yermanós' list but posed by another delegate, Sotíris Charalámvis, who, pressing his palms together and raising them before his face in the Turkish manner, asked slily: once the Turks were removed, to whom would power pass? Would it be to that crude fellow (pointing to Papaphléssas' brother Nikítas), who had only just learnt to use a fork when eating? No, said Papaphléssas; when Charalámvis' local bey had gone, Charalámvis would take his place, and he proceeded through a list of prominent Turks distributing their offices among those present.[10] Charalámvis had in fact put his finger on the question – who takes over power from the Turks? – which was to bedevil the Greek enterprise and lead ultimately to civil war between rival factions.

The consensus of those at the meeting, as summarised by Yermanós, was clearly for caution. Most Greeks, they thought, still had no idea about the coming struggle. After the experience of the failed Orlov revolt fifty years before, to start the revolution in the Peloponnese without reliable support would be madness. The attitude of the European powers, especially Russia, was unknown, and virtually all supplies needed to make war were lacking. The conclusion was inescapable: the time was not yet ripe for revolution. Some practical decisions flowed from this, mainly to do with disseminating and gathering information. Envoys were sent to tell the leaders of other regions in the Peloponnese about the result of the conference, and in particular the bishop of Monemvasía was sent to inform Pétrobey, probably the most powerful figure of the Peloponnese not present at Vostítsa. Further messengers were sent to collect information, some to probe the intentions of the two crucial naval islands, Hydra and Spétses, others to Kapodhístrias to discover Russia's attitude, and to the exiled bishop of Árta, now in Pisa, for information about the other European powers.

Finally, a decision was taken on how to respond when the bishops and leaders of the Peloponnese were next summoned to Tripolis for the regular six-monthly meeting with the Ottoman authorities on taxation and public order. If they went, they might be seized as hostages, whereas if they refused they would arouse Turkish suspicions. On balance it was decided that they should make excuses not to attend, should announce that they were going to Constantinople to put their grievances to the Sultan, and should go into hiding in their own districts or in the islands until the situation became clearer. As it turned out, it was easier to adopt this resolution than to put it into practice.

The acting governor of the Morea, Mehmed Salik, issued the

expected summons to Tripolis at the beginning of March. He also announced, on top of the impositions already made to help finance the war against Ali Pasha, a doubling of the harach, the poll tax. The Greek response to the summons to Tripolis was patchy, and by no means everybody followed the line agreed at Vostítsa to prevaricate and stay away.

Yermanós, of course, made his excuses, as did most of the other bishops who had been at the Vostítsa meeting. He first pleaded that an attack of rheumatism in the feet confined him to bed, but when that excuse wore thin a more elaborate pretext was constructed. He set out with his fellow bishops from Kalávrita with a Turkish escort for Tripolis, and on the road a previously concocted letter, ostensibly from a friendly Turk in Tripolis, was delivered to them. The letter warned them that their lives would be in danger if they completed the journey and was ostentatiously read out in the presence of the Turkish escort. The charade completed, Yermanós and his party returned to Kalávrita and took refuge in the nearby monastery of Áyia Lávra, and after further inconclusive discussion about what to do next dispersed to different villages in the Kalávrita region to avoid seizure en masse. There they awaited events. It was clear that the cat-and-mouse game could not be played much longer.

LYIT LIBRARY LETTERKENNY

8

The Storm Breaks

The Greek revolution broke out in a number of different places during the latter part of March 1821, in some places by the raising of a Greek flag and the swearing-in of armed men, in others with concerted attacks by Turks on Greeks or by Greeks on Turks. There are four towns which can claim to be the place where the revolution began, claims that are disputed to this day: Areópolis in the southern Peloponnese, and hereditary stronghold of the Mavromichális family; Kalamáta in the outer Mani, where Pétrobey and other leaders soon assembled; Vostítsa on the Gulf of Corinth, where the important pre-revolutionary meeting had been held; and Kalávrita in the hills high above Vostítsa, close to the monastery of Áyia Lávra where Pouqueville set his dramatic story.

The sequence of events can become confused because at this period there were two different sets of dates, the Julian or Old Style, and the Gregorian or New Style which ran twelve days later, the New Style resulting from calendar reforms initiated by Pope Gregory XIII in 1582. British and other European writers used the New Style of dating, while Greek writers used the Old Style or, as in proclamations addressed to a foreign audience, gave both. The event officially recognised as the start of the war of independence is the legendary raising of the standard at Áyia Lávra on 25 March Old Style, which is 6 April New Style. But the occasion is commemorated nationally on 25 March in the New Style, which Greece adopted later; so the annual celebrations are, strictly speaking, always twelve days early. As 25 March is such a key date in the Greek calendar, dates in this chapter are Old Style, while elsewhere in this book dates are New Style unless otherwise specified.

In Areópolis, in a little square the size of a tennis court, stands the church of Áyios Michaíl, with whitewashed walls and a terracotta Byzantine roof. Set into the wall opposite the church is a twentieth-century plaque depicting a mansize Archangel Michael holding aloft a laurel wreath ready to crown the victor. The inscription reads: 'From this historic square was launched the great uprising under the leadership of Pétrobey, 17 March 1821'. Areópolis immediately emphasised its warlike credentials by changing the town's name, previously Tsímova, to its modern version, the City of Ares. Thus Areópolis claims primacy.

Outside Kalamáta armed Greeks began to assemble from 20 March onwards, a force under Papaphléssas on one side of the town, and on the other 2,000 men under the command of Kolokotrónis and the heads of the Mani's leading families. Kolokotrónis described their progress: 'As we went along all the Greeks showed the greatest enthusiasm; they came out and met us everywhere, carrying the sacred eikons, with the priests chanting supplications and thanks givings to God. Once I could not forbear weeping, on account of the ardour which I beheld. So we went on, followed by crowds. When we came to the bridge of Kalamáta we exchanged greetings, and I marched forward.'[1] On 23 March the Turks of Kalamáta, faced with these overwhelming forces, surrendered on the promise that their lives would be spared, but not many survived; in the chilling phrase of a contemporary, 'the moon devoured them'. The capitulation was followed by a great celebration at Kalamáta's main church, which Finlay, for once unrestrained, described in these words: 'Twenty-four priests officiated, and five thousand armed men stood round. Never was a solemn service of the Orthodox Church celebrated with greater fervour, never did hearts overflow with sincerer devotion to Heaven, nor with warmer gratitude to their church and their God. Patriotic tears poured down the cheeks of rude warriors, and ruthless brigands sobbed like children. All present felt that the event formed an era in the history of their nation.'[2]

The victorious Greek leaders immediately set up a so-called Senate of Messénia (that is, of the south-west Peloponnese), and Pétrobey was proclaimed both leader of this senate and 'commander-in-chief of the Spartan forces'. It was in this dual capacity that Pétrobey issued on the day of the Turks' surrender a call to the nations of Europe which wove together a number of themes that were repeated continually in the course of the struggle. The Greeks were now united, Pétrobey's document claimed – 'All our intestine discord is plunged into oblivion' – and were determined – 'We have resolved to be free or perish.' Their cause was 'a just and sacred enterprise', and Europe owed them a debt – 'Greece, our mother, was the lamp that illuminated you and she now reckons on your active philanthropy.'[3]

What of the other claims to have led the revolution? At Vostítsa the Turks, hearing rumours of insurrection, fled across the Gulf of Corinth and took refuge in the inland town of Salóna, modern Amphíssa. The Greeks under Andréas Lóndos did not hinder them, and on a date which was probably no later than 23 March, when Kalamáta fell, Lóndos raised over the town a Greek flag of a black cross on a red background (a design soon to be superseded). Thus Vostítsa was one of the first towns to be liberated from Ottoman control. At Kalávrita matters were resolved with equal despatch. On 21 March a force of 600 Greeks compelled the Turks to take refuge in their fortified buildings, and on the 26th the Turks surrendered. In the following August, when the French philhellene Maxime Raybaud visited the town they were still alive in captivity, but, reports Raybaud sadly, 'ils périrent peu de temps après'.[4] The Greek losses at Kalávrita were reported as two killed and three wounded, including one of their commanders, while their gain was a hundred or so guns to swell their own arsenal.

Thus, in summary, the chronology of the first days of the revolution seems to have been: on 17 March, revolution proclaimed in Areópolis; on 20 March, Greek forces move on Kalamáta, and on 23 March the town surrenders; about 23 March Turks abandon Vostítsa; on 21 March, Turks are attacked at Kalávrita, and are taken captive on 26 March. But, whatever the exact sequence of events, Áyia Lávra is likely to remain, thanks to Pouqueville, the defining venue of the start of the revolution.

In these four towns the Greeks were successful against limited or no resistance. The rising at Patras in the last days of March was a different matter. Patras was the leading commercial town of the Peloponnese, described by Gordon as 'the most flourishing and populous city of the peninsula of Pelops, the emporium of its trade, and residence of the foreign consuls and merchants; seated in a delightful plain of the Achaian shore, at the foot of lofty hills, surrounded by a fertile country, and containing 18,000 inhabitants, two-thirds of whom were Greeks'.[5] There had been a fortress on the high ground north-east of Patras for over a thousand years, a mark of its persisting strategic and commercial importance, and Byzantines, Venetians and Turks had all contributed to its massive defences. Patras was immediately opposite the Ionian islands, which were under British control, and ships carrying passengers and goods regularly crossed the intervening stretch of water. Thus disturbances at Patras immediately raised the question of whether Britain would support the Turks, a friendly power, or the Greeks, for whom there was considerable sympathy, or would maintain some form of neutrality.

At the beginning of 1821, there were eight European consulates in the town: those of the five major powers – Britain, France, Russia, Prussia and Austria – plus Holland, Spain and Sweden. The two consuls who played the most important roles in Patras were those of France and Britain. The French consul was Hugues Pouqueville, younger brother of the historian François, whom he had succeeded as France's representative at the court of Ali Pasha. After his years in that difficult post Hugues Pouqueville had had enough of Greece, but on returning to France found to his dismay that he was immediately sent back as consul at Patras. Long extracts from Hugues' diary are quoted by François, to support his case that the English were primarily responsible for the calamities of the Greeks at Patras.

The British consul was Philip Green, with his brother Richard as vice-consul, and their combined record was published in 1827 as *Sketches of the War in Greece*. In his preface Philip Green makes a scathing attack on François Pouqueville, accusing him of using his 1824 history 'to give credit to falsehoods the most daring, to a distortion of facts the most ingenious and in every falsehood, in every mis-statement to pursue the grand object of blackening the English name. . . . Myself and my brother are the individuals in whose persons he has most frequently sought to pander to the vitiated taste for such abuse that unhappily exists among our Gallic neighbours.'[6] Green also includes a vigorous rebuttal of other allegations against him, but nevertheless he is still regularly castigated by Greek historians as pro-Turk and anti-Greek.

'There are many rumours of war afloat,' reported Philip Green from Patras in early January 1821, adding that Greek resentment of the Turks had been heightened by the 'unlooked for and arbitrary exaction' of a levy to pay for the war against Ali Pasha.[7] By the middle of March the Turks living in the town were moving their families and possessions into the citadel, and the Greeks were hiding their property or shipping it off to the Ionian islands. The many Ionian residents of Patras were at first forbidden by the Turks to leave, but Green managed to get this order rescinded. The Greeks were also arming themselves, and by mid-March there was no powder or shot to be bought in the Patras bazaar.

The spark that ignited the revolt came, as it were, from a burning house. On 23 March the Turks tried to search the house of a leading Greek citizen of Patras on suspicion that he was hiding weapons, and finding the doors barred set the building on fire. The flames spread quickly, destroying some 200 houses in the next twelve hours, and street fighting broke out between Turks and Greeks. Many Greeks who had withdrawn to the surrounding hills for safety could see the conflagration and poured back. Hugues Pouqueville described his feelings on the following morning:

> A terrifying night has been followed at last by a day such as I never hope to see again. . . . A consuming heat, combined with the brilliance of a burning sun, and with the force of the sirocco, would be enough to destroy us if the danger of each minute did not give us supernatural strength. The flames roar; explosions are heard every moment; sometimes I can feel the ground shake beneath my feet; beams and sections of wall, collapsing into the heart of the conflagration, send columns of flame bursting upwards.

And Pouqueville adds, in a rare criticism of the Greeks: 'Great God! Those who incite revolution have much to answer for!'[8]

The street fighting quickly gave way to siege warfare. The Turks barricaded themselves in the fortress, from which they commanded the town, and the Greeks brought up six small-calibre guns to a house some forty yards from the castle walls. Neither side's fire had much effect. Many of the Turkish heavy cannon had no carriages and so could be aimed only by being manhandled into position and propped up with pieces of wood, while the Greek four- and six-pounders, even if accurately aimed, made no impression on a fortress which had been strengthened over the centuries. Thus the exchange of shot produced,

Richard Green wrote, 'a constant noise with little execution'.[9] Sharpshooting was more effective, and the Greeks lost their best gunner, an Italian, to a single shot from a sniper on the Turkish ramparts.

Both sides were anxiously awaiting reinforcements, and help for the Greeks arrived first. On the evening of 25 March, Bishop Yermanós, having put behind him the doubts expressed at the Vostítsa conference, arrived on the plain outside Patras with a party including Andréas Lóndos and a force of 200 men, and next morning entered the town. The new arrivals, with leading Greeks of Patras, formed what Philip Green called 'a sort of council for the general direction of affairs'. On the first day they recognised the importance of international support, as Pétrobey had done at Kalamáta two days earlier, and addressed to the foreign consuls an appeal similar to Pétrobey's: 'We are firmly persuaded that all the Christian Powers will recognize the justice of our Cause, and far from opposing obstacles, will assist and succour us, in calling to mind how useful our ancestors were to humanity. In acquainting you with this, we beg you will be pleased to procure us the protection of your August Court.'[10] Four days later a discouraging British response reached Patras, a proclamation by the Ionian governor Maitland which forbade Ionian subjects from taking part in the disturbances on either the Greek or Turkish side, under pain of losing Ionian government protection. Not surprisingly, the copy of the proclamation which Green put up opposite his consulate was immediately torn down by the infuriated Greeks.

The Turks were now shut up in the citadel of Patras, while the town was held by some 5,000 armed Greeks. The Greeks were digging a mine under the walls of the citadel, whose reserves of water were fast running out, the pipes having been cut on the first day of the siege. The Castle of Patras would very probably have fallen to the Greeks within a few more days if Turkish reinforcements under Yussuf Pasha had not come to their aid. Yussuf had left the forces besieging Iánnina to take up a new appointment as pasha of Évvia, the large island off the east coast of Greece. Learning of the disturbances at Patras when he reached Mesolongi, he directed his troops, variously reported as between 300 and 1,000 men, across the narrows of the Gulf of Corinth. While Yussuf was still at the Castle of the Morea on the southern shore, Green sent a deputation to assure him of British neutrality, as demonstrated by Maitland's proclamation, and to ask for British and Ionian property in Patras to be respected if Yussuf attacked. Yussuf promised to give strict orders to his troops about British property, and intimated that he would have to await reinforcements before trying to relieve Patras. The deputation was taken in by this indication of delay and therefore, as Philip Green wrote, 'You may imagine their surprise and our consternation, when at day-break this morning [3 April] we were alarmed by the news that the Turks were entering the place.'[11] The Greeks too were taken by surprise. Yermanós had earlier sent a detachment of 400 troops to guard the road between the Castle of the Morea and Patras and to give warning of Yussuf's approach, but to his disgust they had stayed at their posts for only a day before returning to Patras to join in the looting of Turkish houses.

The events in Patras in the ten days or so between the outbreak of revolt and the arrival of Yussuf Pasha gave rise to several allegations against Philip Green, all vigorously rejected by him. First, he was accused of sending Captain Hunter to Préveza to warn the Turkish commander there of the plight of the Patras Turks. Not so: Hunter sailed to Corfu, to give warning to the Ionian government, not to the Turks. Second, Green was accused of sending a letter to Yussuf at Iánnina urging him to come to Patras; this is most unlikely. Third, Green was accused of helping Yussuf by showing him the way into the Castle of Patras (how could Yussuf have missed it?) and by sending to Yussuf standards of two colours and a cross as carried by the Greeks, so that he could deceive his opponents. Gordon, even though no supporter of Green, rejected this as ridiculous: 'The idea of a single pacific individual's introducing a body of troops into a fortress blockaded by five or six thousand men, is so absurd, that it needs no refutation.'[12]

The day that Yussuf entered Patras, 3 April, was Palm Sunday, and the Greeks had been preparing to celebrate their religious festival. Instead, surprised in their beds by Yussuf's dawn arrival, all who could took flight, some 8,000 souls by Green's reckoning, of whom 6,000 were men capable of fighting and so greatly outnumbered the Turks. With the Greeks in retreat, Yussuf gave orders, on the day after his arrival, for the houses of the Greek leaders to be set on fire, thus restarting the conflagration of ten days before. This time, with the sirocco still blowing, some 700 houses were burnt down, and Green saved his consulate only with the help of the crew of a British ship and of Yussuf in person with his troops, who pulled down a dozen houses to create a firebreak. No such consideration, of course, was shown to the Greeks. The Turkish troops went on the rampage, and about forty Greeks were beheaded and their bodies thrown into the street, though Green says he managed to save nine or ten captives, for one of whom the order for decapitation had already been given.

The consulates were now the only places of refuge for Greeks who could not yet board ship for the Ionian islands or had no hope of doing so, and of the eight consulates only the English, French and Spanish remained standing. Green recorded his own humanitarian efforts: 'Numbers of Greeks, chiefly old men, women, and children, took refuge in the Consulates: the French Consulate, from its extent, accommodated the largest number: I received as many as I possibly could. The Greeks in their flight abandoned the wounded in the hospital. . . . I have persuaded a Zantiot, practising as a surgeon, to remain here and attend the wounded: I have superintended the dressing of their wounds, but fear no skill can save them.'[13] Meanwhile the larger French consulate was sheltering 300 to 350 on Green's reckoning, though Hugues Pouqueville quadrupled the number to 1,500 and his brother doubled it again to 3,000.

These events led to a further accusation against Green, that he had turned away refugees from his consulate. 'For the sake of plunder,' wrote Yermanós, 'and because of his basic ill-will towards the Greeks, Green showed every sort of inhumanity in this situation, and when defenceless women with infant children sought refuge in his consulate, turned them away and shut them out.'[14] Pouqueville predictably repeated this charge. It is quite possible that Green did turn people away but only because he had to. His consulate, smaller than the French, could shelter only so many asylum seekers, and by Green's own account he did all that he could for those whom he could accept.

Philip Green was no simple altruist. He later, as agent of the Levant Company, defied the English naval blockade to sell supplies to both sides in the war, and was accused in England of doing so for personal rather than company profit. These later activities do not generally contribute to the Greek animus against Green – after all, they helped

Greeks as well as Turks – and it is his conduct at Patras in the early days of the war which is condemned by Greek writers, then and now. The main reason seems to be that the Greeks expected him to support their cause openly, but Green was English, not a Greek national like some of the other consuls, and was accredited to the Ottoman government with which his own country had good relations. In any case he was under instructions from Maitland, Britain's governor in the Ionian islands. François Pouqueville's book hurt Green's reputation further, reckless as it was in repeating and often embroidering any rumour to Green's discredit that circulated in the fevered atmosphere of embattled Patras. Finally, the Green brothers' book cannot have endeared them to the Greeks. It not only belittled Greek efforts but also ridiculed the actions of the Turks, and where was the glory for the Greeks if their foe was not regarded as formidable? Also Richard Green, though not his brother, wrote all too often in a tone of supercilious mockery of what he called the 'warfare between these two semi-barbarian people'.[15] It was a style which might make gentlemen chortle in their London clubs, but was bound to antagonise men battling for a cause in which they profoundly believed. So the animus against Green is understandable, but the accusations against him do not stand up, and it cannot be right still to apply to Green in cavalier fashion the derogatory epithets of *philótourkos* and *miséllinas*.[16]

As for poor Patras, the struggle continued, the Greeks periodically reoccupying the town and trying to capture the fortress, the Turks periodically being reinforced and holding out. By the end of 1821 the town was a wasteland, with only ten or twelve houses of the original 4,000 still undamaged. The citadel of Patras remained in Turkish hands throughout the war, as did the Castles of Roumeli and the Morea, and the three strongholds formed a compact triangular bridgehead which gave the Turkish troops vital access to the heartland of Greek resistance.

9

The Land War

In the early stages of the war on land the Greeks had three immediate objectives. The first was to prove that Greek resistance would not crumble under the first counter-attack by the Turks; this was achieved in May 1821 by Kolokotrónis at the battle of Valtétsi, in the foothills five miles south-west of Tripolis. The second objective was to show that the Greeks were capable of capturing a stronghold held by the Turks; this was demonstrated by the Greek siege, successfully completed in early August 1821, of Monemvasía, perhaps the most impregnable fortress in the whole Peloponnese. The third aim was to block the two routes by which Turkish troops could march south to the Gulf of Corinth, one in the west through the mountainous country of the Makrinóros, and the other in the east past ancient Thermopylae. In this third aim the Greeks had only temporary success.

In the heady early days of the revolution Kolokotrónis had marched triumphantly into Kalamáta through cheering crowds, but in the weeks immediately following few things went right for him. On the day after the taking of Kalamáta Kolokotrónis headed north to Karítena, an isolated village on a rocky outcrop in the central Peloponnese some twenty miles west of Tripolis, where a group of Turks was besieged in the village's small fortress. The Turks in Tripolis learnt that their compatriots were under siege in Karítena and sent out a force of 3,000 infantry and cavalry to relieve them.

Kolokotrónis stationed himself on a hill with his telescope, which he would let nobody else use, to warn of the approach of the Turkish forces, but when he gave the signal the Greeks, instead of mustering to oppose them, turned and fled. Kolokotrónis was left alone, and had to hide in the trees as a Turkish unit passed. When he rejoined his fellow captains they were for moving away to besiege the south-western fortresses of Methóni, Koróni and Navarino, but Kolokotrónis, who consistently argued for the capture of Tripolis first, refused. 'I shall stay here on these hills,' he said, 'where the very birds know me; better that they, my neighbours, should eat me than any others.' His account continues:

> I was left alone, I and my horse at Chrysovitsi. But Phlessas turned back and said to a boy, 'Stop with him lest the wolves devour him.' I sat down until they had disappeared with their flags. After some time I descended the hill until I came to a church on the road, dedicated to the Blessed Virgin (the Panagia at Chrysovitsi), and there, where I threw myself down, I wept for Hellas. 'Holy Virgin!' I cried, 'help us now, that the Greeks may take heart once more.'[1]

Thus it was to the double invocation, fundamental to the Greek cause, of ancient Greece, Hellas, and of the Orthodox faith that Kolokotrónis turned in his darkest hour.

Kolokotrónis' despair was short lived, and he was soon back with Greek forces round Tripolis. His first task was to rebuild the army of the central Peloponnese, on a sounder basis so that it did not vanish at the first threat. The forces which had gathered around Karítena and had now dispersed had been chaotic. The assembly was like a village carnival, said one observer. The men stayed with their own family or group, under no overall authority. Their weapons were knives, spits and anything else which could be used as a weapon. They relied on their womenfolk to bring them food and drink. The captains had no agreement on a common objective. Kolokotrónis now began to introduce some system into the disorder. Officers were appointed formally, with written commissions. A central commissariat was developed. Recruiting methods became harsher; Kolokotrónis' son Pános was sent out with orders to burn the houses of those who would not rise, and to distribute their possessions to the revolutionary forces. Kolokotrónis also insisted on a proper count of the numbers in each band, an unpopular move since it now became more difficult for captains to draw excess rations and weapons, and for men to desert to other groups or simply to their own homes.

Such attempts to establish military structures were almost wholly unfamiliar to the Greeks. A few, like Kolokotrónis, had served as mercenaries for foreign powers in the Ionian islands, while for the rest any experience of fighting was as armátolos or as klepht. Armátoli had for centuries been hired by the local Turkish authorities, initially to guard the mountain passes and later for the general maintenance of law and order. The main threat to law and order came from armed bands of klephts, who lived by brigandage in the mountains. Their numbers were constantly swelled by Greeks fleeing injustice, others fleeing justice, many simply seeking a more rewarding and adventurous life than that of a villager under a feudal Turkish overlord. However, there was no simple pattern of opposition between law-breaking klephts and law-enforcing armátoli. The armátoli were often recruited from klephtic leaders: who else had the necessary experience? Armátoli as well as klephts would rob rich and poor alike. Armátoli and klephts would sometimes join forces in campaigns of brigandage and jointly resist Turkish forces sent against them. The captain of either klephts or armátoli would be the leader of a band from his own extended family or at least from his own village. The favoured method of attack was to trap the enemy in a narrow pass or when crossing a river, create havoc by firing from above, and finally charge into the confusion. Defence was from the safety of rocks, stone walls or buildings from which scatological insults were hurled as often as bullets. Despite all the later attempts by a central government of insurgent Greece to establish a regular army on west European lines, this was the form of warfare, *klephtopólemos*, which the Greeks traditionally and instinctively favoured, and the only way most of them trusted to defeat the Turks. But to succeed by this means the bands needed something of the order, discipline and co-ordination which Kolokotrónis was now trying to impose.

During April of 1821 the Greek forces in the area round Tripolis were slowly augmented by men from the nearby villages and by the return of many of the captains who had earlier headed south. Kolokotrónis was now recognised as the man for overall command, and in early May he was formally appointed *archistrátigos*. Armed camps of Greeks were established in a rough semi-circle of villages to the west of Tripolis, where the mountains come down to the plain: at Levídhi, Piána, Chrisovítsi, Vérvena and, closest of all to Tripolis, Valtétsi. The Greek reorganisation had come only just in time. In mid-May Mustafa Bey, the newly appointed lieutenant-governor of the Morea, reached Tripolis from Epirus, standing in for Khurshid, who was still away besieging Iánnina. This new pasha of the Morea was a warlike and able man, in Kolokotrónis' view, and was the most formidable opponent the Greeks of the Peloponnese had yet had to meet.

It was clear to the Greeks that Mustafa was going to waste no time in moving to crush them decisively. The Greeks therefore prepared to make a stand at Valtétsi. This village was in the centre of the semi-circle of the Greek-held posts west of Tripolis, it was on a defensible hill in the plain, and it was much closer to Tripolis than the other villages, so that if the Greeks held it they would be a step nearer to the capture of Tripolis itself. The village church of Valtétsi was now fortified, and three *tamboúria* were built, redoubts of stone wall about three feet high, with apertures for firing and a ditch running round the inside so that the defenders' heads were below the parapet. The captains who had returned from the south were ready to give support from nearby villages. Two members of Kolokotrónis' family, his nephew Nikítas and his son Yennéos, were away in Árgos collecting lead from roofs for use as shot. Kolokotrónis himself was everywhere: 'I slept at Valtetsi, dined at Piana, and supped in Chrysovitsi.'[2]

Mustafa planned a pincer movement on Valtétsi, attacking from north and south while a smaller third force was to move behind Valtétsi to cut off the Greeks' expected flight. At dawn on the morning of 24 May Kolokotrónis' watchers on the hills immediately above Tripolis lit their signal fires to show that Mustafa's forces had set out, and two hours later they attacked the Valtétsi fortifications.

Against Turkish expectations, the Greeks did not flee but maintained their positions. Kolokotrónis joined the battle from Chrisovítsi and harried and divided the Turkish forces. The Turkish cavalry were useless when trying to attack up a rocky slope against a fortified position, and the Turkish gunners were not skilful enough to lob cannon shot into the fortifications. The battle continued all day, and at nightfall both sides remained in position, each hoping that the other would have retreated by daybreak, but at dawn both sides were still in position. After an hour of further ineffectual cannon shot Mustafa began to withdraw his forces and their retreat soon degenerated into a rout, in which the Turks lost some 600 to 800 killed or wounded, while the Greeks, though claiming a far smaller number, probably lost about 150.

If Kolokotrónis had not established some degree of system in the Greek fighting units, the battle of Valtétsi would have been lost. Had that happened, it is quite possible that the rest of the Peloponnese would have succumbed, and that the revolution of 1821 would have gone the way of the failed Orlov rebellion of fifty years earlier. Kolokotrónis was thus well justified in claiming that 'this battle established the good fortunes of our country; if we had lost it we might never have made another stand'. He said as much in his speech to his men at the end of the battle: 'We must all fast, and render up thanksgivings for this day, which should be kept holy for ever, as the day upon which the people made a stand, whereby our country achieved her freedom.'[3]

For centuries the castles which ringed the Peloponnese had been crucial to control of it as it was occupied successively by the Byzantines, the Venetians, Franks diverted from the Crusades, and the Turks. Their importance was recognised as early as the fourteenth century, when the Franks held the Peloponnese: it was said that if they had lost the Morea, the possession of one fortress only would have sufficed to reconquer the whole peninsula.[4] Some of the fortresses remained in Turkish hands throughout the war, others were taken by the Greeks and then retaken by the Turks. One Greek capture which they never relinquished was the first, of Monemvasía.

This spectacular citadel lies just off the east coast of the southern Peloponnese, linked to the mainland by a causeway, the single entrance (*móni émvasis*) which gives the place its name. The rock is about a mile long on its east–west axis and something under half a mile wide. A fifteenth-century Byzantine book described it as an island high, oblong and abrupt, on all sides surrounded by sheer and impassable cliffs, and commanding the sea as if competing with the sky itself.[5]

The lower town on the north side has been a busy commercial centre since the twelfth century, and Monemvasía gave its name to Malmsey, the wine shipped from the harbour beneath the lower town but produced in Tínos and other Aegean islands. From the lower town a single steep path of worn and uneven stones leads to the upper town, whose ruins are now half hidden by thistles, wild garlic and gorse, but in 1666 a Turkish visitor, Evlija Chelebi, described it in glowing terms. There were, he said, 500 well-built houses, each like a castle, with red-tiled roofs; they had gardens and courtyards, albeit small, though no vineyards; and each was of such beauty as to merit worldwide recognition. White as swans, he concluded, all the houses were rich and elegant, worthy of a king.[6]

At the outbreak of the revolution the Greeks immediately laid siege to Monemvasía with what troops they could muster, but this amounted only to about 1,400 men, largely inexperienced in fighting, and enough to blockade but not to capture the rock. As some went away to fetch food and others drifted back to their villages the original force was at times halved to 700, and the Greeks fell back on the stage-army technique of sending men away at night to return next day as, in Turkish eyes, fresh reinforcements. The Greeks had some support from the island of Spétses, forty miles or so to the north, but as with the Greek land forces the number of ships from Spétses, sometimes five, sometimes twelve, was enough to contain but not to capture. The Turks at Monemvasía eventually tried a sortie. On one night at the beginning of June they sent men by boat to the shore to the north, intending that this party should attack the besieging Greeks in the rear while a force from the rock attacked them in front across the causeway. But the plan was betrayed, and when the Turks landed on the north shore they were killed or captured. The siege of Monemvasía had by then lasted for two months, and no end was yet in sight.

Hunger now became the dominant factor in the siege, and with it the swirl of report, rumour and fantasy that accompanies starvation conditions. It was said that the Turks were eating century-old maize, left behind by the Venetians, and rationing even that, that they were eating animals which were unclean to them – donkeys, dogs, rats and mice – and after that roots and berries, and finally that they were practising cannibalism. As starvation became worse among the Turks they began to allow individuals to surrender. The Greeks treated them well, but soon stopped accepting such surrenders in order to increase the pressure of starvation. Some Turks tried to reach the mainland by jumping from the cliffs and swimming with the help of planks or inflated wineskins. Finally, the leading fifty Turkish families moved into the upper town, the fortress on top of the rock, closing the gate of the single path to it, taking the remaining food with them and leaving the others in the lower town to survive as they might.

Finally, in early June the Turks offered terms for surrender of the fortress, but because they were afraid of being slaughtered by the besieging Greek forces they insisted on submitting to Dhimítrios Ipsilántis, brother of Alexander and his successor as head of the Philikí Etería, who had recently arrived in the Peloponnese. The besiegers were outraged. It was the Peloponnesians, they said, who had used their resources and spilt their blood in the siege of Monemvasía, and the surrender of the fortress should therefore be to the Greek people, *to Ellínikon éthnos.* The Turks however replied that they did not know of any such thing as 'the Greek people'. The Turks got their way over this, and Ipsilántis and his deputy Prince Alexander Kantakouzinós remained in control of the negotiations, which dragged on for another month. There were arguments over what weapons and other possessions the Turks could keep, where they might be shipped to and at whose expense, and what reparations they should pay. Ultimately, Kantakouzinós offered final terms, to be withdrawn if not accepted within twenty-four hours. On 2 August the instrument of surrender was signed, the keys of the fortress were ceremonially handed over on a silver dish to the besiegers, and two days later they took possession of Monemvasía. Throughout its history Monemvasía had been the last fortress to fall in the successive attempts to take control of the Peloponnese; in this war it was the first.

Of all the strongholds in the Peloponnese, Monemvasía probably offered the least military gain, and certainly far less than the twin fortresses above the Bay of Navarino which fell to the Greeks a few weeks later. Monemvasía, thought Gordon, because of its restricted harbour and its isolation by the surrounding mountains, was of minor consequence as a military post, and in fact little was heard of it for the rest of the war. It was a token objective, and the significance of its capture was almost wholly psychological. Of its fall a contemporary wrote: 'For all Greeks, and especially those living abroad, the news of the capture of the castle was astounding, like something from legend.'[7]

Of the two main routes through Greece by which Turkish forces could come down from the north, the eastern route followed the coast, roughly on the line of the main Thessalonika–Athens road today, and led into the

Peloponnese across the isthmus of Corinth. The natural point at which to block this road was where it squeezed between two mountains near Thermopylae, about ninety miles north-west of Athens. It was at Thermopylae that in 480 BC Leonidas and his 300 Spartans died heroically resisting the Persian advance under Xerxes, and it was near here that, a century after the war of independence and in action against another occupier, Greek resistance forces with British help cut the country's main railway line by blowing up the Gorgopótamos bridge. The western route ran from Iánnina to Árta and then to Mesolongi, leading to the Peloponnese by a short sea crossing of the Gulf of Corinth. The dangerous part of this route was the five miles of mountainous country east and south of Árta along the slopes of the Makrinóros. To block these two routes was strategically a great deal more important to the Greek cause than a quick morale-boosting victory or the capture of a symbolic objective.

In the previous January, when a Greek rising was clearly imminent, superior Greek commanders for East and West Roumeli had been appointed by a meeting of military leaders on Lévkas: for Eastern Roumeli Odysseus Andhroútsos, who as Ali Pasha's lieutenant had held Livadhiá for him the previous summer, and for Western Roumeli Iannis Varnakiótis, who had also served Ali Pasha. The reputations of both Varnakiótis and Andhroútsos were later tainted by accusations of treachery, for which Varnakiótis lived to make amends but Andhroútsos did not.

By the end of April 1821 Turkish troops from Lamía under Omer Vrionis were already trying to clear the Greek forces from the area of the eastern route. One of the first clashes ended in a Greek defeat. A Greek captain, Athanásios Dhiákos, found himself with a handful of men trying to hold the bridge over the river at Alamána, a few miles south-east of Lamía. Most of Dhiákos' party were killed, including the bishop of Salóna who was fighting with them, and Dhiákos himself was captured and, on the orders of Omer Vrionis, impaled. The sickening reality of impalement was that the victim was spreadeagled face down, and held in place by ropes attached to each leg while a man with a heavy mallet drove a long sharpened pole into his anus. The pole was then set upright and he was left to die of his internal injuries. Dhiákos' service to the Greek cause was short, but his memory as a proto-martyr is still honoured.

The Alamána bridge was now open to the Turks, and in August a

Turkish force, variously estimated at 5,000 or 8,000 strong, crossed it on its way to the Peloponnese to relieve their countrymen besieged in Tripolis. The Greeks concentrated their forces at the deserted village of Vasiliká, where the road was wooded and ran through a long narrow pass.

In the first days of September the Turkish forces entered the pass. The Greeks were led by Iannis Goúras, lieutenant of Odysseus Andhroútsos, who was later to play a part in his leader's downfall, while Odysseus himself was away further south in his territory. The Greeks first poured down heavy fire on their enemies in the pass and then attacked, emboldened, it was said, by a rumour that Odysseus had arrived. The Turks were forced back to Lamía, destroying the Alamána bridge behind them to block pursuit, and abandoning wagons, animals, military stores and seven cannon, all of which fell into Greek hands. Here at last was a significant Greek success, which came at an opportune moment, since it was too late in the season for the Turks to make another attempt to reinforce the Peloponnese by that route before winter. 'Thus was Thermopylae once more the theatre of a battle most important to Greece,' wrote Gordon, 'inasmuch as it ruined the enemy's plan of campaign'[8] – but only, of course, until the next year's campaigning season.

The western route south from Árta through the Makrinóros is now made easy by a modern road, but until that was built the journey presented formidable obstacles. A Greek writer in the 1940s described in vivid terms its grandeur and impenetrability: 'The gigantic mountains are ranged one behind the other in endless ranks, separated by dramatic valleys, deep gorges and narrow hollows: their jagged ridges leap upwards, and their sharp peaks seem to touch and pierce the blue dome of the sky. The narrow tracks, dangerous paths, deep ravines, waterless canyons, and the rivers and their tributaries, the streams and the springs make the valleys a highly complicated spider's web.'[9] This was ideal terrain, of course, for the guerrilla ambushes at which the Greeks were so adept. It was also, for those who could find their way through it, a place to take refuge, or indeed to rob refugees. Makriyánnis, then a young captain, took charge of a group of refugees from Árta – more than 500 families, he claims – and led them into the Makrinóros in a pitiable condition, without food or proper footwear. 'There was one woman with four young children, the oldest seven years old. She had abandoned two of them and I took pity on them. I tied them together, took them on my shoulder and saved them.' The refugees were in danger not only from the Turks but also from fellow Greeks: Makriyánnis rescued a woman who had been stripped of all her belongings and wounded in the foot by men he described with heavy irony as 'some sterling patriots'. She had only with difficulty persuaded her attackers to break the ring on her finger rather than cut off the finger. Makriyánnis was horrified: 'When I saw this glorious deed, I became disgusted with the Greek cause, because we were a lot of cannibals.'[10]

Although in terrain such as the Makrinóros the ambushers had the advantage, their task was by no means easy. It involved hours and often days of patient waiting, with minimal sound or movement and enduring thirst and hunger, until the chance came to attack. It was proverbially said that ambushing was the test of a true warrior. Panic was never far away. 'More than once', commented Raybaud, 'I have seen in these circumstances – a night sortie, a bivouac, some confusion on the march – a frightened man, or even a joker, say the word "Turk" with tragic consequences.'[11] All would be thrown into confusion, with wild firing and total loss of discipline.

A Turkish attempt in June to force a passage to the south was repulsed. In the next few weeks Khurshid Pasha, still at Iánnina, sent reinforcements for another attempt, and in July a force of 1,800 Turkish troops moved against some 200 entrenched Greeks. 'The Ottoman troops', wrote Gordon, ' . . . made repeated attacks upon the Greeks without success; their horsemen could not act among thick woods . . . and the insurgents having blocked up the paths with large stones and trunks of trees, poured on them a heavy fire of musketry. Entirely baffled, the Turks retired with a loss of near 150 killed . . . neither did they for the fifteen subsequent months make any further attempt upon Makrynoros.'[12] By the time the next attempt was made in the following year matters were very different. The area commander Varnakiótis and other Greek captains had made their accommodations with the Turks, and Ali Pasha was dead, so Turkish forces were no longer tied down at Iánnina. Thus when in late 1822 Omer Vrionis marched south with 6,000 men, he found the Makrinóros unguarded, and at the end of the year was able to besiege Mesolongi, the first in a series of sieges which was to end with the town's fall to the Turks in the spring of 1826.

10

The War at Sea

Greeks have been sailors since the days of Odysseus' twenty-year voyage home from Troy. Part of the reason is Greece's geography; there has always been the need to travel between hundreds of scattered islands, and on the mainland it has often been easier to sail round the rim of such a mountainous country than to travel and transport goods overland. The temperament of the Greeks, ancient and modern, was suited to the type of seafaring which called for a small band of more or less equals, serving a captain for the duration of a voyage, reacting with impromptu vigour to the unpredictable changes of wind and water. In this they were the antithesis of the Romans, who were at home on land, with large hierarchical permanent armies, structures of efficient imperial administration and long straight roads.

The Greek revolutionary fleet was drawn almost exclusively from three small and separated islands: Hydra and Spétses off the north-east coast of the Peloponnese and Psará in the northern Aegean about a hundred miles south of the entrance to the Dardanelles. These islands enjoyed much more freedom than the mainland. Nominally under the control of the kapitan pasha, they were left alone provided they paid their relatively light taxes, which they collected themselves, and provided they contributed the annual quota of sailors to the Turkish navy. There was virtually no Turkish presence. The islanders were also well used to making their own voice heard. On all merchant ventures, since everyone down to the cabin-boy was to receive a share of the profits, decisions before and during the voyage were taken only after the captain had consulted the crew.

The three naval islands had prospered from their grain-carrying merchant fleets, which they had developed over the previous century, and more recently from running the British blockade of the southern French coast during the Napoleonic wars. On Hydra, the richest of the three, this wealth had gone into grand houses, which are still there, and a luxurious lifestyle. The town of Hydra was described by Gordon as 'one of the best cities in the Levant, and infinitely superior to any other in Greece: the houses are all constructed of white stone; and those of the primates, erected at an immense expense, floored with costly marbles, and splendidly furnished, might pass for palaces even in the capitals of Italy'.[1] However, this opulence was now under threat. The fall in value of the Turkish piastre was cutting profits. The defeat of Napoleon had brought not only an end to lucrative blockade-running but also a big reduction in the price of grain in Europe, and a particularly good harvest in 1820 reduced the price still further. Revolution offered a way out of economic decline.

The temperament of the islanders reflected their origins, Psará having been settled during the previous century by Greeks from Asia Minor, and Hydra and Spétses by Albanians. The Albanians were generally regarded as tough, intelligent and industrious, and were ready to emigrate to pursue their fortunes. They were willing to serve as mercenaries with whoever would reward them best, and in the course of the war of independence were to be found both on the Greek side, winning Byron's alternating admiration and exasperation, and on the Turkish side as part of the Greeks' conglomerate enemy the *tourkalváni*. Contemporaries regularly commented on the distinctively Albanian character of the people of Hydra and Spétses, and contrasted it with the Greek temper of the Psarians. In Gordon's view 'the Hydriots and Spezziotes are of genuine Albanian race, rude, boisterous, unlettered, addicted to intemperance, and, with few exceptions, uncivilised: they are bigoted, and have an aversion to strangers. The Psarrians, Asiatic Greeks, although eminent among their countrymen for spirit and enterprise, are of a more humane, sprightly, and pliable temper.'[2] Making a similar comparison, the English traveller George Waddington wrote that 'vivacity, levity, vanity, attract and amuse you in [the Psarians], and are well contrasted by the sedateness, pride, almost insolence of [the Hydriots]'.[3] Gordon and Waddington were thus agreed about the quicksilver temperament of the Psarians, and it is no surprise that sailors from Psará were the first to use against a Turkish fleet that most hazardous form of naval attack, the fireship.

Rarely in the field of maritime conflict have two opposing fleets been as mismatched as those of the Turks and the Greeks in 1821. The Turkish navy consisted of ships designed and built for battle, with their supporting vessels. It was a unified force, under the command of the kapitan pasha, who stood third in the Turkish hierarchy after the Sultan and the grand vizier. It had an established base in Constantinople where it had every facility for refitting and reprovisioning, and which was totally secure from attack because protected by 160 miles of the narrows of the Dardanelles and the Sea of Marmara. The Greek ships however were designed not as warships but as merchantmen, though they were regularly equipped with guns to fight off pirates. Command in the Greek fleet was anything but unified. Squadrons from different islands sometimes sailed under a single admiral, but co-operation between commanders depended on arrangements made at ad-hoc meetings in the cabin of one of their number. Even command on a single ship scarcely deserved the name. The traditions of trading days persisted, sailors would usually serve only for the month for which they had been paid in advance, and for any significant change of plan the captain had to get the agreement of the crew.

Given the purposes for which they were built, it was inevitable that the Turkish ships were enormously superior to the Greek in size and in firepower. Following the categories of Britain's navy, sailing ships of the eighteenth and nineteenth centuries were named as ships of the line, frigates, corvettes, brigs and so on, and were classified in a confusing number of different ways: most loosely, by the number of masts; most generally, by the number of guns carried; most precisely, by tonnage, though this could be measured by several different calculations. The largest were ships of the line, that is those fit to stand in the line of battle. They had three masts and were divided into six classes or rates, though by the beginning of the nineteenth century only the first three were considered powerful enough for battle. A first-rate ship of the line carried a hundred or more guns, a second-rate eighty-four to ninety-eight and a third-rate seventy to eighty, all with guns on two or more decks. For example, Nelson's flagship the *Victory* was a first-rate ship of the line of 2,162 tons with three masts, three gun decks and in all a hundred guns, with a crew of 850. Next in size after ships of the line were frigates, generally two masted, carrying between twenty-eight and fifty guns and used as scouts and protectors of the fleet. Smaller still were corvettes and brigs, also generally two masted but with fewer than twenty-eight guns. The relationship between tonnage, number of guns and number of crew for Nelson's *Victory* was much the same over the whole range of early-nineteenth-century fighting ships: each gun required about twenty tons burden and about eight crew members.

The Turkish navy at the beginning of the nineteenth century consisted of about twenty three-masted ships of the line, each carrying about eighty guns and so comparable with second- or third-rate ships of the British navy; seven or eight frigates, with about fifty guns; five corvettes with about thirty guns; and forty or so brigs and smaller craft carrying fewer than twenty guns. By contrast, the Greeks at the outbreak of the revolution could muster only a mixed squadron of armed merchantmen, about forty ships in roughly equal proportions from the three naval islands; in size they were only 250–300 tons and none carried more than twenty guns, most only eight to twelve. It was almost as if an assembly of lightly armed coastal cutters had set out to oppose Nelson's Trafalgar fleet.

However, the Turks' advantage was a great deal less than it appeared. Their superior size of ship and firepower was of use only in a set battle at sea, in which success depended on precise seamanship – attacking ships needed to sail in line astern along the enemy's line in order to fire broadside at it – and on accurate gunnery. The Turks were poor on both counts. 'Nautical skill may truly be said not to exist among the Turks,'[4] wrote Richard Green from Patras in October 1821, and as for gunnery, even in 1825, the fifth summer of the war at sea, the Turks kept their guns at the same elevation throughout an action instead of using wedges to change the trajectory. Moreover, in the age of sail a set battle was usually easy to avoid. An attacking fleet would have to be sailing more or less downwind to approach the enemy, who on the open seas could make use of the same wind to sail out of danger.

The Turks were also at a disadvantage because they relied on Greeks and others to provide their crews. 'The vessel is sailed and steered by Europeans,' wrote Richard Green of the Turkish 1821 navy, 'while the fighting part belongs exclusively to the Turks.'[5] On the outbreak of the revolution nearly all the Greeks in the Turkish navy naturally defected, so that the Turks had quickly to recruit new sailors by their customary method of impressment. This commonly meant that the owner of a Constantinople waterfront bar would discover a ship's captain's need for crew, and then ply enough of his customers with drink until they signed an irrevocable service agreement, a practice called 'crimping' in the British navy, which also resorted to it when manpower was short. These new recruits then had to be trained, as Richard Green describes:

> The confusion on board a Turkish vessel is absolutely ridiculous. One half of the men are, perhaps, horribly sea-sick, sprawling about the deck; while the other half are pulling at ropes, of which they have no knowledge. The Chaouses [officers] are seen running here and there, bastinadoing right and left, and forcing the men to their duty. Indeed, the way in which the sailors are taught to handle and know the different ropes is, as I was informed, quite on a par with the rest of the system. Vegetables, pipes, pieces of cloth, &c are attached to the rigging and the cordage, and then the command is given, 'haul up the long pipe; let go the cabbage,' &c.[6]

Despite Green's implied scorn, the use of vegetables and homely objects to identify bits of rigging was rather a good idea: a precursor of today's colour coding. Nearly a century later a similar system was used by the Greek army in the Balkan wars. Illiterate recruits did not know left from right, so were made to hang a clove of garlic on their left ear and an onion on their right, and were taught to turn to the garlic or the onion.

The balance between the Turkish and Greek fleets was further redressed by two Greek advantages. The first was manoeuvrability: their ships were lighter and could get under way and tack more quickly than the Turks'. Their racing skills and boat design had been so far developed for beating the blockade of the southern French coast that when the British captured three Hydriot blockade runners they regarded the masts as dangerously high for the size of boat, and shortened them before using the vessels themselves. The second and crucial Greek advantage, the stone in the sling of David against Goliath, was the use of fireships.

Fireships were not a new invention. Thucydides describes their use in the fifth century BC, they were employed successfully against

Alexander the Great, unsuccessfully against the Turks at the fall of Constantinople, and to devastating effect at the battle of Palermo in 1676 by the French, who for another century retained separate ranks for the bruloteer crews of their fireships. Some Greek historians like to emphasise the long history of the fireship to demonstrate that it was not a fiendish and somehow unfair weapon of war which pre-eminently they exploited.

The Greeks had achieved a memorable success with fireships in support of Russia against Turkey at the time of the Orlov revolt in 1770. The Turkish fleet had been driven into the harbour of Chesme near Smyrna, and under cover from both darkness and the smoke from an exchange of gunfire four Greek fireships, with Greek crews mainly from Psará but with Russian or English captains, sailed into the middle of the crowded Turkish fleet. At least one fireship found its mark, and the flames spread to other Turkish ships. By daybreak the Turkish naval force was destroyed, only one of their fifteen ships of the line and a few smaller vessels remaining undamaged, and it is estimated that of their total crew of 15,000, many of them Greeks, only 4,000 survived.

Fireships were substantial vessels, typically brigs of around 200 tons and about seventy feet long, with two masts carrying enough sail to enable them to sail rapidly downwind against the enemy, and needing a crew of twenty-five to thirty men. A single deck covered the hold, in which a trough about six feet wide was constructed along both sides to contain the combustible material. A simple form of this was dried furze dipped in pitch and oil and sprinkled with sulphur, a more elaborate one was a compound of gunpowder, alcohol, naphtha, sulphur and powdered charcoal rolled into balls. Smaller transverse troughs led to barrels of powder. Twenty or more openings, about two feet square and covered by hatches, were cut in the deck so that when the hatches were opened air would feed the flames below. Hold, deck and masts were smeared with pitch, and the sails soaked in turpentine. The captain and crew remained on board until the fireship was firmly attached to its target by hooks fixed to the ends of the yards, and also if possible by the prow being rammed into one of the enemy's lower gun ports, which would have been only five or six feet above the water. At the final moment the fireship crew scrambled into the escape boat which had been towed behind – in the French navy by a chain, to ensure that this vital lifeline was not cut. The captain left last, lighting a powder train from the stern as he did so. As captain and crew rowed away, fire spread through the fireship's hold until it reached the powder barrels whose explosion blew open the hatches and turned the vessel into a blazing inferno. The target ship now caught fire, and when the flames reached its powder store was blown to smithereens.

That is what happened if all went to plan for the Greeks, but fireships often failed to attach themselves to the enemy ship, and fireships were expensive. All Greek boats were privately owned, and the owner would have to be paid the equivalent of about £800 in the currency of the day for a ship, even an old one, to be converted. The conversion cost another £800, and the crews were paid above the normal rate. Success added to the cost: the crews then received a further payment of 100 to 150 piastres depending upon the size of the enemy ship destroyed, a bonus equal to about two months' pay of an ordinary seaman in the British navy of the time. The captains, however, were said to refuse this bonus, as they would 'consider it a disgrace to accept a recompense for doing their duty to their country'.[7]

Spétses was the first of the three islands to join the revolution on Palm Sunday 1821, the very day when at Patras the Turks under Yussuf Pasha surprised the Greeks in their beds. Psará followed Spétses a week later, on Easter Sunday, in spite of its exposed position only forty miles from the Turkish coast and in the direct path of any Turkish fleet issuing from the Dardanelles. After a further week independence was proclaimed at Hydra, where the two leading captains were Iakoumákis Tombázis and Andréas Maioúlis. In the first months of the war a Greek fleet under Tombázis had the Aegean Sea to itself, carrying calls for revolution to other islands and seizing isolated Turkish merchant ships. But at the beginning of June the Turkish fleet sailed out of the Dardanelles under Kara Ali as kapitan bey or admiral. It had two principal aims: to restore Turkish control over the Aegean islands that were in revolt, and to support Turkish garrisons beleaguered in fortresses round the Greek coast.

During the rest of the summer of 1821 there were three separate Turkish naval expeditions, each opposed with varying success by Greek fleets. The first Turkish naval expedition in early June was challenged by the Greek fleet before it had sailed a hundred miles from the mouth of the Dardanelles. The Turkish fleet took shelter in the Bay of Sígri on the north-west coast of the island of Lésvos, but their second largest ship of the line, a seventy-six-gun vessel, was let down by poor seamanship. Although the wind was favourable, it failed to join the rest of the fleet in the Bay of Sígri and found itself isolated at the wide sandy beach of Eresós, a few miles to the south. This was an ideal opportunity for the Greeks to make use of fireships. There was nobody who knew how to prepare them except a few old men in Psará, survivors of the fireship success at Chesme fifty years before, and it was a Psarian shipbuilder who came forward with the necessary skills. One fireship, with a Hydriot captain and crew, was launched against the isolated Turkish vessel at Eresós, but failed because the powder train was lit too soon. Nothing could be done on the next two days because of calm or contrary winds, but on the third day two more Greek fireships were despatched, manned by Psarians. One of them failed, but the other was successfully attached and fired. The Turkish captain cut his cables and his ship drifted on shore, making escape easier for his crew, but after three-quarters of an hour the flames reached the powder store of the Turkish ship, which was blown to pieces with the loss of some five or six hundred lives. The Turkish fleet retired to the Dardanelles having accomplished nothing and the Greek ships returned in triumph to their home ports.

A month later, in mid-July, the Turks were ready for a second naval venture, this time with the specific purpose of subduing the island of Sámos. Sámos had joined the revolution early, and parties of Samians were raiding the nearby Turkish coast, plundering houses and driving away livestock. The Turkish fleet under Kara Ali now consisted of four ships of the line, five frigates and about twenty smaller ships, and the plan was to bring across to Sámos an army of 12,000 or so assembled at Kuşadasi on the coast opposite. However these troops, kept waiting for transport, became increasingly disorderly, fell to plundering and slaughtering the Greeks of the town, and largely dispersed with their plunder. Kara Ali tried to land small parties of soldiers on Sámos, but they met fierce resistance and were driven back. By the time that he had managed to assemble ten transport vessels full of troops, perhaps 1,000 men in all, the Greek fleet had arrived. It numbered ninety ships from the three naval islands with some from Kásos to the south, and was one of the largest Greek fleets to put to sea in the whole course of the revolution. The Greeks forced Kara Ali's transports back to the Turkish mainland, the Turkish troops were driven away from the shore by grapeshot and the transports burnt. Kara Ali made no further attempt to land on Sámos, and the island remained unsubdued, attempting in the following year to involve its peace-loving neighbours of Chios in the conflict. Kara Ali sailed south to Rhodes, where he joined forces with a flotilla from Egypt, under the command of Ismael Gibraltar. By mid-August the Turkish fleet with its Egyptian allies was back within the Dardanelles, and the Greeks, after touching at Sámos where they received a blessing from the exiled patriarch of Alexandria, were again in their home ports.

After only a few weeks' respite, the Turkish fleet under Kara Ali, with its allies from Egypt, sailed out on their third and last venture of the summer. This time they switched their attack to the west, to the Ionian rather than the Aegean Sea. This gave them several advantages. First, they were well away from possible interference or attack by the Aegean islanders of Hydra, Spétses and Psará. Second, the British authorities in the Ionian islands, despite their declared neutrality, still allowed Turkish ships to use their harbours: it was not until the end of October that belligerents on both sides were barred from Ionian ports. Third, on its voyage round the Peloponnese the Turkish fleet could fulfil one of its main obligations, the support and provisioning of the Turkish-held strongholds on the coast.

This they proceeded to do. Kara Ali's fleet brought provisions for the Turks in the citadel of Methóni, and at Koróni joined the Turks beleaguered in the fortress in driving back the Greek besiegers. The Turkish fleet tried to land troops at nearby Kalamáta, but were repulsed by energetic resistance. After taking on provisions at Zákinthos without objection from the Ionian authorities Kara Ali's fleet reached Patras, where it was joined by ships from the Epirus coast which had been withdrawn from operations against Ali Pasha. At the sight of the Turkish fleet, the Greeks besieging Patras by sea withdrew to the Gulf of Corinth and the shelter of the harbour of Galaxídhi. Thus all three of the remaining Turkish-held fortresses on the western side of the Peloponnese – Methóni, Koróni and Patras – were now more securely in their hands.

The Turks' next target was the flourishing merchant port of

Galaxídhi on the north coast of the Gulf of Corinth. The Greek ships blockading Patras had withdrawn there, but the port was defended only by a few guns on an island at the mouth of the harbour and by 200 Greek irregulars. Kara Ali despatched to Galaxídhi a flotilla consisting mainly of Egyptian ships and commanded by Ismael Gibraltar, accompanied by around 1,000 soldiers and by Yussuf Pasha, the Turkish commander at Patras. The defenders of Galaxídhi withstood two days of Turkish bombardment but to no avail: their guns on the island were eventually silenced and the Greek irregulars, with most of the population, made for safety in the hinterland. The Turks landed, seized the best thirty-four of the ships in the harbour, burnt the town with the rest of the ships, and took some thirty Greek sailors captive. The Greek fleets of Hydra, Spétses and Psará were now roused to action, having been inactive for a month because of disagreements between Hydra and Spétses, but could do no more than harass the Turkish fleet on its way back round the coast of the Peloponnese. Kara Ali, after stopping again at Zákinthos, which was still open to him, finally reached Constantinople at the end of November with the thirty-four ships captured at Galaxídhi, from the yard-arms of which, as grisly trophies, hung the bodies of his thirty Greek captives. As a reward for his services Kara Ali was promoted from kapitan bey to kapitan pasha, supreme commander of the Turkish navy and governor of the Greek islands.

Kara Ali had not done very much to justify his elevation, though Gordon's judgement that his conduct was 'a tissue of folly and cowardice'[8] is probably too harsh. He had failed to crush the revolt on Sámos, he had failed to inflict any serious damage on the Greek naval fleets and he had failed to develop a defence against the Greek fireships. His successes lay in the supply and reinforcement of fortresses on the Peloponnese coast, and the destruction, by his Egyptian colleague Ismael Gibraltar, of the inadequately defended merchant port of Galaxídhi. Whether it was deserved or otherwise, Kara Ali was not to enjoy his new status for long: in the following summer off Chios he lost his flagship and his life in an attack by the Greeks' primary weapon, a fireship.

Why did the Turkish fleet not make a direct attack on the three main naval islands, and so gain for itself freedom of action at sea? Although Hydra was well defended – 'every peak was bristling with a battery,'[9] wrote a visitor in 1825 – Spétses according to Gordon was 'incapable of defence' and Psará was very far from help from the other naval islands or the Greek mainland. Hydra and Spétses were never directly attacked, and Psará only in the fourth year of the war. One might also ask why the Turks did not pour in troops by sea to the Peloponnese fortresses they held, as Ibrahim Pasha of Egypt did in 1825 with devastating results. The Turks were better placed than the Egyptians to carry out such an operation: Ibrahim's voyage from Alexandria, with a stop at Crete, was across over 600 miles of open sea, while the distance from the mouth of the Dardanelles to the southern Peloponnese was less than half that, about 250 miles.

The answer to both questions seems to be simply that, as contemporaries often remarked, the Turks were no sailors. When the Athenians of Pericles' day had been building alliances among the islands of the Aegean and sending naval expeditions as far as Sicily, the Turks had been fighting from horseback on the steppes of Asia. Their subsequent empire was land based. Their furthest advance westward had been overland to the gates of Vienna, and they were used to defending land frontiers on their eastern borders in today's Iran, Syria, Iraq and Saudi Arabia. The Turks were also faced with the threat of the extensive use of fireships, as terrifying as the advent of the torpedo a century later. It is easy to see that the Turks at sea lacked the individual and collective confidence to attempt the bold maritime moves which might quickly have extinguished the Greek revolt.

11

The Turkish Reaction

The outbreak of revolution in 1821 had repercussions in virtually every town with a mixed Turkish and Greek population in Greece itself or in Asia Minor. Where the Greeks quickly achieved dominance, as in much of the Peloponnese, it was the Turks who suffered most. In other parts of Greece, however, and in the mixed townships of Asia Minor, Turks outnumbered Greeks and a combination of Turkish government policy and local feelings of resentment, fuelled by news of Turkish reverses, often put individuals, families and whole communities in danger.

Makriyánnis nearly died at the hands of the Turks in Árta. He had been in Patras when the revolution broke out, but arrived in Árta a week later, on Easter Sunday, to give news of the revolt to his fellow members of the Philikí Etería. There he was promptly arrested 'as an unreliable subject of the Sultan, since I had been over to the Morea'. Twenty-five of his fellow prisoners were hanged, but he was thrown into a dungeon for further questioning under torture. His account continues:

> There were one hundred and eighty of us there. The place was full of rotten loaves of bread and we had to empty our bowels on them because there was nowhere else. The filth and the stink were abominable, none worse in the whole world. We pushed our noses against the keyhole of the door to get fresh air. And they beat me and inflicted innumerable tortures on me and almost finished me off. As a result of the beating, my body swelled up and became inflamed and I was at death's door.[1]

However, Makriyánnis bribed a guard to let him out to see a doctor, escaped, and survived to take part in that summer's operations in the Makrinóros and in many of the revolution's later battles.

At Smyrna, which was a prosperous centre of international trade on the west coast of Asia Minor, the whole Greek community was in danger. Turkish forces were assembled there before embarking to fight the rebels in Moldavia–Wallachia or the Peloponnese, but with little to do and no proper arrangements for feeding them these troops soon turned to plunder. The situation was inflamed at the beginning of June when news arrived of the destruction by Greek fireships of a Turkish frigate at Eresós, only eighty-five miles away on the coast of Lésvos. As Gordon recorded, '3000 ruffians assailed the Greek quarter, plundered the houses and slaughtered the people; Smyrna resembled a place taken by assault, neither age or sex being respected.'[2] The marauders sought from the mullah a *fatwa* justifying a general slaughter of the Christians; the mullah refused, and was himself killed. The consuls in Smyrna sent a joint letter of protest to the Turkish governor pointing out that the European merchants were there under the guarantee of the Sultan's protection, and had brought great wealth to the town; if disorder continued, they would leave, and the trade on which Smyrna had flourished would collapse. Furthermore, the Turks had their international reputation to consider: 'Reports of the present misdeeds will spread throughout Europe, and even reach America.'[3] It was a prophetic statement, though one that was probably of little concern to the Smyrna governor at the time. The events at Smyrna in the summer of 1821 were given dramatic treatment in the classic 1897 story by Dhimítrios Vikélas, *Loukís Láras,* in which a young boy, the eponymous hero, survives with his family the terrors of Smyrna only to be caught up a year later in the massacres on Chios. As Vikélas wrote, the history of the struggle consists not only of military victories but of the persecution, slaughter and dishonour of the defenceless and weak, and of their fortitude in affliction.

The most dramatic example of the Turkish reaction to the revolution was at Constantinople, and stemmed not from harsh policing as at Árta or from the habitual unruliness of troops on the move as at Smyrna, but directly from Ottoman government decisions approved or promulgated by the Sultan himself.

The Sultan, Mahmud II, had ascended the throne in 1808, and held it until his death in 1839, making his reign one of the longest in Ottoman history. Mahmud had come to power by a hard route, and was no stranger to acts of ferocity. His two immediate predecessors, both his cousins, were Selim III (1789–1807) and Mustafa IV (1807–8), and the reigns of both had been dominated by the question of reform of the army. By the end of the eighteenth century the janissaries were no longer the Sultan's elite troops of earlier times, but had become a much enlarged, disorderly and self-indulgent rabble, protesting with force against any attempt to curtail their privileges. As a counterweight to the janissaries, Selim III set up in 1792 the so-called Army of the New Order, initially a small body of a few hundred men with a European nucleus of Germans and Russians, trained on European lines and with European discipline. In its early years it was kept out of the public view, but by 1807 it had grown to a force of some 22,500 and Selim felt strong enough to begin incorporating the janissaries into it. However he had underestimated his opponents. When in July 1807 a pasha went to announce the start of incorporation to the janissaries stationed in the Bosphorus fortresses, they turned on him and killed him and his guards. This was a signal for the whole corps of janissaries to gather in force outside the Sultan's palace, and, despite Selim's craven attempt at appeasement by formally abolishing the New Order, they now demanded his replacement by his cousin Mustafa. Selim was allowed to retire to imprisonment in the harem, and Mustafa IV was acclaimed sultan.

His reign was short lived. A new military force now entered the picture, the experienced troops in the Bulgarian provinces led by Bayrakdar Mustafa Pasha, a supporter of the New Order. In July of the following year Mustafa Pasha marched on Constantinople with the intention of restoring Selim III. When these forces surrounded the palace, the Sultan sent his executioners to strangle, with the traditional silken cord, both the deposed Selim and the young Mahmud, calculating that if these two last survivors of the house of Osman were eliminated he himself could not be deposed. Selim was found and executed, but Mahmud escaped detection, fleeing through the palace's warren of passages and chambers, and was proclaimed sultan in Mustafa's place. The deposed Mustafa was imprisoned in the same rooms as Selim had occupied, but within months was himself strangled on Mahmud's orders. Mahmud was now the last of the house of Osman, whose founder had died nearly five centuries earlier.

The first decade of Mahmud's reign was dominated by two concerns. One, inherited from his predecessors, was to build an army both to support his authority in the capital and to control the unruly provinces of the Ottoman empire. In Arabia the desert warriors, the Wahabis, had captured first Medina in 1804 and then Mecca in 1807, the two holy cities of the empire. In 1817 the Sultan was forced to grant limited autonomy to Serbia, and in Epirus Ali Pasha was a continuing threat. Mahmud's second concern was the encroachment of Russia. Turkey had been forced by the Treaty of Kutchuk-Kainardji of 1774 to make major concessions to Russia, which were extended by further treaties in the following decades. In both his domestic and foreign concerns Mahmud's conduct was distinguished by patience, determination, a willingness to concede when necessary before advancing where possible, and a readiness to act forcefully and brutally at the decisive moment. The Sultan's adviser, Halet Effendi, was said to have quoted a Turkish proverb that described Mahmud's method: 'The mole works in silence and darkness but he makes his way as he purposes. The pace of the tortoise is slow, but if he makes sure of every ascending step, he at last reaches the hilltop. The scorpion conceals his sting, and is a quiet and contemptible reptile, until he can dart it with death into his foe.'[4] Why then did Mahmud choose, as his most dramatic response to the Greek rebellion, the public execution at Easter of the Greek Orthodox patriarch Grigórios, an act which did nothing to help quell his rebellious subjects and violently antagonised the Greeks' fellow Orthodox nation and potential ally, his old enemy Russia?

The Sultan's action against Grigórios was the culmination of some weeks of increasingly disturbing news of Greek activities. First in early March came the discovery of a plot, by Greeks serving in the Turkish navy, to set fire to the dockyard arsenal, assassinate the Sultan, seize the capital's artillery and arm the Greek population. It was a bold, perhaps hare-brained scheme, but in the event it was discovered in time and its leader, a captain from Hydra with a senior command in the Turkish navy, was arrested and imprisoned with his associates. Then, with Easter still a month away, information reached the capital of the killings of Turks at Galatz and Iaşi in Moldavia which had marked the start of

Alexander Ipsilántis' campaign. Finally, reports were brought to Constantinople a week before Easter of the outbreak of revolution in the Peloponnese and the attendant killing of many thousands of Turks.

The reactions of the Ottoman authorities became increasingly fierce as the news became more alarming. On the discovery of the plot to burn the dockyard they did no more than expel non-resident Greeks from the city and institute a search for hidden arms. When news of Alexander Ipsilántis' expedition arrived, the patriarch was ordered to denounce him, which he did in uncompromising terms. The authorities arrested seven bishops and held them as hostages for Greek good behaviour, and brought in troops from outside the city, who soon began to murder Greeks and plunder their houses. All Greeks in Constantinople had now become suspect, even the educated and prosperous phanariot Greeks, and news of the rising in the Peloponnese initiated a series of executions. The victims included a phanariot holding the high office of dragoman of the Porte, two former dragomans of the fleet, a member of the distinguished Mavrokordhátos family, a number of merchants and bankers, and three men suspected of a plot to poison Constantinople's water supplies. Three monks and two priests are also recorded as having been executed, but, though bishops had been taken as hostages, until Easter Sunday no senior member of the clergy had been harmed.

In the early hours of darkness on Easter Sunday, the Christians were summoned by the crier to celebrate the risen Christ. They made their way without hindrance through the janissaries who thronged the streets to the patriarchal church of Áyios Georgios where the patriarch Grigórios was to preside over the Easter service. Grigórios was now an old man, and in his third period of office as patriarch. Born around 1750 in Dhimitsána in the central Peloponnese, he had risen rapidly through the church hierarchy, becoming bishop of Smyrna in 1785 and patriarch for the first time in 1797. It was at this period that he formed a lasting friendship with Yermanós, later to be bishop of Old Patras. Grigórios was deposed after eighteen months for favouring the French at a time when Napoleon had invaded the Ottoman province of Egypt. He was banished to Mount Athos, but was re-elected patriarch in 1806 when Turkey became France's ally against Russia and Britain. However, the wheel turned again when in 1808 the army from Bulgaria moved into

Constantinople and installed Mahmud II as sultan. Grigórios fell foul of the army's commander and was dismissed, spending another ten years on Mount Athos before returning as patriarch for the third time in 1818. Robert Walsh, chaplain to the British embassy in Constantinople, visited Grigórios during his final patriarchate and described him as 'thin, pale, very aged, apparently past eighty years, with a venerable white beard; his dress was a robe of simple crape, which covered his head'.[5]

The outbreak of the Greek revolution put Grigórios in an impossible position. As patriarch he was responsible for the good behaviour of the Christians, under the original agreement between Mehmed, the conqueror of Constantinople, and Yennádhios, the first patriarch under the Ottomans. However, Grigórios had no means of controlling the Greeks' behaviour since the bishops, even his old friend Yermanós, and the lower clergy paid no attention to his calls for submission to the government. In denouncing rebellion when Alexander Ipsilántis initiated it, he was not only following the instructions of his temporal master, but also probably trying to save his flock from self-destruction. In the end the denunciations did nothing to satisfy the Ottoman authorities, failed to divert the Greeks from their course, and served only to alienate Christian clergy and laity from the head of their church.

Having concluded the service on Easter Sunday 1821 Grigórios returned to his own quarters as dawn broke. Almost immediately he was summoned to a hastily convened meeting of the Holy Synod by the dragoman of the Porte, who was accompanied by a secretary. The secretary then produced two edicts, the first deposing Grigórios as 'unworthy of the patriarchal throne, ungrateful and unfaithful to the Porte, and guilty of intriguing', and the second calling on the Synod to elect a successor immediately, a choice which fell on Evyénios, the bishop of Pisidia. Grigórios was led away, but at noon on Easter Sunday was brought back to the patriarchate and there hanged from the hasp fastening its central doors, which in memory of the event are to this day painted black and welded permanently shut. According to Walsh's account, 'His person, attenuated by abstinence and emaciated by age, had not weight sufficient to cause immediate death. He continued for a long time in pain, which no friendly hand dared to abridge, and the darkness of night came on before his last convulsions were over.'[6] That same evening, it is said, the grand vizier Benderli Ali and later the Sultan himself came and gazed at the patriarch's body. A statement of the Ottoman accusations, lengthy but vague, was attached to the corpse. After three days the patriarch's body was taken down and as a final insult a party of Jews, regarded as inveterately hostile to the Christians, was ordered to drag it through the filthy streets and throw it into the harbour. In the Jews' defence it was said that they performed their office under duress and 'with great calmness and decency'. The body was retrieved from the water by the captain of a ship from Kephaloniá, and taken to Odessa where on the instructions of the outraged Tsar the funeral ceremony was conducted with every elaboration of ritual and every mark of respect.

In the weeks that followed the execution of the patriarch, the Turkish authorities appeared to be doing everything possible to antagonise Russia still further. The banker to the Russian embassy was arrested on suspicion of providing funds for Greek rebels, and all efforts by the Russian ambassador, Count Stroganov, to intercede for him or to be shown proof of his guilt were brusquely rejected. These personal insults were followed by commercial aggravation: the Turks began seizing grain ships flying the Russian flag as they passed Constantinople on their way from the Black Sea to the Aegean. The pretext was that the city was short of food because supplies from Moldavia–Wallachia had been interrupted by Ipsilántis' incursion, but the real reason, it was thought, was to stop grain reaching the rebels in Greece. Violent affronts to the Orthodox faith also continued. Churches were wrecked, and senior members of the clergy, including all the seven bishops held as hostages, were executed.

Stroganov tried to enlist the support of the other ambassadors at Constantinople in his protests against these actions. He sought a collective condemnation of the execution of the patriarch, but to no avail, and was equally unsuccessful with his proposal that the ambassadors should jointly ask for naval vessels to be sent to Constantinople for the protection of themselves and the Christian population. When Britain's ambassador Viscount Strangford refused to go along with the latter idea, Stroganov is said to have 'presumed publicly to say to the British ambassador, "that his name would descend to posterity, stained with blood"', and, on leaving the room, he is believed to have addressed to him these words: 'My Lord, I would wish *you* too, good-night, were I not assured that with such a conscience you can never sleep.'[7]

The Tsar's own approaches to the other powers, embodied in a memorandum of 4 July, fared no better. Metternich, the inveterate opponent of revolutionary movements, had of course ranged Austria firmly on the side of the Turks. Castlereagh for Britain replied that he viewed the Greek revolt as another symptom of 'that organised spirit of insurrection which is systematically propagating itself throughout Europe'.[8] Prussia initially favoured collective action, but this made no headway against opposition from Metternich and Castlereagh. France's counsels were divided and her reaction ambivalent; the French government, it has been said, was inclined to run several contradictory policies at the same time in the confident expectation that they could not all fail.[9]

Tsar Alexander therefore proceeded with an ultimatum of his own to the Ottoman government, though one that implied much greater support from the other powers than he had in fact obtained. The document was drafted by Kapodhístrias, and made the strongest case against the Turks and in favour of the Greeks that Kapodhístrias was ever to pen for his master. The Turks were accused of insulting the Orthodox faith, proscribing Russia's fellow Christians, breaking Russo-Turkish treaties and, most important of all, threatening 'to disturb the peace that Europe has bought at so great a sacrifice'. Unless Turkey acceded to the Russian demands for restoration of the damaged churches and for justice in determining the guilt or innocence of individuals, Russia would issue a formal declaration that:

> the Ottoman government has placed itself in a state of open hostility against the Christian world; that it has legitimized the defence of the Greeks, who would thenceforth be fighting solely to save themselves from inevitable destruction; and that in view of the nature of that struggle, Russia would find herself strictly obliged to offer them help because they were persecuted; protection, because they would be in need of it; assistance, jointly with the whole of Christendom, because she could not surrender her brothers in religion to the mercy of a blind fanaticism.[10]

Stroganov presented this ultimatum to the Turkish government on 18 July, and as instructed allowed seven days for a reply; when none was received by then, he broke off diplomatic relations and prepared to leave. The Reis

Effendi, the Ottoman foreign minister, did produce a reply one day later but Stroganov rejected it as being out of time, and after a fortnight's frustrating delay because of bad weather sailed from Constantinople on 10 August, his five-year mission at an end. He had failed to achieve any collective action by the ambassadors at Constantinople, just as the Tsar had failed on the wider European stage to win the support of any of the other powers, in spite of his talk of acting 'jointly with the whole of Christendom'. It was clear that if Russia went to war with Turkey she would have to act alone, and this she was not prepared to do.

The Ottoman authorities gave their reasons for executing Grigórios in the document of some 500 words which was attached, as was customary, to the hanging corpse. The document began by saying that the duty of the leaders of subject peoples was to watch their conduct day and night, report any misdeeds to the government and prevent such misdeeds by advice, threats or if necessary punishment. However, the statement continued, it was impossible to regard the patriarch as uninvolved in the revolution; to all appearances he was a secret participant in it; in fact he was the prime cause of the disturbances, bringing harm to the government and the imminent total destruction of the Greek people. Hence his execution.[11]

The document clearly fails to establish a case against Grigórios. He had done all that he was asked to do in condemning revolution, most recently in his fierce denunciation of Alexander Ipsilántis and all who supported him. No evidence was offered to substantiate the progression from 'not uninvolved' in the revolution to 'secret participant' to 'prime cause'. The British ambassador Strangford was told by the Reis Effendi that only on the day before the patriarch's execution 'a fresh mass of the most convincing evidence against him had been submitted to the Sultan, who, in a fit of violent anger and indignation had ordered his immediate execution'.[12] However, this mass of evidence was never shown to Strangford or to anyone else; and the Sultan was the last person to allow a fit of anger to determine a highly political action.

Some later historians have tried to demonstrate Grigórios' involvement with the rising; this would enhance his standing as a Greek patriot but would also, of course, go some way to justify his execution. Their main evidence is a letter of July 1819 from Grigórios to Pétrobey Mavromichális, commending his plan to establish a school in the Mani and sending a contribution to it of 45,000 piastres. It is suggested that 'school' was simply the Philikí Etería's code for 'revolution', and that this was the purpose for which the society's agent Perrevós used the money. Donations to the Philikí Etería were often disguised as contributions to schools, but it is only speculation that Grigórios was using 'school' in this coded sense, and many schools were in fact founded in the years before the revolution. Neither Grigórios' Greek supporters nor his Turkish accusers have ever convincingly demonstrated his secret support for his compatriots' revolt.

Was the object of Grigórios' execution simply to intimidate the Greeks into submission? If so, the action was ill judged: the patriarch had so distanced himself from the revolution in his public pronouncements that his death could hardly be seen as a blow to it. The Greek reaction seems to have been neither fear nor outrage but, surprisingly, indifference. There is very little reference to his execution in the memoirs of the participants, and Grigórios' old friend Bishop Yermanós makes no mention of it at all. Another possible explanation might be that the Ottoman authorities wanted a more compliant figure on the patriarchal throne. But Grigórios could hardly have done more to carry out their wishes, and when his successor Evyénios was called on for another denunciation of the Greeks in August 1821 he could only attempt to outfawn the obsequious words of Grigórios, condemning the Greeks' 'weakness and madness' in opposing 'this invincible Government which has ever loved and cherished all alike'.[13]

The most likely interpretation is that among the Sultan's advisers there was a continuing conflict between hawks and doves, and that the patriarch's execution represented a token victory for the hawks. According to Finlay, Mahmud had by now come to distrust two of the apparent doves, 'both Halet Effendi, hitherto his favourite minister, and Benderli Ali, his grand-vizier, whom he considered too favourable to the Greeks and too fearful of Russia'.[14] Halet Effendi, who memorably compared Mahmud with the mole, the tortoise and the scorpion, was a cautious conservative, protecting the traditional status of both the janissaries and the Greek phanariots. He later fell from favour, and was executed at the end of the following year. Benderli Ali lost his post of grand vizier a few weeks after the patriarch's death, and under his successor the executions of Greek clergy and other leaders immediately intensified. It is possible that Benderli Ali's visit to view the patriarch's corpse, ascribed by some to triumphalism, was actually an indication of regret. It was part of Mahmud's policy throughout his reign to control the factions that surrounded him by giving first one and then the other a freer hand. On this interpretation the execution of the patriarch was a demonstration by the newly installed hawks in the Sultan's inner circle of advisers that they would stop at nothing to crush the Greek rebellion, even the killing of the titular head of the Greek community without trial and without producing evidence of guilt, and despite the lip-service he had paid to the Ottoman government. Insofar as they considered the Russian response, they reckoned, on this scenario, that they could get away with it – as, in the event, they did.

12

The Capture of Tripolis

From the first days of the revolution Kolokotrónis had insisted that the Greeks concentrated their efforts on the taking of Tripolis in the central Peloponnese. Equally determined to defend it was Mustafa, the kihaya bey or lieutenant-governor, acting for his superior Khurshid, pasha of the Morea, who since January 1821 had been away at Iánnina besieging Ali Pasha. Tripolis takes its name from the three derelict classical towns of Tegea, Mantinea and Palladion, which it was built to replace in the fourteenth century. It lies in the middle of a featureless plain about 2,000 feet above sea level, reached from the coast near Navplion by a steep and winding road. Behind the town, to the north and west, stands an amphitheatre of barren mountains on whose lower slopes, the Tríkorpha, the Greek forces were ranged.

In 1821 the town was ringed by a wall about two miles in circumference, some six feet thick and fourteen feet high on the outside, with a continuous parapet and towers at intervals, from both of which defenders could fire on attackers. Within the walls was a small citadel, a last refuge for the besieged. From the besiegers' point of view the town was very different from most of the other strongholds ringing the Peloponnese into which the Turks had retreated. At Monemvasía, Navplion, Corinth and Árgos the fortresses were on top of a steeply sloping pinnacle of rock, while Tripolis was on an open plain. The citadels at Patras and Koróni were perched above the town and could be held even if the town itself was lost, whereas the Tripolis citadel was within the town. Methóni was defended by the massive and cleverly designed ramparts of the Venetian military architects, but Tripolis had only a primitive stone wall. Also Tripolis was landlocked, so the Turks could not support it from the sea. It was thus not only a desirable objective for the Greeks, from its central position and because it contained so many leading Turks and their wealth; it should also, in theory, have been a relatively easy target. But practice was a different matter.

When the kihaya bey Mustafa came south in May 1821 to take up his post in Tripolis, he brought a body of seasoned troops with him, the most formidable of which were 1,500 Albanian mercenaries under their commander Elmez Aga. Mustafa's total garrison in Tripolis amounted to some nine to ten thousand men under arms. He had two bodies of specialist soldiers. One was a force of cavalry, which was valuable as an escort for foraging parties, and would have been more useful in attack if they could have brought the Greeks to battle on the open plain, an encounter which the Greeks were canny enough to avoid. The second specialist group was a complement of a hundred gunners brought from Constantinople. These might have been more useful if they had had reliable artillery, but by the end of the siege only seven of their thirty cannon were in even reasonable repair.

The total population of Tripolis, including the armed garrison, was estimated at about 30,000, roughly double the pre-war numbers, since though most Greeks had left many Turks had come in from the surrounding countryside. There was therefore an increased number for whom food and water had to be found, and the crowded conditions in the town were a breeding ground for disease. Among the distinguished Turks trapped in Tripolis were two provincial governors and the wife of the absent Kurshid Pasha, as well as his harem. Also in the town were a number of eminent Greeks, held as hostages since the early days of the revolution, including five bishops. Few of these Greek captives survived.

As the months of 1821 passed the Greek forces around Tripolis steadily increased from the two or three thousand who had been present in May to about 6,000. By late summer they were drawn up along the Tríkorpha foothills, to the north and west of the town and just out of the Turks' cannon range, in four main groups. Kolokotrónis was on the left of the line and subordinate to him were Anagnostarás in the centre and Iatrákos on the right. On the higher slopes above them was a reserve force under Pétrobey Mavromichális.

His position in reserve was appropriate while the experienced captains held the forward positions.

An army of thousands stationed for months in rocky foothills on the edge of an arid plain obviously had to be supplied from elsewhere. Thus ovens in neighbouring villages were taken over and the villagers brought bread to the camp on donkeys and mules. Sheep and goats were also presented to the troops, and Karítena, twenty miles to the west behind the Greek lines, contributed 48,000 animals in the course of the siege. The Greeks also needed ammunition, so lead was stripped from roofs for use as shot, and libraries and monasteries were ransacked to provide paper for cartridges. The mountain village of Dhimitsána to the west was the main provider of powder, and was therefore spared any other requisitions.

In July 1821 a newcomer arrived at the Greek camp: Dhimítrios Ipsilántis, whose brother Alexander had led the disastrous revolt in Moldavia and Wallachia earlier in the year. On his way from Russia to Greece via Trieste, Dhimítrios Ipsilántis came across a Frenchman named Baleste, a veteran of Napoleon's armies who had lived in Crete and so knew the language and conditions of Greece, and engaged him to organise the first regular Greek army, the earliest of many attempts, all ultimately failures, to introduce European systems into the Greek forces. Ipsilántis and Baleste sailed from Trieste for the Peloponnese in a ship flying the Russian flag, and Baleste was dropped off at Kalamáta to begin his task of organising regular troops while Ipsilántis went on to Monemvasía and then Tripolis. He came expecting to move smoothly into the leadership of the revolution in the Peloponnese, and brought with him three means of influencing events: a commission from his brother Alexander, written before his surrender to the Austrians, grandiloquently naming Dhimítrios as plenipotentiary of the General Committee of the Council of the society; the implied prospect of Russian help for the Greek cause, which was still hoped for in spite of the Tsar's stated refusal to become involved; and a sum of money variously estimated at between 200,000 and 300,000 piastres.

Dhimítrios Ipsilántis knew virtually nothing of soldiering; his military experience was only a short period as a young captain on the Russian general staff at the end of the Napoleonic wars. Furthermore, he was a most unimpressive figure: less than five feet tall, skinny in body

and limbs, prematurely balding, with a speech impediment and a diffi-
dent manner which came across as coldness, and lacking the decisive-
ness which might have overcome these disadvantages. However, all who
had dealings with him recognised his high-mindedness.

With the arrival of Dhimítrios Ipsilántis a three-way split among the
Greeks in front of Tripolis quickly became apparent, a split that became
ever wider as the war went on. One party supported Ipsilántis, who
remained popular even after news arrived of his brother's disastrous
defeat in the Danube provinces. A second element backed the military
leaders, of whom Kolokotrónis was the acknowledged head. The third
group, itself divided by personal feuds, consisted of the senior clergy and
the civilian leaders. The civilian leaders, variously called *proésti* or *prókriti*
in Greek, *kojabashi* in Turkish, and notables or primates in English, were
in effect the aristocracy of the Peloponnese, mainly rich feudal landowners who had held considerable local governing powers under the Turks.
Their aim, said their opponents, was simply to replace the Turks as rulers
of their domains, and to make use of the military to bring this about.

Shortly after reaching the camp at Tripolis, Ipsilántis made an
extremely high-handed move. In June a government for the whole
Peloponnese, the Peloponnesian Senate, had been established, which
replaced the local councils set up at Kalamáta, Patras and elsewhere
when revolution first broke out. Ipsilántis now proposed that this
should be replaced by a new government under his direction, and that
he should become commander-in-chief of all the Greek forces. The
civilian primates were outraged by these proposals, but Kolokotrónis,
surprisingly, supported them. He could no doubt see that he would
continue to exercise the chief military command, whatever nominal
title was given to this spindly youth. Also Kolokotrónis was alert to the
international repercussions of Greek discord, and when his men wanted
to attack the primates he climbed on to a rock and addressed them:

> We have taken up arms against the Turks, and therefore it is regarded by
> the whole of Europe that we Greeks have risen up against tyrants, and
> all Europe is looking on to see what will be the upshot. . . . If we kill our
> primates, what will the kings say? Why, that these people have not risen
> for freedom's sake, but to slay their own colleagues, and that they are bad
> men, and *carbonari*; and then kings will give help to the Turks, and we
> shall have a heavier yoke than that which we have borne hitherto.[1]

Thus the troops were pacified. A compromise was reached, that the existing Peloponnesian Senate should be retained, not replaced as Ipsilántis had demanded, but that Ipsilántis should become its president, and have the role of commander-in-chief. Both Ipsilántis and the primates had had to make concessions, but Kolokotrónis had yielded nothing of substance.

As the summer sun blazed down on the dry plain of Tripolis, one of the first acts of the Greeks had been to try to deprive the besieged of drinking water. One account says that they cut off the channel which supplied water from outside to the town's fountains. Kolokotrónis says that his men polluted this supply with a poisonous plant which he calls *phlómos*, probably of the spurge or figwort family, both of which were traditionally used as medicines but which in excess could be fatal. It is very doubtful if this ruse could have produced high enough concentrations to do any harm. In any case, Tripolis was not wholly dependent upon water from outside, since it contained a number of wells within its walls. As the siege progressed the Albanian troops of Elmez Aga took possession of the best wells and demanded payment for their use. Thus water was short in the town, but not short enough to bring an immediate capitulation.

Food was a more pressing problem for the besieged, but this was lessened by the Greeks themselves. Men of the Mani in particular would set up markets at night under the walls and sell the besieged bread and fruit, which the buyers often resold at a huge profit. For a time the Turkish cavalry provided protection for foraging parties, but this came to an end in late August when Greek forces under Kolokotrónis and Anagnostarás surprised an escorted group that had gone to fetch grain from a village a few miles north of Tripolis. The Turks were driven back into the town and lost the train of mules and horses carrying the collected provisions. A hundred or more Turks were killed, and Kolokotrónis had their severed heads carried before him as he returned to the Greek camp. 'The Turks did not again venture forth from Tripolitsa,' recorded Kolokotrónis. 'This was the last time. They now fought only from the walls, and they despaired of being able to procure any more provisions.'[2] The Turks' horses too were deprived of fodder, and were reduced to grazing on the withered grasses below the city walls. Before long they were killed for food.

Overcrowding and lack of water and food soon led to the outbreak of disease in the embattled town. The American philhellene Samuel Gridley Howe was not at Tripolis, but as a doctor he vividly imagined the situation. 'To make misery even greater,' he wrote,

> a disease broke out in the place and swept off hundreds every day. Sometimes it would seize upon a family, every member of which would be sick at the same time with it, and they lay in lonely misery, for not a friend came near them; or, if he came, it was only to see if a little bread or water might be plundered. Humanity had been frozen up by misery; and without a hand to bring a draught of water, or close the dying eyes, they gasped out their existence in sight of one another, and their bodies lay and rotted away in the solitary chambers.[3]

Starvation and disease might reduce the town in the end, but a quicker means of victory seemed to be offered by the delivery to the Greek camp of three mortars seized after the fall of Monemvasía. Initially nobody knew how to use them, but in late August an Italian named Tassi presented himself, claiming to be an expert in gunnery. Among the philhellenes serving with the Greeks was the young French artillery officer Maxime Raybaud, who could see at once that Tassi was a charlatan, with no knowledge of guns, trying to impress his hosts by casually dropping the names of Castlereagh, Metternich and Kapodhístrias into his conversation. Raybaud was a witness to Tassi's first, and last, artillery experiment. In an earthwork at the safe distance of a mile from the town Tassi placed and loaded the best of the three mortars, while Ipsilántis looked on and the Greek soldiers sat on the surrounding heights to watch the anticipated spectacle. Tassi lit the fuse, but a muffled explosion made it immediately obvious that the firing had gone wrong, and that the mortar was smashed. The Greeks were furious, not least Kolokotrónis, and Tassi kept out of sight for a few days until Ipsilántis, good-hearted as ever, enabled him to slip away quietly. Tassi was later killed, with many other foreign supporters of the Greek cause, in the disastrous battle of Péta in the following year.

Raybaud was now persuaded to take charge of the Greek artillery at Tripolis. It was no easy task. Of the three mortars from Monemvasía, one had been wrecked by Tassi and the other two had been spiked. The Greeks ultimately possessed a further eight guns. Three sixteen- or eighteen-pounders were brought by Thomas Gordon, who arrived at Tripolis in early September, also bringing with him troops and weapons, and the remaining five cannon were smaller pieces. All needed attention, either to the guns themselves or to their mountings. Mountings could be improvised from tree trunks bound together by iron hoops, but repairing the guns was extremely difficult. 'A piece of work', wrote Raybaud, 'which would scarcely have taken an hour in a workshop with the necessary tools, consumed whole days, and even then the job was botched.'[4] Raybaud's repairs were ultimately successful, but the Greek guns never did any damage to the walls of Tripolis.

Though conditions were hard for the Greeks on the hills, and grim for most of those in the town, the siege had its more light-hearted moments. When opposing troops were within earshot of each other, insults were genially exchanged. When a hat appeared above the ramparts of either side it drew a hail of bullets, and there were exultant cheers when the hat was revealed to be on a stick and not on a head. At other times the two sides fraternised. In the heat of the day, when fighting was regarded as impossible, a party of Greeks would cautiously approach the walls, from which a party of Turks would cautiously emerge. The two groups would then sit down for long conversations on the outcome of the siege and other matters, smoking their pipes the while. In the cool of the evening Raybaud would find Greek soldiers dancing to the music of a tambourine and a sort of oboe, or listening to a singer accompanying himself on a mandolin while chanting a warlike song or the verses of the revolution's revered forerunner Rígas Pheréos.

Within days of his arrival in early July Dhimítrios Ipsiántis offered surrender terms to the besieged Turks, terms which were rejected with disdain. However, in the following months the town's predicament worsened. The Greek forces had been steadily increased, to numbers variously estimated at between 10,000 and 20,000, by the expectation of plunder. At the end of August a major blow to Turkish hopes of resistance came with the news that the Greeks had successfully blocked the advance of a Turkish army from the north down the Thermopylae route on the east coast; this meant that Tripolis could not be relieved that year. Thus divisions began to appear among the besieged. One party led by the lieutenant-governor Kihaya Bey Mustafa proposed fighting their way out through the encircling Greeks and joining their compatriots in the fortress of Palamídhi at Navplion twenty miles to the east. The Albanians under Elmez Aga looked for the outcome most profitable to themselves, which was likely to involve a separate agreement with the Greeks. The third group, which included most of the eminent Turks trapped in the town, supported a negotiated surrender. In short, the first group wanted honour, the second money and the third safety.

The surrender party in Tripolis now decided to open negotiations by making use of the Greek hostages who had been held in the town since the beginning of the siege five months earlier. These had been kept in appalling conditions. Their bodyguards had been killed, and the hostages with their servants, thirty-eight in all, were confined in a cramped cell with one small window. Masters were shackled by one chain round their necks and servants by another, so that if one on the chain stood up or sat down all of them had to follow. The Turks now in mid-September prevailed on the hostages to write a letter to their compatriots outside, calling on them to lay down their arms and throw themselves on the clemency of the Sultan, a ridiculous demand obviously, but a way of starting the process of parley. As such it was successful, and two days later representatives of the two sides met in a tent pitched between the Greek encampment and the town. The Greeks demonstrated that they were negotiating from strength by keeping the Turks waiting for an hour before joining them. Discussions continued in a series of meetings over the next ten days, the Turks' demands being steadily whittled down.

It was only now, when negotiations for the long-expected surrender of Tripolis had begun, that the Greek leaders drew up a formal arrangement for the division of the spoils in the town. If Tripolis surrendered by agreement the troops, who had received no pay since the siege began, were to get two-thirds of the booty and the national treasury one-third. If it fell to attack the troops would be rewarded with a larger share: three-quarters instead of two-thirds. Country units absent guarding the mountain passes would get the same share as those besieging the town. There was provision for the families of Greeks killed during the siege, and a reward was offered for capturing alive any of the distinguished Turks in Tripolis. In the event these tidy formulae were almost totally ignored, and the national treasury got nothing.

Within a few days of the start of negotiations and the agreement on division of the spoils, something very odd happened: Dhimítrios Ipsilántis left the camp. He was followed by Gordon and all the philhellene officers except Raybaud and a few others, and took with him the regular troops who had come up from Kalamáta after training by Baleste. Ipsilántis' party was accompanied by Kolokotrónis' eldest son Pános. It was Kolokotrónis who took the lead in persuading Ipsilántis to leave, on the grounds that the Turkish fleet had, for the first time, arrived off the west coast of the Peloponnese and that Ipsilántis should go and oppose it. However, Ipsilántis took with him only one two-pounder mountain gun, 'a redoubtable artillery', commented Raybaud with heavy irony, for facing the might of the Ottoman navy.[5] There is little doubt that Kolokotrónis wanted the principled Ipsilántis out of the way when Tripolis fell, and that the job of Pános Kolokotrónis was to see that he stayed away. It also seems likely that Ipsilántis and his companions, foreseeing what would happen when the Greeks entered the town, were ready to accept an excuse, however flimsy, for absenting themselves.

In the following days negotiations with the main Turkish representatives dragged on, but a separate agreement was quickly reached with the Albanians under Elmez Aga. They were to be allowed to leave for Epirus, with their weapons and possessions, on condition that if possible they joined the forces of Ali Pasha fighting the Turks, and in any case did not fight against Greeks. Other deals between groups or individuals were concluded. The Turks from the town of Vardhoúni in the Mani surrendered en masse to their former neighbours, and were allowed through the Greek lines to herd miserably behind the camp with other such refugees. Bobolína, the renowned lady ship's captain who commanded a ship of the Spétses fleet after her husband's death, arrived at Tripolis – with her ships, reported an Italian journalist who had obviously not looked at a map – and entered the town to haggle with Turkish women for costly gifts in return for their safety. Fighting was virtually halted while these various negotiations were being carried on.

The lull lasted only a few days more. After the equinoctial squalls of late September the heat of summer had blazed out again. 'On Friday 5 October,' wrote Raybaud, 'the sun rose brilliantly. The heat was stifling, and the atmosphere painfully oppressive. Only the monotonous sound of the cicada broke the silence of the day, which seemed like a return to the dog-days of July.'[6] On that somnolent morning when negotiations were continuing and a truce had been orally agreed, the tower near the gate to Navplion in the south-east wall of the town, and so on the far side from the main Greek encampment, was left unguarded. The few Turkish sentinels on the walls allowed a party of Greeks to approach to sell them grapes and these seized their opportunity, scrambled over the walls and opened the main gate to their compatriots.

The Greeks poured in in their thousands, intent on plunder and indiscriminate slaughter. The corpses of those who had died earlier of famine or disease and which lay unburied in the streets were now covered with new bodies. Those which had been buried were exhumed for their valuables, producing a further spread of disease. Women and children sheltering in their houses were thrown from the windows. Packs of stray dogs followed the victorious Greeks to tear apart and eat their victims. Fires from burning houses intensified the heat of the day, and a pall of smoke hung over the town in the windless air. The town resounded with the guttural Greek war-cry, which took on a deeper animal growl in the act of killing. Raybaud was in the town for most of the three days of carnage and managed to rescue a few of the inhabitants. He described the scene as a hell of fire and blood.

On the day of the assault the Albanians under Elmez Aga withdrew to the governor's palace at the northern end of the town, and demanded fulfilment of the agreement that they should leave for Epirus. Before nightfall the Greeks, relieved not to be fighting them, allowed them out to bivouac temporarily in Kolokotrónis' encampment. On the next day Elmez Aga and his troops left for the north, but even though deprived of their Albanian mercenaries the Turkish troops put up a stout resistance, either in houses or in the citadel at the southern end of the town. From the citadel forty Turks managed to fight their way out and get to Navplion, though without the kihaya bey Mustafa, who had always favoured this course; he and the other Turks of distinction were taken captive in the hope of a future ransom. The citadel, with no food and no source of water, surrendered on the third day to Kolokotrónis, who remained within its walls for several days, allowing nobody else entry, while he assembled for his own use the riches that had been put there for safe keeping.

While the citadel was still holding out, the most callous act of all was committed by the Greeks. Those who had earlier left the town by agreement had remained at the Greek camp; they numbered some 2,000, mostly women and children. A breakaway party of Greeks were determined to be rid of them, and leading them to a gorge where the plain meets the mountains killed them in cold blood. Raybaud had followed, and managed to rescue one young girl; he gave her into the care of a Corfiot living in the southern Peloponnese, who brought her up as one of his own family. Raybaud passed the scene of the massacre shortly afterwards, while the stench of putrefaction still hung over it, and again the following year when the bones had been picked clean by wild animals and birds of prey. Even as skeletons, he recorded, some of the victims still clasped each other in their last embrace.

How many died in the storming and sack of Tripolis? The population of the town, estimated at 30,000 when the siege began, had, when the town fell, probably been halved to about 15,000 by fighting, voluntary exodus, starvation and disease. Gordon believed that over half of the remainder, some 8,000, were killed at the time of the sack, for the loss of about 300 Greeks killed or wounded. Among the casualties were all but three of the surviving Greek hostages; the others, Gordon reported, 'soon died through a too sudden change of diet, and transition from want and fear to joy and plenty'.[7]

There was nothing to justify the horrific carnage at Tripolis in the centuries-old military conventions which, brutal as they sound, did set some limits to conduct in war. These conventions laid down that, if a fortress was taken by assault, the garrison could be slaughtered and the town sacked for twenty-four hours, but that civilians should be spared. At the fall of Tripolis the Greeks treated the Turkish civilians as animals to be exterminated, and a particularly dishonourable act was their killing of defenceless refugees in the gorge. The mind-set which dehumanises one's opponents is as old as war itself, and the Greeks and Turks were no stranger to it. Significantly, the Greek word for pursuing the enemy was to hunt, *kinigó*. This phraseology, if not the conduct, has persisted to our own day even in regular armies: in 1944 Montgomery's message to the troops embarking for D-Day ended with 'Good hunting!'

When Ipsilántis, Gordon and the other philhellenes left Tripolis just as negotiations for surrender began, they could not have foreseen that the talks would be ended by an opportunistic surprise assault by the Greeks. The most likely outcome at that stage was that surrender terms would be agreed and then disregarded, and that slaughter would follow. This was what had happened at the most recent fall of a Turkish-held fortress, New Navarino, at the end of July. Ipsilántis had a further motive for departure at this point: he needed to remove the regular troops from the scene. What chance would there be of turning them into a disciplined body if their first experience of combat was the sacking of a town in the company of the plunder-crazy irregulars?

Ipsilántis' progress after leaving Tripolis achieved nothing. He could only watch helplessly from the southern shore of the Gulf of Corinth while the Turkish fleet burnt the Greek ships in the harbour of Galaxídhi on the northern side. He was still on the gulf when news reached him and his companions of the fall of Tripolis, to which they returned a few days after the sack had ended. There is no doubt that he, and Gordon who returned with him, were horrified by what they found, and Gordon shortly afterwards left Greece in disgust, not to return until five years later. Gordon's own account of the fall of Tripolis is less than frank about his own part. He does not mention that he departed and returned, and seems to condemn Ipsilántis for doing just that: Ipsilántis' decision to leave was, says Gordon, 'impolitic and intempestive', and his march along the shores of the Gulf of Corinth 'an useless military promenade'.[8] If, as implied, Ipsilántis should have stayed, Gordon should have stayed too. They might at least have succeeded, as Raybaud did, in saving a few lives. Nevertheless, it is hard not to sympathise with the predicament of decent men who had come to support, as they thought, a noble cause, and found instead what they saw as a dirty war.

It is doubtful if anyone could have restrained the Greeks during the sack of Tripolis. Kolokotrónis wielded the greatest authority, and Raybaud reports that he and his fellow commander Iatrákos entered the town soon after the sack began, and tried unsuccessfully to get the rampaging soldiers to leave, which may have been from a desire to save booty from destruction rather than to save Turkish lives. Kolokotrónis in his memoirs only speaks, laconically and impersonally, of the conclusion of the sack: 'The end came, a proclamation was issued that the slaughter must cease.'[9]

It was Kolokotrónis who gained most from the siege and sack of Tripolis. He had outmanoeuvred both Ipsilántis and the civilian leaders, he had brought to a successful conclusion the plan which he had continually urged of capturing Tripolis first, and he came away with a huge quantity of booty for himself, booty which enabled him to reward his men and so maintain the military force on which his position rested. He continued as the military leader in the Peloponnese, under the nominal and light-reined command of Ipsilántis, whose influence was now in decline. Kolokotrónis went on to further and less tarnished military successes, until he fell foul of the government and his fortunes were dramatically reversed.

LYIT
LIBRARY
LETTERKENNY

13

Forming a Government

By the end of the summer of 1821, with the war only six months old, the Greeks were riding high. They had captured the four fortresses of Monemvasía, Old and New Navarino and Tripolis, they had blocked Turkish advances down both eastern and western routes north of the Gulf of Corinth, and at sea they had had their first success with a fireship. These Greek victories had thrown a crucial question into sharp relief: who runs the war? Various bodies had been set up to control operations, at least in name, in the different places where the revolt had spasmodically broken out. At Patras in the Peloponnese the insurgents set up 'a sort of council for the general direction of affairs', and similar bodies with equally vague responsibilities were formed in other Peloponnesian towns. These were pulled together in June 1821 into a single Peloponnesian Senate. However its remit was no more specific than before: its members were to act for the common good and prosecute the war 'in whatever way Divine Providence guides them and they think appropriate'.[1] Also its powers were temporary, lasting only until the fall of Tripolis and the summoning of a national assembly.

In mainland Greece north of the Gulf of Corinth two separate regional governments were established towards the end of 1821. In West Roumeli a Senate was set up, based on Mesolongi and headed by Alexander Mavrokordhátos. In East Roumeli the government was called the Aríos Págos, borrowing the name of the oldest judicial council of pre-classical Athens, and was dominated by Theódhoros Négris. Négris was a phanariot who had risen sufficiently high in the Ottoman hierarchy to be appointed secretary to the Turkish embassy in

Paris, and was on his way there by ship when he learnt that the revolution had broken out; he immediately headed for Greece. In both West and East Roumeli the military were to be subordinate to the civilian government, reflecting the European outlook of both Mavrokordhátos and Négris. The East Roumeli constitution had one unusual feature: it was the first revolutionary document to envisage a future king for Greece, but that was a long way in the future. In December 1821 the Greeks came together at a site near ancient Epídhavros, east of Navplion, for their first national assembly. The aim of the assembly was to form a single national government.

It is easy to think of the Greeks of the war of independence as a single body politic, and easy to assume that unity against the Turks and the bonds of religion and language submerged all other differences. In fact, however, Greek society was criss-crossed by a large number of fault lines, and was so divided that perhaps it should not be called a society at all.

On land the Greeks had taken up the war in three main regions: the Peloponnese and, north of the Gulf of Corinth, West Roumeli and East Roumeli, the last two being divided by the southern spurs of the Píndos mountains. The war at sea was in the hands of several Aegean islands, notably Hydra, Spétses and Psará. Each of these geographical divisions looked for recognition of its own status and interests in any centralised government: the Peloponnese as the region which had been cleared of Turks, apart from a few isolated fortresses, and in which the revolution had been successfully begun; East and West Roumeli as the areas most exposed to Turkish attack from the north; and the islanders as the defence against the Turkish navy. As well as having different interests the people of different regions often heartily disliked each other. As a modern historian has put it, 'The Roumeliots looked on the more prosperous and peaceable Peloponnesians as untrustworthy and effete. The Peloponnesians regarded their northern brothers as backward and boorish. The Islanders displayed an insular contempt for all mainlanders.'[2] There was also ill-feeling within regions: the men of the Mani were regarded as dishonest and disreputably rapacious by other Peloponnesians, and Hydra and Spétses were in constant disagreement with each other.

A second major split was between different social groups, the three main ones being the civilian leaders, the military captains and the so-called westernisers, those who had arrived from abroad with ideas of government on western European lines. The civilian leaders comprised the landowning primates and the senior clergy, and both bodies had had considerable authority in their own localities under the Turks. The bishops, of whom there were forty-one, decided civil (but not criminal) cases between Christians, and mediated with Greek or Turkish leaders over individual disputes. The other civilian element, the primates, were in effect the operators of the Ottoman system of local government. In the Peloponnese they met annually as a provincial assembly to advise the governing Turkish pasha, and two members of this assembly were chosen as virtual ambassadors of the Peloponnese to Constantinople, where they could seek remedies for injustice and even influence the appointment of a new pasha. Because of their close co-operation with the Turks the primates were widely distrusted, and Dhimítrios Ipsilántis castigated them as men 'who, sharing the sentiments of the Turks, wish to oppress the people', and as 'the friends and companions of tyrants'.[3]

The primates were drawn from the rich, and their wealth was based on land. In the Peloponnese the primates, with the monasteries, held about a third of the productive land or roughly 700 square miles. With the revenue derived from land the primates were able to bid for the lucrative tax-farming contracts from the Ottoman government. Because they collected both rents and taxes in kind rather than cash, and they alone had the resources to get the produce to markets or ports, they were able to exert a virtual monopoly control over prices. Thus the wealth of the primates multiplied, a wealth regarded by the peasantry as the fruits of blatant exploitation – another reason to distrust them.

The second main social group consisted of the military captains. Many had previously been either a brigand klepht or an armátolos hired by the Ottoman government to control the klephts, and a captain would often alternate between the two roles. Others had held the rank of kápos, leader of a primate's armed force and under his authority, with no independent command granted by the Turkish administration; Kolokotrónis himself may never have been more than a kápos, in spite of his claim to the more glamorous title of armátolos. Here was a source of friction between captains and primates. Many a captain would previously have been either a threat to the primates as a klepht, or a competitor with independent status as armátolos, or a subordinate kápos now risen to greater prominence than his former employer. Of all the groups the captains had the closest link with the common people, from whom they had usually come and from whose ranks they recruited their troops. Some of the captains had served in foreign armies, and had learnt, as Kolokotrónis certainly had, how the revolution was likely to be viewed by foreign powers, and the importance of conciliating them. Thus these captains had certain common ground with recently arrived westernisers, men otherwise totally different from them.

These westernisers formed the third social group, and were drawn from three main categories: merchants in the Ottoman empire and in the major cities of Europe where the Greek diaspora had settled; phanariots, the senior civil servants of the Turkish government, especially in the administration of Moldavia and Wallachia; and Greek professional men who had been educated abroad. The most prominent of the westernisers was Alexander Mavrokordhátos, from one of the leading phanariot families. When the revolution broke out he was living at Pisa in Italy, where he had been part of Shelley's circle. From there he took ship to Marseilles, collected supplies for the Greeks and a number of philhellene volunteers, including Raybaud, and landed at Mesolongi at the beginning of August 1821, where he began improving the town's defences and establishing his own leadership. Still only thirty, his travels had given him mastery of seven languages, and experience in the government of Wallachia had introduced him to the arts of diplomacy. His portraits, with circular spectacles or elegant cravat, present him as a somewhat owlish figure, perhaps an academic or a civil servant rather than a leader of men. But appearance was deceptive. 'His manners are perfectly easy and gentlemanlike,' wrote Howe,

> and though the first impression would be from his extreme politeness and continual smiles that he was a good-natured silly fop, yet one soon sees from the keen inquisitive glances which involuntarily escape from him, that he is concealing, under an almost childish lightness of manner, a close and accurate study of his visitor. . . . His friends ascribe every action to the most disinterested patriotism; but his enemies hesitate not to pronounce them all to have for their end his party or private interest. . . . Here, as is often the case, truth lies between the two extremes.[4]

Mavrokordhátos understood the arts of politics better than any other Greek participant in the struggle, and as government bodies formed and re-formed in the course of the war it was often Mavrokordhátos' influence, sometimes behind the scenes, which was dominant.

The westernisers believed that the new Greek state should have four main characteristics. First, it should be a constitutional state, guaranteeing individual rights and based on popular elections; this was naturally favoured by the common people. Second, though Orthodoxy would be the state religion, the state should be secular, with the church having no special powers such as it had enjoyed under Ottoman rule; this was of course unpopular with the ecclesiastical leaders. Third, it should be based on western legal codes and systems of administration; this cut at the traditional powers of the primates in regional government. Finally, it should have a regular army, paid and controlled by the government and trained on western European lines; this was never fully achieved, but the prospect of it antagonised the military class, who were still convinced with some justification that their irregular bands, operating as klephts had always done, were the best means of defeating the Turks.

The new national government which the Epídhavros assembly was to hammer out needed to achieve three things. It must be effective in prosecuting the war. It must satisfy the foreign powers, whose support was recognised as crucial. Finally, it must balance the conflicting claims of the various interest groups. The proceedings of the assembly were therefore not just a drily rational exercise in constitution-making; they were a covert but fierce competition for power.

The assembly which came together in the last weeks of 1821 was named the Assembly of Epídhavros, and its outcome the Constitution of Epídhavros. The name Epídhavros had all the right associations – birthplace of the healing god Asklepios, site of the magnificent classical Greek theatre – but in fact the assembly was held at the nearby coastal village of Piádha. Raybaud thought it a delightful setting and, probably with a touch of hyperbole, wrote of its 'pleasant woodlands and a sky ever pure: arbours of orange trees provided shade, and before them lay the island of Sálamis'.[5] There were delegations from the Peloponnese, East and West Roumeli and the Aegean islands, fifty-nine members in all, meeting in a barnlike chamber in the middle of the village. Mavrokordhátos was elected president of the assembly. None of the captains attended, and an even more notable absentee was Dhimítrios Ipsilántis, who at the beginning of December had gone to take command of the siege of the fortress of Corinth. He was hoping to enhance his standing as a national leader by a military success, but by the time Corinth fell to the Greeks in early 1822 the assembly had finished its work and a government had been formed.

The first act of the assembly was to appoint a committee to draw up a constitution, a committee composed of twelve members, three from each of the four main regions in a careful balancing of their interests. This committee was dominated by Mavrokordhátos and Négris, and worked fast, drawing in part on the regional constitutions which had already been formulated and in part on the constitutions of the United States and France. Within a fortnight the Constitution of Epídhavros was drafted, approved by the assembly and signed, being backdated by a few days to 1 January 1822 (Old Style) to mark the beginning of Greece's first calendar year of independence. The constitution was firmly labelled as provisional, and was to be reviewed after one year. Many saw it as a holding operation until Greece acquired a king, many of the articles were obviously too loosely drawn to be permanent, and in any case nobody then knew what the future extent of the Greek state might be and what other interests might have to be accommodated.

The constitutional document began with a brief and dignified preamble. 'In the name of the Holy and Indivisible Trinity: the Greek nation, under the fearful domination of the Ottomans, unable to bear the heavy and unexampled yoke of tyranny and having with great sacrifices thrown it off, declares today, through its lawful representatives gathered in National Assembly, before God and man, its political existence and independence.'[6] It then laid down the essentials of religion (the state religion to be Greek Orthodoxy) and civil rights (equality before the law; security of property, honour and personal safety; no taxation without a previous law). The rest of the document established the machinery of the state, with three largely independent arms of government providing checks and balances against each other, very much on the American model. The Senate, elected for a year by the people, would pass laws, and specifically would vote on declarations of war and peace treaties and on an annual state budget. The Executive of five members, appointed by the Senate also for a year, would run the government and prosecute the war, appointing eight ministers to be responsible for departments of foreign affairs, internal affairs, finance and so on. A crucial part of the system of checks and balances was that Senate and Executive could each veto the acts of the other. The third arm of government was to be a judiciary independent of the other two branches and charged with drawing up new laws; a supreme court was to function at the seat of government, and local courts throughout the country. But these provisions for a judiciary remained a dead letter, and the framers of the constitution may have foreseen this when they stipulated that, until new laws were drawn up, Byzantine law should govern all criminal and civil cases, except in commercial matters where French law should apply.

Such was the machinery of government, designed with its checks and balances to work like a well-regulated clock, but whether it did so would depend upon who filled the posts created. Mavrokordhátos, one of those representing West Roumeli, had dominated the assembly and became president of the Executive, in effect the national president. Of the ministers, Négris was the most prestigious, holding the foreign affairs portfolio and presiding over ministers' meetings. The most impressive minister was Iánnis Koléttis, responsible for internal affairs, who a month later also took over the war ministry. He had been trained in medicine at Pisa, whose university could provide better education than any Greek institution. He had also been schooled in ruthless intrigue as a physician at Ali Pasha's court, and practised a sort of masterly inactivity. 'With patience and stolid silence,' wrote Finlay, 'he profited by the blunders of his colleagues, always himself doing and saying as little as possible. He trusted that others, by their restless intrigues and precipitate ambition, would ruin their own position, and leave the field open for him. His policy was crowned with success.'[7] He also had undoubted presence; Howe noted that a stranger who saw him in a crowd would turn to look at him again, and mark him for an extraordinary man. From the civil strife of 1823 and 1824 Koléttis emerged as the most forceful of all the Greek leaders.

The Senate was to comprise those elected as delegates to the assembly, and Ipsilántis, still away besieging Corinth, was appointed its president. He was influential enough to be offered this olive branch, though the post fell far short of the position of national president and commander-in-chief which he had demanded the previous summer. Vicepresident of the Senate was Pétrobey Mavromichális, a man never far from the centre of power, who acted as president in Ipsilántis' absence.

The three aims of those who drew up the Constitution of Epídhavros were to create a government which would balance the interests of the competing groups, would impress foreign powers and would be effective. Did they succeed?

Balance between the regions was very precisely maintained in terms of appointments. All four regions were represented more or less equally on the twelve-member committee which drew up the constitution, on the five-member Executive, in the group of eight ministers and in the Senate. However, no balance was achieved in two important areas. First, there was no definition of the relationship between the new national government and the existing regional governments; the national government was simply given broad general powers, while regional governments were left to carry on as before. This nettle was not grasped until a second national assembly fifteen months later, which decreed the abolition of the regional governments. The other imbalance concerned the military captains. They had no representatives at the assembly, they were offered no posts in the government and they became nominally subordinate to the Executive, which was charged with the overall direction of the land and sea forces. This too changed at the second national assembly, where captains attended as delegates, and the conflict between them and their opponents became open and violent. The captains had more than enough power to insist on representation at Epídhavros if they had wanted it. However, some of them may have felt that they would be outmanoeuvred in constitutional debate by smooth-talking theorists, others may have believed that it was better not to be associated with arrangements that were likely to try to clip their wings, and the strongest of the captains may have thought that the new government was anyway an irrelevance and would not be able seriously to curtail their powers as the dynamos of the revolution. So the captains played no part at Epídhavros.

Of the impact of the new government on foreign powers, Finlay wrote caustically: 'A good deal was done by the Greeks at Epidaurus to deceive Europe; very little to organise Greece.'[8] This was unfair. What Greece wanted from Europe was recognition and money. After Epídhavros money could be raised by borrowing abroad, as Greece now had a properly established government to which loans could reasonably be made. The new government lost no time in exploiting this opportunity and six of the seven laws passed in the government's first two months concerned the raising of loans abroad. When a loan was finally secured in London two years later, the deception lay not in the Constitution of Epídhavros but in the overblown accounts of Greece's resources and prospects for which Greece's philhellenic friends were mainly to blame. As for recognition, this was slow in coming. When in the following March the Greek government asked the Ionian government for the return of an impounded ship, the reply from the governor Sir Thomas Maitland was withering: 'His Excellency has just received letters from persons who give to themselves the name of the Government of Greece, by a messenger now in this port. . . . His Excellency is absolutely ignorant of the existence of a "provisionary government of Greece," and therefore cannot recognize such agent. . . . He will not enter into a correspondence with any nominal power which he does not know.'[9]

Finally, was the new government designed to be effective? There was probably only one way in which the government could fully co-ordinate its war effort, and that was for wide powers to be given to a few, and if possible to one man. This is what Kapodhístrias, Greece's future president but at present at the Russian court, had urged some months before the assembly met, but Kapodhístrias was out of touch with the reality of the Greek situation. The competing interests were not going to hand over power to a restricted oligarchy, and there was no one man, no George Washington, who had emerged as an accepted leader with widespread support. The government formed at Epídhavros was the exact opposite of the strong central administration which Kapodhístrias had called for. As both arms of the government had the power of veto, neither Executive nor Senate could act without the consent of the other. Members of both served for a year only, and so had to think constantly of the next election rather than the conduct of the war. There were probably far too many ministers: as Bishop Ignátios wrote from Pisa, 'even second-class kings have only two or three ministers'.[10] Perhaps the most fatal weakness was the failure to define the relationship between the central and regional governments and the powers of each. Balance had been achieved, but at the cost of potential paralysis.

This point was put strongly by the English utilitarian philosopher and jurist Jeremy Bentham, who sent the Greek government his comments on the new constitution a few months later. His opening remarks delighted the Greeks: 'To find the provisional Grecian Constitution in so high a degree conformable to the principle of the greatest happiness of the greatest number has been matter of considerable and no less agre[e]able surprise to me,' he wrote.[11] However, he saw a danger in the constitution's plethora of potential vetoes, which he called 'latent negatives'. The president of the Senate, for example, was empowered to call the Senate into session, and it was open to him never to call it into session at all. Other individuals were required to sign, countersign or seal resolutions, and simply by doing nothing could block the government's actions. Bentham also deplored the excessive number of ministers, and would have done away with them altogether, making members of the Executive responsible for a reduced number of departments. But his most fundamental criticism was of the division of powers between the arms of government, which underlay the whole principle of checks and balances. The bodies among whom power was divided would, he thought, compete against each other in their own interest, not in the interests of the people. It would be better, Bentham maintained, for the Executive and the judiciary to be dependent on the Senate, and the Senate in turn to be dependent upon the will of the people through universal suffrage. The tenor of all Bentham's comments was that every branch of the government should be as responsive as possible to popular sovereignty, which he saw as coinciding more or less with the greatest happiness of the greatest number.

Bentham was right to treat the work of the assembly at Epídhavros as a serious attempt to produce a workable system of government. But Epídhavros was also the arena of a competition for power, and in this Mavrokordhátos was the main beneficiary. He had achieved all he could have hoped for: a constitution drawn up under his guidance, and the leading position in the newly formed national government. Then, surprisingly, he went away. He left first for Hydra; the island's support was going to be vital in the defence of Mesolongi against the Turkish navy. Then in May 1822, with the Senate's agreement, he returned to Mesolongi and continued preparations for the defence of the town and the process of building up support throughout the region. Thus Mavrokordhátos spent hardly any time filling his role as president of the Executive and his absences clearly demonstrate his priorities: prestige might lie with the provisional government of Epídhavros but his power base in Mesolongi and West Roumeli was much more important to him. Nevertheless, he was astute enough to grasp the presidency of the Executive to ensure that nobody else could use it to build his own influence. A contemporary coined a pleasing analogy for Mavrokordhátos' tactics: 'He imitates the cunning of the hedgehog who, they say, flattens his needles and makes himself thin to enter his burrow, and once inside fluffs them out again and becomes a ball of prickles to stop anyone else getting in.'[12]

14

The Eyes of the World on Greece

In the first years of the Greek revolution the governments of the major European powers had little sympathy for it. Those governments' subjects however often took a very different view. Travellers had increasingly visited Greece when the Napoleonic wars had made the Italian Grand Tour impossible, and had written glowingly of their experiences. The study of Latin and Greek was the mainstay of higher education. Many saw the Greeks as representing Christianity embattled against Islam, and as the birthplace of Europe's civilisation resisting the barbarism of Asia. Perhaps only in the foreign reactions to the Spanish civil war of the 1930s has there been such a sharp contrast between the cold abstention of governments and the passionate involvement of individuals.

The shocks of the Napoleonic wars shaped the policies of the European powers in the following decades. In November 1815 at the close of the Congress of Vienna the victors over Napoleon – Britain, Russia, Austria and Prussia – signed a treaty continuing for twenty years their Quadruple Alliance, which was pledged to uphold by force the post-Napoleonic settlement in Europe. Three years later France under the restored Bourbon monarch Louis XVIII was added to the grouping, making it a Quintuple Alliance. To sustain the so-called concert of Europe, the powers were to meet at regular congresses 'for the purpose of consulting upon their common interest and for the consideration of the measures most salutary for the maintenance of the peace of Europe'.[1] It was from the second of these congresses in 1821 that Tsar Alexander sent his uncompromising denunciation of Alexander Ipsilántis' incursion into Moldavia and Wallachia.

In parallel with the Quadruple and later Quintuple Alliance, and often confused with them, was the Holy Alliance, initiated in September 1815 by the Tsar when his fluctuating religious fervour was at its height. The Holy Alliance's original members were Russia, Austria and Prussia, who undertook 'to consider themselves all as members of one and the same Christian nation, the three princes looking on themselves as merely delegated by Providence to govern three branches of One Family, namely Austria, Prussia and Russia, thus confessing that the Christian world, of which they and their people form a part, has in reality no other Sovereign but Him to whom power alone really belongs'.[2] The signatories were to take as their sole guide the precepts of the Christian religion. In time the Holy Alliance was endorsed by all Europe's rulers except the Pope, the non-Christian Sultan naturally, and Britain on the ostensible grounds that George III was incapable and the Prince Regent not yet the monarch. The Holy Alliance was anathema to progressives. As Shelley wrote in the preface to *Hellas*, in a passage which his cautious publisher omitted from the first edition: 'This is the age of the war of the oppressed against the oppressors, and every one of those ringleaders of the privileged gangs of murderers and swindlers, called Sovereigns, look to each other for aid against the common enemy, and suspend their mutual jealousies in the presence of a mightier fear. Of this holy alliance all the despots of the earth are virtual members.'[3]

However, those who joined or endorsed the Holy Alliance were far from enthusiastic about it: Metternich dismissed it as 'a high-sounding Nothing', Talleyrand as 'a ludicrous contract'. Nevertheless the formation of the Holy Alliance seemed to signal a commitment by governments to act from religious principle rather than self-interest. In theory this might mean that Greek appeals to altruism would win support from governments in the same way as from individuals. But there was of course an inherent and disabling contradiction in the principles of the Holy Alliance when applied to the Greek situation: the Alliance's commitment to uphold the Christian religion meant support for the Greeks, but its commitment to uphold government meant support for the Sultan. Thus in the Greek conflict the influence of the powers of Europe would inevitably spring from their own national interests, and the only hope for Greece was that these interests might come to coincide with her own.

*

A Polish ex-soldier who after a fight with the captain of a boat on the Mississippi had been put ashore and had lived on wild berries in a cave with an Indian woman . . . A watchmaker's apprentice from Alsace who pretended to be deaf and dumb . . . A tall blond Piedmontese who murdered the girl behind the cash desk at the Café du Parc in Marseilles. The list sounds like the ingredients for a thriller, as propounded in John Buchan's *The Three Hostages*: 'Let us take three things a long way apart. . . . Not much connection between the three? You invent a connection – simple enough if you have any imagination, and you weave all three into a yarn.' For our three disparate characters there is no need to invent a connection: all of them took ship in 1821 to go and fight for the cause of Greek independence.

Not all the philhellene volunteers were so exotic. Maxime Raybaud had joined the French army as an eighteen-year-old in 1813, but at the end of 1820 had fallen victim to the army's manpower cuts. Excited by the news of Alexander Ipsiléntis' venture – 'I learnt with a thrill that Greece was shaking off her chains'[4] – he left Paris for Marseilles, where he joined the Hydra brig commissioned by Mavrokordhátos to carry war supplies to Greece. It sailed in July 1821 carrying five French officers, three Italian officers from Piedmont who were political exiles, a doctor, several junior officers, and sixty or so expatriate Greeks. On the first morning out these passengers were divided into four groups for daily arms drill under the officers, the polyglot Mavrokordhátos obligingly translating for those Greeks who did not understand the French or Italian commands. In Raybaud's account the voyage had its diversions, as when they were becalmed off Sicily and watched the sailors dive from the highest yards and swim with dolphins for hours at a time. It also had its excitements, as when a storm drove them along at ten or eleven knots under a single sail, to the accompaniment of Albanian shanties from the Hydriot sailors. They expected to land at Patras, but learnt on arrival that Patras and virtually all the Peloponnesian strongholds were still in Turkish hands. They therefore sailed further north to Mesolongi, where the governor and the other Turkish families had been imprisoned after the Greeks seized the town. There at the beginning of August they transferred into small boats to travel through the shallow lagoon at the approach to the town, and they eventually stepped ashore to enthusiastic cries of 'Long live Freedom!', being the first supporters from abroad that the town had seen.

Marseilles was the point of departure for most of the early philhellenes as it was for Raybaud. Eleven ships sailed from there between the outbreak of the revolution and the end of 1822, carrying in all some 360 volunteers, the largest contingents coming from the German states, France and Italy. At the end of 1822 the French authorities closed the port to ships bound for Greece, perhaps because France was now following Metternich's pro-legitimacy lines, or because reports of returning philhellenes showed all too plainly that, as one of them put it, volunteers would find only misery, death and ingratitude. But in the early days optimism and idealism ran high. Throughout France, the German states and Switzerland politicians, churchmen and university professors proclaimed the triple message that Europe owed its civilisation to the ancient Greeks, that the modern Greeks were their descendants, and that Greece could be regenerated by driving out the Turks.

The message appealed particularly to the idealistic young. A youthful doctor in Mannheim said that the call went through him like an electric shock. A theology student in Prussia was excited by the idea of fighting where Epaminondas and Themistocles fell. A Danish student wrote: 'How could a man inclined to fight for freedom and justice find a better place than next to the oppressed Greeks?'[5] The other two main groups who rallied to the Greek cause were demobilised soldiers and political refugees, and many volunteers were both. Among the ex-officers who achieved fame in Greece were the Frenchman Baleste, appointed by Dhimítrios Ipsilántis to form a regular Greek army; Colonel Thomas Gordon, the wealthy educated Scot who wrote one of the best contemporary accounts of the war; Captain Frank Abney Hastings, who had been dismissed from the British navy for challenging his superior officer to a duel; and the Württemberg count General Normann, who had fought both for and against the French in the Napoleonic wars and was thus not welcome in any army, and who led a motley German battalion to Greece from Marseilles in January 1822. Among the ex-soldiers who were also political exiles were Tarella and Dania, both from Piedmont and both with service in the French army. Tarella later took over the small and barely trained body of troops which Baleste had put together, in which Dania became a battalion

commander. Both men were dead within a year on the battlefield of
Péta.

Apart from those with an obvious motive for going to Greece – idealism, soldiering, exile – the philhellenes included a clutch of eccentrics:
a Bavarian china manufacturer intending to set up a factory in Greece,
an out-of-work French actor, a dancing master from Rostock, and even
a Spanish girl dressed as a man. The youth from Alsace, mentioned
earlier, pretended to be deaf and dumb to avoid questions about his
claim, made in sign language, that he was Prince Alepso of Árgos. His
ruse was discovered when he arrived in Greece and after a drinking bout
was heard talking in fluent German.

Many of the volunteers were rich enough to pay for their own travel on
the road to Marseilles and on the voyage to Greece, but many others, especially the idealistic young, depended on the goodwill of others, and committees were therefore formed to raise money to help the volunteers on
their way. The most numerous were in democratic Switzerland,
unaffected by great-power politics, where virtually every town had an
active Greek society. The most practical were in the German states. In
Leipzig, for example, a pamphlet identified the Greeks' need for officers
trained in artillery and military engineering, and called on the Greek societies not only to raise money but to establish contacts in Greece to receive
the volunteers. Thus the enthusiastic young philhellene on the way to
Marseilles became a familiar sight on the roads of Europe. 'In different
parts of the country,' wrote one English traveller, 'I met with numerous
companies of young men on foot, with knapsacks at their backs, on their
way to Marseilles, there to embark for Greece. These parties appeared to
be composed chiefly of young German recruits and runaway students,
and from the boisterous enthusiasm which they generally manifested, it
was my endeavour always to avoid them as much as possible.'[6]

Associations to help the Greek cause were not restricted to the central
parts of Europe, nor to raising money to help individual volunteers on
their way. Greek committees were established in Spain, France,
England, Russia and America. Their activities included raising subscriptions to help the Greeks directly by sending money or supplies,
organising relief for Greek refugees from the conflict, and pressing their
governments to act on the Greeks' behalf. In Spain Madrid has a claim
to have formed the very first Greek committee. France was last in the

field. There was an early outpouring of French pamphlets supporting the Greek cause – over thirty in 1821–2 – but a specifically Greek committee was not established until February 1825 in Paris. By then Greece had moved into the foreground of public and government concern, partly because of the profound impression made by the death of Byron, partly because the outcome of the war came to be more clearly seen as affecting France's national interests.

In England the question of support for Greece became entangled in domestic politics. Its earliest expression was in October 1821 from Dr Lemprière, author of the famous classical dictionary, with an appeal for funds published in the *Courier*, normally a paper reflecting the views of the Tory government. But the *Courier* quickly abandoned support for the Greeks; as a contemporary wrote, the editor 'changed his note in a very few days when he found that [his sentiments] were unpalatable to our Government'.[7] With Castlereagh as foreign secretary the Tory government line was that neutrality meant not attempting to support the Greek cause with funds, men or equipment; a Tory philhellene was thus virtually a contradiction in terms. Canning however, succeeding Castlereagh in September 1822, took the view that private subscriptions could go hand in hand with official neutrality, so that England's influence in Greece could be strengthened without jeopardising the alliances of the powers. Thus in March 1823 the time was ripe for the formation of the London Greek Committee, but even this was a reflection of domestic politics. Out of nearly forty members of Parliament in the committee of eighty-five, virtually all were Whigs, Radicals or Independents. Another feature of the list was the number of Scottish and Irish names, suggesting, as one historian has put it, that 'perhaps philhellenism provided a kind of surrogate for nationalist emotion, which lacked expression at home'.[8] The London Greek Committee was, in short, a protest movement, and opposition to the government was the prime qualification for membership of it.

In the United States Greece found an immediate champion in Edward Everett, one of the most brilliant men of his generation. He was elected professor of Greek at Harvard in 1815 at the age of twenty-one, and visited Greece three years later. In 1820 he became editor of the *North American Review* and in 1824 a member of Congress, and so had two platforms from which he could speak to the nation. His later career was no less distinguished – governor of Massachusetts, ambassador to Britain, secretary of state. In 1863 it was Everett, now a US senator, who was invited to give the funeral oration at Gettysburg, a two-hour speech highly praised at the time but since overshadowed by Lincoln's 272 words. In 1821 Koraís, Greece's champion living in Paris, sent Everett the Greek appeal 'To the Citizens of the United States', which stated confidently that 'it is in your land that Liberty has fixed her abode', so that 'you will not assuredly imitate the culpable indifference or rather the long ingratitude of the Europeans'.[9] In November 1821, at Everett's instigation, this appeal appeared in the newspapers. There followed a cataract of pro-Greek articles in the press, in the eastern seaboard states, as far west as Illinois and as far south as Mississippi. They praised Greek heroism, condemned Turkish atrocities while ignoring or explaining away Greek ones, and publicised local pro-Greek activities.

These activities were many and various. Some of the earliest groups sent provisions to Greece; in the winter of 1821–2 Charleston, South Carolina, sent fifty barrels of dried meat, and Springfield, Massachusetts, sent flour, fish, meat and sugar. Fund-raising associations sprang up, most of them channelling their contributions through the prestigious committee of New York, the city where a spectacular fund-raising ball was held at the beginning of 1824. By the end of that year the New York Committee alone had raised the equivalent of some £8,000, which the London *Morning Chronicle* ruefully admitted was 'a sum, be it known to the shame of the United Kingdom, almost as large as all the subscriptions which the Greek Committees have been able to obtain in this country after eighteen months' exertion'.[10] Some of the fund-raising activities were imaginative. A New York City hatter promised to contribute 25 cents to the Greek cause for each of his new Greek-style hats sold, raising $140 in three months. A Louisville barber offered a week's takings. 'Let those who value freedom, both civil and religious,' he announced, ' . . . give me a call and thereby participate in the thrilling pleasure which I shall feel in contributing to the relief of an intelligent and refined people, who are now manfully contending for independence.'[11] Sometimes imagination went too far. In Ithaca, New York, three vagrants were arrested for begging with forged papers purporting to show that they were collecting for the Greeks.

In Russia there was fervent and widespread sympathy for the Greeks, based not only on the usual grounds, but also on Russia's special debt to Greece as the bringer of Christianity to Russia. Prince Alexander Golitsyn, a government minister and one of Russia's leading philhellenes, wrote of the desire 'to help the sons of that country which fostered enlightenment in Europe and to which Russia is even more obliged having borrowed from it the enlightenment of faith, which firmly established the saving banner of the Gospels on the ruins of paganism'.[12] There was no incompatibility in Golitsyn's position as both minister and philhellene since aid for the Greeks was government policy from the Tsar downwards, but this aid was to be restricted to two purposes only: relief for Greek refugees from the conflict, and the ransoming of Greek captives who had been enslaved. It was no part of the policy to send military supplies to Greece, and when on one occasion weapons on their way to Greece were intercepted they were sold and the money given to refugee relief.

Golitsyn was the prime mover in raising funds for the Greeks. In a government announcement of August 1821 he called for subscriptions to be made through the church in the confidence that 'pious Christians, in faith and love, will certainly lend a helping hand'.[13] Golitsyn also urged military governors to seek donations from the people of their regions, and civilian officials to approach the local merchants to participate in this 'philanthropic work, which alone can bring eternal treasure and before which all the riches of the world are nothing'.[14] By mid-August 1822 Golitsyn's initiatives had raised 973,500 roubles, then the equivalent of over £9,000. Large individual donations helped swell the Russian total: 100,000 roubles from the Tsar himself, 15,000 roubles from the Dowager Empress, and thousands of roubles from members of the aristocracy. The Second Army, stationed in Bessarabia in south-west Russia and so closest to the Greek conflict, raised 4,000 roubles. In St Petersburg the merchants raised 25,000 roubles for refugee relief, and the craft guilds 5,000 roubles for ransom money. Contributions came even from the peasants in remote rural communities, where donations of as little as ten kopeks were touchingly recorded. Fund-raising did not slacken after an initial burst, as happened elsewhere. Continuity was ensured by the Tsar's allocation of 13,000 roubles a month from the imperial treasury to refugee relief, though for aristocratic refugees only, a payment continued by his much less philhellenic successor Nicholas I. By the end of the decade Russia had raised several million roubles for the Greeks.

The number of Greek refugees needing help was formidable. Golitsyn in his first call for donations claimed that nearly 4,000 had reached Odessa in a single day, probably an exaggeration since the total for the year of 1821 was 12,000. A further 40,000 Greek refugees crossed into Russia from Moldavia and became the responsibility of the relief committee of Kishinev some hundred miles west of Odessa. Help was given not only in money but also in medical care, shelter, education for the young, and later in attempts to find employment. Money was distributed according to family size, but a heavier weighting was given to social status. Thus the family of a manual labourer might receive 60 roubles a month, the family of a merchant 120 roubles, an individual senior cleric 170 roubles, and an aristocratic family up to 2,500 roubles. It is no surprise, though it would cause an outcry today, that in Odessa aristocratic refugees, comprising only 5 per cent of the total, received nearly half the money distributed.

The second aim of Russian philhellenic activity was the ransoming of Greeks enslaved by the Turks, but this proved far more difficult than helping refugees. The ransom effort began in the summer of 1822, a year after Golitsyn launched the refugee relief programme, and was prompted by the distressing reports of slaves, many of them women and children, taken after the Turkish destruction of Chios. The initiative came from three Greek clerics in Bessarabia, who were particularly concerned about the forcible conversion of the enslaved Christians to Islam. Their object, they said, was 'to save from the abyss of perdition as many Christians as providence will allow',[15] and Golitsyn wrote of those enslaved as 'burdened by all the woes of captivity and confronted with the threat of being torn from the Church of Christ'.[16]

The first estimate of the scale of the problem gave the number of captives as 100,000 and the total ransom money needed as 500,000 roubles, a sum that was in fact raised in the next twelve months. But how was it to be applied? There was no expectation that all the captives could be ransomed, at an average cost of five roubles each, equivalent only to a few English pence. In February 1824 the ransom committee received a request to pay 3,250 roubles a head for a captive family of four, and later that year the current ransom fee was still increasing because the captors kept raising their prices. Even if an acceptable sum could be agreed, how should the money be transferred to the seller? If it was channelled through the senior Greek clergy in Turkish territory, this would simply lead to Turkish suspicion of the clerics and confiscation of the money. Alternatively, ransom money might be passed to the Greek government, but this would imply recognition of that government and violate Russia's neutrality. In the event, although some enslaved Greeks were ransomed by the private initiative of wealthy Greeks or benevolent representatives of foreign governments, there is no evidence of a single successful ransom by the Russian organisation. About half the ransom money was later transferred, with the Tsar's approval, to refugee relief, and the rest eventually passed to Kapodhístrias' government to combat hunger and poverty in Greece itself.

Russian philhellenic activity was thus unusual in several respects. It sprang from a particularly close association between government and people, the Tsar publicly supporting an enterprise in which everyone from aristocrat to peasant joined. Also the church in Russia played a far bigger role in the Greek cause than elsewhere, naturally enough given the bond of shared Orthodoxy. In Russia alone there was an officially sponsored effort to ransom captives, an effort which was a total failure. The final unusual feature of Russian philhellenism is that, though Greeks from Russia went to fight for Greece's cause, not a single Russian appears to have done so. Russians do not figure in contemporary accounts of Greece's war. No death of a Russian philhellene is recorded: the monument to the philhellenes in the Roman Catholic church in Navplion displays the names of 274 foreign philhellenes who died in Greece, over a hundred from the German states, forty or so each from France and Italy, smaller contingents from Britain and elsewhere, a handful from Spain, Hungary, Sweden and Denmark, and a single Portuguese, but no Russian. It is remarkable that not one Russian idealistic youth or discontented soldier was apparently prepared to flout government policy and risk official disapproval like the Tsar's denunciation of Alexander Ipsilántis, or if prepared to do so was unable to find a way of evading border and harbour controls in order to reach Greece. Nevertheless, it meant that Russians were spared the generally miserable experiences of the volunteers from other countries, whose high hopes of contributing to a noble cause were so often ended by a battlefield bullet or by a lingering disease.

15

The Philhellenes in Action

On reaching Greece most of the Philhellene volunteers urgently needed to find a military unit which they could join and which would feed and support them. This was not easy. The Greek forces were almost wholly made up of bands each attached to a virtually independent captain, who appointed his relations as his officers and drew his men from his own locality. For Europeans, joining such a band was out of the question. They would not have been accepted into it, and even if they had been they would have been unable to stand the life of eating badly if at all, sleeping rough, ever present filth and lice, difficult marches and rough companions with whom they could not communicate. Only one body of troops constituted an army in anything like the European sense, and this was the Regiment Baleste, the force which Baleste, on Dhimítrios Ipsilántis' instructions, had begun to put together at Kalamáta in the summer of 1821.

Baleste had the rare combination of military experience from service under Napoleon and fluent command of Greek from his subsequent years in Crete, where his father was a merchant. With the help of a handful of French and Italian officers he set about recruiting for the Regiment Baleste, which was intended to be the core of a Greek regular army run on European lines and to be paid and controlled by the Greek government. France's military system was adopted, which, said Raybaud, gave extreme satisfaction to the French volunteers. However, creating this force was a slow and difficult business. Virtually none of the Greek irregulars joined, preferring independence to discipline, plunder to putative pay, and the company of kinsmen and friends to

145

that of strangers. There were some recruits from the Ionian islands, where Greeks had served in British regiments and were familiar with European military systems, but most of the Greek volunteers for the regular force were refugees from northern Greece or Asia Minor and so were strangers in the Peloponnese, without friends or family and with no refuge other than with Baleste's troops. The number of Greek regulars fairly quickly reached 200, but then rose more slowly and probably never exceeded 600 in the lifetime of the force. Nevertheless, a uniform was devised and distributed, black with a national emblem in three colours on the headgear, and a system of ranks was drawn up with the intended rates of pay for each. These military trappings were plentiful, but basic necessities were almost nonexistent: for food and lodging Baleste's recruits were dependent upon the generosity of the people of Kalamáta, where they were based.

The first effort of the Regiment Baleste was an assault on the Palamídhi fortress at Navplion in December 1821. It was a total failure, and it was of this incident that Kolokotrónis said: 'The Greeks were not equal to taking castles such as those by assault; it was folly to attempt it.'[1] The affair at Navplion eroded yet further any trust the Greeks had in European methods of fighting. Some of the philhellenes also became disillusioned, notably Baleste, who left shortly afterwards to join the revolution in Crete and within a month was captured and killed in a failed assault on Réthimno.

Nevertheless Mavrokordhátos, now president of the Executive in the newly formed government, was convinced that the Europeans could play a useful role in the revolution, but now accepted that they should form a unit of their own. This unit was to be a part of the regiment of regular troops initiated by Baleste, but would not include all the philhellenes; a number of them, especially the more senior officers, were needed to provide a European element in the command of the regiment as a whole. By the beginning of the summer of 1822 the philhellenes had assembled at Corinth, for the moment the seat of the government which had been established at Epídhavros, and there at the beginning of May the new units were presented with their standards. The regular forces were organised as one regiment of two battalions, one battalion of Greeks and one of philhellenes. Mavrokordhátos became the formal head of the regiment, with Normann, head of the German volunteers, as his chief of staff. Colonel of the regular regiment was the Italian Tarella, with another Italian, Gubernatis, as his lieutenant. The Greek battalion, 400 strong, was made up of five companies, while the philhellene battalion of 120 men under Dania as battalion commander formed two companies, one mainly of Germans and Poles under a Pole, and the other mainly of French and Italians under a Swiss. A small group of philhellenes was in charge of their pathetically small artillery of two field guns. The presentation of standards took place at the foot of the towering crags of the Akrokórinthos and Dania's units were given the title of the Battalion of Philhellenes.

By the summer of 1822 the Turks were in a much stronger position to repeat their attempt of the previous year to march south. Mavrokordhátos' strategy for resisting them was shaped by two main considerations. First, the Souliots were still holding out in their mountainous enclave against Turkish attacks, and could put into the field some 4,000 fighting men. If they could be supported they would be a permanent threat to any Turkish army moving south from Iánnina. Second, Mavrokordhátos now had under his command a regiment of regular troops including a battalion of philhellenes, and he wanted to use them and to demonstrate the effectiveness of European military methods. Thus he was led to challenge the Turks to a setpiece battle on the plain of Péta, within sight of Árta where the main body of Turkish troops was assembled under Omer Vrionis and only a dozen miles from the entrance to the Soúli region.

First the Mavrokordhátos forces needed to be brought up from Corinth. One party with the two field guns went by ship as far as Vostítsa, which lies halfway along the Gulf of Corinth. The rest set off for Vostítsa overland; this group included Mavrokordhátos himself and his general staff, a party of Souliots under Márkos Bótsaris, a company of Ionian islanders from Zákinthos, Kephaloniá and Ithaca, and several hundred Greeks from the Peloponnese. Raybaud, as one of Mavrokordhátos' staff officers, was in the overland party and described the journey, emphasising the contrasts as he usually did: a wretched first night camping on marshy ground in pouring rain; a splendid welcome on the second night at the monastery of Áyia Iríni, where whole sheep were roasted for them and there were goatskins to sleep on; the sun breaking through on the third day and sparkling from the rocks of

Delphi and the double peak of Parnassos on the north side of the gulf. The two parties were reunited at Vostítsa and continued overland, skirting the Castle of the Morea with its Turkish garrison and marching to a point beyond Patras from which eight brigs took them across to Mesolongi at the beginning of June. There Mavrokordhátos spent ten days organising food supplies for his troops, while the philhellenes drilled and manoeuvred. 'It was unimaginably difficult', wrote Raybaud, 'to train the men in the harsh and precise details of service in the ranks, in strict discipline and in the advantages of systematic instruction, when these men were Europeans of a generally difficult temperament and different in their habits, education, language and weapons.'[2] These differences could become violent, and while in Mesolongi a German shot a Frenchman dead in a duel.

Mavrokordhátos' forces, about 700 regulars and twice as many irregulars, were far too small to tackle a Turkish army of nine to ten thousand men. Mavrokordhátos and his troops therefore moved north to Kombóti, a few miles south-east of Árta, to get the support of the local captains, the most prominent of whom were Georgios Varnakiótis based at Kombóti and Gógos Bakólas at Péta. The loyalty of Bakólas was very much in doubt. Now aged seventy, with a lifetime as alternately klepht or armátolos leader behind him, he was highly respected by his men, not least for a successful battle against the Turks on his home ground of Péta the year before. He was now in open communication with the Turks. According to him, this was simply a ruse to get the Turks to provide his troops with supplies, and he was still totally committed to the Greek cause. However as well as using these supplies for feeding his own troops he was making a profit by selling them on to other Greek forces. He became, said Raybaud, the monopoly supplier of wine, rum, biscuit and coffee, and even adjusted the exchange rates for foreign currency to suit himself A further problem was that Bakólas was believed to be responsible for the death on Ali Pasha's instructions of Márkos Bótsaris' father: would he now be a reliable comrade in arms of the son?

By the beginning of July Mavrokordhátos' forces, regular and irregular, local and imported, reliable and unreliable, amounted to barely 2,000 men, whereas he had hoped to raise three or four times that number. Mavrokordhátos was further weakened by the temporary absence of some of his best soldiers. Márkos Bótsaris and his troops, accompanied by two other Greek captains and their men, had left on an expedition which proved fruitless to help the Souliots beleaguered in their homeland. To bring the Turks to battle by an attack on them was therefore out of the question; the best option was to occupy a good defensive position and wait for the Turks to do the attacking. Péta offered just such a position, and it was there on 4 July that the philhellenes, the regulars and the Ionians established themselves under the command of Normann. Mavrokordhátos, with a small staff, withdrew to a village some ten miles south of Péta, and he was later criticised for playing the château general too far from the scene of action.

It was fortunate that Márkos Bótsaris and his companions returned from the unsuccessful venture into Soúli ten days later on 15 July, since by then Mavrokordhátos knew from a Greek in Árta that the Turks would attack next morning. The final disposition of the troops at Péta was now hurriedly agreed. The village of Péta is on a low hill at the edge of a plain, with Árta a few miles to the west and the Makrinóros mountains to the east. Behind the village to the east is a north–south ridge some two miles long, and in front of it a parallel ridge, lower and shorter, the low hill of the village providing a link between the two. By the night of 15 July the Greek forces were in position. On the higher ridge Bakólas occupied the right at the northern end, two other Greek captains Varnakiótis and Vlachópoulos the centre, and Márkos Bótsaris and his Souliots the left; the two old enemies, Bakólas and Bótsaris, were thus kept as far apart as possible. On the forward ridge the Greek regulars under Tarella were in the centre, the Ionians on the right with the two field guns and their philhellene crew, and the main body of philhellenes under Dania on the left, the position regarded as the one of maximum danger. There were some 1,200 men on the upper ridge, and only about 500 on the lower.

An hour before dawn on 16 July the whinnying of horses and other sounds of an army on the march confirmed the expected attack. The Turks advanced on the Greek positions in a huge crescent, with 600 cavalry on their right wing, and as they approached the forward ridge, firing as they came, they were amazed to find that their fire was not returned. Only when they were within a hundred paces did the regulars, in a controlled display of European tactics, let loose a lethal fire, supported by an enfilade from the two cannon at the northern end of the ridge. During the next two hours the Turks repeated their assault on the forward ridge with no greater success, and their left wing, attacking the Greek irregulars on the upper ridge, was driven back by fire from the traditional *tamboúria* earthworks. It seemed that European methods had proved themselves, and that it was after all possible for regulars and irregulars to act together.

Even Bakólas seemed to be co-operating when his troops drove off a body of Albanians attacking his position on the right of the upper ridge. However, some fifty of the attacking Albanians took cover rather than retreating, and then scaled the ridge at a point which Bakólas had now left unguarded. This turned the battle. First Bakólas' troops fell back along the ridge, then those of the captains in the centre and finally even the Souliots of Márkos Bótsaris, all retreating to the shelter of the mountains behind them, leaving the Turks in possession of the upper ridge and the regulars at their mercy below. The Turks poured down, using the village of Péta as a sort of stepping stone on which troops from the plain joined them. The forward ridge too was rolled up from the north. The Ionians succumbed first and the two cannon were put out of action, then the regulars in the centre were cut to pieces trying to withdraw through the village, and finally the philhellenes fell back to a small hill in the plain a few hundred yards from their original position, cut off by the Turkish cavalry from further retreat.

Here the dream of the philhellene volunteers that they might play a noble part in the liberation of Greece came to an end. Their commander Dania was killed in hand-to-hand fighting, their standard bearer died still holding the battalion's flag, and, with the casualties from earlier in the battle, sixty-seven philhellenes are known to have died at Péta. Tarella and virtually all the European officers of the regular regiment were killed, though Tarella's lieutenant Gubernatis survived the battle and succeeded Tarella as the regiment's commander. Raybaud would probably have been among the dead if he had not been in Mesolongi that day, on a mission from Mavrokordhátos to secure supplies and more cannon. Perhaps Mavrokordhátos wanted to keep out of harm's way the faithful companion who had been with him since they left Marseilles together a year before. Of the philhellene dead, thirty-four were German, twelve Italian, nine Polish, seven native or naturalised French, three Swiss, one Dutch and one Hungarian. Fewer than thirty philhellenes got away from the hill where most of their comrades died, and with the Turks in pursuit fled through the ravines and undergrowth of the nearby mountains. In a final twist on a day when support given or withheld swung the battle and determined who lived and who died, this small band was saved by a sudden outbreak of shots from the heights above them, covering fire provided by the troops of Bakólas.

Was Bakólas then a traitor? The surviving Europeans were convinced that he had thrown the battle to the Turks by leaving his position undefended according to a prearranged plan. They were deeply suspicious of his earlier communications with the Turks which had secured him such generous supplies. Three days after the battle Bakólas openly joined the Turks and remained with them until he died the next year. What further proof of his bad faith was needed? Others were not so certain. Bakólas himself claimed that he was simply extracting provisions from the Turks and would sooner or later lead them into a trap, an explanation which Mavrokordhátos accepted. Bakólas' crucial withdrawal from his position might simply have been a mistake made because he believed he had repelled the Turkish attack; Gordon stated even-handedly that his action could have been due either to 'the blackest treachery' or to 'one of those chances which exercise such an influence over the fate of battles'.[3] Bakólas' troops provided cover for the escaping philhellenes. Apologists for Bakólas also point out that he presented himself with the other captains at Mavrokordhátos' camp on the day after the battle, still professing his loyalty to the Greek cause, a profession which Mavrokordhátos still accepted. On this view Bakólas went over to the Turks only because of the general distrust of him in the Greek camp.

The covering fire from Bakólas' men at the end of the day may well have been spontaneous rather than under orders, so the case for Bakólas rests on two things: first, his own professions of his loyalty, which he would have made whether loyal or not, and second Mavrokordhátos' support for him. But Mavrokordhátos too had motives for concealing his real thoughts. Before the battle he was trying to secure Bakólas' loyalty by proclaiming his belief in that loyalty. After the battle Mavrokordhátos needed to present the outcome in the least damaging light, claiming a week later that his military venture had been useful in drawing part of the Turkish troops south and away from Soúli, but 'had failed due to mistakes such as men often fall into' and that the culminating battle of Péta 'while it certainly brought us some gain was lost only because of a trivial occurrence'.[4] This was blatant whitewash; as the contemporary politician and historian Spirídhon Trikoúpis wrote, 'In a word, the outcome of Péta was not a defeat, it was a disaster.'[5]

Almost certainly therefore Bakólas was guilty of treachery, and brought about in a single day the deaths of more of his own side than most traitors encompass in a lifetime of deceit. His actions need to be seen in context. The chieftains of West Roumeli were used to co-operating with the Turks, as both they and their present opponent Omer Vrionis had seen common service under Ali Pasha, and Omer Vrionis himself had deserted Ali Pasha for the Turks. The strong Albanian elements in both Greek and Turkish forces made a change of sides less abrupt. Above all a Greek chieftain needed to hold on to his local territory and in the early days it was far from certain that Greek victory would secure it for him; to keep his base as a satrap of the Turks, at least temporarily, was better than to lose it altogether. Finally ostensible agreements with the Turks were sometimes actively encouraged: for example, later that summer Varnakiótis, one of the captains at Péta, was instructed by Mavrokordhátos to start pretended negotiations for submission to Omer Vrionis. Before long, Varnakiótis had actually joined the Turks, only returning to the Greek side in 1828 when Greek success was assured. But even in an era when loyalties were fluid there were degrees of treason. To change sides during a lull in military activity was less reprehensible than aiding the enemy in the course of a battle. To change sides when the Greeks were losing was not as bad as treacherously undermining a potential Greek success. If the detractors of Bakólas are right, then his action was of the last kind and was indeed the blackest treachery.

The aftermath of Péta was painful. Ten days after the battle twenty-five surviving philhellenes attended the funeral service in Mesolongi for their dead comrades. Their battalion was then formally disbanded, those who could left for home, and the sick and wounded remained in Mesolongi, most of them to die during the following winter. Normann, lightly wounded at Péta, died in Mesolongi at the end of November. The Souliots in their homeland, deprived of support, capitulated by agreement and many of them were evacuated to the Ionian islands.

Mavrokordhátos fell back on Mesolongi, whose low mud walls and sur-rounding lagoon were now the only barrier between the western Turkish army and the Peloponnese. After Péta the flood of volunteers to fight for Greece slowed to a trickle – none except Byron and his party in 1823, perhaps seven in 1824, and never again as many as the 500 or so who arrived in 1821–2. The disaster at Péta might also have permanently discredited the whole idea of philhellenism had it not been revived by Turkish atrocities which stunned the world and were carried out during that summer on the island of Chios.

16

Chios

In the years preceding the Greek revolution no part of the Ottoman empire was more blessed by good fortune than the island of Chios. The Italian influence was strong, from intermittent occupation, going back to before the crusades, of Venetians, Genoese and Florentines; hence the Italianate names of many of the leading families, and the island's contemporary name of Scio. The Chians had become rich through commerce, hiring the ships of Psará and Hydra for transport of goods, and wealthy Chians were established as commercial agents in major cities from Marseilles to Odessa and from Moscow to Alexandria. The products of the island included cotton, silk, citrus fruit – whose blossom, it was said, could be smelt five miles out at sea – and the famous mastic which is still cultivated. This is a resin which oozes from small cuts made in the bark of the *Terebinth lentiscus* bush, which grows in the southern part of Chios in the twenty-two villages known as the *mastichochória*, which were then the personal appanage of the Sultan's sister. This area produced over fifty tons a year of the gum, which was, says Gordon, 'a substance highly prized by the Eastern ladies, who amuse their indolence by chewing it, deriving from that practice as much gratification as their male relations enjoy by inhaling the fumes of tobacco'.[1] Chewing mastic is like chewing the end of a Biro, with an extra whiff of petroleum; some pieces remain as hard granules in the mouth and others dissolve into glutinous gobbets. The attraction of mastic is therefore hard to understand, and it is now best enjoyed as a flavouring for ouzo.

The Turkish presence on Chios was minimal, consisting only of a governor, a *cadi* or judge, and a few hundred soldiers in the Genoese citadel which dominates the north side of the harbour of Chóra, the island's main town. Civil power rested with the local demogeronts, elected by the leading merchants from their own number; sixteen were of the Orthodox faith and two Catholic, a sectarian balance designed for peaceful coexistence. Taxes were light; the main one was the poll tax, for which even the richest paid no more than eleven piastres a year, at a time when two piastres was reckoned as the cost of a day's food. Combined with all these advantages, and funded by the island's wealth, was a welfare state in miniature: a free school, a hospital for 200 patients accepting no fees except donations from rich visitors from other islands, and special hospitals for lepers, and for victims of the plague, which was a frequent occurrence. There were even arrangements for finding homes for foundlings, for visiting prisoners and for settling the poll tax of those imprisoned for non-payment. It is thus not surprising that the people of Chios had a reputation for cheerfulness; it was said that if you had met a serious-minded Chian you had seen a green horse. A description of the Chian women, by a visitor in early 1822, has a modern ring and sounds rather more Italian than Greek:

> They wear pink, green and white dresses, mostly very short, white or blue stockings, and little red shoes embroidered like a sultan's slippers: their long hair falls to their shoulders, from which they put it up by attaching it to the head with gold pins. They paint their eyebrows, but never their cheeks, and constantly chew the mastic which is gathered in the southern part of the island. These young girls have a certain boldness combined with great artlessness; they are innocent without being modest; and if their upbringing has not made them reserved and studiously grave, it has taken nothing away from their natural simplicity and enjoyment of life.

And the visitor, writing later after the island's destruction, asks, 'Poor young girls, of the most beautiful island in the sea, what has become of you?'[2]

In early May 1821 a fleet from Hydra and Psará, commanded by Iakoumákis Tombázis of Hydra, arrived off the east coast of Chios to persuade the Chians to join the revolution. A deputation of leading Chian citizens had already met Tombázis on Psará, and begged him to leave them undisturbed as they could contribute nothing to the struggle. Tombázis now tried a direct appeal to the people, sending an emissary round the villages to stimulate revolt. His message was a mixture of encouragement (the Greeks were already victorious in the Peloponnese), promises (the Greek fleet would soon close the Dardanelles), exhortation (how could Chios, the richest island, stand apart from the revolution?) and threats. However, the villagers were no more responsive than their leaders and eleven days after its arrival Tombázis' fleet sailed away.

The departure of Tombázis signalled not a return to tranquillity but, as Gordon put it, 'an end to the peace and happiness of Scio'. The Turks took forty hostages from the leading Chian citizens and held them in the fortress at Chóra as guarantees of the islanders' good behaviour; it was later agreed that the original forty should alternate month by month with another forty. The hostages included the archbishop Pláton, two deacons and representatives of the most distinguished Chian Greek Orthodox families – Argenti, Mavrogordato, Ralli, Rodocanachi, Vlasto. In addition five or six Catholic hostages were taken. Weapons belonging to the Chians were confiscated and the Turkish governor requested help from Constantinople. As a result some 1,000 disorderly troops crossed from Chesme on the opposite coast and roamed through Chóra and the nearby countryside, attacking and mur- dering the citizens and plundering their houses. Three of the Chian hostages – a Rodocanachi, a Skilitsi and a Ralli – were sent to Constantinople, conveyed overland to ensure that they could not be rescued by a Greek ship. Thus Turks and Greeks on Chios awaited developments.

In the following spring the Samians, who had joined the revolution early, made their own attempt to involve Chios in the struggle. The Samian leader was the forceful Likoúrgos Logothétis, and he was sup- ported by an expatriate from Chios, Antónios Bourniás, formerly an officer in the French army. On 22 March 1822 a Greek fleet under Logothétis and Bourniás, carrying some 1,500 armed men, anchored off Áyia Eléni a few miles south of the island's capital.

When the Samian troops landed the local Turks retreated into the citadel, where the garrison had been increased to 4,500. Battle was now joined, with exchange of cannon fire between the Turks in the citadel and the Greeks from the shore below the citadel, and from the hills of

Tourlotí and Asómati above it. The Greeks took possession of the town, burnt down the customs house and stripped the lead from the roofs of two mosques for use as bullets. Logothétis moved into the palace of the imprisoned archbishop Pláton, deposed the demogeronts who had previously represented the people of Chios, and established in their place a revolutionary committee of seven ephors, an arrangement about which Finlay was characteristically scathing: 'Lykourgos did nothing, the ephors had nothing to do, and the camp became a scene of anarchy.'[3] Logothétis and his fellow commander Bourniás quickly fell out, both demanding the title of Saviour of Chios, and settled the dispute by allotting the northern part of the island to Bourniás and the southern part, with Chóra, to Logothétis. They thus abandoned any possibility of joint action, and divided up territory as if the battle was already won, instead of only just beginning.

The Sultan's reaction was prompt and decisive. Seven wealthy Chians in Constantinople were taken hostage, in addition to the three already sent from Chios itself. The kapitan pasha, Kara Ali, was ordered to Chios with a powerful fleet and with orders to convey 15,000 men to Chios from Chesme, where 30,000 had now gathered. Many were volunteers, including it was said a whole infantry regiment of Muslim priests, and most were simply attracted by the riches of Chios. The British consul at Smyrna reported that 'we have got rid of all our ruffians, who have gone to take part in the plunder of Scio'.[4] Strangford, Britain's ambassador in Constantinople, was worried about the control of such large numbers of unruly troops.

> If the Captain Pasha [Kara Ali] should have been charged with the supreme command of the land-forces, and that the other Pashas should have been placed under his orders (which I hope may be the case) the reduction of Scio will be effected according to the usages of civilised war. If however his command should be merely a Naval one, I fear that he will not be able to repress the barbarous spirit of vengeance which will undoubtedly animate the Turkish Army, and which will then overwhelm Scio.[5]

On 11 April 1822, which was the Thursday before Easter, Kara Ali's fleet reached Chios. There was short-lived resistance from the Greeks, and a minor success when a Turkish ship with eighty men on board stuck on a shoal, and most of its complement were killed by Greek musket fire. Otherwise the Greeks were powerless against the incursion of troops from Kara Ali's ships, which was combined with a sally of the Turkish garrison from the citadel. Logothétis and his Samian followers fled, and after a brief resistance at Áyios Georgios, a hilltop town six miles south-west of Chóra, were taken off by Psarian ships from the west coast. Chios was now abandoned to its fate.

The scenes that followed were as appalling as any that had yet occurred in the bloody annals of the revolution. 'The horrors of civil war were never more fearfully displayed than at Scio,'[6] wrote Strangford. Gordon likened them to those following the sack of Tripolis, and of the events on Chios wrote: 'Mercy was out of the question, the victors butchering indiscriminately all who came in their way; shrieks rent the air, and the streets were strewed with the dead bodies of old men, women, and children; even the inmates of the hospital, the madhouse, and the deaf and dumb institution, were inhumanly slaughtered.'[7] When after a few days there were no more inhabitants in Chóra to be attacked or goods to be looted, the terror spread to the countryside, augmented by the Turkish troops who continued to pour across to the island from Chesme. Within a week two grisly consignments from the governor of Chios had reached Constantinople. They contained the heads and ears of rebels who had been killed or, worse still, the ears of some who had been taken alive, and a notice to this effect was posted outside the Seraglio.

For those not seized immediately, remote monasteries, with their walled enclosures, water cisterns and ovens to feed a community offered the three things the refugees most needed: shelter, water and food. At Néa Moní, in a beautiful setting in the hills near the centre of the island, 2,000 refugees gathered in the walled complex of monastery buildings; all were killed when Turkish bands broke through the outer wall. Even more Chians lost their lives at Áyios Minás, on a hilltop south of Chóra from which the 3,000 huddled asylum seekers could see the boats carrying their predators crossing from Chesme. On Easter Sunday 14 April the monastery, packed with Chian families, was set on fire by the Turks. It burnt to the ground and all the refugees inside perished. Áyios Minás has been rebuilt on the former site, and the dark stains on the original stone floor are said to be from burnt human flesh. In the chapel are glass cases containing the neatly stacked skulls and bones of those who died. These ossuaries raise disturbing questions about whether the dead, even if unidentifiable, should have been given a proper burial, or whether the destruction of Áyios Minás and its refugees was such an extreme atrocity that the relics of its victims must be set before each succeeding generation lest they forget.

For a time the mastic villages were safe. Kara Ali, within a week of his landing and as soon as the Samians had left, sent three of the foreign consular agents out to the villages with an offer of amnesty, supported by a letter from the distinguished hostages urging acceptance. The amnesty being accepted, protection of the villages was entrusted to Elez Aga, according to Gordon 'a chief distinguished for generosity and probity'. Outside the mastic villages, a fortunate few found refuge in the consulates, which Kara Ali had agreed to respect; the French consulate sheltered some 1,200, and almost the whole Catholic population was protected by the Austrian consulate.

Otherwise, people went into hiding in the hope that the storm would pass, or struggled to reach the little harbours on the west coast from which ships from Psará or other islands might take them off. Nearly a century later a Chian schoolmaster, Stilianós Víos, published descriptions of the refugees' experiences, some from themselves in great old age, others from their children and grandchildren. Over time some of the accounts had blossomed into dramatic legends. In one story, for instance, three Turks who tried to seize a priest were struck blind, and in another two Turks of a party that killed the fugitives in a cave were turned to pillars of stone 'which can be seen to this day'. In a particularly colourful episode, a Chian fell in love with the Sultana in Constantinople, who gave him, as a token of her affection, a gold sword encrusted with diamonds. The Chian, when his house on Chios was searched on the orders of the suspicious Sultan, threw the sword down the well, but when the winch was turned the sword came up in the bucket. Though the story ended with the unfortunate gallant being taken to Constantinople and executed, it was obviously a deeply satisfying one, quite apart from the reverse Freudian imagery of *her* sword being plunged into *his* well. It showed that the Sultan could be cuckolded like any other man, and cuckolded by a Greek.

Most of the accounts, however, have the ring not of myth but of harsh reality. When Turks appeared, often only in ones and twos, the first hiding places were in the cellar, roof or even the oven of the house, or somewhere near by: a barn, a church crypt, an old Genoese tower, a hollow olive trunk, the outlet pipe of a mill. A wet-nurse saved her two small charges by lowering them into a well, and is still remembered with gratitude by their descendants. When refugees felt unsafe in their own houses and villages, they took to caves in the hills, especially those in the mountainous north-west corner of the island, from which the rocky outline of Psará, whence salvation might come, could be seen in the distance. Getting food and water then became a pressing problem. Small groups would leave their cave at night and gather pulses and fruit, still unripe in the early spring, and sometimes manage to bake bread, but of this there was never enough, and one group spent twenty breadless days.

A continual worry was that the crying of babies would reveal hiding places. 'Before they went into hiding,' runs one account, 'there was an argument, because the husband insisted that the baby should be hidden elsewhere, and the mother did not want to be parted from her child. The Turks who were roaming the mountains took up position above the cave and fired at anyone they saw. At the first gunshot the baby started to cry and so they were revealed. The wife, who was beautiful, was taken into slavery with the child, and the husband was put in front of a large plane tree and shot.' Sometimes the child was sacrificed. One was thrown down a ravine. Another, a girl of eighteen months, was left outside a cave, ignored by Turks who were looking only for adults and covertly watched by her anxious father; after three days the danger passed, she was brought in and revived and, says the teller of the tale, 'she grew up, got married and had as many children as me'. In another story danger was averted by quick thinking. Turks were having a party near some refugee caves and a Chian was playing the violin and singing for them. Hearing a child's muffled cry he sang: 'Better kill the child, my dear, Otherwise you won't get clear.' The Turks asked what he was singing. 'Just a refrain,' he replied. The child stayed quiet, it seems, and all those in hiding were saved.

The Turks used tricks of their own. They cooked some meat and went round the mouths of caves crying in Greek, 'Fine meat! Fine meat!' They left bread at the entrance of a cave to see if anyone came out for it. Neither ruse was successful. Sometimes, though, a friendly Turk was helpful to the fugitives. One Turk was approached by a Chian traitor who offered to show him where two girls were hidden; the Turk killed the informer and put the refugees on the road to Mestá. One Turkish official sent his men to protect fugitives from attack by a roving party of Turks, a rare instance of any control being exercised over the marauders.

The Chians put up what resistance they could. Near Kardhámila in the north-east a priest, who had the only gun left in the village, came across a Turk dragging off a woman and her children, and from ambush shot him dead. A father and son were found hiding under a fig tree by a Turk on his own; the father knocked down the Turk with a branch of the tree and killed him with a stone. Women resisted too. A Turk was leading to Chóra a group of captive women, among them the narrator's aunt Amília. The Turk stopped at a well, and sat on the edge smoking his pipe. 'The women then thought of drowning him, but were too frightened. Then my aunt Amília called on the Mother of God to give her strength. She gave the Turk a great shove and pushed him into the well. Afterwards they took to the hills and reached Lithí, where a ship from Psará rescued them.'

Rescue by ship was for all the refugees the best hope. As the east coast was clearly visible from the Turkish mainland the only chance of escape was from the west coast, where much the best anchorage was the long bay leading to the harbour of Mestá, which is some two miles from the town itself. At one time the cramped houses and narrow streets of medieval Mestá were said to shelter 5,000 Chians waiting to get away by sea. The rescue ships were mainly from Psará, and there was considerable resentment against Psarians who demanded money before accepting fugitives. Other rescue ships came from Sámos, Hydra and Spétses. One woman, with a newborn baby and still bleeding from the birth, plunged into the sea in desperation and was picked up by an English ship which took them both to the island of Síros. Síros, a hundred miles south-west of Chios, was a common destination for refugees, since Psará, the first stop for many, was too poor to support them. Some went on to other islands, some to the mainland to join the fight for independence there. Many eventually returned to Chios and most, it seems, cherished the dream of ultimate return.

While the countryside presented this picture of fear and flight, destruction and disorder, seventy-seven of the eighty Chian hostages (three had been sent to Constantinople) were still being held in Chóra, forty-nine of them in the citadel. They had been in captivity since the visit of Tombázis' fleet in March 1821, on an alternating basis until all were called in on the landing of the Samians in March 1822. Only the Catholics had been released, through the combined efforts of the French vice-consul on Chios, the French consul-general in Smyrna and the French ambassador in Constantinople. Further hostages were still being held in Constantinople, the three sent from Chios and seven residents of the capital. The usefulness of all was now at an end. On 5 May Kara Ali, on direct orders from the Sultan, took out the forty-nine hostages held in the citadel and hanged eight from the yards of his flagship and the remainder from the trees in the road which runs below the west wall of the citadel, now named the Street of the Martyrs. This choice of location was brutally theatrical. The Chians who took this road would see, as they looked up, the bodies of their compatriots and above these the ramparts of the citadel, symbol of Turkish dominance. Turks, looking down, would see the ghastly results of their reprisal and, passing beneath, the citizens whom these hanging corpses were intended to cow. All the great families of Chios lost leading members, and Archbishop Pláton died with them. Two weeks later the Chian hostages held in Constantinople were publicly beheaded.

The Turkish troops on Chios soon turned from slaughter to the more profitable business of enslavement. Gordon estimated that by the end of May, some two months after Kara Ali's landing, 45,000 Chiots had been taken as slaves, among them the women and children of the leading families. 'Whole cargoes were shipped off to Constantinople, Egypt and Barbary,' wrote Gordon, 'and for a long period the slave market at Smyrna displayed the bustle of active trade, and attracted Moslem purchasers from all parts of Asia Minor.'[8] Kara Ali at one point imposed a ban on the export of slaves from the island, but revoked it when he found that the soldiers were killing their prisoners instead. Strangford protested to the Turkish government in Constantinople about the taking of slaves and received a subtle if casuistical answer: that enslavement of the wives and children of enemies was not only permitted but enjoined by Muslim laws and religion; that the Christian powers of Europe had tolerated slavery for centuries, purely for gain and without the sanction of religion; that the Ottoman government had a right to act as it pleased towards its own subjects; and, in a final rhetorical flourish, 'why do not the Christian Sovereigns interfere to prevent the Emperor of Russia from sending his subjects into Siberia? Because they know very well what answer they would receive!'[9]

Some of those taken as slaves managed eventually to escape. Some were fortunate enough to be ransomed, particularly by Chian merchants of Smyrna who through an agent would buy back the captives and arrange their shipment to Trieste or elsewhere. But this was an expensive business; the cost of rescuing the wife of one of the Turks' hostages and her two young daughters was almost 15,000 piastres. Other captives were handed over to the British vice-consul on Chios, Giudici, because their captors could find nobody on Chios to ransom them and could not ship them to the mainland. Some hundreds were saved in this way, again at considerable expense, for which Giudici was still vainly seeking recompense a year later. Finally in mid-June an imperial order was sent to the Constantinople slave market prohibiting the further sale of Chian captives, an order said to have been instigated by the Sultan's sister, proprietor of the mastic villages. But by then the supply of captives was already virtually exhausted.

The Greek fleet now moved into action, its failure to do so earlier being attributed by some to lack of supplies and by others to dissension between the three main naval islands. It was too late to help Chios; their present object was to stop Kara Ali's fleet from joining up with another Ottoman fleet from Egypt, a combination which the Greeks feared would give the Turks complete dominance at sea. On 10 May 1822 a combined Greek fleet of ships from Hydra, Spétses and Psará, consisting of fifty-six warships and eight fireships, under the command of Andréas Miaoúlis of Hydra, set out from Psará to attack the Turks in the channel between Chios and the mainland. For some weeks thereafter only skirmishes took place, the Turks trying ineffectually to sink Greek ships by cannon fire, the Greeks trying to use their fireships with equally little success.

The Greek opportunity at last came on the night of 18 June when the Turkish fleet, anchored outside the harbour of Chóra, was celebrating the end of Ramadan. The wind was from the north that day, and two Greek ships spent the daylight hours beating northwards against it up the Turkish coast, giving the impression that they were trying to round the cape that lies across the entrance to the Gulf of Smyrna. In fact the two vessels were fireships, one commanded by Andréas Pipínos of Hydra and one by Konstantínos Kanáris of Psará, and they were working towards the necessary upwind position for attack. After sunset they turned to sail downwind towards the Turkish fleet. The night was dark, with only a sliver of moon, but the Turkish ships were illuminated for the celebrations, those of the kapitan pasha Kara Ali and of his vice-admiral being easily identified as the most brightly lit. The design of fireships had been improved since the Greeks' first experiments the previous autumn, being now reinforced with copper to prevent them disintegrating before their target ship had time to catch fire.

At midnight Kanáris bore down on the kapitan pasha's flagship, ramming his bowsprit into an open port near the flagship's prow. The fuse was lit, Kanáris and his men were taken off and within minutes flames driven by the wind were sweeping over the flagship. The other fireship under Pipínos damaged but failed to destroy the vice-admiral's ship, being cut loose before the flames fully caught, and it drifted on shore to burn away without doing further harm. Kara Ali's flagship however was soon a mass of flames. People in Smyrna fifty miles away were amazed by the fiery glow in the sky to the west. Turkish sailors took to the lifeboats, but two were so overcrowded that they sank. There were many Greeks taken as slaves locked up on board, who shouted in vain for release. Kara Ali entered a lifeboat, where he was struck on the head by a spar falling from the blazing rigging. He was taken to land, but died the next day, and was buried in the little Turkish cemetery of the Chóra citadel, where his marble tomb still stands. After three-quarters of an hour the flames on the flagship reached the powder store, and the ship exploded. Of the 2,286 reportedly on board, only some 180 survived.

On Chios the loss of the kapitan pasha and his flagship prompted the Turks to a final act of reprisal against the remaining islanders. The mastic villages had until now been protected by Elez Aga after their acceptance of an amnesty in April. Survivors from other parts of the island had taken refuge there, especially in the village of Tholopotámi, which clings to a steep hillside above the plain. A horde of Turks, said to number 20,000, now descended on the *mastichochória*. The villages were laid waste and the inhabitants killed or taken as slaves.

The final toll on the suffering island could now be assessed. Before the catastrophe there were between 100,000 and 120,000 Greeks living on Chios, and by the end their numbers were reduced to some 20,000. Gordon's even more shocking figure of only 1,800 survivors on the island is almost certainly wrong, perhaps a mistake for 18,000, though he may be right to say that 'the most populous villages had only twelve indwellers'. The number of Greeks killed was put at 25,000 and of those enslaved at 45,000; that is, the catastrophe left about a quarter of the population dead and nearly half taken into slavery. Probably between 10,000 and 20,000 escaped, some to return, some to settle on other Aegean islands, some to continue the great family names of Chios – Ralli, Rodocanachi, Argenti, Vlasto – as they found fortune or fame abroad.

How did this near-destruction of a population come about? Later historians of Chian descent lay the blame squarely on Logothétis and his incursion from Sámos; Philip Argenti for example writes that 'the Samians . . . were seeking personal adventure and therefore decided to coerce the Chians *nolentes volentes* into "liberty", assuming to themselves a doctor's mandate and knowing better what was good for Chios than did the Chians themselves. After all, if the expedition failed, what did it matter? could they not retreat to Samos or elsewhere?'[10] But the root cause of the disaster was that the Ottoman response to Logothétis' incursion was so wildly disproportionate. The number of Samians landing was probably no more than 1,500, and it was clear to the Turkish authorities that the invaders would get little support from the Chians. The Turkish garrison on the island, 4,500 strong, in itself outnumbered the Samian forces. Kara Ali was then instructed to bring a further 15,000 men across from the mainland, where many more were waiting to join in the plunder of Chios. Not all these thousands of Turks were on the island at the same time. It seems that most collected their booty of goods or captive slaves and returned to the mainland to sell them, and most of the accounts of the Chians themselves mention small groups or single marauders, not troops en masse. Nevertheless the sheer number of Turkish troops pouring into and out of the island presaged disaster, particularly because Kara Ali was unable properly to control his varied forces, just as Strangford at Constantinople had feared. If the Turks had limited their response to the small-scale Samian invasion merely to the minimum force needed to repel it, Chians at home and abroad could have continued in prosperity as an important contributor to the Ottoman economy, and the Turks would not have suffered the international odium which their savagery on Chios provoked. A destructive act of policy by the Ottoman government was thus, as on other occasions, ultimately self-destructive.

The execution of the hostages seems to have been on the direct orders of the Sultan, and behind him we glimpse again the shadowy figure of his minister Halet Effendi. A year earlier, at the time of the execution of Patriarch Grigórios, Halet Effendi seems to have been a cautious moderate but by now he had changed his stance. Strangford describes him as urging the execution of the Chian hostages, in opposition to other ministers, and writes of 'the barbarous system of terrorism which Halet Effendi pursues, for the sake of diverting public attention from his own misdeeds'.[11] In this he failed, or at least he failed to ingratiate himself with the Sultan; he was shortly afterwards exiled to Konya, where before the end of the year he was beheaded on the Sultan's orders, another victim of the deadly pavane in which advisers of the Sultan moved in and out of his favour.

Waves of shocked reaction to the fate of Chios spread throughout Europe. One of the most immediate concerned money: the prosperous and widespread Chian commercial houses owed, in the natural course of trading, considerable sums to European firms, and these were now largely irrecoverable debts. Thus the Italian vice-consul in Smyrna wrote as early as 31 March 1822, when Kara Ali's fleet had only just reached Chios: 'Our trade has been gravely prejudiced by this insurrection because of the sums owed by Chians to Europeans, which probably cannot be paid.'[12] On 17 June, the day before the destruction of Kara Ali's flagship, the British consul in Smyrna reported that the Chian merchants there owed the English merchants a staggering 195 million piastres.

Revulsion, however, was the overwhelming response. It was forcibly expressed by Lord Londonderry, Britain's foreign secretary, in a despatch to Strangford of 9 July 1822 after the destruction of Chios was complete. Londonderry acknowledged receipt of Strangford's despatches, 'which convey the painful and disgusting recital of the bloody scenes growing out of the Scio War', and which he said had been laid before the King. The execution of the innocent Chian hostages in

Constantinople particularly concerned both Londonderry and the King, and, though Britain could not regard the Chian hostages as in any sense under her protection, Strangford was given a stern message to transmit to the Turkish government:

> By a repetition of such deeds of blood, they will not only render all pacific arrangements impracticable, but they will leave to friendly and allied States, no other alternative but to withdraw their Missions from being, as it might seem, the approving witnesses of Transactions for which no human offences can furnish a pretext, much less a justification, and which, if repeated, must stamp the Council of the State that tolerates them, with the reproach of the most ferocious and hateful barbarism.[13]

Within a year the British government led the way in recognising the Greeks as belligerents, rather than rebels, by its acknowledgement that the Greek blockade of the Turkish coast was legal. Thus Britain took the first steps down the path of involvement in the Greek revolution, an involvement which was to culminate at Navarino.

A second crowned head of Europe added his authority to the appalled response to the events on Chios. At the Paris Salon of 1824 Delacroix exhibited his painting *Scènes des massacres de Scio*. In the foreground women, children and the wounded sit or lie in disconsolate attitudes. Behind them a Turk on horseback has seized and manacled two women. In the distance a fleeing crowd is being attacked, and far away towards the sea the blackened countryside is still burning. Théophile Gautier, a friend of Delacroix, described the impact of the work, with its feverish and convulsive drawing, rushing brushstrokes and violent colours, which aroused the disdain of the classicists and the enthusiasm of the young. The painting stirred public opinion in much the same way as today's television pictures of tragedies in distant parts of the world. At the end of the exhibition Delacroix's picture was bought for the Louvre by King Louis XVIII of France.

17

The Expedition of Dramali

In the summer of 1821 the Greeks had successfully blocked the Turkish army's progress down the eastern route to the Peloponnese by a victory at Vasiliká near Thermopylae. By the summer of 1822 the Turks were preparing for another attempt, and were in a much better position to do so. Ali Pasha's death had released the Turkish forces besieging Iánnina, and the Turkish commander Khurshid Pasha was able to assemble at Lárissa, halfway between Athens and Thessalonika, a force estimated at between 20,000 and 30,000 men, many times the size of the army which had been defeated at Vasiliká. The man directly appointed by the Sultan to lead this massive force into the Peloponnese was Mahmud, pasha of Dhráma east of Thessalonika and so commonly called Dramali. This appointment was variously said to please Khurshid Pasha because it allowed him, now a sick man, to remain at Lárissa, or to displease him because Dramali now became his rival. While the Turks' position was a good deal stronger than a year earlier, the Greeks' was far weaker because of violent dissension among their leaders.

This dissension was at its fiercest in East Roumeli, where a contemporary reported that 'almost every political and military chief was engaged in a plot to supplant or assassinate some rival'.[1] The leading captain was Odysseus Andhroútsos, who first fell out with the regional government, the Aríos Págos, over military tactics. In June 1822 the national government, at the request of the Aríos Págos, sent two representatives to bring Odysseus under control; both were killed on Odysseus' orders. Thus the first six months of 1822, during which the threat of Dramali's advance became ever clearer, were wasted on murderous internal disputes.

On the see-saw of Greek fortunes the structural failure to organise the defences of East Roumeli was offset by one success: the capture of the Akropolis of Athens. Athens was a town of some 10,000 inhabitants, half of them Albanians and the rest Turks or Greeks, 'an impoverished community', thought Finlay, 'consisting of torpid landed proprietors and lazy petty traders'.[2] Most occupied the twelve to thirteen hundred houses packed around the north and west sides of the Akropolis, the areas that had been populated since classical times and probably since the Neolithic era. The houses of Athens may have been mean, the streets squalid and the population unprepossessing, but Byron on his visit in 1811 found the place intensely romantic: 'I am living in the Capuchin Convent, Hymettus before me, the Acropolis behind, the temple of Jove to my right, the Stadium in front, the town to the left, eh, Sir, there's a situation, there's your picturesque! nothing like that, Sir, in Lunnun, no not even the Mansion House.'[3]

On the outbreak of the revolution most of the Greeks in Athens fled for safety to the island of Sálamis, as their ancestors had done before the advance of Xerxes' Persian army over 2,000 years earlier. Returning after a few months they began a blockade of the Turks in the Akropolis, but this was interrupted by the arrival of Omer Vrionis in July 1821 to relieve the siege. Omer Vrionis was responsible for the infamous 'Greek hunts', which Howe described: 'One of his favourite amusements was a "Greek hunt", as the Turks called it. They would go out in parties of from fifty to a hundred, mounted on fleet horses, and scour the open country in search of the Greek peasantry, who might from necessity or hardihood have ventured down upon the plains. After capturing some, they would give the poor creatures a certain distance to start ahead, hoping to escape, and then try the speed of their horses in overtaking them, the accuracy of their pistols in firing at them as they ran, or the keenness of their sabres' edge in cutting off their heads.'[4] Those brought in alive were tortured to death or impaled. This appalling sport came to an end when Omer Vrionis left in November 1821 to command the Turkish forces in West Roumeli and the Greek blockade of the Turks in the Akropolis was resumed.

Within a few weeks the Greeks made an assault on the west end of the Akropolis at its main gate. The attack failed, but the Greeks were able crucially to seize the well outside the walls on the southern slope, the source of healing waters for the ancient worship of the god Asklepios and the only supply, apart from collected rain, of drinking water for the Turks in the garrison. In case they were later repulsed, the Greeks polluted the well by throwing into it the bodies of dead Turks. In the spring of the following year the Greeks resumed their efforts to capture the Akropolis. In early March 1822 the minister of war, Koléttis, supplied the besiegers with two mortars and ammunition, to be supervised by the Frenchman Olivier Voutier, one of the philhellenes who now joined the operation. Voutier's bombardment was completely ineffective, and was only continued, in Howe's view, because of the philhellenes' enthusiasm for it: 'The whims of several fanfaronading European officers, who were continually talking about approaches and contravallations and blinds and gabions, must be complied with.'[5] At the beginning of April another tactic was tried. A mine was started and after thirty-three days of digging had reached the wall at the south-west corner of the Akropolis. When the explosive was detonated a portion of the wall collapsed and a party of Greeks and philhellenes rushed the breach, but were yet again repulsed.

Where mortars, mines and manpower had failed, thirst and the accompanying disease was now doing its work. The rains failed the embattled Turks, as Waddington vividly described:

> The winter and next the spring was passing away, and not a shower had yet fallen. They watched every cloud, as it rose from the Egean sea, and came rolling towards them; and, as it appeared to be approaching, they spread out their bowls and their spunges, extended their shawls and their turbans, and the very veils of their women, that not one precious drop might be lost, while the names of Allah and the Prophet were loudly and frequently invoked. *Not one drop ever came to them.* The clouds . . . were invariably broken by the Acropolis, as if they shunned the red flag which was floating there.[6]

By the early summer the Turks could last out no longer and on 22 June capitulated on terms distinctly favourable to them. The life and honour of all would be safe; they could keep half of their money, plate and jewels; they would be provided at Greek expense with passage to Asia Minor in foreign ships; and, perhaps most surprisingly, those Turks who wished to remain could live in Athens without hindrance.

Agreeing to favourable terms was one thing, sticking to them was quite another, as all those in authority realised. The representatives of the national government and of the Aríos Págos, as well as the Athenian civic leaders, all urged restraint. An oath to respect the agreement was sworn on the Bible by the Greek captains in front of the archbishop of Athens. The foreign consuls had been asked by the Turks to guarantee the terms. The consuls wisely refused this request, having no powers to enforce observance, but they undertook to use every effort to uphold the terms, and it was on their initiative that foreign transport ships were summoned from Síros. The capitulation agreement was signed in front of a large assembly in the spacious Austrian consulate, after a passionate address by the French consul Fauvel, who had held the post for some thirty years and so knew the temper of his audience: 'Athenians! . . . The attention of the world is today directed towards Greece and is especially turned on this town of glorious memories. Like you, the world waits impatiently for your prolonged struggle to succeed. Let not the day which tells it of your triumph tell it also that you have besmirched that triumph by bad faith. . . . Swear to succour the weak, swear to be merciful to the unfortunate.'[7] Fauvel's views and efforts were shared by two other consular representatives, Gropius of Austria and Origone of the Netherlands. The English consul, who might also have backed them, was absent and terminally ill.

The mood of the people of Athens however was one of post-liberation bloodlust. The previous year's 'Greek hunts' of Omer Vrionis had not been forgotten. The Turks of the garrison which he left behind had further infuriated the Athenians by killing the ten Greek heads of families whom they had taken as hostages and hanging their bodies over the Akropolis wall. Present in Athens were refugees from the Turkish destruction of Chios and of Kidhoníes. Also Greek casualties during the siege of the Akropolis, some 300 lost in action, had been particularly heavy. The ugly mood of the Athenians was further inflamed by reports in early July that a large Turkish army had passed Thermopylae and was marching on Thebes, modern Thíva, and Athens. Reprisals began almost immediately. On the day after the capitulation ten Turks were abducted and killed on the same spot where the ten Greek hostages had died. Two days later two women and two children were slaughtered. By mid-July and the arrival in Piraeus of the first two French transport vessels, nearly half the 1,150 Turks who came down from the Akropolis had been massacred by the Athenian soldiery. Of the rest some died immediately of disease, and the remaining 550 took shelter in the consulates. The captains of the two French ships had to escort their charges to Piraeus through an angry mob, with an armed guard and their own swords at the ready, and between them took off 325 Turks. In the course of the following year the remainder were rescued, four-fifths of the total on French vessels and the rest on those of Austria or England, the last handful finally departing in October 1823.

The two French captains and the three foreign consuls came best out of this sorry affair. However, we find François Pouqueville in his history making charges against the Dutch vice-consul Origone very similar to those he made against the English consul Philip Green at Patras. Describing Origone dismissively as a Corsican, Pouqueville accused him of giving daily signals to the Turks in the Akropolis about the progress of Greek mining operations or their preparations for attack. Origone rejected this accusation with spirit in a letter to Gordon:

> Faithful to the principles of humanity, and to the instructions of his Majesty the King of the Netherlands, I always observed the strictest neutrality towards the belligerents, but did whatever I could to alleviate the miseries of war. In proof of this assertion, I am able to cite various Greek families redeemed from slavery at my expense, the gratuitous distribution of grain to women in a state of destitution; and lastly, the fact, that for two whole months the consulate was open to hundreds of poor people who had no refuge but the Dutch flag.

Origone concluded with a fine flourish: 'As for the epithet of Corsican, which he applies to me as a term of reproach, Monsieur de Pouqueville ought to recollect that, if it had not been for another Corsican, he would never have attained to a rank he does not show himself worthy of.'[8] It seems that Pouqueville's obsessive nationalism led him to deny credit for helping the Greeks to anyone but the French.

One result of the fall of the Akropolis was to exacerbate yet further the dissensions among the Greeks. The divisive question was: who was

1. Callet, *L'Embarquement des Parganiotes*. The people of Párga leave their homes on
Good Friday, 1819

2. The two prophets of revolution, Koraís and Rígas, raise the
suffering maiden Greece to her feet

3. Ali Pasha being rowed in state on the lake at Butrint in southern Albania

4. Ali Pasha's Iánnina. It was on an island in this lake that Ali met his end

5. Monemvasía, the first fortress captured by Greeks in the summer of 1821

6. On 25 March 1821 Bishop Yermanós initiated the Greek war of independence by raising the flag of revolt at the monastery of Áyia Lávra, or so the legend says

7. Theódhoros Kolokotrónis

8. Makriyánnis

9. Three portraits of Mavrokordhátos: in Geneva in 1819 (*above left*); as apparently, in Howe's words, 'a silly fop' (*above right*); and as a military commander (*left*). Only the nose and mouth are common to all

10. Byron as glorious youth

11. Byron aged 35

12. Delacroix, *Scènes des massacres de Scio*

13. The mountainous region of Soúli, fiercely defended, lost and regained by its warlike inhabitants

14. Thomas Gordon

15. Andréas Miaoúlis

16. Edward John Trelawny

17. Odysseus Andhroútsos

18. Delacroix, *La Grèce sur les ruines de Missolonghi*

19. Horace Vernet, *La Retraite*. An Arab horseman in the marshes of Mesolongi

20. Theódhoros Vrizákis, *The Exodus from Mesolongi*. The reality was less dramatic but equally dangerous

21. Panayiótis Zográphos, *Siege of Athens*, 1826–7. One of a series of twenty-four pictures of the war of independence commissioned by Makriyánnis and first exhibited in 1839

22. The Battle of Navarino, 20 October 1827

23. Iannis Kapodhístrias, first President of Greece

24. The assassination of Kapodhístrias in Navplion, 9 October 1831

to be in command of this prestigious fortress? The natural choice would have been the commander of the local forces in Athens, but on the day of the surrender one of the Greek cannon, being fired off to celebrate the success, exploded as he was ramming it down and killed him. In his place his brother was designated commander of the Akropolis by the representatives of the surrounding villages but was rejected by the Aríos Págos, which regarded the appointment as a usurpation of its own powers. Eventually, at the end of September, a conference was held in Athens of the leading citizens of all the major centres of East Roumeli: Athens, Livadhiá, Thebes, Sálona, Atalánti and the island of Évvia. These delegates assumed for themselves the control of East Roumeli, and totally rejected the authority of the Aríos Págos. Further, they appointed as commander of the Athens Akropolis the old enemy of the Aríos Págos, whom the Aríos Págos was now describing as *ethno-katáratos*, cursed by the nation: Odysseus Andhroútsos. This marked the final extinction of the influence and authority of the Aríos Págos, while Odysseus had risen to a yet higher position on the slippery pole of Greek internal politics.

On 5 July 1822 Dramali's army which had been assembled at Lamía crossed the river Sperchíos on its way south. Its objectives were to cross into the Peloponnese by the isthmus of Corinth and recapture the citadel of Corinth, the Akrokórinthos, which had been taken by the Greeks in the previous January; to relieve the Turks who were still being besieged at Navplion, though close to surrender; and finally to recapture Tripolis. If Omer Vrionis in the west could cross the Gulf of Corinth and reinforce the Turks in Patras, and the Turkish fleet could support both operations, the Greek insurrection would be crushed.

Dramali commanded the largest force seen in Greece since 1715, when the Turks had finally driven out the Venetians. Estimates of the number of Dramali's troops varied widely, as usual, but probably amounted to about 20,000 fighting men, a massive force to crush a few thousand guerrilla fighters: even at Waterloo Wellington and Napoleon had each commanded only 70,000 men. Cavalry made up a large proportion of Dramali's army: estimates vary between one-third and two-thirds. The fighting men were accompanied by a small train of artillery (six six-pounder brass guns), several thousand camp followers and a huge train of pack animals: 30,000 mules and horses and camels. How was this multitude to be fed and watered? Some of the necessary provisions would be carried by the pack animals, but they too (except perhaps the camels) would need fodder and water, as would the cavalry horses, and then there were the human needs to satisfy. It was clear from the start that Dramali's campaign would have to be short, sharp and effective, and that even so his army would largely have to live off the land. There was a further constraint on Dramali. His army was composed of contingents under seven different pashas, most from the north like Dramali himself and only one, Ali, a former bey of Árgos, with experience of the territory they were about to invade. This led to disruptive disagreement about tactics.

Initially all went well for Dramali. Within a week of crossing the Sperchíos he had taken and burnt Thebes, sixty-five miles to the south. Odysseus Andhroútsos put up no resistance, which he later justified by saying, 'I had not 4000 men under my command, not 400 good soldiers, and not forty to whose courage I would trust my life,'[9] which says little for Odysseus' ability to inspire loyalty in his troops. The members of the Aríos Págos, the now discredited local government of the region, fled first to Sálamis and then for greater safety to a village in the far north of Évvia. Dramali's incursion might have been halted at the narrow neck of the isthmus of Corinth, but the Greek force there of a thousand men retreated, claiming in justification that the Turkish army was four times its actual size. The Greek garrison of a mere 300 in the Akrokórinthos, on its towering crag south of the town, abandoned their position before Dramali reached it. Within ten days, and without a single battle, Dramali was well on the way to fulfilling his mission.

His next objectives were to occupy Árgos and to relieve the Turks besieged in Navplion. The Navplion Turks had held out since the beginning of the revolution, but by June 1822 their provisions were exhausted. A capitulation agreement of the standard form was signed, allowing the Turks to leave by sea once they had surrendered the fortress and most of their property. Hostages were exchanged to guarantee observance. However, the actual surrender of the fortress and the departure of the Turks was delayed. The national government sent in clerks to make an inventory of the property to be surrendered. Individual Greeks made bargains with the Turks, obtaining their valuables for cash or by offering help with safe conduct. The Turks found they could now buy provisions from the Greeks, and once they learnt that Dramali was on the way were anxious to spin out negotiations until his arrival. The prospect of sharing in the booty of Navplion drew Peloponnesian bands, many from the Mani, to nearby Árgos, where terror and confusion now reigned.

Árgos was the current seat of the national government, which had moved there from Corinth in the previous month. Nearly all its members now fled, leaving on Greek ships which were waiting in the bay near Navplion to take away the surrendered Turks. Their flight was seen as cowardice in the face of the enemy, and the standing of this first national government never recovered from it. The civilian population, some of them survivors of the catastrophes at Chios and elsewhere, tried to escape by the same means as the government, and were robbed as they fled by the troops from the Mani who, said Gordon caustically, 'would have reputed it a disgrace to have gone back to their mountains as poor as they left them'.[10] Even aboard ship the refugees were not safe, and lost the last of their possessions to the Greek boatmen. Meanwhile a contingent of Turkish cavalry galloped through to Navplion, assured the Turks there that help was at hand, and returned without meeting any opposition.

While Dramali established himself in the fortress of Akrokórinthos which he had secured so easily, the Greeks started to take steps to counter his lightning incursion. First, they burnt the crops in the path of his advance, including the stores of grain. If the garrisons of citadels could be brought to their knees by starvation, so too perhaps could an army in the field. Second, they occupied the citadel of Árgos, which like its sister fortress the Akrokórinthos crowns a steep hill just outside its town, and which had not previously been occupied by either side. The initial Árgos garrison was only a handful of men, but their numbers were soon increased to about 700 by the arrival of a body of troops under Dhimítrios Ipsilántis, who had refused to flee with the other members of the national government and gained great credit for undertaking this dangerous duty. Third, Kolokotrónis was appointed commander of the forces resisting Dramali, an appointment made by the Peloponnesian Senate now that the national government had left the scene and abandoned its responsibilities.

Dramali, having reached Corinth and occupied its citadel so easily, was now faced with a choice. This was debated at a council of war which was joined by Yussuf Pasha, the Turkish commander at Patras which was no longer under immediate threat. Yussuf and the other pasha with local knowledge, Ali of Árgos, proposed that, provided the Akrokórinthos was strongly garrisoned to protect their rear, the army should be split into three sections, one to press on towards Tripolis, a second to occupy the region around Kalávrita halfway along the Gulf of Corinth, and a third to move to Patras at its far west end. Thus the Turks would be marching on the Peloponnese on a far broader front, would force the Greeks to divide their much smaller forces, and crucially would have a far better chance of finding provisions. The proposal was a reasonable one, though any advance south from Kalávrita would have been through the perilous mountains of the northern Peloponnese. However, though Yussuf and Ali of Árgos were supported by some of the other commanders, they were overruled by Dramali, who was determined to lead the whole army to Tripolis, unwilling it seems to give up the chance to become the sole hero of the subjection of the Peloponnese.

While the Turks' problem was how to deploy their strength, Kolokotrónis' was how to remedy his weakness. First he had to assemble his forces, and by his own account: 'I went to the Senate and said, "As many among you as have any acquaintance with letters, let them come hither." Then we sat down and wrote all through the night and sent to every district to gather men together as quickly as possible.'[11] His calls were heeded, and before long his own band of 2,000 men was swelled to some seven to eight thousand. His plan was to block the Turkish advance from Árgos to Tripolis, to cut off their retreat by placing troops in the narrow passes between Árgos and the isthmus of Corinth, and thus to bottle the Turks up in the plain of Árgos. Valuable time for making these dispositions was gained by the resolute defence of the citadel of Árgos by Ipsilántis and his few hundred men, since the Turks were unwilling to leave at their back an enemy garrison in such a strong position. Ipsilántis managed to give the impression of much greater strength than he had: in Gordon's account, when the Turks sent in a summons to surrender, 'Prince Demetrius received the bearers of this proposal with apparent indifference, regaled them out of the small stock of luxuries reserved for his own table, and declared his resolution of holding out for six months.'[12] But the citadel of Árgos had no water supply, and its surrender could only be a matter of time. In the last days of July Ipsilántis profited from a diversionary attack by the Greeks to lead out a part of the garrison, and the fortress was finally abandoned on the night of 3 August. As the last defenders left, the captain of the garrison, Kariyánnis, who had been in the citadel since it was first occupied, was deep in an exhausted sleep, and woke to find the Turks already beginning to plunder the fortress. In a fine display of the panache which the Greeks call *levendía*, he seized a cooking pot, put it over his head to avoid recognition, and walked out in the guise of just another Turk with his booty.

Meanwhile Dramali's difficulties were multiplying. The army's source of meat, the live cattle which it had brought with it, was finished, more quickly than it might have been because some had been handed over to the Turks besieged in Navplion and some had been sold off to the Greeks. The grain crops had been burnt by the Greeks, and the Turkish commanders quarrelled over what scanty provisions were available; the troops were forced to rely on unripe fruit and many contracted dysentery. Water too was short as it was a particularly dry summer. There were operational as well as supply problems. The Turkish fleet, which had appeared off Hydra at the end of July and caused great alarm among the Greeks, had sailed on round the Peloponnese to Patras without giving Dramali any support. The plain south of Árgos where the Turks were now operating was an area of vineyards, ditches and intersecting water-courses, disastrous for Turkish cavalry but ideal for Greek sharpshooters. At Navplion the armistice during surrender negotiations had ended, and the Greeks were once again besieging the Turkish garrison, so Dramali could have no hope of capturing the town quickly. Kolokotrónis' forces blocked the way to Tripolis. The only course for Dramali was to lead his army back to Corinth.

However Dramali, with amazing lack of foresight, had failed to leave guards on the narrow passes through which his retreating army would have to move. There were basically three routes which Dramali could take, which today's roads still follow. The most direct was through the Dhervenákia, the deep ravine on the main Árgos-to-Corinth road leading to the plain beyond. A second route led in a wide loop to the west over comparatively flat country through the village of Áyios Georgios, rejoining the main route just beyond the Dhervenákia. A third route ran to the east through Áyion Óros, and this like the first led through some hazardous defiles. Kolokotrónis now made his dispositions. He himself took his stand with 1,000 men near the far end of the western route. The central and eastern routes were covered by Papaphléssas, Kolokotrónis' nephew Nikítas, and Ipsilántis, with some 3,000 men. Iatrákos, one of the captains at the previous year's siege of Tripolis, was stationed between Árgos and the passes, to fall on the Turkish rearguard and prevent the army's retreat back to the plain of Árgos.

On 5 August came the first break-out of Dramali's troops. His Albanian infantry passed to the west of the Dhervenákia, not following the western road but keeping to the mountains and avoiding the obvious paths, and they reached Corinth with the loss of only three men. But cavalry and trains of pack animals had to follow well-beaten roads not mountain tracks, and on the following day Dramali sent his advance party forward through the Dhervenákia. The Greeks under Nikítas and Ipsilántis had slowed their passage by felling trees and heaping up stones, and waited till the Turkish column was well inside the defile before opening fire from the rocks above with devastating effect. Hand-to-hand fighting followed, in which Nikítas took the lead, and it was from his exploits on that day that he earned the name of 'Tourkóphagos' or Turk-eater. Some of the Turks got through after abandoning their mounts, some retreated towards Árgos, but the ravine was left strewn with abandoned weapons, dead horses and human corpses. Dramali himself had not yet moved, but two days later on 8 August he led the remainder of his army northwards along the eastern route. When they were caught there by the forces of Papaphléssas, Nikítas and Ipsilántis, the slaughter in the Dhervenákia was repeated at Áyion Óros. Dramali himself got through protected by his bodyguard. He was jeered and hooted at by the Greeks, who recognised him, and lost his sword and his turban. The destruction of the Turkish army would have been even greater if Iatrákos had followed orders and attacked from the rear, but he failed to do so. 'So much for Iatrákos,' is the mild English translation of Kolokotrónis' comment in his memoirs, but the deleted expletive in the Greek original was doubtless much stronger.

The booty seized by the Greeks was immense. Gordon estimated that they had gained possession of all the Turkish army's valuables and baggage, 400 cavalry horses, 1,300 pack-animals and most of the 700 camels, and he went on to comment: 'The captors afterwards sold camels at half-a-crown a head, and fine steeds at the price of a few shillings, and for a month the towns of the Morea resembled auction marts, rich dresses and arms being hawked about the streets from morning till night.'[13] Gordon also reckoned that the Turks lost some 2,000 dead in the actions on 6 and 8 August, while the Greeks claimed that only forty-seven of their men were killed or wounded. The estimated imbalance may, for once, be accurate; encumbered horsemen trapped in a narrow pass stand little chance against plunging fire from sharpshooters hidden in the rocks above.

While the depleted army of Dramali, defeated, demoralised and disease-ridden, settled in Corinth for the winter, the aftermath of the disaster at the Dhervenákia brought further setbacks for the Turks. The western Turkish army under Omer Vrionis advanced through West Roumeli to the outskirts of Mesolongi, but was unable to achieve anything and withdrew. Khurshid, the overall commander of Turkish forces north of the Gulf of Corinth, confronted with the failure of both arms of his attack on the Peloponnese, committed suicide by poison. Dramali died of fever at Corinth before the end of the year. Thus, with the death of Kara Ali off Chios in the previous summer, the Sultan had lost three of his most senior commanders in the space of six months. At Navplion the Turks in the twin fortresses of Palamídhi and Akronavplion continued to hold out, but by early December they were starving. Turks coming down from Palamídhi in search of food were too weak to go up again, a predicament which anyone who has climbed Palamídhi's precipitous pathway will appreciate. On 12 December, appropriately the feast day of Andréas, patron saint of the Peloponnese, the Greeks entered Palamídhi unopposed and a few days later the Turks in Akronavplion surrendered on terms. On this occasion the terms were honoured, largely thanks to Captain Hamilton of the English frigate *Cambrian*, who insisted on their observance and himself took on board 400 Turks. Sixty-seven of these died on the voyage but the rest were safely landed at Smyrna. Thus the Greeks took control of Navplion, which was to become the first capital of independent Greece.

The architect of the Greeks' signal victory against Dramali was without doubt Kolokotrónis. One of the keys to Greek success was the denial of provisions to the Turkish army by a ruthless scorched-earth policy, initiated by others but vigorously pursued by Kolokotrónis once he arrived on the scene. It was thanks to him that the Greeks assembled in sufficient numbers to confront the Turkish army. It was he who saw the importance of first blocking Dramali's advance from Árgos to Tripolis, whose possession he consistently believed was vital to the revolution's success, and then at the crucial moment switching his forces to the passes north of Árgos in order to cut off Dramali's retreat. No wonder that, in Gordon's words, 'his name became a sort of talisman, the people every where sung ballads in his honour, his political adversaries humbled themselves before him, and for some months he was absolute in the Morea'.[14] It is appropriate that today a heroic statue of him should stand on the slopes above the Dhervenákia, gazing northwards across the plains towards Corinth over which Dramali's shattered army withdrew. On the plinth of the statue is a verse which bleakly recognises that the reality of war is not heroism and glory but corpses on a barren hillside:

> Here lie the beys from Roumeli and agas from the Morea;
> Their headless bodies sleep above the pass of Dhervenákia.
> Black earth now makes a bed for them, the stones provide their mattress,
> And snow and ice, when winter comes, are all they have for blanket.

18

The Greeks Divided

The year 1822 had brought success for the Greeks, mainly in the Peloponnese, but failures elsewhere. They had suffered a terrible defeat at Péta, and at sea the destruction of Kara Ali's flagship had come too late to save the island of Chios from devastation. However they had captured Athens and Navplion, and Kolokotrónis after early setbacks had won a great victory at Dhervenákia. But Kolokotrónis' success had raised again the crucial question: should the military be under the control of the civilian government?

The provisional Greek government established at Epídhavros had been intended to last only for a year, until the end of 1822, when local elections were to be held for members of a new assembly. This assembly would revise the constitution and set up a new government. It is no surprise, given the ravaged condition of much of Greece, that these elections were not completed in time, and that the second national assembly was not ready to meet until early April 1823. It is a credit to the Greeks that they held elections at all, which are commonly suspended by nations at war. Nor is it surprising that the electoral rules were not always observed. Officially the members of the new assembly were to be chosen in secret ballot by the whole male adult population. In practice some delegates were elected by acclamation rather than by secret ballot, some were chosen only by the soldiers rather than the whole population, some simply appointed themselves, and some districts sent two delegates representing different parties. Members of the outgoing Senate were also entitled to attend. As a result the numbers at the second national assembly were vastly increased, to some 260 compared with the 59 at Epídhavros. Representatives came from as far away as Crete in the far south and Tríkeri near Vólos in the north. The largest regional group were the 113 from the Peloponnese, nearly half the total. Forty-six members attended as military captains, who had not been represented at all at Epídhavros a year earlier, but had by now realised that the government exercised significant power and that they must have a voice in it. At this second assembly, said Trikoúpis, everything was irregular, disorderly and alarming, and it was as rowdy as the first was tranquil.[1]

There had been debate about where the new assembly was to be held. Navplion was an obvious choice, but since its surrender to Kolokotrónis in the previous December it had been under the control of his son Yennéos, who refused the government entry on the ground that its mandate had now expired. The assembly was therefore held near Ástros, about twenty miles by road south of Navplion on the east coast of the Peloponnese.

Here the delegates assembled on 10 April 1823 but as two distinct bodies rather than one. The larger element, broadly the supporters of the politicians grouped round Mavrokordhátos, occupied a village near Ástros, while the backers of the military, headed by Kolokotrónis, took up position in an adjacent village, the two being separated by a deep ditch. Both camps contained armed men: 800 on the military side and three times as many with the politicians. The conflicting objectives of the two groups were obvious: the politicians wanted to control the military, while the role of the politicians, in Kolokotrónis' view, was simply to provide the military with supplies. However the membership of the groups had become far less clear-cut than before. Some of the politicians, notably Dhimítrios Ipsilántis, had allied themselves with the military, while a number of captains had joined the politicians. Some of these captains were from West Roumeli, where they were under the influence of Mavrokordhátos, others were from the Peloponnese, including Iatrákos who was obviously out of favour in the military camp after failing Kolokotrónis at the battle of Dhervenákia. But for the revolution to survive the two groups needed each other: the military depended upon the politicians' skills, especially on the international scene, while the politicians were nothing without the captains. Thus the dispositions in the twin villages outside Ástros exactly mirrored the aims and needs of the two sides: they had to stick together, partly for mutual support and partly from mutual suspicion, but between the two was a deep rift.

The main deliberations of the assembly took place on the more numerous and politically sophisticated side of the divide. President of the assembly was Pétrobey Mavromichális of the Mani, the position held at Epídhavros by Mavrokordhátos, but Mavrokordhátos now had the less prominent but more influential post of president of the committee overseeing the revision of the Epídhavros constitution. This committee declared first that the fundamental principles of the constitution should be retained unchanged, since 'they had demonstrably saved the people', though the people had in fact been saved by the captains and principally by Kolokotrónis. The principles of the constitution were therefore not altered but a number of changes were made to it, most of which looked like minor adjustments but which in fact had far-reaching implications. First, it was decided that the members of the Executive should be chosen by the Senate, not as before by the members of the constitutional assembly, and that the Executive could no longer veto, but only delay, acts of the Senate. Both moves strengthened the Senate against the Executive. Second, responsibility for foreign affairs was transferred from a minister, hitherto Négris of East Roumeli, to the Executive as a whole; relations with other countries were becoming far too important to be left in the hands of one man. Similarly, in a third change, the war minister, previously Koléttis, was replaced by a three-man committee, like the three-man committee controlling the navy, and in a transparent move to rein in Kolokotrónis the position of commander-in-chief was eliminated. Fourth, the regional governments of East and West Roumeli and the Peloponnese were abolished, thus cutting the Gordian knot of their tangled relationships with the central government.

As well as revising the constitution, the assembly at Ástros passed two resolutions which were highly contentious. First, the whole of insurgent Greece including the Aegean islands was divided into sixty districts, each under the control of an official directly appointed by the central government. The alternative was to let the country become a mere patchwork of fiefdoms under virtually independent captains and primates, or in Gordon's words 'to subject Greece to more than thirty companies of robbers, who would have been constantly fighting with each other'.[2] However this proposal was flatly rejected by the islanders of Hydra and Spétses as giving them less autonomy than they had enjoyed under the Turks. Second, there was a proposal to raise money for the war by selling off the so-called national property, the *éthnika ktímata*, that is the property previously owned by departed Turks. What exactly did 'property' mean? Many suspected that it included not only the vacated buildings but also the land on which they stood. Disposal of this land was regarded as a sale of the people's birthright, probably at knock-down prices due to favouritism, and a mechanism for the already rich to enrich themselves still further by selling at a profit later. There was a further reason for not selling the national lands: they were going to be needed as collateral, of a rather artificial sort, for the loans raised abroad. To show their displeasure at the scheme the troops in the military camp wrote 'Land sell-off' on a piece of card and used it for target practice. In the face of this opposition the proposal was withdrawn.

The next step was for the Senate to elect holders to the new offices. The presidency of the Senate itself went, in a surprise move, to Iánnis Orlándos, a primate of little personal repute, brother-in-law of the leading primate of Hydra, Georgios Kondouriótis, and therefore seen as representing Hydra's interests. This enraged the representatives of Spétses and Psará, and Orlándos' presidency of the Senate lasted only a few weeks. In making appointments to the Executive, the Senate tried to placate Kolokotrónis and exert some indirect control over him by giving office to his friends. Thus the Executive was made up of Pétrobey Mavromichális as president, and three further members: Andréas Zaímis and Charalámvis, both primates with a military following from the northern Peloponnese but from rival factions, and Metaxás of Kephaloniá, who had brought a contingent of Ionian islanders to join the revolution. These three were all firm allies of Kolokotrónis, and Pétrobey was broadly sympathetic to him. The fifth member of the Executive was to be chosen by the islanders. These appointments clearly reflected the dominance of the Peloponnese, the growing influence of the islands and the virtual exclusion of East and West Roumeli.

There was no post in the new government for two important figures from the previous administration: Négris and Dhimítrios Ipsilántis. Mavrokordhátos was appointed to a position of no great prominence but of potentially great influence: general secretary of the Executive. As such he was charged with processing and presenting to the Executive the foreign affairs issues which were now its responsibility. Mavrokordhátos could probably foresee more clearly than anyone that Greek success would depend upon these issues: on foreign diplomatic support, on foreign loans and ultimately on foreign intervention.

Its work completed, the assembly at Ástros dispersed and the new government, both Senate and Executive, moved to Tripolis, which was now clear of the plague that had followed the Greek capture of the town eighteen months earlier. But the shakiness of the government's foundations quickly became apparent. Those disappointed of office or influence, led by the infuriated Négris and supported by Kolokotrónis, who was not appeased by the appointment of his friends to the Executive, moved to Karítena, some twenty miles west of Tripolis, where Kolokotrónis' influence had always been strong. There they declared their intention of holding a new assembly. The only way left for the Senate to bring Kolokotrónis under its control was to persuade him to become a member of the Executive himself, and thus the Senate at the beginning of June offered him the vacant Executive position, which had initially been reserved for the islands, coupled with the Executive vice-presidency. The offer was couched in extraordinary terms:

> If you do not accept this offer which the people and the government are making, and if you do not instruct your supporters to cease all action against the government, then the two government bodies will be in the unpleasant position of denouncing you and your fellows as rebels and pursuing you as defectors and enemies of the people; and if in the ensuing struggle you are victorious (which we cannot believe possible) . . . then the Greeks of Roumeli and the islands will be compelled to make an honourable peace with the Turks, which they desire and have offered us . . . and then you in the Peloponnese can have rebellion and licence and anarchy and anything else you like.[3]

Kolokotrónis accepted and the Senate, with an olive branch in one hand and a cudgel in the other, had asserted its authority.

A month later in July another dispute arose which revealed the differences not only between the government and its opponents but also between the government's two bodies, the Senate and the Executive. In the face of widespread opposition to his appointment Orlándos resigned as president of the Senate. Who was to succeed him? Anagnóstis Dheliyánnis put himself forward, a member of the powerful Dheliyánnis clan from Karítena and supporter of Kolokotrónis. To keep him out the Senate almost unanimously elected Mavrokordhátos as its president, even though he was currently general secretary of the Executive. Mavrokordhátos, under pressure from the Senate, initially accepted, but within days he resigned from the post in a long letter explaining the dissension his appointment would cause, and withdrew as he had done before to Hydra. However, the Senate refused to accept his resignation, though it was repeatedly offered, until August of the following year, and throughout that time Mavrokordhátos was regularly referred to as the president of the Senate even in his absence. But there was no avoiding the breach which his resignation was designed to heal: the Kolokotrónis–Dheliyánnis faction was angry at the defeat of its candidate, and the Executive regarded the Senate's choice of Mavrokordhátos as an attempt to poach one of its key officers. Probably the only thing that would have prevented these rifts widening further would have been the need for unity against a major Turkish attack, but for a number of reasons this failed to materialise during the campaigning season of 1823.

The final phase of Dramali's expedition completed this Turkish disaster. As we have seen, the remnant of his army had withdrawn in the autumn of 1822 to the citadel of Corinth, where before the end of the year Dramali himself died. Navplion had by now fallen to the Greeks and the only hope for the Turks in Corinth was to escape west to their fellow countrymen in Patras. Thus at the end of January a garrison of 800 was left to hold the Corinth citadel, 1,000 sick and wounded were sent by sea along the Gulf of Corinth to Patras, and the remaining 3,500 set off for Patras along the gulf's southern shore. With half their journey completed, at the point where the road narrows at Akráta to bridge a river, they found themselves trapped by Greek forces in front and behind. Yussuf Pasha sent ships from Patras to rescue them, but a storm wrecked the attempt. The Turks held out for six weeks, eating first their horses and then, it is said, the bodies of their dead comrades. Finally in mid-March a second flotilla from Patras, accompanied by three European ships, succeeded in reaching the trapped remnant of

Dramali's army. The surviving 2,000, 'more resembling blackened skeletons than men', said Gordon, reached Patras, where they died at the rate of twenty a day.

In early 1823 therefore the Turkish forces were back to where they had started a year earlier. Nevertheless, the Sultan persisted in a similar plan of campaign for 1823: to march troops down from the north to subdue the Peloponnese. This time, however, the main army was to cross into the Peloponnese not by the isthmus of Corinth but by the narrow stretch of water near Patras, thus exploiting the one major Turkish stronghold in the northern Peloponnese. Meanwhile separate forces were to crush the revolt in East Roumeli, both operations to be supported by the Turkish fleet.

This main army was assembled at Ohrid, in the south-west corner of modern Yugoslavia, by Mustafa Pasha, governor of Shkoder in northern Albania. His troops were Albanian mercenaries and said to number about 10,000. In July they moved south, and to avoid the dangers of the Makrinóros on the west coast moved first to Tríkala, halfway between the two coasts, and then westwards across the Píndos mountains to Karpenísi, which at 3,000 feet is the highest provincial capital in Greece. Here they met their first opposition. Márkos Bótsaris, leader of the Souliot contingent at Péta the year before, had survived that battle and had remained with Mavrokordhátos at Mesolongi. Bótsaris now moved out against Mustafa's army with 350 men under his own command, but on the way from Mesolongi to Karpenísi persuaded other captains to join him, making a total force of 1,200. This was still far too small for any pitched battle with Mustafa's 10,000, but Bótsaris persuaded his fellow captains to make a surprise night attack. As men of Bótsaris' force were Albanian-speakers like their opponents and were dressed similarly, a reconnoitring party from Bótsaris' camp was able to enter the enemy lines two nights before the planned assault and spy out their dispositions undetected. On 21 August the attack was launched in the middle of the night, and Bótsaris' men at first created total panic and confusion among the enemy, though his fellow captains largely failed to support him. Bótsaris continued leading his troops in spite of a wound in the groin, but when he incautiously raised his head above one of the enemy's defensive walls a single shot killed him. His companions concealed his death, and his men continued fighting till dawn, and they then retreated. They had not halted Mustafa's advance, but they took away a rich haul of booty: nearly 700 pistols, a thousand muskets and many horses, mules and sheep. In Finlay's description: 'Horsehair sacks filled with silver-mounted pistols, yataghans [curved swords], and cartridge-cases, were fastened over pack-saddles like bags of meal, and long Albanian muskets were tied up in bundles like fagots of firewood.'⁴ The body of Márkos Bótsaris was taken back to Mesolongi for a magnificent funeral, and his name has ever after been revered as a patriot whose loyalty was never in doubt, and as a heroic commander who died in battle at the head of his men.

A surprising aspect of the battle of Karpenísi was that it was fought solely between Albanians. No Greek or Turk took part in it, and in fact very few Turks fought in the whole land campaign of 1823. That the Sultan now had to rely almost wholly on Albanian mercenaries against the revolt in Greece points to one of his major difficulties: manpower. The campaign in Greece was not the only call on the Sultan's army. Relations with Russia were still uneasy, and Turkish forces had to be maintained on the Russian borders in case of an attack from that quarter. Also the Sultan was at war with Persia from October 1820 until July 1823, so the Persian war ended too late to release men for that year's Greek campaign. The Sultan's manpower problem was further exacerbated in early March 1823 by a massive fire in the capital's military complex at Tophana on the Asiatic side of the Bosphorus. This destroyed the arsenal with its store of ammunition and the cannon foundry containing artillery for the army and navy, as well as fifty mosques and thousands of houses. Without military supplies, the still unruly janissaries could not leave the capital, and popular rumour held them responsible for the fire.

It is therefore not surprising that the Sultan, with his own troops stretched, insubordinate or immobilised, turned increasingly to the use of mercenaries, but this brought its own problems. Whereas regular troops could be kept in the field for some time on reduced pay or no pay at all, mercenaries generally had to be paid promptly and in full or they left. The solution was to debase the Ottoman coinage by progressively reducing its precious metal content, with the result that in a few years of the early 1820s the Turkish piastre lost over half its international value. Thus the Sultan's difficulties in mounting a campaign against the

Greeks in 1823 were compounded of demoralisation after the failures of 1822; the distractions of the Russian threat and the Persian war; the fire at Tophana, due to accident or arson; reliance on mercenaries; financial difficulties and a debased coinage; and as in previous years the dissension between Ottoman commanders who temporarily joined forces as independent pashas and never easily accepted the commands of one of their number or co-operated with each other.

Nevertheless a Turkish fleet, as well as land forces, was made ready in early 1823 under a new kapitan pasha, Khosref. For operations against the Greeks the Turks had now stopped using line-of-battle ships, which were impressive but unwieldy, and highly vulnerable to attack by fireships. So when Khosref sailed out of the Dardanelles at the end of May 1823 his fleet was made up of smaller ships: fifteen frigates, thirteen corvettes, twelve brigs and forty transports, supported by a squadron from Algiers.

The fleet first sailed to Évvia, without hindrance from the Greeks, and disembarked troops to reinforce the Turks in the stronghold of Káristos. It then sailed on round the Peloponnese, supplying the fortresses of Methóni and Koróni, and towards the end of June reached Patras, where it stayed for two months, achieving little. Khosref landed some troops in an attempt to take Mesolongi, but they succeeded only in burning two coastal villages before they were driven back. Khosref also tried to send provisions by sea to the garrison still holding out in the citadel of Corinth, but the citadel is a good three miles from the shore and as soon as the stores were landed a Greek band of 2,000 came down from the neighbouring hills where they had been lying in wait, drove off the Turks and seized the supplies. Starvation finally led the garrison of the Corinth citadel to surrender to the Greeks in the following November.

Gordon described Khosref as 'an old lame man, addicted to pleasure', and believed that he had little interest in naval or military success: 'The business he really applied himself to was the sale of permissions to Austrian, Maltese, and Ionian vessels to enter the gulf and trade with the insurgents, who exchanged their currants for arms and ammunition.'[5] Leaving Patras at the end of August, Khosref's fleet spent the rest of the year patrolling the Aegean, without opposition until a combined Greek squadron of forty armed ships and six fireships put to sea under

Miaoúlis of Hydra. The Greeks were unable to exploit their fireships; to this extent the new Turkish naval policy of using smaller vessels was effective. The Greeks' major success came at the end of October, when Miaoúlis' fleet captured a particularly elegant twenty-eight-gun corvette, bought in England, and four brigs. Thus when Khosref sailed back into Constantinople in early December he had this loss to report and to balance it the capture of only a few small Greek ships and virtually no useful contribution to the year's campaign.

After the death of Márkos Bótsaris at Karpenísi the Souliot bands, now numbering some 2,000 men, made another attempt to hold up Mustafa's army a few miles further on in the ravines of Mount Kaliakoúdha, but without success. The Turks pushed on to Agrínion, where they were joined by an army under Omer Vrionis, and in mid-October the combined force moved towards Mesolongi. The Turkish commanders decided that they must first capture the islet of Anatolikó, modern Etolikó, in Mesolongi's lagoon. The Turks mounted a large battery to bombard it but the Greeks held out, and at the end of November after six weeks of unavailing siege the Turkish armies again withdrew, Mustafa to his base in faraway Shkoder. Within days of the Ottoman withdrawal Mavrokordhátos returned to Mesolongi as once again governor-general of West Roumeli, and was ready to receive Byron.

In East Roumeli the Turks' campaign of 1823 had done no more than their other efforts to take the war to the heart of the rebellion in the Peloponnese. They strengthened their hold on Évvia and on some of the major towns of the region – Salóna, Aráchova near Delphi, Livadhiá and Thebes – but made no serious attempt on Athens. Resistance from Odysseus Andhroútsos, combined with memories of Dramali's fate, deterred them from any attempt to cross the isthmus of Corinth. Thus in the course of 1823 not a single additional soldier from the Ottoman army entered the Peloponnese, and the opposing Greek factions there were left undisturbed to pursue their self-destructive rivalry.

From the summer of 1823 until the end of the year the broad division among the Greeks was between those who supported the Executive and those who backed the Senate. Support for the Executive meant in effect support for Kolokotrónis, who had joined it under duress in June. Of the other four members of the Executive, two – Charalámvis and

Metaxás – sided with Kolokotrónis; its president Pétrobey Mavromichális was regarded as a supine figurehead, and only Andréas Zaímis opposed his Executive colleagues. Kolokotrónis was backed by a number of powerful Peloponnesian clans. Ranged against the Kolokotrónis faction and broadly supporting the Senate were Andréas Zaímis, Executive member and primate of Kalávrita, and his ally Andréas Lóndos, primate of nearby Éyio, the pair being often referred to as the two Andréases. Gordon gives contrasting portraits of them.

> Zaimis was endowed with political talents, gravity of manners, sound sense, and brilliant eloquence; he was upright in his dealings, kind and generous to his inferiors, beloved by the people of his province, and respected by all men, because he respected himself: his faults were pride, ambition, and timidity in the field. Londos possessed abundance of courage, but he was drunken, debauched, rapacious, and oppressive. There was the same contrast in their personal appearance, the first being tall and handsome, the second dwarfish, and almost deformed.[6]

Also supporting the Senate were Mavrokordhátos, the islanders (especially those from Hydra), and a number of the captains. Other splits cut across this broad division between Executive and Senate. The Executive itself was divided, and so was the Senate, eleven of its members ultimately aligning themselves with the opposition to it. There was antipathy between regions, especially between the Peloponnese and the islands, and divisions within regions, notably between the Peloponnesian leaders. There were also the shifting allegiances and disputes between individuals and families. In short, it was as if the mirror of the Greek body politic was now not merely cracked but splintered and about to disintegrate.

This disintegration is demonstrated by the moves from place to place by the two branches of the government during 1823. After the assembly at Ástros in April both branches moved to Tripolis, and in August to Sálamis. However in October they split, the Senate remaining at Sálamis while the Executive moved to Navplion, where it was under the wing of Kolokotrónis since Navplion was still garrisoned by his forces. In November the Senate moved away from Sálamis and closer to its supporters in the naval islands, going first to Árgos and then to Kranídhi, which is within twenty miles of both Hydra and Spétses. But Kranídhi is also only twenty-five miles from Navplion. Thus by the end of the year the Senate and the Executive, having for some time circled each other like fighters in a ring, had taken up positions for confrontation.

A string of incidents had brought this confrontation closer. Kolokotrónis had joined the Executive in June only under threats from the Senate, and from the start had acted as member and vice-president simply for the advantages it might bring him. He made no secret of this. 'Cease singing,' he told his Executive colleagues, 'and my dance ceases.'[7] 'Dancing' here is co-operating and 'singing' is offering inducements. As time went on the inducements for Kolokotrónis to co-operate with the Executive became less. His position on the Executive had not strengthened his hand as a military leader and if anything had weakened it. The soldiers and the common people were coming to regard him less as a great general, the hero of Dhervenákia, and more as just another politician. At the end of October 1823 Kolokotrónis resigned from the Executive. He was thus no longer the puppet of the Senate, and was free to follow his original line of opposing it.

Further disputes between the Senate and the Executive arose over the legality of each other's actions. Iánnis Peroúkas the finance minister, who was answerable to the Executive, imposed a government monopoly on salt. Every family in the land needed salt and would be hurt by a price rise imposed by a monopolistic government. The measure was one of those tax-raising schemes which governments have so often blithely introduced without reckoning on the resultant outcry. The minister had acted without Senate approval, which the law required, and on this ground the Senate dismissed him. But could the Senate legally do so? The Executive pointed out that a Senate vote needed a quorum of two-thirds, that is forty-seven of its seventy members; but eleven members had defected to the Executive side and another score had simply departed, so that only forty or so senators were present at votes. However this argument could be used by the Senate too. The Executive also needed a quorum of three of its five members, and with absences for various reasons was often reduced to two.

Matters came to a head at the end of the year. On 7 December the Senate dismissed from their posts both the erring finance minister and one of the Executive's members, Kolokotrónis' supporter Metaxás, saying it was his absence which had left the Executive without a quorum and so inoperative. In place of Metaxás the Senate appointed its own man, Koléttis. This provoked Kolokotrónis' supporters to action, and on the following day 200 troops from Navplion under its garrison commander Pános Kolokotrónis burst into the Senate while it was in session in Árgos, seized the Senate's records and dispersed the senators with threats and blows, later ransacking their houses. Pános Kolokotrónis failed however in his main object, which was to arrest the senators and carry them off bodily to Navplion. Instead the senators escaped to Kranídhi, where they could rely on the protection of Hydra and Spétses.

In Kranídhi the Senate dismissed its two remaining opponents on the Executive, Pétrobey Mavromichális and Charalámvis, and accepted the resignation of the pro-Senate Andréas Zaímis. The way was now clear for the Senate to appoint an Executive of its own persuasion: the new president was Georgios Koundouriótis of Hydra, vice-president was Panayiótis Botásis of Spétses, and of the other three members one was a supporter of Koundouriótis, one was a member of the Lóndos clan representing the Peloponnese, and the other was Koléttis, already appointed. Mavrokordhátos held no office, but played a crucial role in the background. According to Howe, Koundouriótis said to Mavrokordhátos, ' "Mavrokordhátos, you know I am ignorant of politics: how can I serve if I accept?" "Never mind – never mind," replied the shrewd manager, "you shall be the ship, and I will be the rudder." '[8]

The Senate now called for new elections to replace those senators who had defected to the other side or who had left for other reasons. Meanwhile in Navplion the members of the old Executive refused to accept their dismissal, and the senators who had joined them also called for new elections to replace their rivals in Kranídhi. At the end of January the old ousted Executive and the senators who supported it moved from Navplion to Tripolis, leaving Navplion still in the hands of Pános Kolokotrónis. Thus at the beginning of 1824 Greece had two governments. One was at Kranídhi, consisting of most of the senators and the new Executive which it had appointed. The other at Tripolis comprised the old Executive and the few senators who supported it, and had the military backing of Kolokotrónis. Both bodies claimed legality, and each tried to outmanoeuvre the other. Both of course were also keen to secure for themselves the proceeds of the long-hoped-for English loan, and the support of the newly arrived Lord Byron.

19

Byron's Road to Greece

Byron had not been in Greece since his travels there in 1809–10 with John Cam Hobhouse, but he had altogether pleasant memories of the country, the only place, he said, that he was ever contented in. He had been deeply impressed by his visit to Ali Pasha at his stronghold in Tepelene. He had been enraptured by the view of the Parthenon and other monuments of antiquity from his Athens lodgings. He had enjoyed a light-hearted amorous interlude, probably more mock than serious, with his first Athenian landlady's young daughter Theresa Mákri ('Maid of Athens, ere we part, Give, oh give me back my heart'). 'I like the Greeks,' he wrote, 'some are brave, and all are beautiful.'[1] He had formed a particularly high opinion of the Souliots, who had rescued and entertained him after a shipwreck near Párga, and who were invested, when the incident was related in *Childe Harold*, with all the romance of rugged and good-hearted banditry. Byron's affection for the Souliots was to cause him a lot of trouble when he finally returned to Greece.

The years 1810 to 1816 saw the dazzling rise and fall of Byron's star: wealth and fame from the publication of his verse, starting with the first two cantos of *Childe Harold* in 1812; scandal in the same year from his brazen affair with Lady Caroline Lamb, wife of the future prime minister Lord Melbourne; the even more scandalous matter of his alleged incestuous relationship with his half-sister Augusta; his marriage to Annabella Milbanke, and its failure after the birth of a daughter Ada; dissipation and debt; and his departure from England for good. He lived first in Switzerland and then in Italy, with the Shelleys as his constant companions: Shelley himself, his wife Mary, and Mary's stepsister Claire Clairmont, who had met and declared her passion for Byron while they were still in London. Towards the end of 1816 Byron left Pisa and the Shelleys for Venice, where he arrived in November, and soon afterwards rented the Palazzo Mocenigo on the Grand Canal. Claire Clairmont's daughter by him, Allegra, was born in the following January, and in May 1817 came to live with him in Venice, where Byron, poet and philanderer, was a fond but hardly an orthodox father.

At the end of 1819 he met the object of his last attachment, Teresa Guiccioli. Teresa was 19 and had been married for a year, in a marriage of convenience, to the 58-year-old Count Alessandro Guiccioli, she for the first time and he for the third. It was not long before Byron became Teresa's *cavalier servente* in a triangle of young wife, elderly complaisant husband and *cavalier* who was ostensibly the friend of both and no more than a platonic admirer and shawl-carrier for the wife. The Count's toleration of the obvious affair between his wife and Byron eventually snapped when he returned one evening to find them, as Byron put it, '*quasi* in the fact'. The Count applied to the Pope for a legal separation, which was granted on condition that Teresa lived in the house of her father Count Gamba at Filetto, about fifteen miles south-west of Ravenna. Byron was a frequent visitor to Filetto, welcomed by Count Gamba, who much preferred the poet to his elderly son-in-law, and by Teresa's younger brother Pietro.

Both Pietro and his father had been involved for some time with the Carbonari, the Italian organisations working for independence from the Austrian domination of Italy. 'I vaticinate a row in Italy,' Byron wrote, 'in which case I don't know that I won't have a finger in it. I dislike the Austrians and think the Italians infamously oppressed.'[2] Soon Byron did have a finger in it; by July he had acquired the title of *capo* of one of the local revolutionary bands, though this probably involved no more than romantic night-time meetings in the forests. But in the summer of 1820 a general rising of Italians was crushed by an Austrian army, and Byron and Teresa, with mingled irony and emotion, pronounced its epitaph. 'Alas,' she said with tears in her eyes, 'the Italians must now return to making operas.' 'I fear,' Byron commented, '*that* and maccaroni are their forte.'[3]

One result of the failure of the Carbonari rising was the break-up of the Gamba household at Filetto. In July 1821 Count Gamba and his son Pietro, known supporters of the revolution, were banished from the Romagna, the area around Ravenna and Bologna. Because Teresa's judicial separation from her husband required her to live in her father's house, she had to follow. Shelley found a house for them in Pisa, where in October Byron joined them. The following year, 1822, brought a double blow to Byron. His 5-year-old daughter by Claire Clairmont, Allegra, who had been placed in a convent at Ravenna, died there on 20 April. Teresa described how she broke the news to him: ' "I understand," said he, – "it is enough, say no more." A mortal paleness spread itself over his face . . . I began to fear for his reason; he did not shed a tear. . . . He remained immovable in the same attitude for an hour, and no consolation which I endeavoured to afford him seemed to reach his ears.'4 The second catastrophe followed three months later: Shelley was drowned when his boat was caught by a sudden storm in the Gulf of Spezzia. Byron's tribute to him was a simple one: 'Without exception, the *best* and least selfish man I ever knew.'5 The Shelley circle in Pisa no longer held together and in September Byron moved with Teresa and her father and brother to his last Italian residence, the Casa Saluzzo at Albaro, on a hill above Genoa and looking out over the harbour. Only his feelings for Teresa now kept Byron in Italy, and even his attachment to her was beginning to weaken.

During the winter of 1822–3 at Genoa Byron became increasingly restless. For some years he had been attracted by the idea of a simple but useful life in newly liberated South America, and in the summer of 1822 the project was still in his mind, but balanced by the lure of Greece: 'I had, and still have, thought of South America, but am fluctuating between it and Greece. I should have gone, long ago, to one of them, but for my liaison with the Countess G[uicciol]i; for love, in these days, is little compatible with glory.'6 Byron's interest in Greece was finally tipped over into commitment by a visit in April 1823 from two strangers to him: Edward Blaquiere and Andréas Louriótis.

Blaquiere was an Irishman of the Protestant ascendancy, of Huguenot descent. During the Napoleonic wars he had served in the Mediterranean as a British navy lieutenant, and in the following years lived in Paris, because it was cheap, earning a modest living from his books on Mediterranean countries and his journalism. At the time of the foundation of the London Greek Committee in March 1823 Blaquiere was in London, as was Andréas Louriótis, the agent of the Greek government for raising loans abroad, who at Blaquiere's suggestion had come to try the London market. On 4 March, the day after the London Greek Committee's first meeting, Blaquiere and Louriótis left for Greece to gather information for the Committee on the state of Greece and to persuade the Greek government to send representatives to London to negotiate a loan. It was while en route to Greece that they arrived in Genoa on 5 April and Blaquiere sent a note to Byron asking for a meeting. Byron replied promptly and warmly: 'Dear Sir – I shall be delighted to see you and your Greek friend – and the sooner the better. – I have been expecting you for some time – you will find me at home – I cannot express to you how much I feel interested in the cause. . . . '[9] This meeting proved decisive. Though Byron continued to harbour considerable doubts and reservations, his course was now firmly set for Greece.

Byron's doubts and reservations were of two kinds. The first was over how he could abandon Teresa, who had after all abandoned her husband for him. The matter was eventually settled by events: Teresa's father's exile from the Romagna was lifted on condition that she returned there with him (as already required by her decree of separation from her husband) and on the further condition, imposed by her husband, that Byron did not. When Byron sailed from Italy in July, the parting was marked by passionate grief from Teresa but no more than kindly concern from Byron.

Byron's other set of difficulties revolved round the question of what exactly he should do to help the Greek cause. All that he had gathered from the Blaquiere meeting was that 'Blaquiere seemed to think that I might be of some use – even *here*; – though *what* he did not exactly specify.' In mid-May he was still presuming that the London Greek Committee 'will give me some regular instructions of what they wish to be observed – reported or done – I will serve them as humbly as they please'. But all he received from the Committee was news that he had been elected a member of it, accompanied by a flattering letter. Even when on board ship bound for Greece at the end of July he was writing to John Bowring, secretary of the London Greek Committee, that 'the Committee has not favoured me with any specific instructions as to any line of conduct they might think it well for me to pursue'.[8] Byron was therefore left to use his discretion, based on what he knew of affairs in Greece.

Byron could see at once that the Greek cause would need money. 'Cash is the sinew of war,' he wrote, 'as indeed of most other things – love excepted and occasionally of that too.'[9] Within a fortnight of meeting Blaquiere he wrote to his friend and banker Douglas Kinnaird that he needed all the floating sums he could collect. Byron's letters for the rest of his time in Italy are full of instructions for raising money on his property and from his publications, and for converting it into credits on which he could draw in the Ionian islands. By the time he left Italy in July he had, as he wrote to Bowring, nearly 9,000 pounds sterling to take to Greece, but he also urged Bowring to press ahead with the plan to raise a Greek loan on the London market.

As well as assembling funds, Byron was concerned to get more detailed information about Greece. Blaquiere's letters, of which three reached Byron before he left Italy, were enthusiastic but vague. 'Your presence will operate as a talisman,' Blaquiere wrote, 'and the field is too glorious, too closely associated with all that you hold dear to be any longer abandoned. . . . The cause is in a most flourishing state.'[10] Information from expatriate Greeks in Italy and from returning phil-hellenes was sparse and unreliable. So Byron eventually decided that he must go to Greece himself, and that he must first learn more of the Greek situation from the proximity of the Ionian islands.

By 13 July 1823 Byron's preparations for departure from Genoa were complete. A ship had been chartered, the *Hercules*, a collier-built tub of 120 tons, round-bottomed and bluff-bowed, with Captain Scott in command. Byron was to sleep on board ready to sail the following morning. He remained with the distraught Teresa until five o'clock that evening and then left her in the care of Mary Shelley, now his neighbour in Genoa. Three companions joined Byron on the *Hercules*: Teresa's ardent younger brother Pietro, Byron's recently engaged personal physician Francesco Bruno, and the adventurer Edward Trelawny, who had got to know Byron the year before and who responded at once to his invitation ('My dear T. – You must have heard that I am going to Greece. Why do you not come to me? I want your aid . . . ').[11] Byron had also offered passage to a Greek returning home, Konstantínos

Skilítzis, who subsequently sent him a detailed analysis of the Greek political situation. There were eight servants on board, plus four horses, two dogs (one a huge Newfoundland) and an amazing list of stores, from the military (blunderbusses, gunpowder) to the domestic (tooth-brushes, spectacles), and from the practical (candles, speaking trumpet) to the recreational (cognac, gin and Swift's works in nineteen volumes).

The voyage of the *Hercules* began inauspiciously. On 14 July there was no wind, and the party went ashore again, Teresa fortunately for her feelings having already left. The next day they set out again, but after a day of calm the wind freshened at night, the horses kicked down their partitions, and the ship had to return yet again to Genoa for repairs. On 16 July they finally departed and after five days of slow progress reached Livorno, a mere 100 miles to the south. There they took on board James Hamilton Browne, a young Scot who had been dismissed from his post in the Ionian government by Sir Thomas Maitland for his pro-Greek sympathies. It was on Browne's recommendation that Byron decided to head not for Zákinthos, which Blaquiere had suggested, but for Kephaloniá, which was governed by the forceful philhellene Colonel Charles James Napier as Resident. The *Hercules* anchored in the harbour of Argostóli, Kephaloniá's capital, on 3 August, and on the very next morning, according to Trelawny, a flock of ravenous Souliot refugees rowed out to the ship and clambered over the gunwales to put themselves under Byron's protection. The captain was prepared to drive them off, and Byron's steward, Zambelli, rushed to the money chest and coiled himself on it 'like a viper'. But Byron was tolerant. 'As was his wont,' Trelawny concluded, 'he promised a great deal more than he should have done; day and night they clung to his heels like a pack of jackals, till he stood at bay like a hunted lion.'[12] Byron took forty of the Souliots into his own pay, but not for long. By the end of September he was exasperated by their constant demands for money, and offered them a final month's pay and the price of their passage back to main-land Greece. This they accepted, and the episode ended with Byron's authority restored, with considerable sums of his own money spent to no purpose, but as later events proved with his faith in the Souliots unshaken.

Napier had returned to Kephaloniá two days after Byron's arrival, and the two had long discussions on the Greek situation and what could be done about it. It was soon clear that Napier's and Byron's ideas were very different. It was characteristic of Napier to think big and talk tough: he wrote to Byron that 'A foreign force is the only thing which can give a speedy and decisive turn to the war,' and his solution to the Greek problem, he told Trelawny, was 'two European regiments, money in hand to pay them, and a portable gallows'.[13] Byron's approach was different. 'I am not come here in search of adventures,' he wrote, 'but to assist in the regeneration of a nation.'[14] Byron's discussions with Napier thus failed to show him a way forward; so too did his first direct contact with the Greeks. While still in Italy Byron had learnt of the reputation of the Souliot Márkos Bótsaris as one of the bravest and most honest of the Greek captains, and was willing to spend a thousand dollars a month to support the defence of Mesolongi by Bótsaris and his countrymen. Soon after reaching Kephaloniá Byron got a letter through to Bótsaris, who was then facing the Turks at Karpenísi. Bótsaris replied inviting Byron to join him, and saying that he meant to attack the Turks next day. This was the attack which ended with the death of Bótsaris, the Greek captain whom Byron at that stage felt most deserved his support.

Captain Scott of the *Hercules* was anxious to remove his ship from the danger of attack by Turkish or Greek vessels, and had in any case never seen the point of Byron's expedition: 'Why, my Lord, with your fortune and fame, you ought to be sitting in the House of Lords and defending the right side of the question . . . instead of roaming over the world.'[15] At the beginning of September Byron released Scott to sail back to England, and moved ashore to a house at Metaxáta on the coast south of Argostóli, from whose balcony he could see Zákinthos to the south and in the distance the outline of the Peloponnese. Within days of Byron's move to Metaxáta Trelawny and James Hamilton Browne left for the Peloponnese on a fact-finding mission. However their report from Sálamis, where Senate and Executive were still uneasily cohabiting, was quickly contradicted by another, written from Navplion after the two bodies had split, by Skilítzis, Byron's travelling companion on the *Hercules*. 'Matters are in a wholly different state', he wrote, 'from what Browne reported from Salamis.'[16] Navplion was in ruins, he went on: government was more an idea than a fact, with the Executive's influence confined within the walls of Navplion and the Senate's within

Árgos. A particularly disturbing item was that the Executive was preparing to send its own representative to London to seek a loan in competition with the appointees of the Senate. Skilítzis had warned the Executive that if it went ahead with this there would be no loan at all.

Confusion was further increased by the arrival at Metaxáta, during the remaining months of 1823, of a stream of emissaries from Greece bringing letters to Byron pleading the cause of this or that party or individual. Finlay, then in his early twenties, was with Byron at Metaxáta in October and November and described the torrent of appeals to Byron:

> Kolokotrones invited him to a national assembly at Salamis. Mavrocordatos informed him that he would be of no use anywhere but at Hydra, for Mavrocordatos was then in that island. Constantine Metaxa, who was governor of Mesolonghi, wrote, saying that Greece would be ruined unless Lord Byron visited that fortress. Petrobey used plainer words. He informed Lord Byron that the true way to save Greece was to lend him, the bey, a thousand pounds. . . . Every Greek chief celebrated his own praises and Lord Byron's liberality, but most of them injured their own cause by dilating too eloquently on the vices and crimes of some friend or rival.[17]

Byron was not taken in. The worst tendency of the Greeks, he wrote in his journal, is that 'they are such d----d liars; – there never was such an incapacity for veracity shown since Eve lived in Paradise'.[18]

Byron insisted throughout that he must deal only with the Greek government. In November an opportunity to do so seemed to arise: an emissary of the Executive branch of the government, which could still be regarded as speaking for the government as a whole, invited Byron to join them in Navplion, and he made detailed preparations for doing so. This would have been a disastrous move: Byron would have found himself isolated in Navplion, a town dominated by Kolokotrónis' forces, and in exactly the situation of being sucked into one faction that he had consistently tried to avoid.

Fortunately, only days before departure, a new proposal arrived, a request, this time from the Senate, that Byron should make a personal loan to the Greek government specifically to fund the sailing of a squadron from Hydra and Spétses to patrol the waters off Mesolongi. Byron delayed his departure for Navplion to deal with this, and on 13 November signed a loan agreement for £4,000. Finlay, who was present at the signing, had no illusions about this so-called loan: 'I said, you may bid that money farewell, my Lord; you have taken the last look of it.'[19]

Another development coincided with Byron's funding of the Greek fleet. The Turkish attack on Anatolikó had prompted the civilian and military leaders of Mesolongi to call on Mavrokordhátos to return there from Hydra and undertake the direction of affairs. The Senate approved Mavrokordhátos' appointment at the end of October, and on the same day wrote to Byron, asking him to co-operate fully with Mavrokordhátos in the defence of Mesolongi. Mavrokordhátos reinforced the Senate's request, writing to Byron: 'It is not in order to flatter you, my Lord, that I assure you that I should have hesitated to accept so vast a task had I not based my hopes on your co-operation.'[20] Mavrokordhátos reached Mesolongi after the Turkish besiegers had withdrawn, and with the fleet which Byron had funded, on 12 December 1823.

On the same day Colonel Leicester Stanhope, representative of the London Greek Committee, also arrived in Mesolongi, with orders, as Byron understood it, 'to work along with me for the liberation of Greece'.[21] Byron gently mocked Stanhope's naivety, his commitment to lofty Benthamite ideals and his faith in the universal benefits of a free press, but appreciated his worth. As he wrote to Bowring after meeting Stanhope on Kephaloniá: 'I am happy to say that Colonel Leicester Stanhope and myself are acting in perfect harmony together – he is likely to be of great service both to the cause and to the Committee, and is publicly as well as personally a very valuable acquisition to our party on every account.'[22] Byron reached a decision, and on 26 December wrote to Bowring, in one of his last letters from Kephaloniá: 'I embark tomorrow for Messolonghi.'[23]

Byron had at last found the way forward, after taking a month or more to reject the invitation of the Executive to Navplion and to accept the Senate as the proper authority to speak for the Greek government. He would now be working with Mavrokordhátos, the one Greek leader that he trusted and respected as a statesman ('their Washington, or their Kosciusko'). In Mesolongi he would be better placed than in remote Navplion to oversee the distribution of an English loan channelled through the Ionian islands, and would have easier access to his own funds through his Ionian bankers. Stanhope too was now in Mesolongi, and the two together should be able to speak for the London Greek Committee more powerfully than Byron alone.

Byron's months at Kephaloniá have often been represented as a time of dithering and indecision. When Byron moved from the *Hercules* to the house at Metaxáta, the hyperactive Trelawny commented: 'I well knew, that once on shore, Byron would fall back on his old routine of dawdling habits – plotting, planning, shilly-shallying, and doing nothing.' Byron too contributed to this picture of himself as an inveterate lingerer, saying, according to Trelawny, 'If I am stopped for six days at any place, I cannot be made to move for six months.'[24] But this approach does Byron an injustice. Mesolongi became a possible destination only with the prospect of Mavrokordhátos' arrival there; if Byron had moved before that, he would have had to go to the Peloponnese (as he nearly did), and, as he wrote to Bowring with emphasis, 'Had I *gone sooner they would have forced me into one party or the other.* . . . '[25] The Peloponnese was a political bear-pit, and as Byron admitted he had no capacity for that kind of bear-taming. One of the many dualities in his nature was that between the rational and the intuitive. Finlay, perhaps Byron's most perceptive companion at this period, saw the division as between judgement and sympathy, or the masculine and the feminine:

> Both his character and his conduct presented unceasing contradictions. It seemed as if two different souls occupied his body alternately. One was feminine, and full of sympathy; the other masculine, and characterized by clear judgment, and by a rare power of presenting for consideration those facts only which were required for forming a decision. When one arrived the other departed. . . . Hence he appeared in his conduct extremely capricious, while in his opinions he had really great firmness.[26]

It was only, it seems, when judgement and sympathy, reason and intuition came together, and a decision appeared both arguably right and instinctively right, that Byron would wholeheartedly adopt it. This conjunction finally came at the end of the year, when the fateful commitment to Mesolongi was made.

20

Byron at Mesolongi

The journey from Kephaloniá to Mesolongi turned out to be as dramatic as any that Byron had undertaken. Byron had hired two boats for the voyage, one large and slow, a bombard, to take Pietro Gamba, five of the servants, the horses and the heavy luggage including guns, the other a light fast boat called a mistico for Byron himself with his dogs and the remaining five of his retinue. In case of difficulties with the Turks the papers for both boats gave their destination as the island of Kálamos off Lévkas, part of the Ionian islands and a safe fifty miles by sea from their true destination of Mesolongi. This precaution was quickly needed. The two boats left Kephaloniá on the afternoon of 28 December 1823, and spent the next day at Zákinthos taking on supplies and money: 16,000 Spanish dollars on Byron's mistico and 8,000 dollars on Gamba's bombard. At six in the evening the two vessels set sail in light winds under a clear sky, and for the next four hours they kept station together, the sailors of both crews singing patriotic songs in which Byron joined, their voices mingling across the darkening sea. Eventually the faster mistico with Byron on board moved ahead out of earshot into the night.

At dawn next day Gamba and the crew of the lagging bombard had almost reached the entrance to the Mesolongi lagoon when a large vessel bore down on them, flying no colours. Gamba's worst fears were confirmed when his bombard raised the Ionian flag and was answered with the Turkish one. Gamba decided that he would stick to his story that he was heading for Kálamos on a hunting expedition, which would explain the guns in the cargo. The only totally compromising item on board was the packet containing all Byron's correspondence with the Greek leaders; this was weighted with shot and, sadly for historians, dropped overboard. However, when the Greek captain was summoned aboard the Turkish ship events took a turn which would raise an incredulous eyebrow in the reader of a romantic novel: the Greek recognised the Turkish captain as a man whom years before he had saved from shipwreck in the Black Sea. The Turkish captain, now thoroughly amiable, still had no option but to take his prize back to Patras. There Gamba suffered a searching interview with the Turkish commander Yussuf Pasha, in which he managed to maintain the fiction of the Kálamos hunting trip, and after some days' delay was given papers to proceed. He reached Mesolongi on 4 January 1824, but found that Byron had still not arrived.

This was because Byron had had adventures of his own. During the first night of the crossing the mistico had been surprised by a large Turkish ship looming up in the darkness. When hailed the mistico made no response, all on board kept quiet (even, miraculously, the dogs), and the freshening wind carried it safely away. The only reason why the Turks did not fire on the mistico was, Byron thought, that they took it for a Greek fireship, to be avoided rather than attacked. At dawn the next morning Byron's party could see one Turkish ship chasing Gamba's bombard and another blocking the entrance to Mesolongi, so they put into a little port at rocky Cape Skróphes about eighteen miles west of Mesolongi. Within an hour the approach of a Turkish vessel drove Byron's party to flee another twenty miles northwards to the port of Dhragoméstri, modern Astakós. From there, in response to a message from Byron to Mesolongi, he and his companions were picked up by some Greek gunboats, and were nearly wrecked on the passage back past Cape Skróphes. At last on the morning of 5 January, the day after Gamba's arrival, Byron in his scarlet uniform stepped ashore at Mesolongi to a cacophony of gunfire and martial music and a huge and excited crowd of soldiers and citizens, while Gamba wept tears of joy and relief.

This eventful journey showed Byron at his hardy and insouciant best. He had given up his cabin to a sick member of the party, and as he wrote a week after arrival: 'We had bad weather almost always – though not contrary – slept on deck in the wet generally – for seven or eight nights

– but never was in better health (I speak personally) so much so that I actually bathed for a quarter of an hour on the evening of the fourth inst. in the sea – (to kill the fleas and others) and was all the better for it.'[1] Byron at nearly 37, and with a clubbed right foot from birth, was combining the activities of a man half his age with the health of a man twice his age. He had long been aware of this, writing to his half-sister Augusta in 1816: 'My health is good, but I have now & then fits of giddiness, & deafness. . . . My hair is growing grey, *& not* thicker; & my teeth are sometimes *looseish* though still white & sound. Would not one think I was sixty instead of not quite nine & twenty?'[2] His digestion had by now become shaky. 'Dinners kill a weakly stomached Gentleman,'[3] he remarked of the lavish hospitality he received in Kephaloniá. This, combined with unorthodox eating patterns, had caused his weight to fluctuate wildly. His friend Leigh Hunt, meeting him in Italy in 1822, hardly knew him, as he had become so fat. Later that year Byron embarked on a strict slimming regime which as time went on increasingly became his normal diet. At the age of 18 he had weighed 13 stone 12 lb (his wine merchants, Berry's, recorded such matters for their clients) and in 1823, at 35, only 10 stone 9 lb. Thus the early portraits of a robust and glorious youth had given way to the 1823 sketch of a gaunt Byron, slightly stooped, with his head at the questioning angle of old age, and with a stick that seems more for support than for swagger.

Byron had also suffered several prostrating but unexplained illnesses in recent years. On the journey to his last Italian home in Genoa in October 1822, he had been 'very unwell – four days confined to my bed – with a violent rheumatic and bilious attack – constipation – and the devil knows what',[4] but finally dosed himself and was up on the fifth day, ready to eat cold fish and drink a gallon of country wine. A more serious attack, which apparently drove Byron temporarily out of his mind, occurred in the early days on Kephaloniá, just after a sun-baked and exhausting trip to Ithaca. Byron and his party were dinner guests at a monastery, and Byron was unusually silent. Suddenly he burst into a stream of Italian curses on the abbot and his brotherhood, screamed 'Will no one release me from the presence of these pestilential idiots?'[5] and went off to his room, where he smashed everything in it and hurled a chair at one of his companions who had gone to quieten him. At length he swallowed two of Dr Bruno's pills and slept, and next morning was full of remorse and apologies. Even Byron, it seems, could not treat this incident in his usual light-hearted way, and there is no mention of it in any of his surviving writings.

On arrival at Mesolongi Byron took up residence on the second and top floors of the house where Stanhope already occupied the first floor, and a Souliot guard was soon afterwards installed on the ground floor. The house was on the western edge of the town and Byron's bedroom and sitting room faced south across several miles of shallow muddy lagoon towards the open sea, while two or three further rooms looked east over the courtyard to the town beyond. These damp quarters had little furniture, no heating and no drains (slops went into the lagoon), and all Byron could do to domesticate them was to display his collection of weapons on the walls and put his books on shelves above them. It had rained continuously during his crossing to Mesolongi, and heavy downpours soon kept him confined to his rooms all day. It was in these bleak surroundings, the very opposite of his recent quarters in a palazzo under an Italian sun, that Byron and Mavrokordhátos held regular evening discussions of what could be done to advance the Greek cause.

The first project discussed was an attack on the massive Venetian fortress of Návpaktos, twenty-five miles to the east on the north shore of the Gulf of Corinth. Mavrokordhátos put forward grandiose reasons for this venture: if Návpaktos was in Greek hands the Turkish fleet could be driven out of the Gulf of Corinth, the Castles of Roumeli and the Morea at the entrance to the gulf would fall, and so then would Patras itself. However the real reason was that Návpaktos was for the moment a soft target. Its garrison had not been paid for sixteen months, the Turkish ship with money destined to pay it had been captured in the previous November, and the defenders let it be known that they would surrender after a mere token resistance.

Within days of Byron's arrival in Mesolongi he had undertaken to pay a body of 500 Souliot troops for a year, and these with another hundred on government pay were to be the core of a total force of 2,000 to attack Návpaktos. Though the five or six thousand armed men in Mesolongi were, in Gamba's view, remarkably well behaved, the Souliots were not, constantly demanding their back pay and asylum for their families, and the citizens of the town denounced the Souliots as more of a menace than the enemy. By mid-January Byron admitted to Gamba that he had little faith in the Souliots as elite troops, but that there was nothing better available.

A further element in the plan to attack Návpaktos was that a corps of artillery was expected to arrive soon from England. This was the outcome of a proposal put to the London Greek Committee a year before by Thomas Gordon, who had left Greece after the sack of Tripolis in 1821 and was now back in his home at Cairness in Scotland. Gordon estimated that this project would cost about £10,000, of which he offered to contribute one-third, and it was assumed from the beginning that Gordon himself would go to Greece at the head of this corps.

However Gordon delayed coming to London and making any commitment to lead the corps in person. Necessary action to put the plan into effect – getting estimates for the artillery, equipping a workshop, finding men to serve – was left to Gordon's protégé William Parry. Parry, a former navy fire-master, had been taken to Scotland by Gordon in the spring of 1823, and Gordon warmly recommended him: 'It would be impossible for the Committee to find a man in his situation so capable of rendering essential service.'[6] Doubts surfaced later: in November one Committee member wrote to Gordon that 'I have great fears from Mr. Parry's warm and lusty disposition,'[7] meaning that Parry could be drunk and argumentative, and Blaquiere, reaching Mesolongi after Byron's death, reported: 'It now appears that [Parry] is totally ignorant of nearly all those points which induced the Committee to send him out.'[8] Nevertheless it was Parry who got things done, and by November he was ready to sail for Greece with ten light mountain guns plus several larger ones donated by Gordon, a workshop comprehensively equipped with tools, materials and instruments, and eight skilled mechanics. His supplies included seventy reams of paper for making cartridges, and many of the bibles sent to Greece by missionary societies were put to the same use.

Meanwhile in July Gordon had finally closed the door on leading the corps himself. His principal reason was that even in 1821 when he was chief of staff, had the full confidence of his commander-in-chief and was supported by experienced officers, he found that he could produce no beneficial result. If Gordon, with his military training and knowledge of the Greeks at war, thought he could do no good, how did he expect someone far less well equipped than himself to succeed? Nevertheless, he concluded his valediction, as he called it, by saying, 'I must heartily concur (as a member of the Committee) in the proposition, that the charge and direction of the expedition, be confided to Lord Byron.'[9]

No practical steps to advance the Návpaktos plan were taken until 24 January, when Mavrokordhátos proposed to Byron a command structure for the expedition. Byron would be in overall command, but would co-operate with a council of Greek captains presided over by the Souliot chieftain Nótis Bótsaris, uncle of the late revered Márkos. Byron was to choose his own staff from European officers, and Gamba was to lead the Souliots. Virtually nothing in this something-for-everyone proposal made sense, but Byron, against Stanhope's advice, accepted the proffered leadership. His argument for doing so was that the Greek captains would rather be commanded by a foreigner than by one of their own number; that the Návpaktos garrison would be more likely to surrender to a western European than to a Greek; that nobody else, not even Mavrokordhátos, would accept the post; and that 'as I pay a considerable portion of the Clans – I may as well see what they are likely to do for their money'.[10] Byron maintained an ironic cheerfulness about the expedition's prospects: 'Between Suliote Chiefs – German Barons – English Volunteers – and adventurers of all Nations – we are likely to form as goodly an allied army – as ever quarrelled beneath the same banner.'[11]

A few days after Byron's acceptance of the leadership Parry and his artillery corps finally reached Greece. Parry had left England in November 1823 and on 27 January reached Dhragoméstri, from where some of his supplies were carried overland to Mesolongi to avoid offloading them into small boats to cross Mesolongi's shallow lagoon. Parry arrived in Mesolongi on 5 February, and Byron took to him at once: 'Parry is a fine fellow – extremely active – and of strong – sound – practical talent by all accounts.'[12] It was in any case more enjoyable for Byron to spend his evenings drinking brandy with Parry than earnestly discussing logistics with Mavrokordhátos or Benthamite principles with Stanhope. However no coal for the workshop furnaces had been sent with Parry and coal was hard to come by in Mesolongi, so it was clear that it would be some time before Parry's arsenal was ready to be used: three weeks said Byron, two months and a lot of expense said Gamba. Hopes that Parry could assist in an immediate attack on Návpaktos were dashed.

The plan to attack Návpaktos now began to unravel fast. Parry could be no help for the moment. Yussuf Pasha, the Turkish commander at Patras, learnt of the plot to surrender Návpaktos and, as Green reported, he 'instantly requested the disaffected and traitorous chiefs to proceed to the Morea Castle [Antírio], on the plea of paying the arrears; these he detained, and sent over several hundred Ottoman troops to strengthen the garrison of Lepanto [Návpaktos], not omitting, however, to send part of the pay due to the Albanians.'[13] There would therefore be no easy capture of the fortress. Furthermore the Souliots caused increasing difficulties. Gamba was deputed to muster the 600 Souliots who were to be the core of the expedition. A much larger number applied, attracted by the prospect of pay, and Gamba spent two days, 12 and 13 February, weeding out the very young, very old or sick, and establishing the true and not the inflated numbers serving under each captain. As soon as this was done the Souliots tried a new ruse to increase their pay, demanding officer status, and pay, for two generals, two colonels and so on down the ranks, which would have meant that there were nearly as many officers as common soldiers. Byron's patience was at an end, and on 15 February he wrote a furious note to himself: 'Having tried in vain at every expence – considerable trouble – and some danger to unite the Suliotes for the good of Greece – and their own – I have come to the following resolution. – I will have nothing more to do with the Suliotes – they may go to the Turks or – the devil . . . they may cut me into more pieces than they have dissensions among them, sooner than change my resolution.'[14]

Two further events destroyed any hope of an attack on Návpaktos. First Byron, on the day that he wrote his note on the Souliots, suffered a seizure which he described as 'a strong and sudden convulsive attack which left me speechless though not motionless – for some strong men could not hold me – but whether it was epilepsy – catalepsy – cachexy – apoplexy – or what other exy – or *opsy* – the Doctors have not decided'.[15] Byron ascribed the fit to lack of exercise (due to the incessant rains), to agitation over public matters (the Souliot difficulties), and to the fact that he had been 'perhaps not uniformly so temperate' as before (drinking sessions with Parry). As a cure leeches were applied to his temples, but 'too near the temporal Artery for my temporal safety', and it was some hours before the bleeding could be stopped. A week later he was slowly convalescing, but by then the second disruptive event had occurred. It began innocently enough. One of the Souliot soldiers brought a young nephew of Márkos Bótsaris to look at Parry's arsenal. The arsenal guard ordered him away, as he was instructed to do, but the Souliot soldier refused to leave. A fight broke out, the captain of the guard, the Swedish philhellene Adolph von Sass, was summoned, and in the ensuing struggle the Souliot drew his yataghan and almost severed Sass's left arm from his body, and then shot him three times in the head. Sass died within half an hour, and the Souliot killer was arrested but was released to his compatriots when they threatened to burn down the building. The Souliots now saw no further prospects for themselves in Mesolongi and determined to leave for Árta, where there was more chance of plunder, declaring that they had no relish for attacking the stone walls of Návpaktos. Byron offered them a month's pay on condition that they left and did not return.

The Návpaktos plan was now dead and Byron for the moment deeply depressed. 'I begin to fear', he said to Gamba, 'that I have done nothing but lose time, money, patience and health.'[16] Even success in capturing Návpaktos would have had little importance except symbolically; Mavrokordhátos' domino theory, that with the capture of Návpaktos the Castles of Roumeli, the Morea and Patras would fall, was wishful thinking. But was there ever any realistic chance of success? This could have been achieved only by the charade originally envisaged, whereby a token attack would produce an immediate surrender. Once Yussuf Pasha had learnt of the intrigue and scotched it, the Greeks had to prepare a full-scale military operation. Byron was to lead this assault, but he was not the man for military leadership, and the twenty-three-year-old Gamba was even less suited to be his second-in-command. Eager, faithful and conscientious as he was, Gamba constantly made a mess of even simple tasks. When in the early days at Mesolongi Byron asked him to order some cloth from Corfu, Gamba ordered the wrong material and far too much of it, and when the bill came it was more than ten times what Byron expected. 'But this comes of letting boys play the man', Byron wrote in exasperation, 'all his patriotism diminishes into the desire of a sky blue uniform and be d—d to him – for a coxcomb.'[17] Gamba's competence did not improve, and two months later Byron wrote, of another muddle, 'Gamba – who is anything but *lucky* – had something to do with it – and as usual – the moment he had – matters went wrong.'

The force to be led was as flawed as its leaders. Parry's artillery was not ready for action, and his corps was badly weakened when after only a few weeks in Mesolongi six of his eight mechanics, terrified by the Sass incident, begged passage back to England, for which Stanhope paid. What, in any case, could such an artillery corps actually achieve in Greece? The assumption seemed to be that, since effective western European armies had artillery and the Greeks did not, providing artillery would make the Greeks effective. For attacks on fortresses artillery was virtually useless. It made little or no impression on even flimsy defensive walls, as Raybaud had discovered at Tripolis in 1821 and as the Turks were to find during their prolonged sieges of Mesolongi. When the objective was one of the massive and well-designed Venetian citadels, such as Návpaktos, artillery was no use at all, and the Souliots were for once absolutely right to echo Kolokotrónis' dictum on the folly of attempting assault and to refuse to attack stone walls. Otherwise the Souliots contributed nothing but disorder, rapacity and dishonesty to the cause which Byron had come to serve. Perhaps only Márkos Bótsaris could have united and controlled them, and it may be that the single shot which killed Márkos Bótsaris at Karpenísi also killed any prospect of Byron forming an effective corps from the Souliots whom he had admired for so long and towards whom he had been so patient and so generous.

Byron had indeed, as he said to Gamba, spent a great deal of his money, and to little effect. In the previous November he had advanced £4,000, ostensibly to be repaid from the proceeds of the English loan, to bring out the ships of Hydra and Spétses which conveyed Mavrokordhátos to Mesolongi. Pay for the Souliots, first in Kephaloniá and then in Mesolongi, had come to about £2,000, so the money for the fleet and for the Souliots totalled some £6,000 out of the £9,000 or so which Byron initially had available in Greece. There were other drains on Byron's pocket, quite apart from the living costs of himself and his retinue. He had agreed to advance £600 for the government troops in March; he paid £40 (reduced from £80 after some adroit bargaining) in compensation to the Ionian government for the seizure of one of their ships by the Greeks; he made a loan of £550 to Mavrokordhátos personally; and he paid out around £800 to support Parry, who had arrived from England with no money. Byron was in effect the paymaster for the whole Greek war effort which centred on Mesolongi. It was no wonder that he urged the London Greek Committee, through Bowring, to send money and not supplies, especially as some of the supplies were ludicrously impractical: 'The Mathematical instruments are thrown away – none of the Greeks know a problem from a poker.'[19]

Fortunately for the Greeks, Byron's constant badgering of Kinnaird to raise money had considerably increased his resources. By mid-January 1824 his property of Rochdale Manor, after a long time on the market, was sold for £11,250, and with that boost to his funds Byron estimated that he had upwards of £20,000 at his disposal. Thus Byron in Greece was at least a millionaire in today's sterling, and, almost as remarkable, was prepared to spend it all on the cause. As early as June 1823, before he had even left Italy, he wrote to Kinnaird that 'I should not like to give the Greeks but a *half helping* hand.'[20] Furthermore, Byron did not try to influence the recipients of his money, and declared that even if his loans were repaid it would make no great difference as he would still spend the money in the Greek cause. Byron's financial contribution to the Greeks was thus very great, and amazingly open-handed. All the same, though, there was something reckless about it, as of a man who gave no thought for the morrow because he felt he would not reach a tomorrow, and that all he had should be thrown into one last magnificent venture.

As well as spending big money on big projects which achieved little, Byron took trouble over paying out much smaller sums which effectively helped individuals in distress. In his time in Kephaloniá he had visited Ithaca, and gave £50 to the British Resident for the relief of refugee families there, and took back to Kephaloniá one family named Chalandhrítsanos, whose support cost him £40 in the next three months. At Mesolongi on a number of occasions he secured the release of Turkish men, women and children; he rescued a Turkish sailor captured by the Greeks after falling overboard, for whom he provided clothes and, thoughtfully, tobacco, and who remained under Byron's protection; and he arranged for four Turkish prisoners to be sent back to Yussuf Pasha in Patras, with a request that Yussuf would show the same clemency to captured Greeks.

Byron took a particular interest in two of the youngest refugees. One was a Turkish girl in Mesolongi aged about nine called Hato or Hatagée. Her mother, wife of one of Mesolongi's former leading citizens, was now a domestic servant to the English Dr Millingen, the rest of her family having fled or been killed when the Greeks took over the town. Byron spent nearly £20 on elaborate dresses for Hato, and seriously considered adopting her; for her future he considered sending her to Teresa Guiccioli, or to his half-sister Augusta, or even to his estranged wife as a playmate for his daughter Ada. Ultimately, to avoid separating mother and daughter, Byron sent both to Kephaloniá to be cared for temporarily by his devout friend Dr James Kennedy, and they were reunited with their surviving family soon after Byron's death.

Byron's other particular protégé was Loukás, the fifteen-year-old son of the Chalandhrítsanos family whom he had rescued from Ithaca. Byron took Loukás to Mesolongi as his page, and was much concerned during their storm-tossed journey from Zákinthos that the boy might be captured by the Turks. In Mesolongi he alternated between spoiling Loukás outrageously – new clothes for him cost even more than dresses for the girl – and exasperation at being exploited by him. On his death-bed he gave Loukás a bag of Maria Theresa crowns and a £600 receipt for one of his loans to the Greeks, but the government was in no position to honour this, and Loukás died in poverty six months later. There has been speculation about whether the relationship between Byron and Loukás was homosexual. Byron's last verses seem to be about Loukás, and suggest that his feelings were indeed homosexual – 'I am a fool of passion, and a frown Of thine to me is as an adder's eye' – but that they were not returned – 'And yet thou lovst me not And never wilt.' If so, it was with Teresa Guiccioli and not Loukás that Byron formed his last mutual attachment.

Once Byron had recovered from the illness, and its treatment, which had finally ended the plan to attack Návpaktos, he resumed his daily rides with Gamba whenever he could. But the weather continued atrociously wet, and Byron and Gamba had to take an open boat across the lagoon to find ground firm enough for the horses. Mesolongi was a mud-basket, Byron wrote, while Gamba reckoned that the town's main gate was so choked with mud that it would hardly need defending against an enemy attack. But apart from the constant presence of the faithful Gamba Byron's circle was in continual flux. Volunteers, Greeks and foreigners, were drawn to Mesolongi by the prospect of pay from Byron's generous pocket and of service in a force which bore at least some resemblance to a western European army. By the end of March they formed the so-called Byron brigade of about thirty philhellene officers and between 100 and 200 men (Byron's letters show that he was uncertain of their numbers himself). Finlay returned to Mesolongi after a journey to Athens. Stanhope departed, having established with remarkable speed two newspapers in Mesolongi, *Elliniká Chroniká* in Greek and, for consumption abroad, the multilingual *Telegrafo Greco*.

Stanhope left Mesolongi on 21 February bound for Athens, taking with him the young English philhellene William Humphreys, who had arrived on the same boat as Parry. In Athens Stanhope and Humphreys both fell under the spell of Odysseus Andhroútsos, as Trelawny had done before them. Stanhope wrote: 'I have been constantly with Odysseus. . . . he is a doing man; he governs with a strong arm, and is the only man in Greece that can preserve order. He puts, however, complete confidence in the people.'[21] Humphreys praised his looks ('Very tall . . . sunburnt face and breast, rude attire, immense bushy moustache, and bent brow'), his horsemanship, his graceful manners, his forcible mind and his military sagacity. Stanhope, Humphreys and Trelawny now pushed forward a plan that Odysseus had been nurturing for some time, to hold a congress of Greek leaders at Salóna.

The ostensible objects of the Salóna congress were to unite Eastern and Western Roumeli, and to produce a joint military strategy. The proposal was the idea of Négris, who had seen his position decline from governor of Eastern Roumeli in 1821 and chief minister in the national government of 1822 to mere deputy secretary of the 1823 constitutional congress and nothing at all in the present government. Odysseus had first written to Byron with the Salóna proposal at the end of January 1824, but received no response. Towards the end of February he sent to Byron and Mavrokordhátos a renewed invitation to Salóna, this time with the backing of both Trelawny and Stanhope. Stanhope wrote: 'Odysseus is most anxious to unite the interests of Eastern and Western

Greece, for which purpose he is desirous immediately of forming a Congress of Salona. . . . I implore your Lordship and the President, as you love Greece and her sacred cause, to attend Salona.'[22] Byron promptly agreed to go to Salóna; so too, though more reluctantly, did Mavrokordhátos.

On the face of it the Salóna congress was just the sort of political initiative to promote unity which Byron had come to Greece to pursue. Furthermore the second invitation was backed by Stanhope, Byron's fellow representative of the London Greek Committee, with whom, at least in public, he needed to maintain a united front. But below the surface there were as usual other motives. Négris, the originator of the idea, wanted to recover some of his lost influence. For Odysseus, who had already captivated Trelawny and Stanhope, it was an opportunity to win over Byron, and through Byron to get access to the imminently expected English loan. Mavrokordhátos thought the proposed meeting was both unnecessary, as it would not promote unity, and unconstitutional, as military strategy was the preserve of the government and not of some ad-hoc congress. Nevertheless, if Byron went to Salóna, Mavrokordhátos would have to go too, to prevent Byron being lured away by Odysseus.

The news that Byron would go to Salóna quickly prompted rival invitations from other interests, three in a week in the middle of March. Pétrobey's agent Peroúkas, the former finance minister, wrote asking Byron to come to the Peloponnese to unite all factions; Byron replied that it was his duty at present to stay in Roumeli, though if his presence could really help in reconciling two or more parties he was ready to go anywhere. A few days later an envoy of Kolokotrónis arrived to invite Byron to the Peloponnese. This approach too was rejected on the ground that Stanhope would be going to the Peloponnese so there was no reason for Byron to go. Finally the national government at Kranídhi invited Byron to a conference, and offered him the position of governor-general of Roumeli; Byron replied that he was first going to Salóna, but afterwards would be at the government's command.

It was thus Byron's settled purpose to go to Salóna and refuse for the moment all rival invitations. However the journey to Salóna, fifty miles and two or three days away, was repeatedly delayed. Byron and Mavrokordhátos originally agreed to set out on 13 March but on that day there was a public health scare: a man recently arrived from the Peloponnese died in Mesolongi, supposedly of the plague, though this turned out to be a false alarm. On 22 March Byron and Mavrokordhátos were still at Mesolongi expecting to start in three days' time. This date too was missed, and 27 March was next fixed as the day of departure, but by then the weather was even worse than before, making the rivers unfordable and the roads impassable. A final delay came from an unexpected quarter: an attack by their own side. On 3 April Georgios Karaïskákis, captain of a band in Ágrapha to the north, with 150 of his own men supported by a party of Souliots occupied the lagoon outposts of Anatolikó and Vasiládhi. His justification was that a nephew of his had been assaulted by a Mesolongi citizen, but it was widely suspected that his attack on Mesolongi had been instigated by Mavrokordhátos' opponents in the Peloponnese. For Byron and Mavrokordhátos to leave for Salóna was temporarily out of the question. However, after a show of force by the troops in Mesolongi, Karaïskákis' attack fizzled out, and on 6 April Byron was able to refer casually to 'some tumult here' from the incident and report that 'to-day matters seem settled or subsiding'.[23]

Three days after that Byron went out for the ride which began his last fatal illness, and he never went to Salóna. Nor did Mavrokordhátos; his only reason for going was to be at hand to prevent Byron transferring his allegiance to Odysseus. Mavrokordhátos sent two or three delegates, but explained pointedly that they were not participants, merely observers to see that the national interest did not suffer. Even Stanhope did not attend the congress when it was finally held at the beginning of May, and it produced nothing but a formal declaration of support for the national government. Would it have achieved more if Byron had been there? It is extremely doubtful. The dapper, sophisticated Mavrokordhátos and the charismatic brigand Odysseus were as different as any two Greek leaders could be, and would never have trusted each other, would never have agreed to a joint military plan, and would never have surrendered any of their autonomy in their own regions.

On 9 April Byron went out riding with Gamba; they were caught in heavy rain and chilled through during the half-hour boat journey back to the town. Two hours after his return Byron was seized by shuddering and extreme pain. 'I do not care for death,' he said, 'but these agonies I cannot bear.'[24] Such a remark wrung from the normally uncomplaining Byron indicate that this illness was more serious than anything before. After a day confined to the house he again went riding, without the rain but on a wet saddle, and spent the day after that in bed. Parry, by his own account, prepared a boat to take Byron to Zákinthos, but they could not sail because of a hurricane. Only Dr Bruno, Byron's young personal physician, attended him at first, but on 13 April, four days after the start of his illness, the local Dr Millingen was called in. Now began the infamous bleedings, against Byron's objections, which almost certainly shortened his life. The prevailing mental picture of the human body determined, as always, the treatment given. The doctors saw the body as a bag filled with blood; too much of this liquid would pressurise and inflame the brain, so the pressure must be reduced by bleeding. Byron, on the other hand, was well aware of the dangers of bleeding and thought of the body as a stringed instrument. 'Drawing blood from a nervous patient', he said, 'is like loosening the chords of a musical instrument, the tones of which are already defective for want of sufficient tension.'[25]

Despite his reluctance Byron eventually consented to bleeding, and this was done, sometimes twice a day, by lancet or leech, removing over four pints of blood in some sixty hours. On 17 April two more doctors were called in, one a German, the other a Greek and Mavrokordhátos' personal physician, but they could suggest nothing more than continued bleeding and a bizarre assortment of medicines: during Byron's last illness these included antimony, castor oil, Epsom salts, henbane, cream of tartar, boracic, quinine, extract of tamarind, laudanum, ether and claret. On 18 April, Easter Sunday, the usual celebratory firing of guns was kept well away from Byron's house by the town guard so as not to disturb him. On the same day a boat was sent to Zákinthos to fetch a Dr Thomas, but he was away from home and could not be found. But Thomas would have known no more than the other four doctors what Byron's illness was. Nor in fact do we know now. A variety of diagnoses has been suggested, including rheumatic fever, typhoid fever, uraemic poisoning, malaria, syphilis and, perhaps most likely, some form of brain haemorrhage, the last in a series which had caused Byron's previous attacks. Whatever the nature of Byron's last illness, his impaired physique was unable to resist it, and his doctors' hit-and-miss

methods were unable to cure it. At six o'clock on the evening of Easter
Monday, 19 April, Byron died.

Byron had spent just over a hundred days in Mesolongi, and in one
sense had achieved nothing. He had wanted to use his influence and his
money in three spheres: military, political and humanitarian. The military (Návpaktos) and the political (Salóna) initiatives came to nothing
and would have had little effect even if they had succeeded. If
Návpaktos had surrendered to a force under Byron, no other Turkish
stronghold would have fallen as a result. If Byron had gone to the
Salóna congress he would not have brought Mavrokordhátos and
Odysseus together. Only in the humanitarian sphere was Byron successful, but his rescue of Greeks and Turks impartially, laudable as it was,
had no effect on the war.

In another sense, though, Byron achieved everything he could have
wished. His presence in Greece, and in particular his death there, drew
to the Greek cause not just the attention of sympathetic nations but
their increasingly active participation. Blaquiere, for all his irritating
vagueness about Byron's possible role, had foreseen from the start what
his true contribution would be: 'Your presence will operate as a talisman.' With Byron dead, the Greek cause could not die.

Byron has had his critics, from his own time down to the present;
they have castigated his way of life, especially his treatment of women,
derided his verse and questioned his motives in going to Greece. Much
of the adverse criticism by Byron's contemporaries can be ascribed to
self-seeking or self-justification. Much of the later condemnation can
be put down to the propensity, which seems to be peculiarly English,
to bow before a famous man only to examine more closely his feet of
clay. Despite the critics, Byron is primarily remembered with admiration as a poet of genius, with something approaching veneration as a
symbol of high ideals, and with great affection as a man: for his courage
and his ironic slant on life, for his generosity to the grandest of causes
and to the humblest of individuals, for the constant interplay of judgement and sympathy. In Greece he is still revered as no other foreigner,
and as very few Greeks, and like a Homeric hero he is accorded an hon-
orific standard epithet, *megálos kai kalós*, a great and good man.

21

Gold from London

The Greek government, from the time that it took office at the beginning of 1822, had been desperately short of money. It had three possible sources of income. First, plunder, including ransom money for wealthy captives, but this was generally kept by the captain who had seized or extracted it. Second, taxes and duties were still imposed but these were increasingly hard to collect in a war-torn country from Greeks who felt that the departure of the Turks should mean the end of taxation. Finally, there were contributions from abroad, but these were far too little to finance a country at war. Individuals might contribute some hundreds of pounds sterling, and foreign committees might raise thousands, but the government needed hundreds of thousands – the national budget for 1823–4 showed expenditure exceeding income by the equivalent of £500,000. The only way of raising such sums – tens of millions in today's terms – was through commercial loans from abroad.

The Greek government had been trying to raise money by this means from its inception, authorising the borrowing of £200,000 equivalent from abroad as one of its earliest acts, but had had no success. The government's agent for exploring this avenue was Andréas Louriótis, who went first to Spain and Portugal, but 'the Constitutionalists, being on the brink of ruin, could afford him only compliments and professions of esteem'.[1] In February 1823 Louriótis arrived in London, where he was introduced by Edward Blaquiere to the prominent London philhellenes who were about to set up the London Greek Committee. The Committee held its first meeting at the Crown & Anchor tavern in the Strand on 3 March that year, and consisted at its birth of some two dozen prominent figures, two-thirds of them Members of Parliament and also including Jeremy Bentham, Thomas Gordon and Byron's friend John Cam Hobhouse, with John Bowring as secretary. The Committee's first act, as we have seen, was to despatch Blaquiere and Louriótis to Greece to report on the state of the country and to persuade the Greek government to send to London official agents who could contract a loan on its behalf. Blaquiere and Louriótis lost no time, and the day after the Committee's first meeting set sail for Greece. On the way there they called on Byron in Genoa, and in one visit sealed the fate of their host and reordered the prospects for Greece. In September Blaquiere returned to London bringing with him a ludicrously overblown account of the commercial vitality of Greece which he said could, when liberated, become 'one of the most opulent nations of Europe'.[2] The stage was now set for the launch of the first English loan.

London was the best possible place, and perhaps the only possible place, to raise a loan of the size which the Greeks needed. The underlying reason was that, thanks to Britain's early lead in the industrial revolution, more capital had been generated than domestic agriculture and industry could absorb, so that a weight of money built up in London seeking other outlets. Thus London had developed a group of active traders, often highly disreputable, to promote such outlets: 'With huge pocketbooks containing worthless scrip; with crafty countenance and cunning eye; with showy jewellery and threadbare coat; with well-greased locks and unpolished boots; with knavery in every curl of the lip, and villainy in every thought of the heart, the stag, as he was afterwards termed, was prominent in the foreground.'[3] Other considerations made loans to foreign governments, as in newly independent South America, particularly attractive. In 1822 the interest rate on British government bonds was reduced from 5 per cent to 4 per cent, and in 1824 fell a further ½ per cent on the day after the Greek loan was floated, a conjunction so favourable to the loan that to suspect collusion is hardly cynical. Interest payments had been made more secure by an innovation of Nathan Rothschild whereby interest on foreign securities was paid in sterling, not the local currency. Loan promoters had been further safeguarded by the new syndicate system, whereby the responsibility for the loan was shared among a number of issuing houses and not confined to one.

Finally, there was the puff, intended either to encourage initial purchase of the stock or to maintain its value afterwards. Blaquiere was the
main author of puffs for the Greeks, and followed up his first glowing
report to the London Greek Committee with two books, hurriedly
published in 1824 and 1825, which taken together amount to an
extended false prospectus. 'I should have no hesitation whatever', he
wrote in 1824, 'in estimating the physical strength of regenerated Greece
to be fully equal to that of the whole South American continent.' In the
1825 book he provided long lists of the exportable products of each
Greek region (down to valonia, the husks of acorns used in tanning),
praised individual places (Vivári near Navplion was 'perhaps one of the
finest harbours in Europe', and there was 'not a more productive region
in Europe' than Thessaly), gave optimistic estimates of the government's income, and concluded that there was 'no part of the world . . .
[with] a more productive soil, or happier climate, than Greece'. Thus
'of all the countries or governments who have borrowed money in
London within the last ten years . . . Greece possesses the surest and
most ample means of re-payment'.[4] Those on the spot saw things differently. Philip Green, writing from Zákinthos, recorded his 'sincere conviction that there is not the slightest probability of the re-payment of
either interest or capital'.[5] If the London Greek Committee and its
financier friends had listened to Green rather than Blaquiere there
would have been no Greek loan.

On 21 January 1824 the two Greek deputies with powers to contract
a loan reached London: Andréas Louriótis, the original agent, and
Iánnis Orlándos. Orlándos was a reassuring choice for potential investors. He had served briefly as president of the Senate before making way
for Mavrokordhátos and was linked by marriage to the family of
Georgios Kondouriótis, the president of the Executive and a consistent
opponent of Kolokotrónis. Thus Orlándos' appointment signalled that
the loan money would go to a responsible government and not to a
band of unscrupulous captains. Soon after the arrival of the deputies a
banquet was given in their honour in the splendid setting of the
Guildhall at which Canning, now foreign secretary, another member of
the Cabinet and the Lord Mayor of London were present. On 19
February the deputies, on the advice of the London Greek Committee,
signed a loan agreement with the issuing house of Loughman, O'Brien,

Ellis & Co., and on the following day the loan stock was put on sale to the public.

The bonds of the type issued to raise the Greek loan worked very much like today's government bonds. Each nominal £100 worth of the bonds would initially be offered at a discount, but the interest would be based on the nominal £100 value, so the greater the discount the better the interest rate. During the life of the bonds – indefinite in the Greek case – they would change hands at different prices depending partly upon whether better interest was available from other invest-ments, and partly on confidence in the bonds: confidence that interest on them would continue to be paid, confidence that each £100 bond would eventually be repaid at £100, and confidence, or the lack of it, that repayment would be made at all.

The Greek bonds had a nominal value of £800,000, but the stock was offered at 59 per cent so that the amount to be actually subscribed was only £472,000; this was a huge sum in relation to Greece's true resources, but small compared with the £3 million or more loaned to some of the new South American governments. Interest was at 5 per cent on the nominal value, equivalent to over 8½ per cent on the actual investment, and therefore much better than the interest rate on British government bonds. The issuers retained two years' interest (£80,000) and a further 1 per cent (£8,000) as a contribution to a sinking fund for the eventual repayment of the loan. These retentions, plus commissions to the promoters of some £38,000 (including £11,000 to Bowring), reduced the sum available to the Greeks to something under £350,000. Nevertheless their guarantee to repay the full £800,000 was written on the back of the loan certificate: 'To the payment of the annuities are appropriated all the revenues of Greece. The whole of the national property of Greece is hereby pledged to the holders of all obligations granted in virtue of this loan until the whole of the capital which such obligations represent shall be discharged.'[6] Thus to the London inves-tor the Greek loan appeared to have everything in its favour. It was of a relatively modest size, to an apparently rich country. It seemed to have support at the highest levels of government. Interest was generous and two years of it was already secured. There was the expectation of capital gain when each £59 invested was repaid as £100. Finally, the loan was guaranteed by the total resources of the Greek state. It is no wonder that

Bowring, not then a rich man, bought £25,000 worth with his own money, and that the loan was three times oversubscribed.

Nevertheless before long the loan was in trouble. After an initial rise from 59 to 63, helped by optimistic reports from Stanhope which were fed to the press, the price of the stock began to fall. At first there was no news from Greece and by the end of March the stock had dropped to 54, five points below the issue price; as the *Morning Chronicle* put it, 'The long want of news from the Morea has in no small degree hurt the interest which was early taken in this Loan.'[7] Then there was catastrophic news: on 14 May London learnt that Byron was dead, and the stock plummeted to 44¾. The fall was accelerated by a provision in the loan agreement that the £59 due for £100 worth of stock was to be paid in six instalments paid monthly from the beginning of March. This had a ratchet effect: as the price dropped in the early months, investors would cut their losses and sell off their partly paid stock, thus depressing the price still further. One remedy was to use money raised by the loan to buy up stock to support the price, and in April Bowring and others persuaded the Greek deputies to do this. Bowring and many of his associates had invested heavily with their own money, and so faced a personal crisis. Bowring extricated himself by selling his stock to the reluctant deputies at 49, ten points below what he had paid but six points above the current price of 43. In a similar manoeuvre Joseph Hume MP, a founder member of the London Greek Committee, sold to the deputies his £10,000 worth of stock, which had cost him £5,900, for £4,600, three points above the current price, limiting his loss to £1,300; when the stock improved he asked the deputies for the £1,300 he had lost plus £54 interest, and got both.

Relations between the loan's promoters and the Greek deputies were further soured by disagreement about how the loan money should be applied. Bowring and the loan's issuing house had agreed that the distribution of the loan should be in the hands of British commissioners in Greece, to be nominated by the London Greek Committee. The first nominees were Byron and Stanhope, but within weeks of the loan's launch the Greek deputies were complaining that this purely British arrangement impugned the honour and damaged the interest of Greece. They therefore proposed as a third commissioner Lázaros Koundouriótis, elder brother of the president of the Executive, brother-in-law of Orlándos, and owner of one of the finest houses on Hydra. But there were objections to Koundouriótis as being bound to favour Hydra and the islands, so Bentham, called upon to mediate, proposed an intricate solution: that there should be an additional Greek commissioner (giving Greeks parity with British), that he should be of the anti-government party (to provide balance), but that he should be nominated by Orlándos and Louriótis (to ensure acceptability). It is highly doubtful if this ingenious plan would have worked in practice, but it foundered on Bowring's objection that the two Greek commissioners 'would unite in a scheme of depredation for mutual benefit'.[8]

There were further difficulties over who the British commissioners should be. Byron died on 19 April. In May Stanhope learnt that as a serving British officer he had been recalled to England by the army authorities. Napier, Gordon and John Cam Hobhouse all declined the appointment. Thus when the first £40,000 of the loan – £30,000 in gold sovereigns and £10,000 in Spanish dollars – reached Zákinthos on board the *Florida* at the end of April and was deposited with Samuel Barff, Byron's banker, Barff retained it on the grounds that only the commissioners could order its release and that Byron's death invalidated the commission until a successor was appointed. The second instalment arrived in the *Little Sally* on 13 June and was similarly retained by Barff. This second delivery prompted the Ionian government to issue a proclamation forbidding such deposits and imposing heavy penalties on anyone involved in forwarding them to Greece. The impasse was finally broken at the end of July when Barff reportedly defied the Ionian government and took a firm stand, declaring: 'If the money is intended for the Greeks, to the Greeks it shall go, though I should be obliged to go along with it.'[9] However Barff may not deserve the praise he has received for his boldness, since in early June the colonial office in London had overridden the Ionian ban by ruling that the Greek loan was a commercial transaction in which the government should not interfere, and news of this would very probably have reached Zákinthos before Barff took his initiative. Whatever the reasons for Barff's decision, the first £40,000 of the Greek loan was now despatched to the Greek government, followed a few weeks later by a second £40,000. The loan money arrived in Navplion during a lull in the civil strife that tore Greece apart during virtually the whole of 1824.

22

Civil War in Greece

At the beginning of 1824 Greece had two governments, or at least two bodies which claimed to be the legitimate government of the country. One was the new Executive, led by Georgios Koundouriótis, and the senators who backed it, based at Kranídhi east of Navplion; the other was the old Executive with its supporting senators, based in Tripolis, and dominated by Kolokotrónis. Kolokotronis' son Pános held Navplion for his father's faction, and his persistent refusal to hand over that town to the new government made civil war between the two sides unavoidable. How should one label these two sides? In some accounts the opposing parties are called the Koundouriotists and the Kolokotronists, but this is to distort the conflict into one simply between two personal factions, and ducks the issue of which side had the greater claim to legitimacy. It was the Senate which had the constitutional right to appoint the Executive members, and there is no doubt that the balance of legitimacy rested overwhelmingly with the new Executive and the Senate which backed it. So the most fitting descriptions of the two sides are government and rebels.

There were in fact two civil wars in 1824 between government and rebels, of markedly different character. The first can be dated from Pános Kolokotrónis' attack on the senators in Árgos in December 1823 and ended with his surrender of Navplion to the government in June 1824. In this war the participants on both sides were almost exclusively from the Peloponnese, Hydra and Spétses. The government side was dominated by islanders (Koundouriótis) and Peloponnesian landowning primates (Zaímis and Lóndos), the rebel side by Kolokotrónis and his sons and their fellow military captains. Somewhat surprising outsiders were Bulgarian mercenaries, including cavalry, employed by both sides.

Of the government's military supporters many had personal reasons for opposing their natural allies, Kolokotrónis and his captains. Iatrákos had been criticised by Kolokotrónis for his conduct at Dhervenákia; Makriyánnis served with Kolokotrónis' son Yennéos in the early months of 1824, but disgust at Yennéos' rapacity soon drove him to join the government side; Moúrtsinos, in whose house Kolokotrónis had stayed on arrival in the Peloponnese in early 1821, was a rival of the Mavromichális clan, and therefore opposed to the old Executive of which Pétrobey Mavromichális was president. On the rebel side, Kolokotrónis was backed by many of his old comrades in arms, most of them part of his immediate or extended family. Among them were two of his sons Pános and Yennéos, and his nephew Nikítas, who at Dhervenákia had earned the nickname of 'Tourkóphagos'. Some stood aside from the conflict. Sisínis, the wealthy primate of Gastoúni in the north-west Peloponnese, managed to remain neutral until the end of the second civil war though his sympathies lay with his natural allies, the primates Zaímis and Lóndos. Dhimítrios Ipsilántis, now living as a private citizen, tried to reconcile the two sides but failed. Mavrokordhátos stayed in Mesolongi, encouraged to do so by his brother-in-law Trikoúpis, who wrote from the Peloponnese, 'Stay where you are, brother, and unless I write for you to come here, don't come, but attend to the interests of your own region.'[1] In the event Mavrokordhátos stayed in Mesolongi for the rest of 1824, and thus held aloof from the government throughout both civil wars.

By Pános Kolokotrónis' attack on the senators at Árgos in the previous December the rebels had thrown down the gauntlet. After three months of simmering delay the government picked it up on 14 March 1824 by proclaiming Navplion as the seat of government and a week later calling on Pános Kolokotrónis to hand the town over to them. The government's determination to occupy Navplion was underlined by the arrival of the members of both the Senate and the new Executive, on two ships commanded by Miaoúlis of Hydra, at Míli five miles from Navplion across the bay.

However, the government did not move immediately on Navplion but first secured easier objectives. On 25 March the government forces entered Árgos without resistance, and that stronghold again became for a few months the seat of the Senate. A week later the rebel forces in the citadel of Corinth surrendered it to the government without a shot. At the beginning of April the government forces under Andréas Lóndos moved on Tripolis, the seat of the rebel government defended by Kolokotrónis and his supporters. There was a day of skirmishing under the walls of the town. 'Many people reasonably feared', wrote Trikoúpis, 'that a hundred men would fall in the battle, but that day of clashes produced only one casualty, since the troops had no inclination to spill a brother's blood.'[2] Some days later the two sides reached an agreement, the rebels left Tripolis unhindered and by mid-April the government was in possession of the town.

The rebels had now lost three of their four citadels – Árgos, Corinth and Tripolis – but still retained Navplion and were not yet prepared to give up. Kolokotrónis, after leaving Tripolis, withdrew to Karítena twenty miles to the west, and there recruited within days a force with which he returned to Tripolis to besiege the former besiegers. Meanwhile rebel troops from Tripolis under Yennéos Kolokotrónis took the offensive against the government. This force did not move directly towards the government positions in Árgos and Míli, but advanced in a long loop behind the mountains to the north and then to the east and south. In clashes with government forces casualties were light – twenty reportedly killed or wounded on the rebel side, eight on the government side – and no decisive advantage was gained by either. The rebel forces tried to capture Míli opposite Navplion, the harbour for Miaoúlis' ships on which the Senate and Executive were temporarily based, and repeated Pános Kolokotrónis' attempt to capture the senators reinstalled in Árgos. Both efforts failed.

The government had succeeded in holding off the rebel offensive and now took the initiative, sending troops at the end of May to disperse Kolokotrónis' forces besieging Tripolis. Kolokotrónis was by this time ready to surrender on terms, and on 3 June agreed to order the surrender of Navplion on two conditions: that the town be formally handed over to Lóndos and Zaímis, his fellow Peloponnesians, rather than to the government and that the government should give 25,000 piastres to Pános Kolokotrónis to cover the back pay of his Navplion troops. There were no punitive clauses in the agreement, which only required Kolokotrónis' forces to disperse.

The Executive regarded these terms as far too lenient but did not reject the deal because it achieved the government's primary aim, possession of Navplion. The Senate was far more conciliatory, and endorsed the agreement to bring the fighting to an end. On 22 June the senators moved from Árgos to Navplion, and were joined two days later by the Executive in a triumphal entry as guns fired in salute from the heights of Akronavplion and Palamídhi, now firmly in government hands. On 14 July the first civil war was brought to an end by a general amnesty. 'It seemed', wrote Trikoúpis, 'that the situation was peaceful and, in the words of the Senate, under the rule of law. But the laws did not rule, and the Peloponnese did not remain at peace.'[3]

That the peace was fragile was in fact obvious. The government had not won the clear-cut victory which it sought, and now found its two leading captains, Lóndos and Zaímis, in sympathy with the defeated enemy. Gordon summed up the position of Lóndos and Zaímis: 'As great Peloponnesian primates, and consequently Kolokotrónis' rivals, they willingly assisted in pulling him down, but it did not suit their policy to crush him entirely, because they foresaw, that at a future period he might be useful in withstanding the preponderating influence of the islanders.'[4] Rebuffs to the two Andréases followed the end of hostilities: the government refused to pay them for their past services, and control of Navplion was quickly taken out of their hands, the Bulgarian Hadzí Chrístos being appointed garrison commander. Also the government's financial position was about to be strengthened. In June it had had considerable difficulty in raising the 25,000 piastres, equivalent to £500, which was the price of the surrender of Navplion; at the beginning of August the first instalment of the English loan, long delayed at Zákinthos, was in the government's hands.

On 1 August that first instalment, £40,000, reached the government in Navplion, and a further £40,000 arrived at the end of the month. This transformed the government's position. 'There prevailed at Nauplia', wrote Gordon, 'a continual bustle, civil and military adventurers, scribes, and parasites flocking thither, heaping adulation on the men in office, and gaping to catch some drops of the golden shower that was at their disposal.'[5] Much of this golden shower ran to waste, and

Finlay's seething indignation at the way he saw his country's contribution to the Greek cause as being misused still leaps off the page. 'Fireships were purchased and fitted out at an unnecessary expense,' he wrote, 'because their proprietors wished to dispose of useless vessels.' The military captains drew pay and rations from the government for even larger numbers of non-existent soldiers than before. 'No inconsiderable amount', Finlay went on, 'was divided among the members of the legislative assembly, and among a large body of useless partisans, who were characterized as public officials.' The signs of this new affluence were everywhere visible, and in Navplion the expenditure was especially frivolous. 'Phanariots and doctors in medicine, who, in the month of April 1824, were clad in ragged coats, and who lived on scanty rations, threw off that patriotic chrysalis before summer was past, and emerged in all the splendour of brigand life, fluttering about in rich Albanian habiliments, refulgent with brilliant and unused arms, and followed by diminutive pipe-bearers and tall henchmen.'[6] Thus to the catalogue of contemporary animal analogies – the Sultan as mole, tortoise or scorpion, Mavrokordhátos as hedgehog – Finlay added that of the butterfly Greek. But despite this wastage the government now had far more money than before to use against its opponents.

By the time the first civil war ended in mid-summer of 1824 it was clear that the government had lost the support of many of the Peloponnesian captains, especially that of the two Andréases, Lóndos and Zaímis. The government now tried to marginalise them, and in late July despatched to the continuing siege of Patras, well away from Navplion, a force led by Lóndos and including troops under Zaímis and Kolokotrónis' sons Pános and Yennéos. This was perfectly justifiable as a strategic move but the government's underlying motives soon became clear. After the first month Lóndos' adjutant, believed to be a spy in the pay of Koléttis, refused to provide the troops with either pay or rations. By the beginning of October the Peloponnesian captains were in no doubt of their position, Zaímis writing to Lóndos that 'the islanders, for their own ends, are seeking the elimination of any Peloponnesians with persuasive powers and influence'.[7]

As well as marginalising its opponents, the government was anxious to strengthen its own legitimacy. Under the constitution of 1823, which was itself timeless, new elections to government office were to be held annually, and these were now overdue. The government's opponents called repeatedly for a new national assembly, to revise the constitution and, they hoped, clip the government's wings, but these appeals got nowhere. The sixty electors for government posts assembled in Navplion in October 1824, and broadly endorsed the status quo. Georgios Koundouriótis was re-elected president of the Executive, and Koléttis a member of it, with Mavrokordhátos in absentia as general secretary.

The government's opponents were now in a far weaker position than they had been at the start of the first civil war. Then they had held four strongholds – Árgos, Corinth, Tripolis and Navplion; now they held none. Then the government had no money; now it had the English loan, to ensure the loyalty of its own troops and to pay mercenaries from outside the Peloponnese. 'It is baffling', wrote Trikoúpis, 'why men such as the two Andréases and Kolokotrónis embarked on this struggle in the midst of such difficulties.'[8] The reason, as Trikoúpis himself makes clear, was desperation: as Kolokotrónis and his supporters saw it, their influence, their wealth and indeed their lives were at stake.

The spark that ignited the second civil war was a call for resistance in late October 1824 from the people of Arkádhia, now Kiparíssia, in the south-west Peloponnese against government levies on their produce. The Executive, against some opposition from the far more placatory Senate, sent a force of 500 soldiers to deal with the malcontents, with Makriyánnis in command of the troops, and accompanied by Papaphléssas, now the minister for internal affairs, as a sort of political commissar. According to Makriyánnis, Papaphléssas brought with him 'his playthings', that is, a fiddle-player and a prostitute, a woman for whom he sought a replacement among the local population when she was left behind at his camp. Papaphléssas also undermined Makriyánnis' military efforts, withholding ammunition and leading away some of his men. The government's punitive expedition was short lived. Disaffected troops from the siege of Patras, enraged at the government's treatment of them, marched under Kolokotrónis to support the rebel Arcadians, and after two weeks of ragged skirmishing Makriyánnis and Papaphléssas returned to Navplion in mid-November with nothing accomplished.

Within a week of their success in Arkádhia the rebels moved against

Tripolis, which was held for the government by troops mainly from Roumeli. Days of skirmishing followed, in which sixty rebels were taken prisoner and the combined death toll was over one hundred. The most prominent casualty was Pános Kolokotrónis, killed in a battle a few miles outside the town. Contemporaries said that his father was devastated by this death, and perhaps at this point he lost heart for the struggle, though in his memoirs he only records laconically that 'the soldiers came up with Pános, and he was killed'.[9]

The government now took steps to bring in more troops from Roumeli to crush the rebels completely. The government was effectively in the hands of Koléttis, to whom his colleagues on the Executive had delegated the direction of the war while their president Koundouriótis was away ill in Hydra. Koléttis' approach to the Roumeliots was brutally straightforward. He offered them money from the loan and the plunder of the Peloponnese, and by early December Roumeliot troops under a host of captains, of whom the most prominent was the Athens commander Goúras, were pouring into the Peloponnese.

The rebels were now effectively finished, but made one last attempt to take the fight closer to the seat of government at Navplion, a force under Lóndos laying siege to the citadel of Corinth. This was soon abandoned, and the rebels suffered a string of defeats in the villages and mountains of the north-east Peloponnese. Zaímis and Lóndos fled to the protection of Mavrokordhátos in Mesolongi. Retribution spread even to those who had played no active part in the rebellion but had sympathised with it: Sisínis, the rich primate of Gastóuni who had played the neutral, found his family stronghold sacked by Goúras' troops, and after being refused sanctuary on Zákinthos put himself in the government's hands. So too on 11 February 1825 did Kolokotrónis, followed soon after by twelve of his leading captains. A month later Kolokotrónis, his twelve supporters and Sisínis were shipped to Hydra and imprisoned in the fortified monastery of the Prophet Elijah on the heights above the harbour. The government's victory was complete.

Gordon wrote sadly of the effect of the second civil war on the Peloponnese. 'Its prosperity was nipped in the bud by the licentiousness of the northern soldiery, who, however reluctant to kill their countrymen, had no scruples about pillage; and not content with plundering the rich properties of Sisini, Zaímis, &c., robbed all classes without distinction.'[10] Makriyánnis was appalled by the pillaging and dealt fiercely with a group of his men who were guilty of it. He had four of them thrown on the ground and held asprawl, and thrashed all of them in turn till the blood flowed from their buttocks:

> I was worse off than they; my hands were bleeding and I was sick for many days after. Then I had them wrapped in raw sheepskins, gave them a month's pay and gave them free passes. I left them in the village to be tended to till their recovery. I tell you, brother readers, from that time on I never came across a dishonourable or a thievish man in my troop and wherever any of my men went they were welcomed by the country folk like their brothers.[11]

Restraining his troops from brutality was one of the major problems for Makriyánnis as a man of conscience. The other was which side to support in the civil strife. He had served with Odysseus Andhroútsos and Goúras in 1822–3, but had left them in disgust at the mismanagement and cruelty of Goúras as commander in Athens. He had then supported Yennéos Kolokotrónis, but had again left disillusioned. He had finally come to the conclusion that though he had a low opinion of many of the leading figures on the government side – for him Goúras was a robber, Papaphléssas an untrustworthy playboy, and Koléttis a deceitful intriguer – he must support the legitimate government whatever its composition. But he would support it only in fighting the Turks; at the end of 1824 he told the government, 'I'm listening to no more orders for a civil war.'[12] These conflicts of loyalty were soon to be harshly resolved by enforced unity against the invasion from the south of Ibrahim Pasha.

23

Ibrahim in the Peloponnese

By the beginning of 1824 the Turks had achieved virtually nothing in three years of land warfare. In 1821 they had lost some of their fortresses, including the all-important Tripolis in the heart of the Peloponnese, and were bottled up in those which they still held. In 1822 Dramali had been comprehensively defeated after crossing into the Peloponnese by the isthmus of Corinth at the eastern end of the Gulf of Corinth, and in 1823 Ottoman forces at the western end had failed to land a single Turkish soldier in the Peloponnese. To try Dramali's Corinth route again would be putting the burnt hand back into the fire, and any western expedition was under threat from Mesolongi, still unsubdued. At sea the Turks had done little better; they had achieved no convincing successes, and had lost a number of their best fighting vessels to Greek fireships. It was imperative that the Sultan devised a new strategy.

The key to this was the involvement of the Sultan's most powerful viceroy, Mehmed Ali, pasha of Egypt for the previous twenty years. In that time Mehmed Ali had imposed root-and-branch reforms on Egypt which had transformed the country. Agriculture and irrigation were improved with the help of foreign experts, and new crops were introduced – cotton, sugar, rice, indigo. Taxes were raised sharply and state collectors, not tax farmers, travelled along Mehmed's new roads to raise state revenue far more efficiently than before. But Mehmed's main innovation was the creation of a modern army and navy. During the Napoleonic wars he had fought against both French and British and been impressed by the superiority of European military systems over traditional Ottoman methods. He had therefore brought in hundreds of officers and technical experts from Europe, mainly France, set up military schools to train Egyptians, and opened military factories. His partner in these drastic and highly successful reforms was his son, Ibrahim Pasha. The new strategy was to bring a large Egyptian force into the Peloponnese by sea, and the inducement to the Egyptians to co-operate was the promise to Ibrahim of the pashalik of the Morea – once he had conquered it.

Egyptian troops had already demonstrated their effectiveness against the insurgents in Crete, and by April 1824 had crushed the rebellion there. The Sultan's new plan required not just the subjection of Crete as a stepping stone between Egypt and the Peloponnese but command of the whole of the Aegean. The first objective was the destruction of the island of Kásos, thirty miles off the north-east tip of Crete, whose ships had harassed the Egyptian forces throughout the Cretan campaigns. In June 1824 it fell to an Egyptian force sailing out from Crete under its admiral Ismael Gibraltar, while Hussein Bey commanded the troops. The next step was the elimination of the islands where Greek naval forces were concentrated: first the easiest target of Psará, small and isolated, which was sacked a month later by a Turkish fleet under the kapitan pasha Khosref. The next objectives were Hydra and Spétses, though in the event the Sultan never managed to assemble sufficient forces to tackle these more formidable opponents. A subsidiary part of the strategy was the reduction of the still rebellious Sámos.

At both Kásos and Psará the Greek fleets of Hydra and Spétses arrived too late to be any help, and Gordon levelled at them the accusation of Demosthenes from an earlier conflict: 'You run about wherever the enemy chooses to lead you, and, like unskilful boxers, can neither foresee nor guard against a blow until you feel that it is struck!'[1] But in early August the Greeks made up for their earlier ineffectiveness at sea, when a fleet under Andréas Miaoúlis, from Hydra and Spétses and with the surviving ships of Psará, set sail across the Aegean to block the Turkish fleet's next objective, the reduction of Sámos. They successfully did so and the Turkish kapitan pasha withdrew to Bodrum to join forces with the Egyptian fleet awaited from Alexandria.

This Egyptian fleet was a huge armada, the largest seen in the eastern Mediterranean since Napoleon invaded Egypt twenty-five years earlier.

It comprised fifty-four fighting ships and a vast assembly of transport vessels carrying 14,000 infantry, 2,000 cavalry with their horses, and 500 gunners in charge of 150 cannon, the whole fleet amounting to nearly 400 ships. In command was the Egyptian viceroy's son Ibrahim Pasha, and subordinate to him Ismael Gibraltar and Hussein Bey, the victors of Kásos. The fleet left Alexandria on 19 July, and its task was to join up with the Turkish fleet and invade the Peloponnese by sea that summer.

At the end of August the Turkish and Egyptian fleets met at Bodrum as planned, but got no further. The combined Greek fleet, now seventy ships and some 5,000 men, was waiting for them. On 10 September the major sea battle of the year was fought in the open waters north of the Bodrum peninsula off Cape Yérondas. Though this battle was no more decisive than a draw, it was enough to persuade Ibrahim Pasha that he could not invade the Peloponnese that year. In October the Turkish fleet returned to Constantinople, by the end of November the Greeks were back in their home ports, and in December Ibrahim Pasha brought his fleet into Crete's Suda Bay to shelter and refit.

The naval campaign of 1824 was, in Gordon's view, 'the most glorious to the Hellenic arms' of the whole war, but it was far from a total success. The Greeks had thwarted the attack on Sámos, but had failed to defend Kásos and Psará, and Psará was a particular loss because its position had enabled it to give early warning of Turkish fleets sailing out of the Dardanelles; it was an eye of Greece, now put out. With the expenditure of twenty-one fireships the Greeks had destroyed six Ottoman warships with the loss of all hands. But, as that success ratio suggests, the fireship was no longer the all-conquering weapon of earlier years. The Turks were keeping better watch, so the Greeks stopped using fireships at night, when any movement on quiet water was easily detectable. In daylight the Turks would launch small boats to drive off an approaching fireship, and if it got close were ready to fend it off from their hull. Many unsuitable vessels may have been converted to fireships, as Finlay suspected. Also the fireship crews were no longer the fearless operators of before, and in the 1824 campaign there were several occasions when the bruloteers refused to move, even when offered 100 piastres as an incentive. Each fireship needed at least two dozen seamen as well as the captain, and probably there were simply not enough daredevils to fill the ranks.

Since traditionally ships stayed in port for the winter it seemed that any further invasion attempt would have to wait for the spring. However at the end of the year Ibrahim Pasha fell in with Captain Drouault, commander of a French frigate, who had instructions to co-operate with the Egyptians and gave Ibrahim some revealing advice. Forget Sámos, Hydra and Spétses for the moment, said Drouault, and concentrate on pouring troops into one of the three Peloponnesian fortresses in Turkish hands, Patras, Koróni or Methóni. Methóni, besides being extensive and well fortified, gives directly on to the shore, and so was the obvious choice. Drouault went on to point out that winter was not a setback for Ibrahim's fleet but an opportunity. In summer calms Ibrahim's heavy vessels drifted apart from each other and became isolated targets for fireships. The winds of winter gave his ships manoeuvrability but were too strong for the lighter, faster Greek fleet. In short, Drouault was saying that the proverbial General Winter, who had been vital in the Russians' defeat of Napoleon in 1812, could now be Ibrahim's ally against the Greeks. Ibrahim took his advice.

On 23 and 24 February 1825, 'days pregnant with sorrow to Peloponnesus' as Gordon wrote, Ibrahim Pasha's fleet of over fifty fighting ships and transports completed its crossing from Crete to Methóni. Some 4,000 infantry and 400 cavalry disembarked and moved into the citadel or into the camp of 400 tents that was set up on the level ground under the protection of its walls. Methóni is the most impressive of the castles left in the Peloponnese by the Venetians. Built on a promontory jutting out southwards from the coast for almost half a mile, it is protected by the sea on three sides and by a moat on the fourth. Its walls thirty-five feet high, with parapets up to fifteen feet deep and all the defensive elaboration of glacis, scarp, counterscarp and bastion, enclose a space that would accommodate half a dozen football pitches. For the Venetians, who had occupied the Peloponnese intermittently from the twelfth century until finally driven out by the Turks in 1715, Methóni was a vital staging post for journeys to Crete, Egypt, Syria, Constantinople and beyond Constantinople to the trade routes of Asia, 'halfway', it was said, 'to every land and sea'. Hence such a massive and sophisticated structure in such an isolated spot. Within days of their arrival the army from Egypt had seized Koróni, Methóni's sister fortress only fifteen miles away, which the Greeks did not attempt to defend.

Three weeks after the first landing another 7,000 troops reached Methóni from Crete, and by the end of March Ibrahim Pasha's forces were ready to move against the two Greek-held fortresses of Old and New Navarino.

Up to this point the Greeks, distracted by civil war, had done nothing to resist Ibrahim Pasha or even to prepare to resist him, though they had known for some months that Navarino would be his target. Insofar as the Greeks considered an Egyptian invasion in the south they expected it not to happen in winter, and to be easily defeated if it came. 'We will dig their graves with their own bayonets,'[2] said the Greek soldiers, and their friends jokingly asked them to bring back an Arab as a slave. The Greeks were scarcely more impressed when they first saw Ibrahim's troops. They were plainly dressed in red cloth jacket, trousers and skull-cap, in contrast to the glittering apparel sported by many of the Greeks thanks to the English loan. Besides this the Arabs were short and puny-looking, and many had lost an eye from Egypt's endemic eye diseases. But appearances were deceptive; the Arab soldiers were very obedient, quick to learn military manoeuvres which they practised constantly, and extremely hardy, and they had a formidable commander in Ibrahim Pasha.

He too scarcely looked the part. Philip Green described him as 'of middling stature, rather fat, marked with the small-pox, has a reddish beard, and is on the whole not a goodlooking man: he evidently has an excellent opinion of himself, the natural consequence of being surrounded by flatterers and slaves. He is, however, an active man compared with other Turks, and certainly manages, one way or other, to carry his plans into effect.'[3] He lived in impressive splendour at his headquarters, but as simply as the meanest soldier when on operations. He was a fierce disciplinarian, personally cutting down any of his men who broke ranks, and a brutal enemy, as his branded captives shipped to Egypt as galley slaves could testify. On the other hand, he sought the reputation of a civilised prince, was prepared to show clemency when it suited his purpose, and was credited with adhering scrupulously to his word. Ibrahim's army was tougher and better disciplined, and he himself more forceful and more subtle than any enemy the Greeks had so far faced.

The first Greek moves had an element of comedy. On 28 March, a full month after Ibrahim's first landing, Koundouriótis, the president of

the Executive, set out from Navplion to take command of the troops
sent to the Navarino area. 'The president departed from Nauplia with
great pomp,' wrote Finlay, 'mounted on a richly-caparisoned horse,
which he hung over as if he had been a sack of hay, supported by two
grooms. His ungraceful exhibition of horsemanship was followed by a
long train composed of secretaries, guards, grooms, and pipe-bearers.'[4]
His stock expression, 'but on the other hand', was laughed at as the
mark of a ditherer. Reaching Tripolis after a leisurely three-day journey,
Koundouriótis fell sick, and it was not until 17 April that he arrived
within thirty miles of Navarino, which was as close as he got to the
enemy. Koundouriótis was accompanied by Mavrokordhátos as his
counsellor, and, unlike his president, Mavrokordhátos did proceed to
the scene of action. A less fortunate appointment by Koundouriótis was
that of a sea captain from Hydra, Kiriákos Skoúrtis, as field commander
of the Greek forces, a man who knew nothing of land warfare. 'They
might as well have made me an admiral,'[5] Kolokotrónis is said to have
remarked, and Samuel Howe called Skoúrtis 'a stupid old fool of a
general who does nothing but drink and sleep day and night!'[6]

Ibrahim's first aim was possession of the Bay of Navarino, only ten
miles or so from Methóni and the finest harbour in the Peloponnese.
The bay forms a horseshoe with an entrance at the south end, its
western arm being the island of Sphaktíria, which is separated from the
rest of the bay's curve only by a narrow-silted up channel. For Ibrahim
to succeed he needed to dislodge the Greeks from Sphaktíria and from
the bay's two fortresses of Old and New Navarino. Old Navarino,
dating from the late thirteenth century, but already by 1825 an isolated
ruin, crowns the steep cliffs at the northern end of the bay and over-
looks the sandy lagoons below. New Navarino, built by the Turks in 1573
in the aftermath of the battle of Lepanto, lies at the south-east corner
of the bay above the modern town of Pílos.

Ibrahim first eliminated the threat from the Greek land forces which
had come south to oppose him. Some six or seven thousand under the
inexperienced Skoúrtis had taken up defensive positions in the hills
above the village of Kremmídhia a few miles inland from Navarino Bay,
and on the morning of 19 April Ibrahim attacked with half that number
but supported by 400 cavalry. The Greeks held out for some time, but
eventually their centre broke and Ibrahim's cavalry, galloping up a

ravine thought to be impassable, attacked from the rear. Over 500 Greeks were killed and many were taken prisoner. Greek forces were further depleted when as a result of this defeat the men from Roumeli, who made up half the total, departed to protect their own homes and in disgust at the command given to Skoúrtis the sailor general. The days of the Greeks' contemptuous mockery of Ibrahim's Arabs were over, and the battle of Kremmídhia had established their superiority.

Ibrahim's next objective was the island of Sphaktíria. It was held by some 800 Greeks and defended by eight Greek fighting ships in the bay, and to tackle these Ibrahim had to wait for his own fleet to return from its third voyage bringing troops from Crete to Methóni. On the morning of 8 May Mavrokordhátos was on board one of the Greek ships, the *Ares*, breakfasting with its captain, when an Egyptian fleet of thirty-four fighting ships plus troop transports was seen approaching the entrance to the bay. The *Ares* quickly crossed to Sphaktíria, where its captain and Mavrokordhátos landed, and the Egyptians immediately began a bombardment under cover of which fifty launches ferried their troops from the ships to the island. The Greek defenders were over-whelmed and within an hour Sphaktíria was in Egyptian hands. Seven of the eight Greek ships got out of the harbour, but the crew of the *Ares* waited anxiously for their captain to return. They learnt at last that he was dead and, with Mavrokordhátos on board after a last-minute escape, cut their cables and made for the harbour mouth. In a six-hour running battle, one ship against thirty-four, the *Ares* eventually got out of the bay and into the open sea. It was 'an action which can scarcely be paralleled in history', wrote Gordon, and was achieved with the loss of only two Greeks killed and seven wounded.

On the day after Ibrahim's capture of Sphaktíria his troops made an assault on Old Navarino, bombarding it from ships in the bay, from Sphaktíria and from the landward side. The Greek defenders could no longer rely on the water and bread which had previously been ferried over from Sphaktíria, and they now lost possession of their one spring of fresh water. Without provisions, having no artillery, almost out of cartridges and with their ramparts little more than a heap of loose stones, the Greeks' capitulation was inevitable. On 10 May the garrison surrendered and, Ibrahim being in clement vein, they suffered no worse fate than being sent away without money or weapons.

The Greeks' last outpost was New Navarino, the fortress at the mouth of the bay next to the town. Among the defenders was Makriyánnis and his troop of a hundred or so men, and Makriyánnis found New Navarino in scarcely better shape than Old Navarino: 'the fort was rotten and falling to bits'. New Navarino had a garrison of some 1,500 men, most of them rushed in after Ibrahim's landing, and forty pieces of artillery, but gunpowder was short and water was the most pressing problem. The Venetian aqueduct supplying the fort had been immediately cut off by the enemy, so the garrison had to rely on the water in three cisterns. Makriyánnis sealed the one which supplied his troop and distributed the water himself, at first half a pint a day and later only half that. However his men found a way round his precautions, as soldiers habitually do, and bored a tiny hole in the cover to let in a long thin reed through which they could slake their thirst at night. Makriyánnis was furious that his compatriots, only ten miles away and with, he believed, 16,000 men, did nothing to help the defenders of New Navarino. The garrison's situation was hopeless, and on 18 May, only a week after the fall of Old Navarino, Makriyánnis and two other captains were in Ibrahim's tent negotiating a surrender. Within a fortnight Ibrahim had taken Sphaktíria and Old and New Navarino; the Greeks had paid dearly for their failure to reinforce and provision them.

Europeans figured on both sides in the fighting around Navarino. On Ibrahim's side one of the senior commanders was a veteran of Napoleon's campaigns, Colonel Sève, now converted to Islam and called Suleiman Bey. The Italian Gubernatis, a professional mercenary, had fought with the Greeks at Péta but was now in the Egyptian army. Julius Millingen, physician to Byron and to Makriyánnis' men in the defence of New Navarino, accepted Ibrahim's offer of service, changed his name to Osman Bey, and spent the rest of his life in Constantinople as doctor to five sultans. On the Greek side, the most distinguished of the Italian philhellenes Santa Rosa, disappointed of high rank or office in Greece, served as a common soldier on Sphaktíria and was killed there. The American George Jarvis, now every inch a captain of Greek irregulars, helped garrison Old Navarino, and proudly rejected Ibrahim's offer of service after the fortress fell.

Throughout the fighting round Navarino Howe was in the area as surgeon to the Greek forces. He had no pay from the government and supported himself haphazardly by private practice, letting his patients pay as they chose. He had plenty of work. 'I will venture to say', he wrote in his journal, 'that I shall perform more surgical operations in one year than any surgeon in Boston, except at the hospital,'[7] and so it turned out. Some of Howe's operations were battle casualties – removal of bullets, treating wounds from the bursting of guns, amputation of part of a hand – conventional though ghastly enough in pre-anaesthetic days. Other duties were less expected: tending a Greek shepherd shot by marauding Greek troops while defending his sheep from them, treating some Greek soldiers whipped for stealing cartridges, and attending a Greek captain's beautiful young Turkish mistress, of whom Howe wrote light-heartedly, 'her confusion and partial undress made her the more interesting, and entirely destroyed my equilibrium'.[8] Howe's job was made far more difficult by opposition from incompetent Greek doctors. One, to preserve his own monopoly, arranged that Howe's box of medicines should be left behind, and another insisted against Howe's protests on making a huge incision to cure what was no more than a bruise. A third refused to allow a mortally wounded patient of Howe's a decent place in the makeshift ward. He and Howe got into a fist fight – 'with one blow I sent him staggering across the room' – which almost became a pistol fight, but Howe got his way, and as so often after ferocious Greek arguments the doctor 'gradually grew cool, and in two hours was as polite to me as possible'.[9]

From his experiences at Navarino and elsewhere Howe summarised the qualities of a Greek fighter in a warts-and-all but respectful description:

> A Greek soldier is intelligent, active, hardy, and frugal; he will march, or rather skip, all day among the rocks, expecting no other food than a biscuit and a few olives, or a raw onion; and at night, lies down content upon the ground, with a flat stone for a pillow, and with only his capote, which he carries with him winter and summer, for covering; baggage-wagon and tent he knows nothing of. But, he will not work, for he thinks it disgraceful; he will submit to no discipline, for he thinks it makes a slave of him; he will obey no order which does not seem to him a good one, for he holds that in these matters he has a right to be consulted. In a European army, a body of Greeks would be called cowards. They never can be brought to enter a breach, to charge an enemy who

has a wall before him, or to stand up and expose themselves to a fire. The invariable practice is to conceal their bodies behind a wall, or a rock, and fire from under cover. They wear pistols, but never come within reasonable distance to use them; they have yataghans, but the only service they are of is to cut off the head of a slain enemy. As an army, then, and compared to Europeans and Americans, they are not brave; but it may be doubted whether Europeans or Americans, in the same situation, would be any braver.[10]

After the fall of New Navarino, Ibrahim's forces immediately fanned out northwards on their campaign to subjugate the Peloponnese. Ibrahim was acting on the old military maxim that a success is doubled if it is followed up at once, and he took care not to repeat Dramali's mistake of leaving unguarded positions to the rear. The Greek cause was now in extreme danger, and the government embarked on a flurry of measures to meet it.

On 30 May, a week after the fall of New Navarino, the government amnestied all who had fought against it in the civil wars. Kolokotrónis and his companions were released from prison on Hydra, all the rebel leaders attended a service of reconciliation at Navplion in the church of Áyios Nikólaos just back from the harbour, and Kolokotrónis was immediately appointed commander-in-chief of the Greek forces. May also saw another government move, the imposition of conscription to a regular force to be commanded by the French philhellene Colonel Fabvier. Every district in Greece was to provide each year, for every hundred inhabitants, one conscript to serve for three years, and as Greece was reckoned to have 700,000 inhabitants this should in theory have provided a regular army of 21,000 men. Of course it did not: many ravaged districts were quite unable to provide recruits, and most were unwilling to do so, believing that the traditional guerrilla tactics of klephtic fighting were best.

Kolokotrónis and the other amnestied captains and their men could do little more to help the Greek war effort than harass Ibrahim's troops as they advanced from their secure bases at Methóni, Koróni and Navarino. Kolokotrónis' strategic aim was to deny Ibrahim possession of Tripolis, which he still regarded as the key to control of the Peloponnese. It was clear that the Greeks could not hold it, so Kolokotrónis proposed to wreck it. 'If we destroy Tripolis,' he told the government, 'Ibrahim will find no other nest, and I with my armies will drive him out of the Peloponnese.'[11] But he got no support, and when in June on his own initiative he ordered the burning of the town, it was just too late. Ibrahim's troops arrived in time to extinguish the first flames, found the walls and the citadel intact, and occupied the town.

While on land the Greeks reeled back under Ibrahim's attack, at sea they took the initiative. In May Miaoúlis sailed into the thick of Ibrahim's fleet at Methóni with six fireships, and proved that they were still effective by burning seven of the Egyptian warships and a dozen other vessels. A brilliant achievement, the Greeks claimed, while Ibrahim dismissed it as not interrupting his operations for a single hour, and probably both were right: it was a tactical success but of no long-term importance. In August a Greek fleet under Kánaris attempted an even bolder exploit: to destroy by fireship the Egyptian fleet in its own home port of Alexandria. The Greek ships got into the harbour unmo-lested by flying the neutral flags of Russia, Austria or the Ionian islands, a practice not considered dishonourable in that era. But once inside the harbour the Greeks' luck deserted them. The wind changed, the one fireship that was set alight drifted away uselessly, and the rest of the Greek fleet, their identity now revealed, could only escape perilously through a shower of cannon balls. 'Such, such are the few men who redeem the Grecian character,' wrote Howe of the Greeks at Alexandria, 'they shine like diamonds among filth; they are brave, disinterested, enlightened patriots, who are willing and ready to die for their country. Oh, it delights me to think of it.'[12] But for all their boldness they had in fact achieved nothing.

In the land war however the Greeks did achieve one success against Ibrahim which was probably crucial to their survival. This was in June at Míli, or Mills, on the bay opposite Navplion, known as the Mills of Lerna because it was close to the spot where legend says Hercules killed the many-headed monster Hydra, and so a marvellously appropriate place for a few Greeks to confront a mighty enemy. The Mills were vital because they held the main stores of grain and ammunition for Navplion, and because the stream that turned the mill wheels also sup-plied Navplion with water, its own cisterns having been allowed to dete-riorate. The Greek captains defending the Mills were a son of Pétrobey Mavromichális, Dhimítrios Ipsilántis who honourably joined the defence on his own initiative, and Makriyánnis who was determined to compensate for the Greek failure at New Navarino. Makriyánnis wrote an account of the battle which portrays him, perhaps with some exaggeration, as the main protagonist.

According to him, he first spent several days preparing the mill's buildings for defence, extending the walls, and directing the mill stream to flow underground into the enclosure. He then got rid of the two possible means of escape: the horses, which he persuaded his fellow commanders to send to Navplion because they could always escape by the caiques, and the caiques by secretly ordering the crews to sail them away while the soldiers were asleep.

The Egyptian attack came on the evening of 25 June when the midday heat was over, and was watched by Ibrahim himself from an old fort on the heights above. The Egyptians on their first charge got into the enclosure and a fierce gun battle followed; 'the smoke from the muskets was like a mist, a fog', wrote Makriyánnis. Finally the Greeks hit on the tactic of concentrating their fire on the officers. The enemy morale slumped, and the Greeks rushed on them with their swords, one of the war's rare examples of hand-to-hand combat. The Egyptians withdrew, leaving perhaps fifty dead. Greek losses were very few, but among the wounded was Makriyánnis, shot in the arm in the last stages of the battle. He was taken for treatment aboard a French frigate commanded by de Rigny, two years later to be French admiral at Navarino.

After his repulse at Míli Ibrahim did not attack Navplion, probably for a mixture of reasons. He would not want to stay to be harassed by troops of the quality of the defenders of Míli; he did not know how weak Navplion's defences were; and the fortress of Palamídhi above the town would be very difficult to take except by a long siege. Navplion, the seat of the Greek government, was saved, and it is probably fair to say that the defenders of Míli saved it. Had Navplion fallen and the government been driven from the Peloponnese, at best to one of the naval islands and at worst to Turk-dominated Roumeli, it is doubtful if its influence at home, and just as important its support from abroad, could have survived.

By the end of the year, the major towns of the Peloponnese – Kalamáta, Árgos, Místra, Gastoúni – were occupied or sacked and, apart from Navplion and the isolated fortress of Monemvasía, Ibrahim was master of the whole area. He had mastered it, but did not actually control it; as the British Captain Hamilton remarked, Ibrahim marched where he pleased but ruled only where he was. The Greeks had lost several of their leading figures. The old warrior Anagnostarás was killed at Sphaktíria, and the firebrand Papaphléssas met his death in June after a nine-hour battle in the south-west Peloponnese: 'a glorious death', wrote Gordon, of a man whom he described as courageous, good-tempered and generous, and at the same time vain, prodigal and dissipated.[13]

Ibrahim's troops certainly did great damage in the Peloponnese, and some observers were convinced that he intended to make it a waste land. The English traveller the Rev. Charles Swan met Ibrahim, and reported him as saying that he 'would burn and destroy the whole Morea', though Gordon commented that it was pointless for Ibrahim to destroy wantonly 'the principal wealth of a province he hoped soon to possess'. But before the end of the year there was an even more alarming report that Ibrahim intended to remove the whole Greek population from the Peloponnese and to re-people the country with Egyptians. Britain's foreign secretary Canning was horrified at what he described as Ibrahim's barbarisation project, and wrote to the prime minister Lord Liverpool: 'I begin to think that the time approaches when *something* must be done.'[14] It is the common and humane reaction to the news of a barbarity to say 'We must do something' – with emphasis on any one of the four words. Canning was unusual among statesmen in finding a way to do something effective. From now on he actively sought, with other powers, for ways to intervene in the Greek conflict. Ibrahim had defeated the Greeks in the field, but his successes had secured for them allies with huge resources who would ultimately prove too powerful for him.

24

The Involvement of the Powers

Captain Rowan Hamilton was an ebullient Irishman in command of the British frigate *Cambrian*. He was in Greek waters for most of the war, and his friendship for the Greeks stretched British official neutrality to the limits. In the summer of 1825, as Ibrahim's invasion pursued its destructive way, he gave the Greek government some advice: 'While there is a spark of hope, fight on! And when all is desperate, then think of foreign assistance.'[1] Hamilton did not believe that this desperate moment had yet arrived, but the Greeks did. In September of that year a Greek delegation to London presented to the British foreign secretary Canning an Act of Submission that went much further than just a plea for help. This Act of Submission was the only political move during the Greek war which was backed by virtually all the leading figures, and had an unusual origin. It was drawn up by a committee of Greeks on Zákinthos, which circulated separate copies for signature to the Peloponnese, the islands, Athens and Mesolongi, and the document was finally endorsed by the Senate in August 1825. The document could therefore with justice claim to speak for the Greek nation, not just the Greek government. The Act, after a long and wordy preamble about Greece's struggle and her prospects, made one simple statement: 'In virtue of the present act, the Greek nation [*éthnos*] places the sacred deposit of its liberty, independence, and political existence under the absolute protection of Great Britain.'[2]

Here was a diplomatic initiative to accompany the Greek military and naval efforts against Ibrahim. It too failed in its immediate purpose. Canning rejected the proposal as inconsistent with Britain's neutrality, though he offered to promote any compromise between Greece and Turkey and added encouragingly that if the Greeks could win independence by their own efforts 'it was well, and it was their affair'.[3] The offer of submission to another power was a bitter pill for the Greeks to swallow. They had from the beginning hoped for aid from abroad in their fight for independence, but had feared that intervention by a foreign power might, as Koraís had warned, lead simply to a new form of dependence. The powers too, and especially Russia and Britain, had shifted to positions very different from those at the start of the war.

It was Russia which dominated the changes of attitude of the other powers to the Greek question: Russia's actions, Russia's open intentions, suspicions of what Russia's intentions might be, fears that Russia might encroach southward at Turkey's expense, or even bring about the collapse of the Ottoman empire. Russian foreign policy was very largely Tsar Alexander's personal instrument, and in deciding it he was subject to conflicting influences: his desire for stability and peace in Europe, which meant upholding the Sultan's authority; his Christian principles, which meant sympathy if not support for the Greeks; and Russia's territorial and commercial interests, which required a strengthening of Russia's position in the Balkan states and unhindered access through the Dardanelles to the Mediterranean for Russia's navy and her merchant ships. Alexander resolved this clash of motives into two fairly clear lines of policy in relation to Turkey and the Greeks: he would not be drawn into war with Turkey simply to support the Greeks, as his denunciation of Alexander Ipsilántis had shown; but in pursuit of Russia's interests he would apply pressure on Turkey, though stopping short of war unless supported by the other European powers.

Russia's main instrument for bringing pressure on Turkey was the treaty which ended the war of the early 1770s between Turkey and Catherine the Great's Russia: the 1774 Treaty of Kutchuk-Kainardji, a village just south of the Danube in today's Bulgaria. This treaty, the most humiliating that Turkey ever signed, involved Turkish concessions to Russia in three major areas: territory, navigation and religion. The territories of Moldavia and Wallachia were to have a form of independence under ultimate Turkish sovereignty, and Russia was to have a say in the appointment and dismissal of the local governors. At sea the vessels of both countries would have free access to the Black Sea, the

Dardanelles and the Mediterranean. Finally, on religion Article 7 stated: 'The Sublime Porte promises to protect firmly both the Christian religion and its churches; and also permits the Minister of the Imperial Court of Russia to make on all occasions representations in favour of the new Church in Constantinople, and of those who carry on its services.'[4]

The first part of this article might be seen as a fairly innocuous statement of good intent by Turkey, and the second part as giving Russia a very limited right of interference in the affairs of only one particular church. But Russia interpreted the article as giving her the right to intervene in any conflict between the Ottoman empire and its Christian population. Technically, if Turkey harassed or even failed to protect a single one of her Christian subjects, she was in breach of the treaty and Russia was justified in taking action against her. The Treaty of Kutchuk-Kainardji, and particularly Article 7, was the spoon which Russia could use to stir the pot of relations with Turkey whenever it suited her.

The pot almost boiled over into war in the early months of the Greek rising, with the Tsar's ultimatum of July 1821 that unless Turkey acceded to Russia's demands Russia would support the Greeks 'jointly with the whole of Christendom'. But Russia did not have the support of any other power, let alone the whole of Christendom; the threat of war faded, and the points of difference between Russia and Turkey were slowly resolved, largely thanks to the good offices of Britain's ambassador to Constantinople, Viscount Strangford.

Alexander's next Greek initiative came in January 1824, when he issued a *mémoire* inviting the other Quintuple Alliance powers to a conference which would jointly force the Turks to accept a settlement of the Greek question. The settlement he proposed was that Greece should be divided into three semi-autonomous principalities but under ultimate Turkish sovereignty as in Moldavia and Wallachia. The three territories were to be the Peloponnese, perhaps with the addition of Crete, and the eastern and western parts of Greece north of the Gulf of Corinth. The backing of the other powers for Alexander's scheme would have given him the reality of the support of the whole of Christendom which he had previously falsely claimed. However, the other powers, especially Britain, were becoming increasingly suspicious of conferences and congresses, and the joint action into which such meetings might draw them. Also the plan for Greece was seen as a power ploy by the Tsar; with Russia already having influence in Moldavia and Wallachia as well as Serbia, and likely to attain it in the three new Greek principalities, Russia would have six satellites between the Adriatic and the Aegean which revolved round the Russian planet.

If the Tsar's scheme was to work it would need months of confidential negotiation between the powers and with the Turks and Greeks, but the opportunity for this was blown away when at the end of May 1824 the Tsar's *mémoire* was published in a Paris newspaper, possibly leaked by Metternich or by Canning as a way of quashing the proposal. This it certainly did. Even though the plan would have given the Greeks a territory larger than they achieved for nearly a century, they rejected it out of hand as unjust and cruel in settling Greece's fate by the decision of a foreign power. The Turks, even though acceptance would have ended a war in which after three years they had still failed to crush Greek resistance, dismissed the proposal with indignation; the Turkish foreign minister the Reis Effendi was reported, after one of his outbursts against it, as having to stop 'from perfect exhaustion'.

Once Britain's foreign secretary Canning knew that both Turks and Greeks had rejected the *mémoire* he refused to attend a conference to discuss it, and the Tsar blamed Canning for frustrating his plan. On 30 December 1824 Canning received this curt message from the Tsar: 'The Cabinet of London will easily understand that His Imperial Majesty on his side regards all further deliberation between Russia and England on the relations with Turkey and on the pacification of Greece as definitely closed.'[5] The Tsar, said Canning, 'was damned if he would talk Greek to us', and it seemed as if the possibility of intervention in Greece, certainly of intervention by Russia and Britain together, was firmly closed off.

Britain's policy which had brought her to this impasse had in part been driven by fear of Russian encroachment, but there were two other major factors. One was Britain's position as the protecting power, in effect the governing power, in the Ionian islands. The other was her extreme wariness of being dragged into action by her membership of the Quintuple Alliance, and distrust of its congresses.

It was Castlereagh, foreign secretary until his death in August 1822, who had set out the basis of this distrust. In 1818 he rejected the idea that the Alliance should interfere to support established authority 'without any consideration of the extent to which it was abused'. In 1820 he stated that to impose such interference as an obligation on the members of the Alliance was 'utterly impracticable and objectionable'. Canning, succeeding Castlereagh as foreign secretary, was wholly in accord with these views, though he was a great deal more flexible than his predecessor in his implementation of policy and very different in character. Canning was popular with fellow politicians, men of letters and the country at large, whereas Castlereagh, though respected, was seen as remote and austere: a contemporary wrote that Castlereagh 'like Mont Blanc continues to gather all the sunshine upon his icy head . . . . It is a splendid summit of bright and polished frost which, like the travellers in Switzerland, we all admire; but which no one can hope, and few would wish, to reach.'[6] Castlereagh was also unfortunate in attracting odium which was not wholly deserved. As chief secretary for Ireland in 1798 he was blamed for the brutal suppression of the Irish rebellion of that year. 'A high gallows and a windy day,' went the popular song, 'For Billy Pitt and Castlereagh.' As Leader of the House of Commons (as well as foreign secretary) in 1819 he was blamed for the deaths at the Peterloo demonstration. 'I met Murder on the way,' wrote Shelley, 'He had a mask like Castlereagh.' Furthermore, whereas Canning was a masterly communicator with a gift for a pithy phrase, Castlereagh was the opposite; for a statesman of his experience he was an extraordinarily incoherent speaker, and what Byron in *Don Juan* called his 'odd string of words, all in a row, which none divine and everyone obeys' provoked bursts of laughter in the House of Commons.

Canning was temperamentally inclined to be flexible, and he had the skills needed to justify his policy shifts or to convince opponents that they were not shifts at all. He was still proclaiming strict British neutrality when in March 1823 the problem of how the Ionian islands' authorities should treat Greek ships led him to recognise the Greeks as belligerents, to Metternich's fury. The only alternative, Canning explained, was to treat them as pirates, which would lead to endless difficulties. On the other hand he took steps to enforce the Foreign Enlistment Act which barred serving British officers from enlisting in the Greek forces. In March 1824 he did not explicitly support the first London loan to Greece, but he did attend the banquet that launched it. The trend of Canning's policy was on balance helpful to the Greeks, but he had no high opinion of them. 'There is no denying,' he wrote, 'they are the most rascally set.'[7]

At the end of 1824, the Greeks sent Canning a written protest against the Russian *mémoire* that proposed three semi-autonomous provinces, and appealed for Britain's help. Canning replied explaining his position to them. As both Greeks and Turks had rejected the *mémoire*, he wrote, any hope of successful intervention at present was 'utterly vain'. Britain was linked to Turkey by long-standing treaties, and if she took part on the Greeks' side against Turkey she would 'engage in unprovoked hostilities against that Power in a quarrel not her own'. Nevertheless, Britain would not be a party to forcing a settlement on the Greeks against their wishes; and if both Greece and Turkey accepted mediation she would do her best 'to carry it into effect, conjointly with other Powers'.[8] So Canning made clear that he was not as yet prepared to consider force, but was prepared to mediate.

Mediation 'conjointly with other Powers' was a very different matter from being dragged into intervention by decisions of a congress of the Alliance. Canning was consistently opposed to such congresses, and illustrated his opposition with a tale from the Arabian Nights. In this story a young man, to oblige a miller, gets into his mill wheel and agrees to turn it for half an hour, 'but being once in, is whipped on, every time that he attempts to pause; the miller, in the meantime, turning his thoughts to his other business'.[9] The young man was Britain, the mill was the congress system, and the miller was the power that was using the congress system for its own ends. In 1824 that power in Canning's view was Russia, and the British and Russian policy differences led almost inevitably to the Tsar's rejection, in the last days of the year, of any further discussion of the Greek situation between Russia and Britain.

Canning calculated that Britain's rift with Russia could not last because Russia would fall out with the other members of the Alliance, and he was soon proved right. The congress to discuss the Tsar's *mémoire* met in St Petersburg in early 1825, though of course without Britain. The Tsar wanted a mandate to use force to impose his settlement, but neither France nor Austria would agree. Metternich's opposition particularly infuriated the Tsar, who in August instructed all his diplomats that he would no longer work with Metternich, since he, the Tsar, was not receiving 'that reciprocity of services which he had a right to expect'.[10] Russia was now isolated since the Tsar was at odds with all three of his major allies: with Britain for not joining his conference, with Austria and France for attending it but rejecting his proposals. The mill wheel of Canning's analogy had stopped turning.

As the months of 1825 passed Canning began to take steps to repair relations with Russia, and get the Tsar to 'talk Greek' again. Canning cultivated the long-serving Russian ambassador to London, Prince de Lieven, and was anxious that he should not be replaced by some 'great, rough, staring *owski*' who might easily, as Canning put it, snap the thread of Anglo-Russian relations 'which is quite strong enough to hold if it is not strained too hard, and may hereafter be twisted into strength again'.[11] In September 1825 Canning rejected the Greek Act of Submission to Britain since, apart from anything else, acceptance would have made future co-operation with Russia impossible.

A rapprochement between Britain and Russia was finally arranged in an extremely unorthodox way. Princess de Lieven, wife of the Russian ambassador to London, visited St Petersburg in the summer of 1825. She was as politically sophisticated, and some thought as politically influential, as her husband, and on this visit had several meetings with the Tsar and with his foreign minister Nesselrode. Late in the evening of the day before her departure for London she received an urgent message asking her to see Nesselrode next morning before she left. At this meeting the foreign minister told her, in the strictest confidence, that the Tsar was ready to abandon the Alliance and co-operate separately with Britain over Greece; and that, while his curt note of December 1824 prevented him approaching Britain, he would be receptive if Britain approached him. Princess de Lieven was asked to convey this to Canning as a 'living despatch', and in total secrecy. Her meeting with Nesselrode was no doubt fixed for the last hours of her stay to minimise the chances of her leaking the information in St Petersburg. The Princess was amazed at Nesselrode's words: 'Here was the most cautious and discreet of ministers,' she wrote, 'compelled to entrust the most confidential, the most intimate, and most bold political projects to a woman.' Nesselrode explained: 'A woman knows how to make people speak, and that is precisely why the Emperor considers you have a unique opportunity.'[12]

Princess de Lieven returned to England, and she and her husband visited Canning while he was staying near Brighton at the end of October 1825. It was probably there, at an informal meeting away from London, that the Lievens told Canning the secret of the Tsar's willingness to co-operate again with Britain over Greece. At the same meeting Lieven showed Canning, in 'entire personal confidence' and 'without the orders of his Court', the Russian despatch which revealed Ibrahim's barbarisation project. The despatch said:

> The Court of Russia has positive information that before Ibrahim Pasha's army was put in motion, an agreement was entered into by the Porte with the Pasha of Egypt, that whatever part of Greece Ibrahim Pasha might conquer should be at his disposal; and that his plan of disposing of his conquest is (and was stated to the Porte to be and has been approved by the Porte) to remove the whole Greek population, carrying them off into slavery in Egypt or elsewhere, and to re-people the country with Egyptians and others of the Mohammedan religion.[13]

Canning now had both an offer of co-operation from the Tsar and a justification for action, not solely on humanitarian grounds. The barbarisation plan made Russia's intervention almost inevitable – there could hardly be a more flagrant breach of the Treaty of Kutchuk-Kainardji – and Britain did not want Russia to intervene alone. We cannot be certain that the plan was in fact adopted by Ibrahim, or that the Porte approved it. By the summer of the following year both Ibrahim and the Porte had issued denials, though they would not put the denials in writing. But whether true or not, this report of Ibrahim's intentions was a crucial factor in bringing nearer intervention by the powers. Up to this point Canning had consistently opposed the use of force over Greece. Now he stated explicitly that Britain intended 'to prevent, if necessary by force, the accomplishment of the plan imputed to Ibrahim Pasha'.[14]

Then an event occurred which threatened once again to snap the thread of Anglo-Russian understanding. In September Tsar Alexander travelled from St Petersburg to Taganrog on the Sea of Azov which flows into the Black Sea. As he made exhausting journeys round his southern domains, his symptoms of what was known as Crimean fever intensified, and on 1 December 1825 he died at the age of forty-seven. Utter confusion followed. Alexander's natural successor was Constantine, the eldest of his brothers, but by a secret agreement Constantine had renounced the throne in favour of the next brother, Nicholas. On Alexander's death Constantine, now in Warsaw as commander of Russia's military commission in Poland, followed the agreement and swore allegiance to Nicholas. Nicholas in St Petersburg, ignoring the agreement, swore allegiance to Constantine. Thus as the London *Times* put it, 'The Empire is in the strange position of having two self-denying Emperors and no active ruler.'[15]

The revolutionary group who became known as the Decembrists now seized their opportunity. This group, mainly from the aristocratic intelligentsia and with backing from some army units, had been building support since the end of the Napoleonic wars. Its aim was the abolition of the Tsar's autocratic powers, the emancipation of the serfs and the adoption of a liberal constitution, or at least, in the present power vacuum, the enthronement of the supposedly more enlightened Constantine. Nicholas learnt of the Decembrists' plans to act, and accepted the tsardom. On the morning of 26 December the pro-Constantine troops of the Moscow regiment and their officers moved into the Senate Square in St Petersburg, a century later renamed the Decembrists' Square, and there they refused to take the oath of allegiance to Nicholas. Seven hours later the mutinous soldiers had been dispersed by cannon firing grapeshot, and hundreds of Decembrist supporters were later imprisoned and interrogated. Of those found guilty after a mockery of a trial most were sent to penal servitude in Siberia, and five were hanged, still defiantly cheerful on the scaffold and turning back to back so as to shake each other's bound hands for the last time. Nicholas was now firmly established as tsar. But would he follow his predecessor's secretly agreed line over relations with Britain and co-operation on the question of Greece?

To discover the answer to this question the Duke of Wellington, now a member of the cabinet, was sent as a special envoy to St Petersburg. The ostensible purpose of the Duke's visit was to congratulate Nicholas on his enthronement, but the political objective was for him to make clear Britain's position on Greece and Turkey: that Britain was prepared to mediate alone, or in conjunction with Russia, and that if mediation failed Britain was prepared to use force to stop Ibrahim's barbarisation project but in no other circumstances.

However, when Wellington reached St Petersburg on 2 March 1826 he found the new Tsar apparently indifferent to the Greeks and concerned only with forcing concessions from Turkey over the principalities and Serbia. Lord Strangford, now Britain's ambassador to St Petersburg, thought that the Tsar would ignore the Greeks indefinitely, writing that 'the young Emperor Nick does not care a straw for the virtuous and suffering Greeks. He considers armed intervention or indeed any intervention at all as little better than an invitation to his own subjects to rebel.'[16] But the Tsar dealt rapidly with the principalities question by an ultimatum to Turkey, and a few days later Lieven and his wife, summoned from London by the Tsar, arrived in St Petersburg. The Greek question was now actively revived, the diplomatic logjam at last broke, and events moved quickly. On 4 April, only a fortnight after the Lievens' arrival, the Protocol of St Petersburg, a statement of common objectives on Greece, was signed by Nesselrode and Lieven for Russia and by Wellington for Britain. The text of the protocol in French stated that, as the Greeks (by their Act of Submission) had invited Britain's mediation, and as both Britain and Russia wished to mediate jointly, the following arrangement was proposed:

– Greece would become a dependency of Turkey, paying an agreed annual tribute.
– The Greeks would choose their own governing authorities, but in this choice Turkey would have 'une certaine part'.
– Greece would have complete freedom of conscience, of trade and of internal administration.
– To separate Greeks from Turks, the Greeks would acquire (the protocol did not say how) all Turkish property in Greece.
– If mediation was rejected by Turkey, these proposals would form the basis of intervention by Russia and Britain either jointly or separately.
– The future extent of Greece would be settled later.
– Neither Britain nor Russia would seek for herself territorial gains, exclusive influence or commercial advantage.
– Austria, France and Prussia would be invited confidentially to guarantee, with Russia, the final arrangement, but Britain would not be a party to this guarantee.[17]

Such were the terms of the protocol, which offered something to everyone. The Greeks would achieve a limited independence, and the Turks would retain a limited sovereignty. For Russia, the proposals of a single semi-autonomous state for Greece was not unlike the three such Greek states proposed by Tsar Alexander in his *mémoire* of 1824. Both Russia and Britain retained the right to intervene alone as well as together. A guarantee from the other three powers was invited, no more, and Britain would not join the guarantee: that is, the powers of the now defunct Alliance might join the action or not, and Britain in refusing to give a guarantee for the future was emphasising her determination not to step back on to the Alliance treadmill.

The protocol did no more than state the shared aims of the parties, and it would have to be converted into a treaty if obligations were to be imposed on the signatories. Which of the other three powers, Austria, Prussia and France, would sign such a treaty? There was no chance of gaining Austrian support. The protocol effectively marked the end of the Alliance and its unconditional support for authority, which Metternich had in the past been able to dominate. Suppose, he suggested scornfully, that the Irish, in revolt against the British, invited the French to mediate. 'Is England then ready to regard as a Power equal in rights to that of the [British] King the first Irish Club which declares itself the Insurgent Government of Ireland? To regard as justified the French Power which would accept the office of mediator, by reason of the sole fact that the invitation had been addressed to it by the Irish Government? . . . Whither does this absurdity not lead us?'[18] Prussia, the power furthest from the scene of conflict and without the trade or territorial interests of the others, offered vague support but would not sign a treaty without Austria. That left France. After a year of patient diplomacy by Canning France did in fact sign the successor to the protocol, the Treaty of London of July 1827. But that is to take the story beyond April 1826, which brought, besides the signing of the St Petersburg Protocol, another crucial event for the Greeks: the fall after a year-long siege of Mesolongi.

25

Odysseus and Trelawny

During 1825 the war between Greeks and Turks split into three separate parts, virtually three separate wars, as if the main regions of Greece were a thousand miles apart rather than contiguous. In the Peloponnese Ibrahim was almost everywhere victorious. In Western Roumeli a Turkish army arrived before Mesolongi in April to begin the third and final siege of the town. In Eastern Roumeli Turkish forces seized and sacked the town of Salóna in May but abandoned it again in November. Otherwise in that region little happened but skirmishing, apart from two events of a suspect if not mysterious kind: the death of Odysseus Andhroútsos and the near-death of his faithful and fanatical supporter, Byron's companion Trelawny.

Odysseus Andhroútsos seemed to have all the qualities needed for a successful leader of a band of Greek irregulars: courage, of course, combined with a commanding presence, dashing good looks, a total lack of scruple and a taste for intrigue. In Trelawny's eyes he was a glorious being, to others he was only a lesser Ali Pasha of Iánnina, his former patron. At the conference of Greek leaders on Lévkas shortly before the revolution began, Odysseus was made commander of the East Roumeli region, and in May 1821 defeated the Turks at Graviá, a victory regularly cited by his supporters, then and now, as proof of his commitment to the Greek cause. But little military success followed, and when Dramali led his Turkish army south through Odysseus' territory in the summer of 1822 Odysseus did nothing to hinder him, with the lame excuse that he had not enough men he could trust. He failed in attacks on the two Turkish-held fortresses on the island of

Évvia, at Káristos in the south and at Chalkídha where Évvia almost joins the mainland.

As his contribution on the battlefield diminished, so his relations with the government got worse. In June 1822 the newly formed national government had sent two emissaries to bring him under control; both were killed, Odysseus believing, or claiming to believe, that they had orders to kill him. Later that year Odysseus' position seemed to be strengthened when he became commander of the garrison of the Athens Akropolis after the Turks had been forced out, but he was soon replaced by his lieutenant Goúras. In 1824 it was Goúras not Odysseus who was called in to the Peloponnese by the government to help it to victory in the second civil war, and Goúras was rewarded with the overall command of East Roumeli.

By early 1825 Odysseus was receiving no support, supplies or pay from the government, and was losing men to captains who were able to get their hands on some of the English loan, so he made an accommodation, a *kapáki*, with the Turks. Trelawny, as always defending his hero, represents this arrangement as simply a temporary truce, designed to force the government to resume support for him. In fact however Odysseus took his men over to the Turks and fought beside them. But the Turks had no trust in Odysseus and kept him under constant watch. After three months Odysseus took a final gamble and in mid-April slipped away from his Turkish minders on the pretext of reconnoitring new positions, and surrendered to his old associate and former subordinate Goúras.

Odysseus was taken to Athens and imprisoned, in the so-called Frankish Tower which until it was taken down in 1875 stood beside the Propylaia at the western end of the Akropolis. For two months he was kept chained in his cell, tortured it was said to reveal the whereabouts of his treasure. Then on the morning of 17 June the rising sun revealed the lifeless body of Odysseus on the platform of the temple of Athena Nike, a hundred feet below his prison.

What had happened? An Italian doctor living in Athens was immediately summoned to examine the corpse, and reported fractures of the skull, arm, ribs and leg, all on the right side, everything consistent with a fall and nothing to suggest any other cause of death. The doctor's final words made his sympathies clear: 'Death was instantaneous, and appropriate for a wicked traitor to his country' – a rare example of an autopsy report which concludes that it served the victim right.[1] The Athens newspaper amplified the story. Odysseus, it said, had obtained two ropes from donkeys going up to the Akropolis, and while his guards were asleep had lowered himself on one, with the other wound round his waist for a further descent; but the ropes were old and Justice had seen to it that the first rope broke and Odysseus fell to his death. Finally a report was written for Goúras by his second-in-command Mamoúris, Goúras being perhaps intentionally away from Athens at the time. The report stated that Odysseus had been well treated, that he had tried to bribe his guards to let him escape but they had refused, that on the fateful night he had pretended to be ill and persuaded Mamoúris to remove his guards whose presence was oppressive. The account of the two ropes was given as before, and the report ended with crocodile tears: 'I am deeply bewildered and grieved, and your family is inconsolable – I do not know how to bear this heaviness of heart.'[2]

These official versions, besides being obviously partisan, were full of improbabilities. How for instance did Odysseus in a guarded cell obtain and conceal two hundred-foot ropes, and why was Mamoúris so easily persuaded to withdraw the guards? However, foul play remained only a strong suspicion until eyewitness evidence for it emerged over seventy years later. In 1898 a lawyer published an account of the death of Odysseus which he had heard, many years after the event, from one of the guards. That night, said the guard, was pitch dark and a light rain was falling. Some time after midnight four men approached Odysseus' cell, one of them Mamoúris, and the guard was told to go to bed, but instead he hid near by. There was a rattle of chains as Odysseus stood up, and the guard heard Odysseus say: 'I know who sent you and why you are here. Undo just one of my hands and I'll show you what sort of man I am. I don't care about these other rotten-bellies, but why you, Mamoúris?'[3] A commotion and frantic shouting followed, and then all was quiet again. The hidden observer next heard from above the cell a sound as of a pole being driven into a rock and then saw the four men bring a heavy burden out of the cell. The next morning he discovered the pole with a broken rope attached to it, and saw the body where it had fallen. Odysseus' mouth was bloody and swollen, as if he had been beaten with a gun barrel, and his throat was bruised and bore the marks of fingernails, evidence which the examining doctor was told to suppress.

There seems little doubt that this is how Odysseus died: beaten, strangled and thrown from the tower, while a crude attempt was made to disguise the death as a failed escape. It seems too that the orders came from Goúras, anxious to be rid of a dangerous rival, and that Goúras took care to be away from Athens on the fatal night. Gordon says that 'Ghouras subsequently felt remorse for the death of his former friend, heard with pain the mention of his name, and occasionally murmured, "in that business I was misled."'[4] The puzzle over Odysseus' death is not the manner of it, but why Odysseus put himself at the mercy of Goúras in the first place. The bond of their old association may have caused Goúras later regrets, but it was obviously not enough to make Odysseus' cell a safe refuge from his many enemies. He may well have thought that he would soon be freed to take up his command again when his country needed him, just as Kolokotrónis and his fellow prisoners were released from Hydra to fight Ibrahim. Whatever his calculations were, they failed of their object and Finlay concisely described his end: 'In trying to overreach everybody, he overreached himself.'[5]

In 1823, when Odysseus was still the dominant figure in East Roumeli, he took over and fortified a cave high on the slopes of Mount Parnassos. Known as the Mávri Trípa or Black Hole, it was a romantic bandits' hideout which Byron might have imagined. It was reached by an hour's journey over rough country from the nearest village, Tithoréa, and then by three iron ladders bolted to the seventy-foot cliff face, the highest of which could be pulled up through a hole at the lip of the cave floor, so making the place completely inaccessible. A torrent, the Kakórevma, flowed in a gorge hundreds of feet below, and for the visitor stepping across from one ladder to another it was tempting, but most unwise, to glance dizzyingly down. Inside the cave was a series of smaller caves on different levels, and from its mouth, some sixty feet across and thirty feet high, could be seen miles of rugged country to the east and north, and of course any troops approaching over it. Seen from without, the cave might seem a Black Hole, but from within it has been described as more like the terrace of some fantastic Alpine hotel.[6]

It was to this astounding retreat that Odysseus' lieutenant Trelawny came in May 1824, bringing with him from Mesolongi four light cannon which had originally been sent for the town's defence by the

London Greek Committee. Trelawny was accompanied by Gill, one of the English artificers from Mesolongi, and by Thomas Fenton, a Scots philhellene in his early thirties, a tough veteran of guerrilla warfare in Spain, described by Trelawny as 'restless, energetic, enterprising, and a famous walker', and so often sent out as Trelawny's eyes and ears. Trelawny added that 'no querulous word or angry glance ever ruffled our friendly intercourse'.[7] The new occupants now began work to make the place impregnable, building a parapet along the cave mouth with openings for the four cannon, and a guardhouse at the foot of the ladders. They also made it comfortable. Gill built a cistern to catch the stream which flowed into the cave in winter, houses of board and a small chapel were constructed in the inner recesses, and everything necessary was hauled up by a crane with ropes and pulleys, even the ludicrous extravagance of a billiard table brought over from the Ionian islands. The cave was thus a bolt-hole for Odysseus in which he could hold out against any enemy for a long time, and in comfort approaching luxury.

When the young English philhellene William Humphreys visited the cave in the autumn of 1824 he found these improvements in progress or finished, and described military stores and provisions of 'corn, oil, wine, cheese, olives and rakee (brandy), sufficient to supply hundreds of men for twenty years', and sumptuous eating, 'flesh of all kinds, fresh and salt water fish, game and poultry'.[8] Installed in the cave, as well as the garrison, were two of Odysseus' half-brothers, and in the secluded women's quarters Odysseus' mother and his 13-year-old half-sister Tersítza.

In early 1825, as Odysseus saw his position as a Greek leader deteriorating and the need for an accommodation with the Turks approaching, he handed over his one secure base to his one unfailingly loyal ally. In Trelawny's account Odysseus summoned some of his principal followers and said, 'I call you to witness, I give this Englishman the cavern and everything of mine in it,' and then to Trelawny, 'I trusted you from the first day as I do now on the last we may ever be together.'[9] Odysseus' wife and infant son had by now joined the rest of his family in the cave. Trelawny, realising that treachery from within was a far greater danger than attack from without, reduced the garrison to a handful of men of different countries and languages so that they would be unlikely to conspire together: the Scot Thomas Fenton, a Greek, an Albanian Turk, an

Italian, two Greek boys as servants, and as principal bodyguard a Hungarian called Komarone, anglicised as Cameron. For further protection Trelawny kept a huge and ferocious Thessalian mountain dog.

Two other steps were taken with an eye to the future. One night Odysseus, Trelawny and a few of his men left the cave with Odysseus' accumulated wealth – antiquities and £15,000 in gold coin – and buried it outside Thebes, almost certainly not the famous town which was fifty miles away but the nearby village of the same name. Odysseus later removed the markers from the site, and the treasure has never been found. The final action was to bind Odysseus and Trelawny in the most powerful of Greek allegiances, by the betrothal of Trelawny to Odysseus' half-sister Tersítza. The marriage ceremony was held in the chapel in the cave, and within a short time the child was pregnant.

In April 1825, after three months with the Turks, Odysseus gave himself up to Goúras. Goúras now tried a crude deception to get possession of the cave, which was believed to contain a hoard of treasure – though the most valuable part, the gold, had by now been removed and buried – and known to contain scarce armaments and stores of provisions. Goúras therefore sent a detachment of troops to the foot of the cliff, one of whom came forward holding a green bough as a truce flag and announced that Odysseus was with them, was now friendly with Goúras and wanted Trelawny to come down for a conference. Trelawny of course refused. The besiegers made further pleas, which were regularly rejected, and tried scrambling up the cliff to get at the cave from above, to no avail. After four or five days Goúras' men went away, leaving a few behind to keep intermittent watch on the cave. Trelawny was now stuck in his lofty eyrie, tied by loyalty to Odysseus and by fear of capture by Goúras if he left. But while he stayed put he was safe.

This stalemate was dramatically broken by a new arrival, William Whitcombe. Whitcombe, the youngest child of a prosperous London family, was still only 18 when, having offered his services to the London Greek Committee, he reached the west coast of the Peloponnese in the early spring of 1825. He immediately joined the forces moving south to oppose Ibrahim, where Howe noticed him as a young man of striking if rather feminine good looks, dressed in full pallikari panoply, 'a perfect picture of a young Greek, in the person of an Englishman of family and fortune'.[10] Howe got to know him, and when Whitcombe left the camp at the end of April commented that 'Whitcomb is such a fickle-minded harebrained boy that it would puzzle Solomon to calculate his course.'[11] Whitcombe now joined up with the other young English philhellene Humphreys and the pair went together to the main Greek camp at the monastery of Ósios Loukás on the north shore of the Gulf of Corinth. On the night of their arrival at the end of May Humphreys made his way to the cave, which was only about fifteen miles away, and returned with an invitation to the cave for Whitcombe.

Whitcombe arrived there on 7 June and for the next three days fell under the intense influence of the forceful Scot Thomas Fenton. There was nobody else to talk to, Trelawny being aloof and the few guards having nothing in common with Whitcombe, not even language. However Whitcombe, perhaps looking for another person to blame for what followed, came to believe that he had been lured to the cave by Humphreys specifically to become the tool of Fenton:

> Charmed by Mr. Humphreys' account of the excessive intrepidity, honour, romantic situation, &c., &c., of his friend Fenton, added to his good-nature and *bonhomie*, I was induced by the repeated, by the urgent entreaties of that Mr. Humphreys, added to a letter expressing the most pressing invitation from Fenton . . . I was induced, I say, to pay that visit to the cave. On my arrival I was beset by Fenton's utmost talents of duplicity (in which never mortal man has excelled him). Touched by his mournful tales of wrongs, rejection, deprivation of right, viewing him only as the romantic, the injured, the generous hero he had been represented by Humphreys, I swore to stand by him on his resolution to recover his rights or die.[12]

Whitcombe's fourth day in the cave, 11 June 1825, was intensely hot, and after the midday meal, when most of the party had retired for a siesta, Fenton suggested a shooting match on the terrace between himself, Trelawny and Whitcombe. Howe relates what happened next, as he heard it from Whitcombe and as Trelawny's own account broadly confirms:

> It was Trelawny's first fire, and after hitting the mark, he went a little forward, and, in his usual cold, unsociable way, stood with his back to them. Fenton raised his carabine, which was not loaded, and pointing it at Trelawny, snapped. He looked with pretended dismay at Whitcomb,

cocked and snapped again. 'He turned upon me such a look, I knew not what I did. I raised my gun, pulled the trigger, and fell from my own emotions.' These were the words of the mad boy, who had become all but an assassin. Two balls, with which his gun was loaded, had lodged in the back of Trelawny, who was apparently dying.[13]

When Trelawny slumped forward, blood flowed from his mouth, bringing with it several teeth and one of the musket balls, which had broken his jaw. The second ball had broken his collar bone, paralysing his right arm, and remained in his chest. The Hungarian Komarone had been watching. He had long been suspicious of Fenton and now, deciding immediately who was the instigator of the attack on Trelawny, killed Fenton with a single shot. Whitcombe fled in terror, using his sash as a rope to get down the top part of the cliff, and reached the bottom, but was quickly brought back and hung by his ankles from the crane above the precipice. Trelawny's followers wanted to subject Whitcombe to death by roasting over a fire, but Trelawny intervened and Whitcombe was kept a prisoner in the cave. 'He was now mad with terror,' wrote Trelawny, 'he screamed and shrieked if any one came near him, he was in irons and chained to the wall, with no other food than bread and water. I resolved on the twentieth day of his imprisonment to set him free, which I did.'[14]

For those first twenty days Trelawny sat day and night on the terrace of the cave leaning against the rock, kept alive by yolks of eggs and water. Humphreys heard of the assassination attempt and hurried to the cave. After seeing Trelawny's state he set off for Navplion to summon a doctor, but the doctor never reached the cave, and Trelawny might not have welcomed him if he had. 'Nature makes no mistakes, doctors do,' wrote Trelawny; 'probably I owe my life to a sound constitution, and having no doctor.'[15]

Trelawny's first solid food was a piece of cured wild boar the size of a shilling, which he managed to chew despite the agony of his broken jaw. Slowly his strength returned. If he was to leave the cave it had to be with the permission of Goúras, and this was with some difficulty negotiated by the itinerant British ex-officer Major Bacon, 'one of your odd sort of fishes', as Howe called him, 'who has been wandering about in Russia, Turkey and Persia, the devil knows where or what for'.[16] On 7 August Trelawny, his right arm still useless, descended the tottering ladders. His child wife Tersítza came with him, and two days later they were taken off from the north shore of the Gulf of Corinth by a British warship provided by the ever benevolent Captain Hamilton.

There can be no doubt that Whitcombe fired the shots that nearly killed Trelawny, and that Fenton put him up to it: but what can Fenton's motive have been? To strike a blow for Greece? – but Trelawny, for all his warrior trappings, was insignificant as a military captain without Odysseus. To get possession of the cave and its treasures? – but the cave was strategically unimportant, and Fenton must have known that the main treasure, the gold, had already been removed. In any case, given Trelawny's guards, any attempt to assassinate him in the cave was suicidal. For the assassin the gains could not possibly outweigh the costs, so any explanation of Fenton's actions must cover the irrational as well as the rational.

Rational interpretations centre on the plot against Odysseus promoted by Fenton and the American philhellene George Jarvis in the previous October and November, a plot in which they tried to involve Mavrokordhátos. The aim was almost certainly to kill Odysseus and possibly Trelawny too, as Jarvis' journal and letters show. There were good reasons for this scheme. The government in the last months of 1824 was engaged in the second civil war against the dissident captains of the Peloponnese, and the government could win only by bringing in, as it did, Roumeli captains in its support. If Odysseus, never a friend of the government, had backed the dissidents, the government might well have lost. This was the view which Fenton urged on Jarvis, making the most of the danger: 'Odysseus is united with all the important captains of the Morea, and shortly – even soon – all will be over. . . . Certainly such a formidable enemy, with every means of harming us and no loyalties, is well worth the trouble of overturning.'[17] Jarvis in turn tried to convince Mavrokordhátos that the true enemies were not the Turks but 'the others', that is the dissident Greek captains: 'The Turk has never been our most formidable foe. Once the others were defeated it would be a farce with the Tartars [that is, the Turks].'[18] Mavrokordhátos, who was seriously ill in Mesolongi throughout this time, listened to the proposals, and Jarvis told Fenton that 'The Prince does *not* intend to enter into your plans. . . . he *approves* of your plans, however.'[19]

This approval may well have been the product of wishful thinking by

Jarvis; morality apart, Mavrokordhátos' gladiatorial style was to use the net of political manipulation rather than the trident of assassination. Whether or not Mavrokordhátos approved the plan in some sense, he refused any active involvement in spite of Jarvis' increasingly strident pleas. 'It is essential', he wrote to Mavrokordhátos at the end of November, 'that Your Excellency (or the government) gets possession of the cave, and that the traitor's head falls,' and a few days later, 'I beg you, Prince, to give me your decision in writing.'[20] But by this time the rebel captains of the Peloponnese had been defeated, and in early 1825 Odysseus made his accommodation with the Turks. So the justification for a plot against Odysseus – to prevent him joining the anti-government forces – was no longer valid. Jarvis disbanded the troop of Greek irregulars which he had been leading in Roumeli and went south to join the fighting against Ibrahim Pasha at Navarino. Fenton went back to the cave.

Fenton had built enormous personal expectations on the plot against Odysseus; he told Jarvis that 'I would not exchange the glory that I expect for my part in this great enterprise, not even for all the riches which England possesses. Greece – that name alone is enough.'[21] Fenton was a tough veteran, not a starry-eyed youth content with the romance of the Greek struggle, and had come to Greece to do something outstanding for the cause and for his own reputation. The immediate opportunity for this had gone and Fenton was back in the cave with no more arduous task than running errands for Trelawny. Then, after some five months of frustrating inactivity for Fenton, Whitcombe arrived at the cave. Like Fenton he was driven by selfish ambition: 'his only motive in coming', wrote Howe, 'was the hope of distinguishing himself'.[22] He was young, impressionable and as Howe said fickle-minded and harebrained. It was easy for Fenton to overwhelm him with concocted stories of slights and injuries suffered at Trelawny's hands, and to cast himself as an incarnation of the Greece Whitcombe had come to fight for, leading Whitcombe to swear to support Fenton in 'his resolution to recover his rights or die'. Here was a chance for Fenton to achieve at least part of the scheme on which he had built his hopes, to bring down the lieutenant if not the leader. It was as if two schoolboys, the older tough and manipulative, the younger desperate to prove himself, had planned a practical joke on the headmaster or failing him his deputy; there would be enormous éclat, and never mind the consequences. The Hungarian bodyguard Komarone could not understand what Fenton and Whitcombe said to each other, but intently watching their body language he had no doubt where the main responsibility lay; and it was Fenton not Whitcombe whom Komarone immediately shot dead.

Of the actors in this drama only one survived to old age. Odysseus was dead at the foot of the Akropolis within a week of the attempt on Trelawny. Humphreys, who had been responsible, perhaps innocently, for Whitcombe's arrival at the cave, died in Greece of disease in 1826. In the same year Goúras was killed in the defence of Athens, and in the following year Jarvis died of fever in Árgos. Whitcombe, after his release by Trelawny, made his way to Hydra, where Howe met him again and found him distraught, dishevelled and still hag-ridden by nightmares of the cave. He returned to England, served briefly in the British army in the West Indies, and in 1832 at the age of 26 died in mysterious circumstances, perhaps from suicide, in the room of an inn near Bath. Only Trelawny, who had come so close to death in the cave, lived on. He lingered in Kephaloniá until 1828, hoping for a chance to return to Greece which never came. While in Kephaloniá he went through an acrimonious divorce from Tersítza, after the birth of their daughter Zella. Tersítza later married a Greek and in 1840 was still described as distinguished for her beauty. Trelawny returned to England and, as the years passed, told, retold and embellished the story of his adventures. He died at his home in Sussex at the age of 88, with Whitcombe's second bullet, he claimed, still lodged in his breast.

26

The Fall of Mesolongi

The defence of Mesolongi during its final siege has a supremely honoured place in Greek history. 'Here in Mesolongi', wrote Nikólaos Mákris, son of one of the garrison's commanders, 'Hellas, like a towering rock rooted deep in the earth, made light of the storms and withstood undaunted the cannonade of the barbarian hordes against the massive defences of the town. Thus Hellas shook to its foundations the arrogant throne of Ottoman power like a rotten oak, and hurled to the ground the autocratic might of the Sultan, to the amazement and admiration of all mankind.'[1]

Patriotism and filial piety had led Mákris into some exaggeration. The siege of Mesolongi ended in failure for the Greeks, and no more destroyed the Sultan than Dunkirk destroyed Hitler. The walls of Mesolongi were not massive but flimsy, and their effectiveness was all the more remarkable for that. The Greek nation was not, as Mákris implies, united in support of Mesolongi; both the national government and the Greek captains in the surrounding area gave grudging help at best. But Mákris was wholly right to characterise as undaunted the garrison and the people of Mesolongi, whose fortitude did indeed astonish the world as they held off for a year the attacks of besiegers who far outnumbered them.

The siege of Mesolongi which began in April 1825 was not the first it had suffered. In 1822 after the disastrous battle of Péta Mavrokordhátos and his shattered forces fell back to Mesolongi, and were besieged by the troops of Omer Vrionis, the victor of Péta, supported by the cavalry of Reshid Pasha, who three years later was to command the final siege of the town. Omer Vrionis began his siege in November 1822, at the start of the winter rains; mud quickly made the ditch along the landward side of the town virtually impassable, mud deadened the impact of cannon shot falling inside the town, and Mesolongi's low defensive wall of earth proved an effective rampart for the Greeks. Omer Vrionis made a major assault on the Greek Christmas Day, hoping to surprise the townspeople at their celebrations, but the Greeks were forewarned and repelled the attack, holding their fire until the enemy was at close range as they had done at Péta. A week later Omer Vrionis abandoned his camp, which rains and the outbreak of fever had made untenable, and withdrew across swollen rivers and through the marauding attacks of Greek captains to his base at Amphilóchia forty miles to the north.

A year later in October 1823 Mesolongi was again under threat. The main Turkish army had marched south via Karpenísi, where Márkos Bótsaris was killed, and laid siege first to Anatolikó, the small island at the head of the lagoon about five miles north-west of Mesolongi. Water for Anatolikó had to be brought across by boat from the nearby mainland, a traffic which the besiegers immediately stopped, hoping to force a surrender. However to the delight of the Greeks a Turkish cannon ball crashed through their church roof and opened an unsuspected spring of fresh water below the floor. One of the defenders marked this miracle in verse:

> Parched heroes turned for help to God,
> And He, when bombshells struck the spire,
> Revealed a spring beneath the sod,
> And conjured water out of fire.[2]

The garrison of Anatolikó put up a determined resistance, and before the onset of winter the Turkish forces again withdrew.

Thus by 1825 Mesolongi had withstood two assaults, had become linked worldwide with the fame of Byron, and seemed to be under divine protection. Mesolongi was also the only town north of the Gulf of Corinth to have remained in Greek hands since the beginning of the war. How then could it fall? How could it be allowed to fall? Mesolongi had in fact become a symbolic prize for both Greeks and Turks. After Ibrahim's attack from the south, the invasion route for a Turkish army past Mesolongi was much less important, so Mesolongi was now of little strategic value to either side. Indeed some Greek cynics – or perhaps realists – were asking, 'What does it matter if Mesolongi falls? Is Mesolongi the whole of Greece?'[3] On the Turkish side the commander of the besieging army, Reshid Pasha, had been told by the Sultan, 'Either Mesolongi falls or your head,'[4] and he was determined to succeed where his predecessors had failed.

It was Mesolongi's situation which made it so difficult to capture. The town was built on a spit of land projecting into the eastern edge of a huge lagoon, which was only two or three feet deep apart from a few slightly more navigable channels. The lagoon was rich in fish, and at night the waters were dramatically speckled with the flaming torches of the fishing boats, lights which seemed to float independently when a moonless night made the boats invisible. The lagoon was dotted with small islands rising just above the water level, which were to play an important part in the defence of Mesolongi. Prokopanístos, on the southern edge, formed a long thin bar to its entrance; Vasiládhi, a fortified post, commanded the main channel; Mármaris and Klísova lay just off Mesolongi; and at the head of the lagoon Anatolikó with its small town was shielded by the islets of Dólmas and Póros lying just south of it. No Turkish ship of any size could enter the lagoon, and any attempt to use small boats would meet hostile fire from the islands, especially from the three cannon on Vasiládhi. Greek ships however could unload supplies for Mesolongi at the edge of the lagoon into the small flat-bottomed punts called *monóxila*, and these could then make their way to the town through the winding channels which only the locals knew.

The landward side of Mesolongi, about a third of its perimeter, was therefore the best place to attack. Even here the besiegers' task was not easy. To the east of the town lies a wide plain, much of it marshy, stretching away to the foothills of Mount Zígos; a marsh is no place to pitch a large military camp, and the open plain offered no protection against Greek fire from the town walls. These walls were about a mile long, with a deep ditch on the outside as a first obstacle to attackers. At the time of the initial siege in 1822 the walls had been only four feet high and two feet wide, made of earth with stone or brick facing in parts. Since then, on the initiative of Mavrokordhátos and some said at Byron's suggestion, the walls had been raised, broadened and fortified under the direction of an engineer from Chios, Michaíl Kokkínis, though they were still largely built of earth. Along the walls Kokkínis had built seventeen bastions facing north and east, as emplacements for the town's forty-eight guns and four mortars. The most important bastions formed triangular projections, so that defenders could fire along the walls and support each other against attack.

Kokkínis named his bastions after famous men, about half of them distinguished Greeks, among whom Kokkínis included his otherwise obscure uncle. The rest honoured foreigners who had supported revolution in Greece (Byron, Normann) or in their own country: Franklin for America, Skanderberg for Albania, Kosciusko for Poland and, with a nod to England's Glorious Revolution of 1688, William of Orange and his councillor Lord Sheffield for England. Many of the names were soon changed to something more descriptive or familiar: Márkos Bótsaris to Megáli Támbia or Great Bastion, William of Orange to Lunetta, Franklin to Terribile. Sadly only the central bastions now remain; the rest were knocked down successively to provide a cart-track, a railway, a ring road, and finally a slaughterhouse and a public lavatory. Thus do past glories make way for present needs. Kokkínis was proud of his work. 'The rampart will withstand any enemy attack,' he wrote, 'and even the English will be astounded.'[5] Gordon though was scornful, and probably commenting on reports said that these were not bastions in the European sense; Trikoúpis too said that the wall was poorly built and would not impress anyone. But Kokkínis' first claim was justified, and his defences did hold out against virtually every enemy effort to breach them.

In the spring of 1825 Reshid led his army south from Árta. The wooded hills of the Makrinóros, previously a barrier to Turkish advance, had been left unguarded. There was no Greek force to hold up Reshid's crossing of the Achelóos river. A last-minute attempt to halt the Turkish advance from a primitive gun emplacement above the road opposite Anatolikó had to be abandoned, and Reshid's army reached the plain of Mesolongi at the end of April. His forces probably numbered about 20,000, of whom 8,000 were soldiers and some 4,000 were labourers to work on the Turkish entrenchments, 'Christian peasants dragged from the villages of Macedonia and Thessaly' as Gordon described them.[6] The Greek defenders on the walls therefore had the bitter experience of having to fire on their own countrymen.

The garrison of Mesolongi numbered some 3,000 fighting men, including a handful of German and Italian philhellenes, while a further thousand or so defended Anatolikó. A committee of three civilians, appointed by the central government in Navplion, was nominally in charge of Mesolongi, but these three – two merchants and a local official – had no military experience, and the organisation of the defence naturally fell to the troops. These were made up of bands under a number of captains, who met daily to concert plans, and the overall leadership only slowly emerged. By July the acknowledged *primus inter pares* was the Souliot captain Nótis Bótsaris. An unlettered man in his sixties, distrusted by some for greed and ambition, he drove a hard bargain over his generals' pay and quarters, but proved himself by staying at his post for the whole period of the siege. Thus the first orders of the day, dealing with discipline, watch-keeping, food distribution and so on, were signed by eleven military and six civilian leaders, an indication of co-operative effort unparalleled in the Greek struggle.

Among the defenders were three men who wrote accounts of the siege. The twenty-five-year-old Spiromílios, from southern Albania but with military training in Italy, commanded a troop of some 200 of his compatriots; he wrote a crisp military memoir in which he did not hesitate to criticise those he thought were slow to give help. Kasomoúlis, who had two of his brothers with him, wrote a three-volume memoir of the war including his time in Mesolongi, when he acted as secretary to one of the captains. His account is discursive and colourful, unreliable for details but excellent as a picture of the hazards and hardships of life under siege. Míchos, a civilian, wrote a conscientiously detailed account, much of it drawn from the Mesolongi newspaper *Elliniká Chroniká*, which the indefatigable Swiss philhellene Johann Jakob Meyer continued to produce until almost the end of the siege. As well as these three Nikólaos Mákris wrote an account largely based on the memories, and honouring the memory, of his father Dhimítrios, one of the garrison's commanders.

Reshid's army reached Mesolongi in 1825 at the beginning of summer, not the beginning of winter as in the two previous Turkish attempts. His labourers were immediately put to work digging a network of trenches and mounds under the fire of the garrison to bring his troops closer to the town. At some places these earthworks were less than a hundred yards from Mesolongi's wall, close enough for the customary exchanges of banter and insults, and it was said that during lulls in the fighting Greek soldiers would creep forward and light their cheroots from the Turkish fires. There were basically three ways by which Reshid could get past Mesolongi's landward defensive walls. He could batter his way through them, he could undermine them from below, or he could position his troops to attack them from above.

Through failure of co-ordination which so often bedevilled Turkish ventures, Reshid simply did not have enough artillery or shot to blow a breach in the walls. Initially he had only three cannon, and the number had risen only to eighteen by the end of August, whereas the Mesolongi garrison had forty-eight. Turkish ammunition stores were often low as supply by sea, from Patras and then from Reshid's port at Krionéri ten miles east of Mesolongi, was intermittent. When a temporary breach was made in the walls, the defenders drove the attackers back in hand-to-hand fighting, which had been rare in the war up till then. Also breaches could easily be filled. Stone walls will spread impact, and a well-aimed shot at the base of a stone wall can bring down a whole section, whereas earth walls absorb shock. Any damage to the walls was repaired overnight by earth-carrying gangs of Mesolongi civilians, including women wearing men's clothes, so that darkness restored any daylight destruction. It was soon clear to Reshid that bombardment was ineffective.

A second option was to dig a mine under the walls and destroy them from below. The Turks were not expert at this. The chamber in which their explosive was placed was often incompletely sealed to drive the blast upwards; as a result its force was simply dissipated back down the tunnel and did little damage. The Greek mining engineers were much more skilful, and by September they had perfected their technique. They first detonated a small mine under the Turkish earthworks and simultaneously opened fire on the spot; the Turkish forces, expecting a sortie by the garrison, gathered in force to repel it, like a swarm of wasps, said Kasomoúlis, when you hit their nest with a stick. Two hours later the Greeks detonated a second, much larger mine under their massed enemies. The whole rampart shook, Kasomoúlis went on, and the reverberation of buildings was like the groaning of a legendary beast. 'We too were terrified and fell to the ground . . . legs, feet, heads, half bodies, thighs, hands and entrails fell on us and on the enemy.'[7] Mines could be brutally effective, but only if properly laid.

Reshid's third tactic was to attack the walls of Mesolongi from above, by building a huge extended mound from which his troops could fire down on the defenders. The engineer Kokkínis, remembering his military history, called this mound 'Ípsoma tis Enóseos' or Linking Causeway, the name which Alexander the Great had given to his similar construction at the siege of Tyre in 332 BC. Alexander's effort had been a failure, so perhaps Kokkínis did not mind lending this name from Greek antiquity to a Turkish project.

At the beginning of August Reshid began building his mound towards the north-facing Franklin battery, at a thirty-degree angle towards the west so that it was as far as possible from the formidable bastions which flanked it to the east. Within a fortnight the mound was 160 yards long and five to fifteen yards wide, and overtopped the Franklin battery, on which the Turks could now fire downwards from behind screens. The Greeks were forced back from Franklin, but twelve yards inside the walls dug a ditch with a rampart behind it. The attackers were now inside the town but trapped between the walls and the inner ditch, and under fire from the battery on their left, so had become the besieged rather than the besiegers. In this extraordinary contest of competitive earth-moving, the Turks now began building a second mound inside the walls, to overtop the inner ditch and rampart. But by the end of August the Greeks had detonated a mine under the Turks' second mound, and driven them back outside the walls again by an attack in which even stone-throwing Mesolongi boys joined. The Greeks now began the piecemeal removal of the Turks' original mound, carrying away its earth at night to strengthen their own defences. The story went that when elsewhere in Greece or the islands people asked 'What are our people doing in Mesolongi?' the cryptic answer was 'They're stealing earth.'[8]

Finally in a fierce battle the Greeks drove the Turks back from the remains of the original mound, and at the beginning of September, after a month of hectic resistance destroyed it with a mine. Reshid, with his army weakened by casualties, disease and desertion and disappointed by the failure of all three of his methods of attack, pulled back eastwards to the foothills of Mount Zígos.

Reshid would of course have been saved a great deal of trouble if he had managed to negotiate a surrender of Mesolongi. He tried this in July and again in September of 1825, and though some of the Greek captains wavered, and the July negotiations were spun out to give the Greeks a breathing space to strengthen their defences, in the end the Greeks would have none of it. The defenders of Mesolongi, townspeople as well as troops, had quickly become battle-hardened; Kasomoúlis, arriving in Mesolongi in August 1825, said that when bullets flew overhead he was the only one who ducked. But life under siege was tough, as Kasomoúlis describes: 'The defender carried a spade in one hand and a gun in the other. His only relief was to go from fighting to digging and back to fighting. Picture him, with sword or yataghan at his belt beside his pistols, carrying a piece of hide on which to knead dough for bread and a mortar to grind garlic to flavour his fish, preparing them where he stood, night or day.'[9] During lulls in the fighting, he said, the civilians would laugh and chat about the recent battle, while the soldiers patrolled the ramparts like caged lions.

Mesolongi could hold out under these conditions only because its supply line through the lagoon was still open. From June to December Greek fleets under Miaoúlis were intermittently active off Mesolongi. They brought in supplies, mainly from Zákinthos, and in September several more bands of troops, but regularly returned to their home ports to reprovision and to secure the next month's pay. A Turkish fleet under the kapitan pasha also patrolled the mouth of the Gulf of Corinth, supplying Reshid through the port of Krionéri. The Greeks were still using fireships, but the Turks had learnt to counter them and they were no longer the threat they had once been. Clashes between the two fleets were frequent but indecisive. 'Both parties claimed the victory,' wrote Finlay, 'the capitan-pasha because he kept open the communications between Patras and Krioneri, and Miaoulis because he succeeded in throwing supplies into Mesolonghi and in keeping open its communications with the Ionian Islands. But the real victory remained with the Turks, whose fleet kept its station at Patras, while the Greeks retired from the waters of Mesolonghi on the 4th December 1825, and returned to Hydra'[10] – to come back, it must be added, and give support in the following year.

The Greek fleet did what it could, but help for Mesolongi from elsewhere was spasmodic at best. Karaïskákis, Roumeli's most formidable captain, played an enigmatic role. He was prepared to harry Reshid's lines of communication to his base at Amphilóchia further north, and in September he made a successful attack on Amphilóchia itself, but was very lukewarm about any direct help to Mesolongi. Karaïskákis it seems was prepared to help the Greek cause in ways which contributed to his control of his territory in central Roumeli, or which offered the chance of plunder, but saw no benefit in becoming involved in the defence of Mesolongi. Politics too played a part: Karaïskákis was an opponent of Mesolongi's commander Nótis Bótsaris, Karaïskákis being of Koléttis' party in the central government and Bótsaris a supporter of Mavrokordhátos. This central government in Navplion also did little to help Mesolongi, largely because it had no money. Spiromílios refers constantly to the government's failure to provision Mesolongi in advance, to maintain the fleet off the coast, to send reinforcements and supplies, even bandages for the wounded, and to provide pay for the troops.

Nevertheless 1825 had been a triumphant year for Mesolongi. After the failure of his great mound Reshid had withdrawn, leaving only a few troops in his trenches, and in October the winter rains began, making further operations impossible. Mesolongiot wives and children, who had been sent to the island of Kálamos for safety because it was part of the Ionian islands, now returned: an unwise move as it turned out, since there were more mouths to feed later when the siege was renewed. Christmas was celebrated in the traditional way. Dhimítrios Mákris was married in a ceremony attended by his fellow captains, Mesolongi's civilian leaders and many of the garrison. The party went on all night with constant firing of blank cartridges and when next morning the Turks outside the town shouted to ask the reason they were told 'It's the general's wedding.' In a spirit reminiscent of the Christmas 1914 fraternisation in the Flanders trenches, the Turks shouted back 'Long life to them! May they be happy!'[11] The engineer Kokkínis was able to inspect Reshid's entrenchments, and described them as 'earthworks with no coherence, constructions with no logic, and in short by any reckoning a muddle and a hotchpotch. . . . The whole thing is unbelievable – but it's Turkish.'[12] The year 1825 had seen Ibrahim's triumph in the Peloponnese and his recapture of the key objectives of Navarino and Tripolis, but at Mesolongi the Greeks thought they had won.

They might indeed have done so if the Greek captains from other parts of Roumeli had made a determined attack on Reshid's weakened army, and if that army had not been reinforced at the end of the year by the arrival of Ibrahim Pasha, fresh from his victories in the Peloponnese. In the previous autumn Ibrahim's father the Egyptian viceroy had prepared at Alexandria a massive new naval expedition to support his son: a fleet of 135 sail including Egyptian, Turkish, Algerian and Tunisian ships, carrying 10,000 troops, mainly Arabs. In early November this fleet reached Navarino, from where Ibrahim marched north through the Peloponnese with half his army, destroying pockets of Greek resistance on the way, while the rest went on to Patras by sea. By early January 1826 Ibrahim's army was encamped beside Reshid's outside Mesolongi, having brought his stores of artillery, ammunition and provisions into Krionéri on the neighbouring coast.

Relations between Ibrahim and Reshid were understandably cool: if Ibrahim succeeded where Reshid had failed, Reshid would be humiliated – or worse. The story is told that at their first meeting Ibrahim asked Reshid why he had failed in eight months to get past that fence (indicating Mesolongi's walls) while he, Ibrahim, had captured the fortress of New Navarino in a few days. Before Ibrahim could begin his own attack on the fence his supplies had to be brought up from Krionéri ten miles away, on the shoulders of his Arab troops since he had no carts. There was constant rain, the track was either rocky or marshy, the intervening river Évinos was in winter spate, and many of the wretched porters, used to a North African sun, fell sick or died. Those that survived a day's work would light huge fires for warmth which often set fire to the surrounding tents and huts. The labour took six weeks, and during this time two more offers of negotiation were made to the Mesolongi garrison, which as before rejected them with disdain. By the end of February Ibrahim was ready.

The bombardment began at sunrise on 24 February and continued for three days. Some forty Turkish cannon and mortars had been set up in three emplacements, one in the centre opposite the Bótsaris bastion and one at each end of Mesolongi's wall. From a range of only 400 yards, some 8,000 projectiles were poured into the town in the three days; according to Meyer's newspaper, exactly 5,256 cannon shot and 3,314 mortar shells. Though many houses in the town were wrecked, the inhabitants took cover in cellars and ditches and casualties were light. The walls were not breached, and the Greeks drove off three enemy assaults in hand-to-hand fighting. The Arab troops did not live up to their fearsome reputation; they were well disciplined, said Trikoúpis, but not brave fighters. Mesolongi's despised fence had still held.

It was now clear to Ibrahim that Mesolongi could only be reduced by the method that had been used against much more formidable fortresses: starvation. This meant getting control of Mesolongi's lagoon, which was the garrison's source of fish as well as the route for supplies from outside. An attempt on the lagoon had been made in the previous July. In support of Reshid, Yussuf Pasha, commander of Patras, had led into the lagoon thirty-six shallow-draught boats carrying 2,000 troops to attack Mesolongi from the sea, but had failed to capture the fortified island of Vasiládhi and within a few days was driven back. Ibrahim now prepared a larger force of eighty-two vessels, without the masts and keels of Yussuf's craft so that they could negotiate shallower water, plus five large rafts carrying thirty-six-pounder cannon. This flotilla was towed across from Patras by a steamship of the Turkish navy originally built as an English packet-boat, a strange conjunction of the latest example of naval technology acting as tugboat to the most primitive.

Vasiládhi, near the centre of the lagoon and the key to control of it, was the first target. The island was defended by thirty-four gunners, with fourteen guns of twelve or eighteen pounds, and twenty-seven foot-soldiers, under the command of the Italian philhellene Iacomuzzi. They faced a force of a thousand or more, which attacked on 9 March and was led by Hussein Bey, the conqueror of Kásos two years earlier. The island held out all day, but as evening fell their resistance was ended by an accidental explosion of their powder magazine. This may have been from an enemy shell or, as Mesolongi legend has it, because a ten-year-old boy on the island, seeing a gun loaded but unattended, incautiously fired it, igniting loose powder and hence the whole store. Four of the garrison were captured and the rest, including Iacomuzzi, escaped to Mesolongi after a four-hour struggle through the lagoon's muddy shallows.

Three days later the Turks attacked the small islands of Dólmas and Póros, in the north of the lagoon where it narrows in the approach to Anatolikó. These islands are within a hundred yards of the shore, where the Turks set up cannon to bombard them. Both islands fell after a day of resistance, in spite of a diversionary sortie by the Mesolongi garrison from its east-facing bastions. The following day envoys from Anatolikó surrendered the town to Ibrahim under an agreement, which he fully observed, that they should be removed to Árta, where they would be fed for a month. Ibrahim had now achieved his purpose of cutting off supplies to Mesolongi by sea, and once again offered to negotiate a surrender, but on harsh terms: the defenders of Mesolongi should surrender all their weapons, 'not retaining even the smallest dagger',[13] and either leave the town or convert to Islam. The garrison replied that they refused to surrender 8,000 bloodstained weapons, and that the outcome must be in God's hands.

Ibrahim and Reshid now determined to push on towards the seaward edge of Mesolongi by attacking the island of Klísova, about half a mile south-east of the town. The defenders numbered only 120, reinforced when the attack was imminent by a handful of men from the garrison led by Kítsos Tsavéllas, one of its captains. There was a small church on the island, protected by ramparts behind which the defenders' four small guns were placed. On the morning of 6 April Reshid led the first attacks of 2,000 Turkish and Albanian troops in flat-bottomed boats, but even these could not reach the shore of Klísova and the attackers had to jump into the water and wade through the mud. They were easy targets for the defence, and Reshid, himself wounded in the leg, pulled back. Ibrahim now took over, sending in an even larger force of 3,000 Arabs under Hussein Bey, who a month before had taken the fortified island of Vasiládhi. When the Arabs had jumped out into the shallows, they leant on the gunwales of their boats and tilted them as makeshift shields to cover their advance, but were still shot down in numbers. The Greeks knew that these Arabs were regular troops, dependent on orders from superiors, and directed their fire at Hussein Bey and shot him dead. Many claimed the hit, including a young boy perched with his musket on the church roof and nicknamed the wasp, a supposedly sharp-eyed insect. Ibrahim himself joined the battle encouraging and, literally, whipping on his troops, and was wounded. By nightfall the Arabs too had retreated, after what Gordon called 'the bloodiest day Messalonghi had yet witnessed'.[14]

Kasomoúlis visited Klísova the next morning, and viewed the carnage with a coldly triumphant eye:

The lagoon was covered with corpses a gunshot distance away, and they were drifting like rubbish by the shore. . . . one could see bodies floating all round, about 2,500 of them, apart from those whom our boatmen had captured and killed at dawn when they cried out for help. Some 2,500 guns had been found, some with bayonets and some without, plus bandoliers and innumerable belts, from which the Greeks made braces. I made a pair myself, and so did everyone else. But the clothes were worthless apart from those of a few officers; the Greeks got no booty from these, and were much displeased.[15]

Though the combined efforts of the Turkish and Egyptian troops had failed so bloodily at Klísova, they were now masters of the lagoon and Mesolongi's lifeline was cut. The last major supply drop had been at the end of January, when Miaoúlis' fleet had brought in ammunition and 250 tons of maize – just in time, since the population had been reduced to two ounces of grain a day. Even the 250 tons of maize was not going to last long: about two months, allowing a pound a day for each of the town's 9,000 or so occupants. Brave old admiral Miaoúlis, as Howe called him, continued to bring what ships he could muster to harass the Turkish fleet off Mesolongi, and even in the final days of the siege was planning an attempt to retake Vasiládhi and force his way into Mesolongi with supplies. However, his last significant service to the town was to carry a commission of six of its leaders to Navplion in a last desperate attempt to get help from the national government.

This commission comprised representatives of all the different parties sharing in the defence of Mesolongi: two Souliots, from the rival families of Bótsaris and Tsavéllas, two from West Roumeli (for parity), one from the forces who had come in during the siege, and for the Epirus contingent Spiromílios, who wrote a detailed account of the mission. It reached Navplion in late February, and immediately fell foul of the seething political intrigue. On arrival they accepted quarters from Koléttis, and were branded Kolettists. When they protested that they supported neither the Kolettists nor the Mavrokordhatists, they found that neither party would support them. A new national assembly was imminent, so members of the government were thinking of little but their re-election chances. Spiromílios as the mission's spokesman addressed a joint session of the Executive and Senate, asking for an army of seven to eight thousand to attack the Turks and

Egyptians from the east, the reinforcement of Miaoúlis' fleet, a flotilla of shallow-draught armed vessels to retake the lagoon, and meanwhile supplies and pay for the garrison. The government glibly assented to all these demands, but of course there was no money to pay for them. The government once again revived the idea of selling off national lands – illegally, since they were already pledged as security for the first English loan – but there were few buyers, and those there were would offer only a fraction of the price in cash and the rest in promissory notes. Eventually some money was raised by private subscription, but only enough to fund another month or so of Miaoúlis' gallant but inconclusive naval skirmishing.

The mission left Navplion, and Spiromílios wrote a bitter denunciation of all those he believed had let Mesolongi down. The captains of the Peloponnese, he said, had failed to attack Ibrahim's bases there to draw him away from Mesolongi; the president of the Executive, Koundouriótis, expected to be removed at the forthcoming national assembly and so was wholly indifferent; Goúras, commander-in-chief of Eastern Roumeli, had done nothing to help Mesolongi; Karaïskákis' troops at Dhervékista had merely sat there counting the distant cannon shots of the siege. Meanwhile, Spiromílios concluded, a band of 3,500 men had withstood the armies of Turkey and Egypt on land, and at sea the combined fleets of Constantinople, Algeria, Tunis and Tripoli – for twelve months, without pay and often without bread.[16]

Shortage of bread was indeed proving critical. At the beginning of March a rationing committee was set up which requisitioned all the corn in the town – though the Souliots were believed to have continued hoarding supplies – and distributed equal rations to all by the cupful. The Turks now controlled the lagoon so the fishing boats could not venture far, and most of the fish had been driven away by the firing. Any animal would now make a meal: horses, donkeys, dogs, cats, even mice if they could be caught. Seaweed was gathered from the water's edge, but it was so bitter that it had to be boiled five times before it was edible. Even cannibalism was reported. Disease from such a diet was rife, especially diarrhoea, mouth ulcers, scurvy and arthritic swelling of the joints. Those who had suffered worst from malnutrition were skeletal, with livid skin, and some could hardly walk.

There were only two options left for the encircled defenders of

Mesolongi: to capitulate or to break out. In mid-April Ibrahim and Reshid made a last offer of surrender terms which on any rational view the Greeks could have honourably accepted, especially as the terms were not harsh and Ibrahim had a reputation for keeping his word. But the Greeks rejected this offer as firmly as all the previous ones, and began to prepare for a mass exodus.

A council of the military and civilian leaders, including the senior cleric in the town Bishop Joseph, was held in the church of Áyios Spirídhon. There the date for the exodus was set: Saturday 22 April, the eve of Palm Sunday, and the supposed anniversary of Christ raising Lazarus from the dead. The parallel was clear: Lazarus four days dead and restored to life, Greece four centuries oppressed and risen again. Envoys were sent to Karaïskákis and his fellow captains who were encamped at Dhervékista some thirty miles to the east, and it was agreed that Karaïskákis would make a diversionary attack on the appointed night, signalling his arrival by lighting fires on a hilltop out of sight of the enemy. Mesolongi's population numbered about 9,000, made up of 3,500 fighting men, 1,000 civilian labourers and 4,500 women and children. When night fell they were to scramble over the eastern section of the walls, cross the defensive ditch on specially con-structed bridges and then wait behind the earth rampart beyond the ditch. There were to be three groups, one on the right under Dhimítrios Mákris including the women and children, one in the centre under Nótis Bótsaris and one on the left under Kítsos Tsavéllas. Tsavéllas was to keep a few men on the walls till the last moment. When the noise of the planned diversionary attack was heard, all three groups would move forward together.

This was a huge and complex military operation which depended on many different things going right. Could the preparations for the exodus be kept secret, or would the enemy learn of it and block it? When the moment came could 9,000 people, half of them women and children, cross three or four six-foot-wide bridges before the enemy was alerted? Would Karaïskákis' signalling system work? Would he come at all? If all else went well, could such a throng of escapers get through the enemy lines to safety? The plan was full of loopholes, but one must remember that it was devised not by a comfortably quartered general backed by an efficient staff and commanding regular troops, but by men of a divided command who had been fighting almost continuously for a year in worsening conditions, and were now on the edge of exhaustion.

Preparations for the exodus now went forward. A carpenter was commissioned to make the portable bridges, but his first examples were far too heavy – it would take a hundred men to lift them, said Kasomoúlis – and the work had to begin again. The women got ready men's clothes for themselves, and laudanum for the children to ensure that they were drugged into silence on the night. Those too old or weak to leave were assembled in four or five houses, with a powder store below one of them to be blown up when the Turks approached, killing the remnants of the defence as well as the attackers. A mine was placed under one of the main bastions with the same purpose. The problem of what to do with the prisoners was brutally solved: they were all slaughtered in cold blood, and Kasomoúlis' brother boasted of having killed twelve himself. A crazy suggestion that the women and children should also be killed was vetoed by Bishop Joseph.

These preparations did not remain secret: Ibrahim had been told of the Greek plan by deserters from the town, but appeared to do little to forestall it. As darkness fell on the night of 22 April, clouds conveniently covered the ten-day-old moon, and the exodus began. The bridges were hauled over the walls and placed across the ditch; some crossed by the bridges, others struggled through the ditch, throwing pillows and blankets into its muddy bottom to ease their passage. A thousand soldiers went first, followed by the women and children and then the rest of the defenders; all waited, with their faces pressed against the earth of the forward rampart, for the signal to go forward en masse. The signal was to be the noise of Karaïskákis' promised attack on the enemy camp. Although there was no sign of the agreed signalling fires, in the early evening the Greeks had heard gunfire to the east – some 200 rounds – and assumed that Karaïskákis was there in force. But nothing more was heard.

Then the moon came out from behind the clouds, so that the escapers were now visible and the more vulnerable. After nearly an hour of waiting the Greeks lost patience and with shouts of *embrós*, forward, rushed out on to the plain. But some of the garrison were still crossing the bridges when suddenly for reasons unknown the contrary shout of *opíso*, back, went up. From the confused jostling on the bridges some fell into the ditch and drowned, while others pulled back into the town to fall victims to the Turks and Arabs who soon entered over the undefended walls.

Ibrahim knew of the planned exodus, and its timing, a day or two before it happened, and could have prevented it if he had wished. A few well-placed watchmen would certainly have seen and heard the bridges being placed and thousands of people crossing them, and a brief bombardment would have driven them back into the town. But the exodus suited Ibrahim very well. Mesolongi would be his without further fighting. The exodus was an even better outcome for him than a negotiated surrender, which might involve tiresome concessions. The Greeks were much more vulnerable in flight across the open plain than behind their walls. Also Ibrahim needed to keep his main body of troops around Mount Zígos, in case Karaïskákis' attack from the east materialised, rather than in front of Mesolongi's walls. On this interpretation the Greeks did not have to force their way out of Mesolongi as some dramatic paintings represent; Ibrahim let them out.

The Greeks' initial move forward did apparently meet relatively light opposition. Kasomoúlis said that the Arabs in the forward positions kept well down in their trenches, so that their shots flew six feet over the Greeks' heads. Trouble came later. The Turkish cavalry attacked the fleeing columns, and Mákris' group in particular suffered heavy losses. In the foothills of Mount Zígos the Greeks were surprised by a body of Albanian troops who killed many of the men and took the women and children captive. This was where Karaïskákis' troops should have been in position to help them, but only fifty or so under two other captains were there. The fugitives struggled on, and before the mountain slopes hid Mesolongi from view Kasomoúlis looked back at the town, now in flames. 'The torch that was Mesolongi', he wrote graphically, 'shed its light as far as Vasiládhi and Klísova and over the whole plain, and even reached us. The flashes of gunfire looked like a host of fireflies. From Mesolongi we heard the shrieks of women, the sound of gunfire, the explosion of powder magazines and mines, all combined in an indescribably fearful noise. The town was like a roaring furnace.'[17]

Eventually the fugitives reached Karaïskákis' camp after a thirty-mile journey. They found him ill in bed, which partly justified his inactivity, but in tactlessly jocular mood. According to Kasomoúlis he claimed to have counted 1,500 survivors and greeted them with 'Why so many of you? Did the Turks kill only women?' Mákris was incensed. 'We got our backsides here through the gunfire without any help from you,' he told Karaïskákis. 'We have kept our word, and are doing no more. We're going, and you can fight the Turks now.'[18]

Mákris had survived the exodus, as had Nótis Bótsaris and Kítsos Tsavéllas, the leaders of the other two groups, and the Italian philhel-lene Iacomuzzi, hero of the defence of the Vasiládhi island fortress. But many had died, including some of the leading captains, Kokkínis the engineer, six German philhellenes, and Meyer the newspaper editor, who perished with his wife and child in the foothills of Mount Zígos. The total number of Greek casualties in the exodus is impossible to determine; many recorded figures are what Finlay calls 'rhetorical arith-metic'. Finlay's own careful estimate is probably the most reliable: 4,000 dead, 3,000 captured, mainly women and children, and only 2,000 escaped.

When news of the fall of Mesolongi spread it evoked first a gasp of stunned horror as at some unimaginably awful catastrophe, then blame, then a determination to try to retrieve the situation. Kolokotrónis was at the National Assembly meeting to appoint a new government. 'The news came to us that Missolonghi was lost,' he wrote. 'We were all plunged in great grief; for half an hour there was so complete a silence that no one would have thought that there was a living soul present; each of us was revolving in his mind how great was our misfortune.'[19] When Kolokotrónis recovered himself he urged the Greeks to intensify their own efforts, and to look for help to foreign powers. Howe described his feelings in a letter from Navplion. 'I write you with an almost breaking heart. Missolonghi has fallen!' and he saw in its fall 'damning proof of the selfish indifference of the Christian world'. He concluded heatedly: 'You may talk to me of national policy, and the necessity of neutrality, but I say, a curse upon such policy!'[20]

In France, Germany and Switzerland the drama of Mesolongi had stimulated, by the end of the year, a flood of poems, songs, musical plays, essays and sermons. A frequent symbol for Mesolongi's fall was the death of an innocent Greek maiden, and a common explicit theme, as for Howe, was that the Christian powers of Europe had shamefully neglected the Greek cause.

Perhaps the most ambitious rendering of the story was in London, where *The Grand Historical Mimo-Dramatic Spectacle of the Siege of Missolonghi* ran for a week in September 1826. The cast of characters included well-known Turks and Greeks, as well as extras such as Mahmood, supposed to be a Turkish officer but in reality a disguised Greek maiden, and, after scenes of a parade of Turkish troops, the Greek ramparts and a 'grand triumphal ballet' on horseback, concluded with a 'Terrific Explosion, laying the City in Ashes'.[21]

The most potent use of the drama of Mesolongi to help the Greek cause was probably in painting. In July 1826 Delacroix exhibited his *La Grèce sur les ruines de Missolonghi*, completed in a mere three months. The picture is almost filled by the figure of a young woman, hollow-eyed and in disordered dress, half kneeling on the broken slabs of Mesolongi's walls. In the foreground grisly human remains can be seen, and far in the background, to represent Ibrahim's Egyptians, a turbaned black Oriental holds the Crescent flag. The woman's direct gaze and outstretched hands make an appeal for human, not divine aid; her eyes are not raised to heaven, and there is no Cross, no bishop, no angel, no Christ Himself in the sky, symbols common to many representations of Greece's struggle. The message was clear: Greece now looks to her fellow Christians for aid.

The theme was further developed in the Paris Salon exhibition of the following year, when twenty-one works on contemporary Greek subjects were exhibited by Delacroix and others. As one radical art critic wrote, 'The Salon is as political as the elections; the brush and the chisel are party tools just as much as the pen.'[22] From Greeks and philhellenes in Greece and from writers and artists throughout Europe the call went out that the powers of Europe must abandon neutrality and intervene actively to help the Greeks, a call that was ultimately answered at Navarino.

Mesolongi had become a symbol, and the drama of its fall tended to overshadow the reality of its gruelling year-long defence. The leading figures of that defence have their memorial, in the pages of history and in the statues of Mesolongi's Garden of Heroes near the remains of the central bastions. But the common people too played a heroic part, and it is fitting to end with one of them. The story is told that years later a woman of Mesolongi, now ninety and on her deathbed, begged to be buried in the clothes that were at the bottom of her locked chest. When she died her family opened the chest expecting to discover her finest dress, but found instead men's clothing with belt and shoes, preserved from the time that she had worn them as a labourer during the Mesolongi siege and in the final exodus.

27

The Second English Loan

However keen the Greek government was to help the defenders of Mesolongi, there was little it could do because it was, as for most of the war, desperately short of money. Loans from abroad were its only life-line.

The first loan had been floated in February 1824 with the backing of the London Greek Committee, and the proceeds, some £350,000 after commissions and retentions, were passed directly to the Greek government. How the government spent the money was meant to be controlled by commissioners appointed and sent to Greece by the London Greek Committee, but the original commissioners never took up their task (Byron died and Stanhope was recalled to England), nobody of any standing replaced them, and the way the money was spent was unsupervised and, in the view of many, wasteful and downright corrupt. Much of the proceeds of the first loan was spent by the government in fighting the two civil wars of 1824, and by the end of that year the money was virtually gone.

The second loan was floated a year after the first on 7 February 1825, the same month as Ibrahim's first landing in the Peloponnese. It was oversubscribed four and a half times by enthusiastic buyers who obviously had no inkling of the impact of Ibrahim's arrival. This second loan, unlike the first, was arranged independently by the Greek deputies in London, not through the London Greek Committee, and with a different banking house, Jacob and Samson Ricardo. The nominal amount was larger than the first loan (£2 million instead of £800,000) and though the rate was lower (55½ against 59) the amount raised was considerably more (£1.1 million against £472,000). This £1.1 million was immediately reduced by commissions of £64,000, and retention of the first two years' 5 per cent interest (£200,000) and 1 per cent sinking fund (£20,000). More was siphoned off into a so-called rejuvenating fund of £250,000 to buy stock of the first loan whenever its price went down, a move which was unconventional then and would be criminal today. That left £566,000 for the Greek cause.

This time the money was not simply to be handed over to the Greek government, in practice to use as it liked; the promoters had learnt a lesson from the first loan. The money raised by the second loan was to be spent almost exclusively on buying ships and providing other war supplies which would then be passed to Greece. Management of the expenditure was at least formally the responsibility of a four-man Board of Control in London, made up of Samson Ricardo the banker, Sir Francis Burdett and Edward Ellice, both Members of Parliament, and Byron's friend John Cam Hobhouse. The last three were all members of the London Greek Committee, which therefore found itself answering questions about both loans in the controversy over them which erupted in the following year.

Thanks to the second loan it was now possible to conclude a long-nurtured project: to secure the services of Lord Cochrane as commander of the Greek naval forces. Thomas Cochrane, son of the Earl of Dundonald, was the model for several captains in the fiction of Frederick Marryat, who served under Cochrane, and later for C. S. Forester's Horatio Hornblower and Patrick O'Brian's Jack Aubrey. He had had an extraordinary career. As a young captain in the British navy he combined dash and pugnacity with meticulous preparation and extreme care for the lives of his crew. 'Bold and adventurous as Lord Cochrane was,' wrote a contemporary, 'no unnecessary exposure of life was ever permitted under his command. Every circumstance was anticipated, every caution against surprise was taken, every provision of success was made; and in this way he was enabled to accomplish the most daring enterprises with comparatively little danger, and still less actual loss.'[1] But his career was dogged by conflict with authority. As a junior officer he was court-martialled for insubordination (but acquitted); he quarrelled with the First Lord of the Admiralty, the national hero Earl St Vincent, over promotion; as a Member of Parliament but still in the navy he provoked the court-martial of his commanding admiral (the admiral was, probably wrongly, acquitted); he conducted a campaign in Parliament, fully justified, for reform of naval abuses, and in 1814 he was put on trial for Stock Exchange fraud and found guilty, though almost certainly unjustly. Four years later he was in South America, serving in the liberation struggles of Chile, Peru and Brazil, and combining dashing exploits with disputes over his pay. In 1825, with Brazil's independence virtually won, Cochrane resigned from its service, 'heartily sick' of Brazil as he put it, and was available again. This was the naval saviour to whom the Greeks turned, a man of extremes in both action and argument but also, it was said, 'in the estimation of the Old World and the New, the greatest man afloat'.[2]

In November 1825 Cochrane put before the commissioners for the second loan his conditions for serving in Greece. He required payment to himself of £37,000 initially with a further £20,000 when Greek independence was won, and a fleet of six steamships. 'These vessels well manned', he claimed, 'appear to be sufficient to destroy the whole Turkish Naval power.'[3]

The steamship was the nautical wonder of the age, for the first time making ships independent of wind. Their use against the Turks had long been urged by Frank Abney Hastings, the English philhellene serving with the Greek fleets. The steamships of Hastings' design were driven not by propellers, which were a later invention, but by paddle-wheels. The ships usually moved under sail, and the steam engines were used sparingly, only in action or in flat calm. Coal was needed for fuel, as wood did not produce high enough temperatures, and coal was not easily found in the eastern Mediterranean. Another difficulty was that the paddle-wheels took up a large part of the vessel's sides, leaving less space for guns. Hastings' solution was to have powerful guns but fewer of them: a thirty-two-pounder fore and aft, and a sixty-eight-pounder on each side. 'It is not the number of projectiles', he wrote, 'but their nature and proper application that is required.'[4] After a first shot from the bow, the ship would be driven in a tight circle by its paddle-wheels, firing from each gun in turn. Hastings also proposed the use of red-hot shot, hitherto used only on land, to be heated in the ship's furnaces. 'A single shot', he claimed, 'would set a ship in flames.'[5] Admiral Lord Exmouth went even further: 'Why, it's not only the Turkish fleet, but all the navies in the world, that you will be able to conquer with such craft as these.'[6]

Hastings' background and character had much in common with Cochrane's. Hastings too was an aristocrat, grandson of the Earl of Huntingdon and second son of General Sir Charles Hastings. He too served in the British navy, as a ship's boy at Trafalgar and in his early twenties as captain on the Jamaica station. There he fell foul of his admiral and was dismissed the service. In 1822 he arrived in Greece where he was at first suspected of being a spy, a charge he successfully rebutted, writing to Mavrokordhátos: 'I venture to say to your Highness, that if the English government wished to employ a spy here, it would not address a person of my condition, while there are so many strangers in the country who would sell the whole of Greece for a bottle of brandy.'[7] For the next two years this courageous and prickly character served with the Greek fleet. 'Cold and haughty in manner,' writes one historian, 'direct and always to the point, self-opinionated and ungracious, he perhaps tended to belittle the efforts of others. Among the Philhellenes . . . he made no real friends. Yet the Greeks adored him: it was as though his gaucheness did not slip through the barrier of language.'[8]

Hastings was in London to promote his revolutionary ideas when the second loan was launched in February 1825, and within a few weeks had secured a payment of £10,000 from the loan to build the first steamship. The hull was to be built in the Thames shipyard of the firm of Brent, and the engines by Alexander Galloway of Smithfield; Hastings had offered to pay for its guns himself. The hull was quickly and efficiently built, but Galloway's engines, promised for August 1825, were not ready till May of the following year. Engine breakdowns plagued the voyage to Greece and the new vessel, named *Kartería* (Perseverance) and captained by Hastings, finally reached Navplion in September, when it amazed the Greeks. In the next two years Hastings was twice able to use his novel tactics successfully, at Vólos and again in the Gulf of Corinth, in spite of constant failure of the *Kartería*'s engines. This showed that the idea of a rotating steamship firing red-hot shot was not just a fantasy, though it was still a long way from conquering the world.

If the tale of the *Kartería* was one of delays and disappointments, the story of Cochrane's other vessels was worse. Since the *Kartería* counted as one of Cochrane's required six steamships, five more needed to be built. Again the order was placed for the hulls with Brent and for the engines with Galloway, who promised completion by November 1825. Responsibility for the project was already becoming muddled. The Greek deputies in London had undertaken to build the five steamships, as part of their agreement with Cochrane; overall responsibility for expenditure of the loan belonged to the Board of Control (Ricardo, Burdett, Ellice and Hobhouse); but Cochrane was given authority 'to construct, supervise and reject', and did indeed reject the original engines for ones operating at higher pressure. Of the five steamships ordered, the *Epichírisis* (Enterprise) sailed in the summer of 1827, nearly two years late, and was further delayed at Plymouth for repairs to the engines and the rudder. The *Ermés* (Mercury) arrived even later when the fighting was virtually over, and of the remaining three one blew up during trials and two were never completed but left to rot in the Thames.

Worse still was the catalogue of muddle and mismanagement over another use of money from the second loan: obtaining ships from the United States. In March 1825 the Greek deputies in London sent General Charles Lallemand, a former French cavalry officer, to New York as their agent to procure two frigates, buying them if possible (it was not) but otherwise having them built. Lallemand knew nothing of shipbuilding and his only qualification for this mission was his friendship with America's distinguished philhellene Lafayette. Lallemand therefore hired two of New York's most respected naval contractors, the houses of Bayard and of Howland, to direct the building of two frigates. The fixed cost estimates seemed very high at £75,000 to £100,000 for each frigate, so it was decided to build them by so-called 'day's work', that is by buying materials and paying for work as it was completed. With this system the estimated price of each frigate was just under £50,000, but no contract was signed setting an upper limit on costs. The deputies were in a hurry and wanted completion by the end of the year; the day's-work method was expected to save time as well as being cheaper.

Neither expectation was met. At the end of October 1825 the New York contractors Bayard and Howland wrote to the Greek deputies saying that the frigates would now cost £100,000 each and that they should allow for £110,000. A month later the contractors raised their estimate to £185,000 per frigate, and demanded more money, which the Ricardos, the loan's London bankers, refused to pay out. Work on the frigates therefore stopped.

The impasse was broken by Alexander Kondóstavlos, a wealthy merchant from Chios who had been appointed by the Greek government to assist the deputies in London. He arrived in New York in April 1826, and quickly realised that the only solution was to sell one frigate to the United States government in order to pay for the completion of the other. Kondóstavlos was able to go to the top of the administration, being introduced by the long-standing philhellene Edward Everett to the president, John Quincy Adams, and to members of his cabinet and of Congress. The purchase of the frigate required an act of Congress; the process was begun on 10 May, Congress passed the act a week later, and the president signed it on 22 May. 'Everything had been accomplished within twelve days,' wrote Kondóstavlos in amazement. 'Such an example of speed, I do not think one would find anywhere else.'[9] Agreement on the price to be paid by the United States government took longer, but in August this was settled at just under £48,000 for a vessel on which about £88,000 had been paid out; so £40,000 of the sorely needed loan money had been spent for nothing. The other American frigate, the *Hope*, reached Greece in November 1826, a year later than planned, where it was renamed the *Éllas*. It was much admired, and Cochrane used it as his flagship, but it ended the war at the bottom of the sea.

In summary, of the £566,000 raised for the Greek cause by the second loan, nearly £400,000 by Gordon's estimate had been spent on ships. Of the vessels ordered, only one of the two frigates and three of the six steamships had been delivered, all late and the steamships unreliable. A further £67,000 of the loan was spent on war supplies for Greece and further sums on a private yacht for Cochrane, leaving less than £100,000 for the sorely pressed Greek government. Of this sum the last major instalment of £40,000 reached Greece in October 1825, and a final £14,000, which Gordon called 'the last sweepings of the second loan',[10] in May 1826 when the Greek treasury was down to its last sixty piastres.

By the summer of 1826 recriminations about the handling of both loans were flying in London, fuelled by press campaigns in *The Times* and in William Cobbett's *Weekly Register*, and by the fact that the bonds of the first loan had fallen from an original £59 to £10 and those of the second loan from £55½ to £11. The large commissions on both loans were attacked. Bowring came under fire as secretary of the London Greek Committee, and replied that the Greek deputies, not his Committee, were responsible for the misuse of the first loan proceeds, and that the Committee as such had nothing to do with the second loan. As for the second loan, the shambles over the English ships was variously blamed on Galloway the engine-builder for incompetence and delay (perhaps deliberate, as he had a son in the Egyptian navy), on Cochrane who was meant to construct and supervise, and on the Board of Control (Ricardo, Burdett, Ellice and Hobhouse) for totally failing to live up to its name. For the American fiasco the Greek deputies were censored for appointing the unqualified Lallemand, and the naval contractors for overcharging. Even Kondóstavlos was later accused of profiting from the affair, though he was eventually cleared, and Edward Everett paid him a fully justified tribute: 'The frigate's success belonged to the patience and persistence of one man, Contostavlos.'[11]

In the murky events surrounding the two English loans it is tempting to look for one party to blame. The promoters exploited the situation by charging large though not unusual commissions, and so did the Greeks, who borrowed money that there was no prospect of repaying. But in another sense the Greeks were among the exploited, as the loan was floated at a heavy though again not unusual discount. Also exploited were the investors – and this includes the promoters – to whom the loans were sold on false prospectuses. So there is no simple antithesis between predators and victims or between gainers and losers.

The loans and Greece's continuing crippling indebtedness to England soured relations between the two countries for generations. Only in 1878 was an arrangement made by which the debt, now over £10 million with unpaid interest, was reduced to £1½ million, to be serviced by specified government sources of income. In 1826 *The Times* maintained that the loans had delayed Greece's independence, thundering: 'The Greek cause has been betrayed. It has been betrayed in England. It would have triumphed ere now, but for England, and the English Stock-Exchange.'[12] A century and a half later a Greek historian expressed the continuing bitterness about the loans, saying that they had made true Greek independence impossible. 'The undeniable fact remains', he wrote, 'that the two loans, which were contracted to establish the independence of the Greek state, were the basic factors in its enslavement.'[13] There is a Greek saying that good accounting makes good friends; the sorry story of the English loans shows that the converse is equally true.

28

Desperate Remedies

'Greeks only should free Greece,' wrote Byron in *The Age of Bronze*. This was a fine aspiration from the early heady period of the revolution, but by the time of the fall of Mesolongi in April 1826 was obviously wishful thinking. Kolokotrónis on land and Miaoúlis at sea could now do no more than harass the Ottoman forces; the Greeks had no commander capable of a decisive victory in either sphere. The government was split by factions, had no money to prosecute the war or relieve the wretched state of the country, and had failed so far to get the committed support of any foreign power. Also the sharing of authority between the Executive and the Senate was now seen as a mistake. 'The main weakness of the constitution', wrote Trikoúpis, 'was the interference of the Senate in the carrying out of the laws, and the consequent slackening of the Executive's power. Such interference, harmful enough in peacetime, was fatal in time of war.'[1]

The first priority therefore was to reform the government structure. The government headed by Koundouriótis, with Mavrokordhátos as general secretary of the Executive, had taken office for a year in October 1824 as it emerged victorious from that year's civil wars. But in October 1825, when elections for a new government should have been held, Ibrahim was ravaging the Peloponnese and Mesolongi was under siege. The Senate and Executive agreed that simply to elect new holders to the existing offices was not enough and that the perilous times called for a radical revision of the constitution by a new National Assembly.

This eventually met at Epídhavros, site of the first Assembly, in April 1826, when its 127 members were stunned by news of the fall of

Mesolongi. In a brief ten days the Assembly decided on emergency measures to change the system of government. Senate and Executive were to be replaced for the moment by two new bodies appointed by the Assembly. A Government Commission was to conduct the war and run the country, its edicts to have the force of law, while an Assembly Commission was to be responsible for negotiating with foreign powers, and for reconvening the Assembly itself as soon as possible to adopt a more permanent arrangement.

The Government Commission was presided over by Andréas Zaímis, had eleven members including Trikoúpis (who thought the Commission should be much smaller), and was supported by a secretariat of thirty which replaced the ministers. The thirteen-strong Assembly Commission was initially led by Bishop Yermanós, but by June he was dead of typhus, surprisingly little mourned by contemporaries. 'All the fame of this protagonist of the revolution rose and sank in its first days,' wrote Trikoúpis.[2] Gordon's verdict was that 'his death excited no regret, and he was forgotten as soon as the grave closed over him.'[3]

The Assembly Commission responsible for foreign relations took one important step. It sent an appeal to Stratford Canning, Britain's ambassador in Constantinople and cousin of Prime Minister George Canning, to negotiate peace between Greece and Turkey. This was a new approach to the problem of involving Britain on the side of Greece. In 1825 Greeks of all parties had signed the Act of Submission to Great Britain, but Britain had rejected it. In April 1826 the Protocol of St Petersburg opened the way for joint mediation by Britain and Russia, on terms laid down by Britain and Russia and not by the Greeks. Now in the same month the Greeks sent Stratford Canning their own terms, which were a good deal more favourable to themselves than those in the St Petersburg Protocol. All Turks were to leave, handing over all fortresses to the Greeks; the Sultan was to have no authority over internal administration; an independent Greece would include all the provinces which had taken up arms; and these terms were non-negotiable. It was a high-handed document, reflecting faith in the strength of Britain rather than the reality of Greece's extreme weakness. But Stratford Canning refused to take the matter further until a Russian ambassador, the first since 1821, was in post at Constantinople to act with him, and

Russo-Turkish differences delayed the ambassador's arrival until February 1827, nearly a year later. So this initiative was stalled. Otherwise this interim government by two Commissions did little positive. 'The councils were too numerous and too motley to be efficient,' wrote Gordon 'and the action of government being paralysed by its poverty, it soon fell into disrepute.'[4]

When the Commissions took office in April 1826 they were expected to last only a few months until the Assembly reconvened, but there was a succession of delays because of disagreement over where the Assembly should meet. It had to meet somewhere in the north-east corner of the Peloponnese or its neighbouring islands as this was the only area still under Greek control, but each faction wanted a meeting place that would favour its own side. Thus the interim government, initially based in Navplion, issued two calls for the Assembly to meet on the island of Póros, but to no avail. In November the government left Navplion, which was racked by disease and disorder, and moved to the island of Éyina. A third summons to the Assembly to meet on Éyina was also ignored.

The two principals in this disagreement were Zaímis, head of the Government Commission and bent on dominating the forthcoming Assembly which would end his current powers, and Kolokotrónis, who was determined to maintain his own position. Alliances had shifted over the past two years, and sometimes been totally reversed. Zaímis and Kolokotrónis had been opponents in the first civil war of 1824, within months had become allies in the second civil war, and were now opposed again. Kolokotrónis had been imprisoned by Koundouriótis when the civil wars ended, but the two now joined forces in opposition to Zaímis. Koundouriótis in his time as president of the Executive had had the support of Mavrokordhátos, who now backed Zaímis.

The question of where to meet had become so contentious because Kolokotrónis refused to bring his supporters to an Assembly on an island, from which his delegates could easily be turned away as unauthorised. Also the last time he had been on an island was as a prisoner on Hydra at the end of the 1824 civil wars. 'I will not embark on the seas,' he wrote, 'for I took an oath when they had me in Hydra that I would never put to sea again.'[5] His underlying concern, of course, was that on an island he would be isolated from his troops. Ultimately, in

February 1827 Kolokotrónis opened an Assembly with ninety delegates of his own choice at Ermióni on the mainland, while the government had assembled fifty of the original delegates on Éyina. It seemed that there would be a repeat of 1824, with two rival governments and a civil war.

The interventions of three representatives of Britain saved the situation. First to appear was General Sir Richard Church, who had long been a friend and a favourite of the Greeks. As a young major serving in the Ionian islands during the Napoleonic wars he had raised a regiment of Greeks, the Duke of York's Greek Light Infantry, in which Kolokotrónis and other later revolutionary leaders had served. In 1811 the regiment took part in the capture of Lévkas from the French, when Church was seriously wounded, and in 1814 helped retake Páxos. The regiment was disbanded after the Napoleonic wars ended, and Church resigned his British commission for a command in the army of the King of Naples. But as Gordon put it, 'Neither time nor distance weakened the honourable attachment that subsisted between him and his military pupils. His name was constantly in the mouths of Colocotroni, Anagnostaras, Nikitas, Colliopoulo, and other eminent chiefs, who often expressed a hope that he would once more fight at their head.'[6]

In the summer of 1826 the interim government offered Church the supreme command of the Greek land forces, which he immediately accepted. With hindsight it was easy to see that Church, though a popular choice, was not an ideal one. As Finlay wrote: 'Church was of a small, well-made, active frame, and of a healthy constitution. His manner was agreeable and easy, with the polish of great social experience, and the goodness of his disposition was admitted by his enemies, but the strength of his mind was not the quality of which his friends boasted. . . . Both Church and the Greeks misunderstood one another. The Greeks expected Church to prove a Wellington, with a military chest well supplied from the British treasury. Church expected the irregulars of Greece to execute his strategy like regiments of guards.'[7]

Church landed in early March 1827 at Portochéli, ten miles from Kolokotrónis' base at Ermióni, and received a hero's welcome from his old comrades in arms. 'Our father is at last come,' Kolokotrónis proclaimed to his men, 'we have only to obey him and our liberty is secured.'[8] But Church refused to accept any office until the two factions united. Captain Hamilton of the Royal Navy, Greece's wise friend throughout the war, conveyed Church to Éyina to negotiate a settlement, and Hamilton too urged the Greeks to settle their differences, threatening that unless they did so he would tell Stratford Canning that 'Greece was in too disorganised a state to be worthy the care of Europe.'[9] Then Cochrane arrived in his yacht, a week after Church, and took a yet stronger line. He refused even to land, and in forceful quarterdeck style told the delegates that he was disgusted to find the bravest and most famous Greek commanders squabbling over where to hold an assembly while the enemy was destroying the whole country. A compromise was reached, and it was agreed that all the delegates from both parties, whether legally appointed or not, should meet as a single Assembly at Trizíni, Troezen to classical scholars, a few miles inland from Ermióni.

On 31 March 1827 the Trizíni Assembly began its sessions, technically a continuation of the Assembly at Epídhavros a year before but in fact a completely different body with a new agenda. A new constitution was produced. Both Church and Cochrane had by now agreed to serve and had arrived in Greece. Within a fortnight both had been formally appointed and had taken the oath of office. A third resolution with far-reaching consequences was also passed at Trizíni: to offer the presidency of Greece to Kapodhístrias.

Kapodhístrias had resigned as joint foreign secretary to Tsar Alexander I in August 1822 and settled in Geneva. Like many a leader in waiting, he was in constant contact with his countrymen while insisting that he must stand aside from their troubles. 'The more I tried', he wrote, 'to make the Greeks understand that the events of the year 1821 shut me off henceforth from any possibility of existing for them, the less my words and the evidence of my conduct carried conviction with them.'[10] Though no longer Russia's foreign secretary he was still technically in the Russian diplomatic service, and in February 1826 took the oath of allegiance to the new Tsar Nicholas I. After his nomination as Greece's president in April 1827 Kapodhístrias spent the rest of the year preparing for his new role, though he did not formally accept his appointment until he reached Greece at the beginning of 1828.

Preparation meant assessing the support he could expect from the powers of Europe. In March 1827 he was in Paris and from April to June in St Petersburg, where Tsar Nicholas finally accepted his resignation from the Russian service offered six months earlier. In August he was in Prussia's capital Berlin and in London, and in September in Paris again before returning in October to Switzerland. By the end of his travels he had secured the assent of Britain, Russia and France to his presidency, without which he said he could not accept it, but his requests for practical help – foreign troops, subsidies and loans – had produced no firm commitment.

The Greeks had chosen as their first president a man of contradictions. His reputation was international and he had access to the highest levels of government in Europe. His appearance and manner were perfectly fitted to such a role. 'If there is to be found anywhere in the world', wrote a contemporary, 'an innate nobility, marked by a distinction of appearance, innocence and intelligence in the eyes, a graceful simplicity of manner, a natural elegance of expression in any language, no one could be intrinsically more aristocratic than Count Capo d'Istria of Corfu.'[11] But the private man was very different: an ascetic bachelor, constantly in poor health, far from rich, and a solitary despite his wide range of acquaintances in the worlds of politics, literature and the arts. Under the suave exterior of an international diplomat was a driven man. Once the presidency of Greece was offered to him and he dropped the pretence of wanting to be forgotten, he worked tirelessly for the Greek cause without ever accepting reward. In the year of his travels in Europe before reaching Greece this work was primarily a matter of handling his copious correspondence with the governments and his influential friends in Europe, with Greece's provisional government and with his supporters there. This task could last all day and sometimes far into the night, with Kapodhístrias dictating to more than one secretary at a time. Duty was all, but performed in a spirit of melancholy fatalism. 'Providence will decide,' he wrote, 'and it will be for the best.'[12]

Kapodhístrias was in fact being offered tightly circumscribed powers as president. Sovereignty belongs to the nation, declared the Constitution of Trizíni on its first page, and this sovereignty was to be exercised through the Senate. The Senate was to be much more stable than before, only a third of its members retiring in rotation each year somewhat on the American model, instead of all having to seek re-election annually. The president's ministers were appointed by and were answerable to the Senate. The president could only delay an enactment of the Senate, not veto it. The president could not dissolve the Senate. To underline the sovereignty of the people the constitution included a section of twenty-four articles, in effect a Bill of Rights, defining in detail the civil liberties of the citizen. Thus the Constitution of Trizíni was designed to tie down the president like a Gulliver with the strings of lesser men.

For the period until Kapodhístrias reached Greece, a three-man Vice-Presidential Commission was appointed to carry out the president's duties. None of the previous holders of high office had enough support, so the choice fell on three untried men who commanded no respect. One was Georgios Mavromichális, and of the other two one was, in Gordon's words, a Psarian 'enjoying a reputation less than questionable' and the other 'perhaps the most consummate blockhead in all Roumelia'.[13] The trio was derisively described as a boy, a sailor and a cuckold.

The Constitution of Trizíni, like its predecessors, was a balancing act, but the weights to be balanced were now different. One balance had to be struck between the adherents of Britain and Russia. Those who favoured Britain like Zaímis and Mavrokordhátos had the satisfaction of seeing two of Britain's distinguished citizens, Church and Cochrane, in command of the Greek land and sea forces, while those who looked to Russia had as president Kapodhístrias, a Greek distinguished in Russia's service who supposedly still had the ear of the Tsar. The other balance attempted at Trizíni was between the concentration of power in the hands of a president and the retention of sovereignty in the hands of the people. But in the event this arrangement was never put to the test. As soon as Kapodhístrias arrived in Greece he took steps to snap the ties with which the Trizíni Assembly had tried to bind him.

Meanwhile the country was in a terrible state. Its three-man Vice-Presidential Commission was totally ineffective and disorder was wide-spread. At Navplion the rival commanders of the two strongholds, Palamídhi and Akronavplion, bombarded each other. On Hydra the people attacked their leaders, and rival primates fought for control of Místra, Vostítsa and Kalávrita. In the summer of 1827 there were seven distinct civil conflicts by Gordon's estimate. After listening to two rival leaders relating to each other with great glee the incidents of their battles, Gordon concluded that 'civil war, and the misery it occasioned, appeared but a pastime'.[14]

The misery of civil strife was superimposed on the misery already caused by Ibrahim's invasion. Howe graphically described conditions in the Peloponnese. 'Those delightful plains,' he wrote, 'which poets in all ages have sung, but whose beauties have not been overrated, which two years ago were chequered with pleasant little villages, surrounded by groves of lemon and olive and filled with a busy and contented peasantry, were now barren wastes.' The uprooted inhabitants:

> took refuge in the recesses of the mountains, in caverns, in the centre of swamps; in every situation which afforded them security from the enemy's cavalry were seen collected crowds of old men women and children . . . they lived in little wigwams or temporary huts, made by driving poles in the ground and thatching them with reeds. . . . they had no blankets, they had no clothes to change, and their own had become dirty and tattered; they were obliged to wander about in quest of food, and their naked feet were lacerated by the rocks; their faces, necks, and half-exposed limbs were sunburnt, and their hollow eyes and emaciated countenances gave evidence that their suffering had been long endured.

But Howe always looked for signs of resilience and optimism in even the worst situations. 'Yet amid all this misery,' he concluded, 'strange as it may appear, the light and volatile Greek was not always depressed; the boy sang as he gathered snails on the mountains, and the girls danced around the pot where their homely mess of sorrel and roots was boiling; the voice of mirth was often heard in these miserable habitations, and the smile of fond hope was often seen.'[15]

The one significant outcome of the Trizíni Assembly was the detailed definition of civil liberties written into the constitution. 'Its Bill of Rights,' wrote a later historian, 'which embodied the ideal of the rule of law and respect for the rights of the citizen, has survived as the strongest weapon of liberty against autocracy through the many political changes of more than one hundred years of Greek history.'[16] Otherwise the Assembly had made little progress in solving the country's immediate problems. It had established a new form of government which gave power to the president with one hand and took it away with the other. It had nominated a president who would not arrive in the country for many months, and had meanwhile passed the responsibility for government to three incompetents. A potentially more helpful move was the appointment of two commanders of international repute to lead the land and sea forces. But Church and Cochrane were still untried as leaders in Greek warfare, and their abilities were soon to be tested in the battle to drive off the Turkish army which was besieging the Greek garrison of Athens.

29

Athens, the Last Ottoman Success

One of Austria's consuls met Ibrahim at Mesolongi in February 1826 and reported on Ibrahim's plans for the future. 'As soon as Missolonghi has fallen,' he wrote, 'Ibrahim and the capitan Pasha will attack Hydra and then Nauplia by land and sea.'[1] To seize these last Greek strongholds in the Peloponnese was the obvious next step for Ibrahim to complete his conquest. Why did he not take it?

Part of the reason was that he simply lacked the resources. Within weeks of the fall of Mesolongi the Egyptian ships of the fleet that had supported the besiegers were recalled by Mehmed Ali to their base in Alexandria, where they remained for the rest of the year, and because of the growing threat from Russia the Turkish contingent under the kapitan pasha Khosref went back to Constantinople. There was no naval attack on Hydra, and in fact no incentive for the Turkish fleet to make one. Ibrahim had been promised the Peloponnese if he could conquer it, and it was up to him to do so by his own efforts.

Ibrahim was also now much weaker on land. Some 5,000 of his troops had been lost at Mesolongi, and by the end of 1826 the 24,000 who had been brought over from Egypt were reduced to 8,000, of whom 1,500 were in hospital. During the summer of 1826 Ibrahim and his forces roamed the Peloponnese, from Corinth in the north to the Mani in the south and from Ástros on the east coast to Pírgos on the west, destroying villages and carrying off grain and livestock. Battles were usually little more than skirmishes, in which Ibrahim was successful on the plains, mainly thanks to his cavalry, but could not penetrate the hills where his men were at the mercy of Greek sharp-shooters and where the Arabs lost their footing on the slippery rocks. Gordon described Ibrahim's 1826 campaign in the Peloponnese as fruitless marching and countermarching.

Moreover there was now the nagging question of what Ibrahim was to do with the Peloponnese once he had conquered it. The more he wrecked it, the less it was worth. When if ever would the defeated Greeks return to their shattered villages, rebuild them, make the land productive again, and submit to paying taxes to a hated overlord? As a solution to this problem there was a brutal logic to Ibrahim's suspected barbarisation project of replacing the whole Greek population with Egyptians. But whatever the logic of this idea there would have been huge logistical problems in shipping tens of thousands of Greeks across 600 miles of sea to slavery in Egypt, and a similar number of Arabs in the other direction, bringing them from the sunny plains of Egypt to live and work in the harsh and rocky terrain of the Peloponnese. Also if Ibrahim started to implement this plan the powers of Europe would immediately intervene to stop it, as Canning's response to reports of the barbarisation project had shown.

Besides this, the long-term value of the Peloponnese to Egypt had declined. In 1824, when the Sultan first sought help from Egypt, Ibrahim's father Mehmed Ali could see the addition of the Peloponnese to his territory as strengthening his position within a continuing Ottoman empire. In 1826 that empire was showing signs of crumbling, and Mehmed Ali began to think of carving out an independent realm of his own from its remains. These ideas came to fruition a few years later, when Ibrahim siezed the Ottoman province of Syria for Egypt in 1832. But meanwhile Mehmed Ali refused for the moment to keep his fleet in Greek waters or to commit a single extra soldier from Egypt to secure the rapidly tarnishing prize of the Peloponnese.

The problems which had so weakened the Ottoman empire by 1826 were both external and internal. From without, Russia threatened war. One of the first acts of the new Tsar Nicholas I was to issue an ultimatum to Turkey in February 1826, the principal terms of which were that all Turkish troops should be withdrawn from Moldavia and Wallachia, and that the two provinces should be governed in future by locally chosen boyars and not Ottoman appointees. The Turks prevaricated but Nicholas, the gendarme–tsar, insisted, and demanded a conference at Akkermann on the Black Sea, on his territory and not theirs, which, as Gordon said, 'gave a fresh stab to Ottoman pride'. Turkey reluctantly accepted the ultimatum and signed the Convention of Akkermann in October 1826. The threat of a Russian war receded, only to return a year later when Turkey repudiated the Akkermann agreement and Russia did indeed declare war as a result.

The Sultan's problem within his borders lay, as it had done before, with the corps of janissaries. They were now practically useless as a military force, and Mahmud had to fight his wars with mercenaries and with troops raised by local pashas. The janissary regiments in the provinces drew pay and rations in idleness, while those in the capital were an unruly menace, as a contemporary visitor described. 'Lords of the day,' he wrote,

> they ruled with uncontrolled insolence in Constantinople, their appearance portraying the excess of libertinism; their foul language; their gross behaviour; their enormous turbans; their open vests; their bulky sashes filled with arms; their weighty sticks; rendering them objects of fear and disgust. Like moving columns, they thrust everybody from their path without any regard of age or sex, frequently bestowing durable marks of anger or contempt.[2]

In 1807 Mahmud's predecessor Selim III had tried to bring the janissaries under control by incorporating them into his so-called Army of the New Order. The janissaries reacted violently, the new army was formally abolished and Selim lost his throne. In the following year, the first of Mahmud's reign, his grand vizier publicly advocated reforming the janissaries and curbing their abuses, but lost his life in the ensuing janissary revolt.

Thereafter Mahmud proceeded cautiously. By increasing the privileges of the religious establishment he drew clerics away from their traditional support of the janissaries as the one truly Islamic force. He steadily built support within the janissaries by ousting senior officers and replacing them with younger men who supported reform, and appointed as commander of the janissaries an officer loyal to himself. In what has been described as 'a concentrated propaganda campaign unequalled in Ottoman history'[3] he constantly contrasted the successes of the Europeanised Egyptian forces with the failures of the unreformed

Turkish army. After eighteen years of preparation the Sultan was ready to act.

At the end of May 1826 the Sultan announced his reforms. Each of the fifty janissary regiments was to provide 150 men for a new force, to be uniformed, armed and trained on Egyptian lines, Egyptian being a tactful synonym for European. The reform was backed by the religious authorities: 'It is the religious duty of Muslims to learn military drill,' proclaimed their spokesman.[4] The first parade of the new troops was to be in the janissaries' own barracks at At Meydani, near the Blue Mosque and within half a mile of the Sultan's palace. The Sultan's intent was clear: the Janissaries were to be emasculated to create the force which would replace them.

The first parade of the new troops was held on Monday 12 June 1826, and the reaction followed quickly. By Wednesday evening rebellious janissaries were gathering at their barracks, and on the following morning they formally overturned their cooking pots in the traditional renunciation of the Sultan's rations and authority. They then barricaded the barrack gates. The Sultan, backed by the religious authorities, brought up his own loyal troops, whose cannon balls smashed open the gates and whose grapeshot slaughtered the janissaries inside the barracks. Within a few hours the janissary revolt in Constantinople had been crushed, and within a few days a reform needed for half a century or more had been initiated. In the following months the provincial janissaries were dissolved, and rebels in the capital brought to trials which ended in death sentences for thousands.

The destruction of the janissaries was indeed an Auspicious Event, as the Turks called it, since it deprived the Sultan's reactionary opponents of their military force, and opened the way for him to reform not only the army and navy but every branch of Ottoman administration. But the Sultan's reforms came too late to shift the balance in his favour in the conflict with the Greeks.

However there was one prize in Greece which the Sultan could still try to secure: the capture of Athens. Athens had been in the hands of the Greeks since their seizure of the Akropolis in 1822, and after the fall of Mesolongi it was the only remaining Greek stronghold north of the Gulf of Corinth. Athens was an enormously prestigious prize, as the birthplace of the glorious achievements of classical Greece, but it also had an immediate practical value. Some form of autonomy for Greece was by now probable, since the Greek struggle was still alive and the powers of Europe were clearly moving towards imposing a settlement. If the Turks held the whole of Roumeli any new Greek state would probably be limited to the Peloponnese, as Stratford Canning, Britain's ambassador in Constantinople, made clear to the Greeks. Conversely, if the Greeks held Athens they could lay claim to a border further north.

Reshid Pasha had had to concede the honour of capturing Mesolongi to Ibrahim, or at least share it with him, and was now anxious for an unqualified military success of his own. By the end of June 1826, only two months after the fall of Mesolongi, Reshid had brought an army of some 7,000 men, including 800 cavalry, to Athens and had established his headquarters at Patíssia, north of the Akropolis. By the end of July his artillery was in place on the hill of Philopáppos to bombard the south-west flank of the Akropolis. By mid-August Reshid was master of the town of Athens, though not of the Akropolis itself, which was held by a garrison of about 500 men under Goúras, now defending the place where he had encompassed the murder of his old rival Odysseus.

The Greeks' first attempt to dislodge Reshid was an attack from the west by a combined force of Karaïskákis' irregular troops and Fabvier's regulars, numbering about 3,500 men. Karaïskákis the calculating guerrilla leader and Fabvier the correct French officer now met for the first time, and seemed to get on well together. On 18 August 1826 their substantial combined force reached Chaïdhári, five miles west of the Akropolis, but were driven back by Reshid's troops and lost some 300 men. Karaïskákis and Fabvier each blamed the other for the defeat. 'They criticised each other's conduct with acrimony,' wrote Gordon, 'and their followers warmly took up the dispute. . . . any future co-operation became impossible.'[5] It was the first of many disputes which were to bedevil the Greek campaign at Athens.

For the rest of the year the Akropolis remained under close siege and heavy bombardment. On 13 October the garrison commander Goúras was killed by a single sniper shot, and a week later Makriyánnis, serving with the garrison, was wounded three times on the same day, the last wound 'an ugly cut on the back of my head: the shreds of my cap went into the bone to the skin over my brain. I fell down like one dead.'[6] However a month later Makriyánnis was sufficiently recovered to get out with five horsemen through the enemy lines to the government at Éyina with a plea for help, especially for a supply of gunpowder. As a result Fabvier in mid-December landed at Piraeus with 500 of his regular troops, and under cover of darkness got past the Turkish guards and into the Akropolis, each man including Fabvier carrying some 26 lb of powder, a total amount of about six tons. Fabvier expected to leave the Akropolis once he had brought in his supply, and his men had not even brought their greatcoats, but the Greeks of the garrison wanted to escape and leave Fabvier's regulars to take over the defence. They therefore started a skirmish to alert the Turks every time Fabvier tried to leave. Fabvier was now trapped in the Akropolis, and the year 1826 ended gloomily for the Greeks. Though they had managed to hold on to Navplion, Mesolongi's long resistance had finally failed in April, and Athens was still under close Turkish siege.

In deciding their strategy for Athens the Greeks had two main options. One was to cut off Reshid's supplies by attacking the chain of posts which he had prudently set up as links to Évvia in the north and the Gulf of Corinth to the west. This was favoured by Gordon, who was again serving with the Greek forces after a five-year absence, but was rejected in favour of the alternative, a direct attack on Reshid's forces from the coast at Piraeus. Gordon was put in charge of this expedition, which was to be supported by a body of Greeks who were to attack from Elévsis in the west, and by Captain Hastings in the newly arrived steamship *Kartería* with two supporting ships. Gordon did not agree with the venture, which was, he wrote, 'as much opposed to the rules of strategy as the dictates of good sense'.[7] Nevertheless he accepted the command of it.

Gordon's force of 2,300 men landed just east of Piraeus at midnight on 5 February 1827 and quickly occupied the high ground. The Turks meanwhile strengthened their defences and increased the Turkish and Albanian garrison of the monastery of Áyios Spirídhon immediately above the main harbour of Piraeus. This stronghold became the linchpin of their resistance, withstanding repeated cannonades from the *Kartería* at sea and the Greek artillery on land. Twice Reshid brought a force from Athens to dislodge Gordon's troops, and though he failed to drive them into the sea he effectively deterred them from advancing on Athens. This stalemate still persisted, and the monastery of Áyios

Spirídhon was still holding out, when at the end of April 1827 Cochrane and Church arrived on the scene.

By then the Greek army for the attack on Athens had been considerably strengthened. Karaïskákis, fresh from a victory over the Turks in the winter snows of Aráchova near Delphi, had joined it with some 3,000 men. Others had come in from the Peloponnese and Hydra, and the Greek soldiers now numbered about 10,000. But with the arrival of Cochrane and Church counsels became even more divided. Cochrane was for marching straight to the Akropolis, accused the Greeks of cowardice for not doing so, and threatened to leave unless his wishes were met. Karaïskákis, stung by the accusation of cowardice, refused to move while the Turks still held Áyios Spirídhon. Cochrane was for storming this monastery, but Karaïskákis and Church argued successfully for a negotiated capitulation. Under its terms the garrison with its arms was to be conducted by Greek troops to Reshid's camp at Athens, but hardly had the procession left Piraeus on 28 April when a trivial dispute broke out between garrison and escort, a shot went off, firing became general, and before long 200 of the garrison lay dead, only seventy escaping. Gordon resigned his command in horror, as he had done after the bloody fall of Tripolis six years earlier. Church too threatened to resign, but was persuaded to stay, though he was blamed by Gordon for retiring to a schooner in the bay instead of being present at the evacuation. Karaïskákis, with other Greek captains, had marched in the middle of the Turkish and Albanian column as security for its safety, and only he came out of the affair with credit. According to Gordon 'Karaiskaki strove at the hazard of his own life to stop the slaughter, and when he perceived it was to no purpose, cried to the Moslems, "Forgive me, as I forgive you; I can do nothing more for you." '[8]

With the obstacle of Áyios Spirídhon removed, Cochrane resumed his pressure for a march on Athens. It is difficult now to visualise the terrain he was looking at. Today the concrete sprawl of the conurbation of Athens and Piraeus covers the whole area; then one could look straight across from the high ground above Piraeus to the Akropolis about four miles away. To the left were olive groves stretching towards Athens, and to the right an open plain. The coast to the right was the empty shoreline of the Bay of Pháliron. Karaïskákis was still opposed to a march on Athens, especially across the open plain where the Greeks would be at the mercy of the Turkish cavalry, but Cochrane insisted. 'Where I command,' he is reported as saying, 'all other authority ceases.'[9] It was eventually agreed that 2,500 men – regulars, philhellenes and some of the Greek irregulars – would be shipped across to the other side of the Bay of Pháliron and from there march on Athens, while 7,000 Greek irregulars remained at Piraeus and points west to give support to the advancing column.

The last opposition to Cochrane's plan vanished when, in a skirmish two days before the proposed venture, a Turkish horseman shot Karaïskákis in the stomach. He died next day on Church's schooner, remembered variously as the turncoat convicted of treason in 1824, or as the uncertain ally who had failed to support the exodus from Mesolongi, or as the principled and heroic casualty of the battle of Athens. His death removed the only Greek captain with the standing to halt or even to modify Cochrane's risky scheme.

On the evening of 5 May 1827 the attacking force of 2,500 men was shipped east from Piraeus across the Bay of Pháliron, and disembarked at midnight. 'Tomorrow,' claimed Cochrane, 'we will dine in the Akropolis.'[10] But from then on everything went wrong. 'If the plan deserves the severest censure,' wrote Gordon,

> what shall we say to the pitiful method in which it was executed? As the Admiral [Cochrane] had nothing to do with the motions of the troops when once ashore, and the General [Church], satisfied with having sketched a disposition, staid in his vessel till daylight, the captains, all on a footing of equality, acted independently, halting where they chose; so that the column was scattered over a space of four miles, the front within cannon-shot of Athens, the rear close to the sea, and the soldiers, unprovided with spades and pickaxes, dug the earth with their daggers, in order to cover themselves from the charge of horse.[11]

When daylight revealed the scattered Greek forces Reshid attacked. The leading contingent stood firm, but those behind fell back towards the sea and soon the rout became general. The reserve force of 7,000 Greek irregulars did nothing to help and withdrew to the west. When Cochrane and Church finally landed from their ships in the bay they were caught up in the fleeing mêlée and only just escaped to the small boats offshore. The Greek losses were the worst of any single day in the whole war: 1,500 were killed, including 240 prisoners who were beheaded. Of the twenty-six philhellenes in the action only four escaped. Another philhellene, an English surgeon on Cochrane's ship, gave the day a concise label in his poem *The Athenaid*, simply calling it 'The sixth of May, the awful sixth of May'.[12]

Despite this disastrous defeat the expedition's base at Pháliron had been held by a determined last-minute resistance, and Church hung on there with a reduced force for three more weeks. Heat and thirst eventually got the better of them, and on 27 May they left. Church had already recommended capitulation to Fabvier and the others besieged in the Akropolis, which they at first refused, but with Church's departure they accepted defeat. Within a week surrender terms were agreed through the mediation of the French admiral de Rigny. On 5 June the Akropolis garrison of some 2,000 marched out, escorted by Reshid himself and a body of cavalry to ensure that there was no retaliation for the massacre of surrendered Turks at Áyios Spirídhon. This final act of the battle for Athens provoked yet more recriminations. Contemporaries, while accepting that conditions in the Akropolis were harsh, claimed that its wells provided enough water, even if only just enough, and that there was six months' supply of food. The capitulators of the Akropolis were compared unfavourably with the heroes of Mesolongi, and Church was blamed for suggesting surrender, de Rigny for negotiating it and Fabvier for accepting it. But on any rational view the defenders of the Akropolis were right to make terms. After a relieving force of 10,000, under the command of two distinguished foreigners, had tried to save them, failed disastrously and gone away, what was the point in them holding out any longer?

Dissension on the Greek side had marked every phase of the year-long battle for Athens. There was a basic disagreement over whether to starve Reshid into retreat by attacking his supply lines or to make a direct assault on his army at Athens. Cochrane was the most determined advocate of direct attack, but was criticised for arrogant over-confidence and for contemptuously dismissing more realistic Greek proposals. Church was blamed for being too weak to impose his authority, and both Cochrane and Church for staying too remote from the action. As Makriyánnis caustically put it, 'These Europeans, whom we had made our leaders, were for ever carrying out their business from ships: it was from the deck that they did battle with the enemy on land and slaughtered them with speeches and schemes.'[13] The captains of the Greek irregulars tended either to act independently of their nominal European commanders or not to act at all. Both things happened on the awful sixth of May, with catastrophic results.

Was direct assault on Reshid the right strategy? Gordon argued consistently, at the time and in his history, for the alternative of cutting off Reshid's supplies. Gordon had long experience of the war in Greece, but in this case he was probably wrong. Reshid had many potential lines of supply by land and by sea, and attempts to cut them all would have amounted to no more than pinprick attacks. Direct assault was the only way to dislodge Reshid from Athens, and Cochrane, hot-headed and opinionated as he was, was right to back it enthusiastically. But direct assault needed co-ordination, and this was what the forces at Athens disastrously lacked. Cochrane and Church had been appointed in order to unify the Greek war effort on land and sea. When the new commanders were put to the test, the result was even deeper and more acrimonious division.

30

The Treaty of London and the Admirals' Instructions

On 4 April 1826 Britain and Russia, as we have seen, had signed the Protocol of St Petersburg, which stated the intention of the two powers to offer mediation to the Turks and Greeks, to intervene if mediation failed, and to invite Austria, France and Prussia to join them in this endeavour. Metternich for Austria was strongly against the proposal; it gave recognition to rebels and would, he believed, be impossible to execute without war. But Austria delayed outright rejection, and instead tried to sink the plan by putting forward confusing counter-proposals. 'The thicker the shadows,' wrote Austria's foreign minister, 'the sooner these mediators without a mandate will bang their heads.'[1] Prussia followed Austria's lead, so Canning concentrated on winning over France.

Philhellenism in France had waned after the early departures from Marseilles of enthusiastic idealists to join the Greek cause, but the death of Byron in 1824 gave it enormous renewed impetus. The French government however was much more ambivalent than the public. France was intent on extending her influence in the Middle East generally and in Egypt especially. This sprang in part from an ambition to match Britain's position in India, and in part from a determination to balance any Russian expansion southward and stop it going too far. France had already helped Mehmed Ali revitalise Egypt by sending technical and military advisers. At Mehmed's request in November 1824 a further military mission of two French generals and six other officers left for Egypt, but in secrecy. In the following April the French government, after much debate, agreed to build for Egypt two frigates and a brig of war at Marseilles, again in as much secrecy as could be contrived.

If France was to build up her influence in the Middle East and block Russian and British ambitions, where better than in Greece itself? Hence another initiative, again sub rosa, to place a French king on the throne of an independent Greece. The French candidate was the Duke of Nemours, second son of Louis Philippe, Duke of Orléans, the man who was to become king of France in 1830 and whose descendants still lay claim to a restored French throne. In April 1825 the Orléanist General Roche arrived in Navplion to promote the candidacy of Nemours, with the connivance though not the open support of some members of the French government. But Roche was not the only hawker of kingly wares; the so-called English party was at the same time preparing an approach to Britain inviting either Leopold of Saxe-Coburg or the Duke of Sussex to the Greek throne. Roche's mission was effectively ended by the widely supported Greek Act of Submission to England in the summer of 1825.

By the beginning of 1826 therefore France's efforts to extend her influence by acting independently, and largely clandestinely, had come to nothing. In Egypt the French had done a great deal to help Mehmed Ali, but there was no indication that he was prepared to do anything for them. The prospect of a French king for Greece was dead. France was thus now willing to consider joint action on Greece with Russia and Britain, on the lines of the St Petersburg Protocol of April 1826.

Canning formally communicated the text of the St Petersburg Protocol to France on 10 August 1826, though its contents were already well known since it had been leaked to and published in *The Times* in May. Canning followed this up by a six-week visit to Paris in September and October, ostensibly on a private visit. There he found the French King Charles X keen to co-operate, and forged a close bond of friendship with him; Canning was the only commoner ever to be invited to dine en famille with Charles X at the Tuileries. In essence, France was willing to sign a treaty based on the protocol in order to check both England and Russia, just as a year earlier England had signed the protocol as a block to Russia.

The text of a treaty now had to be agreed between the three powers, which was no easy matter, and for the next nine months after Canning's visit to Paris drafts were circulated between the three capitals. Another cause of delay was that Greece was not Canning's only concern as foreign secretary or even the major one. At the end of the year Portugal claimed centre stage. There the government of the Constitutional party, backed by England, was under threat from the Absolutists, who were supported by Spain and France. At the end of November 1826 Portuguese anti-government forces crossed the frontier from Spain and marched on Lisbon, and the Portuguese prime minister called on Britain for military support. On 12 December Canning promised it during a dramatic debate in Parliament. This was the speech in which he famously claimed that, by recognising the independence of Spain's former South American colonies and so weakening Spain, 'I called the New World into existence to redress the balance of the Old.' British troops reached Lisbon on Christmas Day, France and Spain withdrew support from the invaders, and they were driven back by the Portuguese army without the British having to fire a shot. 'By a display of oratory and a military parade,' wrote a later historian, 'Canning had imposed his will on Western Europe.'[2] This happy outcome had a bearing on the Greek question: it encouraged the belief that force had only to be paraded, not used. It was a hopeful precedent for intervention in Greece, but as it turned out a misleading one.

Moves towards a tripartite treaty were further slowed down by an upheaval in the British cabinet. In February 1827 the prime minister Lord Liverpool fell ill and had to resign, and after prolonged political manoeuvring Canning, strongly supported by the King, became prime minister on 10 April. Wellington's opposition to the St Petersburg Protocol had steadily increased, even though it was he who had signed it for Britain, as he had come to doubt the wisdom of intervention; he therefore resigned from the cabinet and from his post as commander-in-chief of the army. Canning's friend Lord Dudley became foreign secretary, and Canning also had the support of the King's brother the Duke of Clarence, later William IV, who was appointed to the revived office of Lord High Admiral. Canning's political position at home was thus much strengthened in the months leading to the signing of the Treaty of London by representatives of Britain, Russia and France on 6 July 1827.

This treaty contained seven open articles and a further three secret articles. The open articles closely followed the St Petersburg Protocol of the year before, proposing limited autonomy for Greece as a tribute-paying dependency of Turkey. There were only two significant changes in the open articles: none of the powers was required to guarantee anything, and there was now no question of any power acting alone. But the secret articles set out what the three signatory powers would now do. They would establish commercial relations with Greece, thus in effect recognising her independent status. If within a month (later shortened to a fortnight by Canning) Turkey, Greece or both had not accepted an armistice, the powers would intervene. Their admirals would be given instructions on how to impose the armistice. If this failed the representatives of the powers in London would take further as yet unspecified steps, using 'les moyens ultérieurs dont l'emploi pourrait devenir nécessaire'.[3] These secret articles did not stay secret for long, as they too were published in *The Times* along with the rest of the treaty a week after its signature. The Greeks were therefore delighted to see that provided Turkey rejected the armistice, as was virtually certain, Britain, Russia and France would intervene. In Corfu, wrote Kapodhístrias' brother Viaro, 'men went mad with joy. The bells were rung, the Christians gave thanks to God, old men danced . . . a day of resurrection.'[4]

While the details of the Treaty of London were being hammered out, another set of negotiations was going on which could, if successful, have transformed the situation in Greece. This was an attempt to detach Mehmed Ali, viceroy of Egypt and father of Ibrahim, from his allegiance to the Sultan. Back in June 1826 Stratford Canning, then British ambassador in St Petersburg, had asked his cousin George Canning if it would be possible 'to enlist the Viceroy of Egypt . . . by holding out to him the prospect of a pashalik in Syria'.[5] On Stratford Canning's initiative the British consul in Alexandria began discussions with Mehmed Ali in September, and learnt that Mehmed was tired of the war in Greece, had purposely told his son to 'loiter about in the interior' of the Peloponnese, and was ready to withdraw from it if Britain would give him open support to 'aggrandise himself towards Arabia'.[6]

However no such open support was forthcoming, and in the following months Mehmed Ali changed tack and took steps to strengthen his position as an ally of the Sultan. During the winter of 1826–7 he threatened to pull out of Greece altogether unless his demands were met, the demands being the replacement of the Turkish kapitan pasha Khosref, whom he accused of gross incompetence in the siege of Mesolongi, and the appointment of himself as generalissimo of all Ottoman land and sea forces in Greece, Turkish as well as Egyptian. The Sultan conceded – he had little choice – and Mehmed Ali began active preparation of his fleet for a new expedition to Greece, with the aim of seizing Hydra and Spétses and so eliminating Greece's naval power. He raised the best part of 15,000 new troops. His ships practised manoeuvres under the supervision of French officers, and from March onwards the ships built for him in France began to arrive. Thus while French statesmen were preparing to sign the Treaty of London to drive Mehmed Ali's forces out of Greece, French officers and shipyards were working to make his intervention in Greece a success.

By June 1827 Mehmed Ali's fleet was fully prepared. It was then that Cochrane, seeking the success as Greece's naval commander that had so far eluded him, brought a Greek fleet to Alexandria in an attempt to destroy the Egyptian fleet, as Kanáris had tried to do two years earlier. Cochrane's ships anchored outside the harbour, and eight fireships were ordered in but only two obeyed, which could do no more than burn one stranded Egyptian vessel. Light winds made it impossible for Cochrane's fleet to enter the harbour, and for two days it lay outside, drifting apart over a distance of twenty miles, before withdrawing back to Greece. If Cochrane had succeeded it might have been he with a Greek fleet and not Codrington with a foreign one who was credited with securing Greece's independence. As it was, Cochrane's attack, even though it failed, demonstrated to Mehmed Ali that he was in danger from Greek ships even in his own harbour, and encouraged him to believe that the Greek situation must be resolved, the sooner the better.

A final attempt to neutralise Mehmed Ali was made in the summer of 1827 by George Canning, now prime minister. At his instigation Major Cradock, an official at the British embassy in Paris, went to Alexandria with instructions to warn Mehmed Ali of the danger of involvement in a conflict between Turkey and the allied powers which might well 'produce some hostile collision in spite of [the powers'] earnest and anxious desire to avoid it'.[7] Canning had high hopes of Cradock's mission. 'If the Pasha's fleet has not sailed before Cradock reaches him,' he wrote, 'I flatter myself it will remain in port.'[8] But when Cradock reached Alexandria on 8 August he was just too late: the fleet had sailed three days earlier. On the same date, 8 August, George Canning, exhausted by the burden of office, died at the age of fifty-seven. 'We have just lost Canning,' wrote Princess Lieven. 'The Mercantile class is in dismay, the people in tears, everybody who is not Metternich is in despair.'[9] So Canning never saw the outcome of the grand scheme of allied intervention in Greece of which he was the prime architect.

The Treaty of London had set the allied and Ottoman naval forces on a potential collision course. At Alexandria the fleet which Mehmed Ali was preparing had been joined by Egyptian ships brought back from the Peloponnese, by a Turkish contingent from Constantinople under Tahir Pasha, and by four Tunisian ships. Ibrahim's brother-in-law Moharrem Bey commanded the Egyptian vessels. The fleet left Alexandria in early August 1827 and consisted of three ships of the line, all Turkish; some sixty other fighting ships, five of the finest having been built in France; forty transports to convey the newly raised troops; and six fireships, one of which was to spark the inferno of Navarino. The fleet carried some 3,500 guns and was manned by over 30,000 sailors. Mehmed Ali was jubilantly proud of it. 'It is not the sort of fleet you have seen hitherto,' he wrote to Ibrahim. 'It is now a brilliant fleet, in modern style, and such as has never been seen before in the Muslim world.'[10] Mehmed Ali wanted to command the fleet in person, but this was forbidden by the Porte. Ibrahim was therefore in overall command of both the fleet and the land forces in the Peloponnese, and it was with Ibrahim that the allied admirals had to deal.

The three allied admirals were Sir Edward Codrington for Britain, Count de Rigny for France, and Count Heiden for Russia. Codrington had spent his life in the navy, as a lieutenant in the battle of the Glorious First of June in 1794, as captain of the *Orion* at Trafalgar in 1805, and from the spring of 1827 as commander-in-chief of the Mediterranean station. He was a fine naval commander, careful in planning, fearless in action, devoted to his officers and men, as they were to him, and prepared to clash with the highest authority to defend their interests. He also showed considerable diplomatic skills in winning the co-operation of his fellow admirals, with both of whose countries Britain had been at war in the previous twenty years.

The French admiral de Rigny had five years more experience of the eastern Mediterranean than Codrington, and had already been involved in the tortuous politics of the region, most recently when he negotiated the controversial surrender of the Athens Akropolis to the Turks in the summer of 1827. Codrington was at first extremely wary of de Rigny, finding in him 'a rooted dislike to the Greeks and a leaning towards the Egyptians with whom he had long been in friendly intercourse'. But Codrington won him over. 'In order to ensure his yielding to me whatever I considered essential,' he wrote, 'I embraced every opportunity of giving way to him in matters of minor importance.' Heiden, the Dutch-born admiral of the Russian fleet, was quite different. Codrington 'saw at once that the Count was a plain sailing open-hearted man' who was 'as ready in every instance to meet my wishes as if he had been an officer of our own Navy'.[11] Codrington had not been formally given the position of senior admiral, but de Rigny, much younger, and Heiden, with much less experience of the Mediterranean, accorded him the position without question.

Co-operation between the allies was the more important because they were heavily outnumbered by their opponents. The allies had only twenty-eight fighting ships, less than half as many as the Turko-Egyptian fleet, and only a third of the Ottoman numbers of men and guns. In the allies' favour, however, was their preponderance in ships of the line, the largest fighting ships, of which they had ten against their opponents' three. Their seamanship was also superior, and Ibrahim consistently referred to the allied fleet as more powerful than his own.

Once the Treaty of London was signed, instructions were sent to the three powers' admirals in the Mediterranean and to their ambassadors in Constantinople. The ambassadors were to present the terms of the treaty to the Ottoman Porte, which they did on 16 August, and the admirals to present them to the Greeks, which they did at the end of the month. The instructions then considered the likely results and laid down what was to be done next. The most probable outcome was that the Greeks would accept the armistice, as they did on 2 September, and more or less keep it, while the Turks rejected it, as they did with increasing vehemence to the allied ambassadors during August and September. In that case the admirals were 'to intercept every supply sent by sea of men, arms, etc., destined against Greece' though force must not be used 'unless the Turks persist in forcing the passage'. At the same time the admirals were told that such interception 'requires the greatest caution' and that 'you ought to be most particularly careful that the measures you adopt . . . do not degenerate into hostilities'.[12]

These instructions were hopelessly inadequate. If carried out as they stood, they would only prevent Ibrahim being reinforced, and would leave him free to use the forces he already had in the Peloponnese in any way he chose, including the long-contemplated attack on Hydra. Even the interruption of reinforcements was paradoxically to be achieved by the use of force if necessary but without hostilities. Codrington therefore sought clarification, as instructed, from Britain's Constantinople ambassador, now Stratford Canning, recently transferred from St Petersburg. Codrington could get an answer from Constantinople in a week, especially if he was off the Turkish coast, whereas an answer from London would take a month or more.

Formal elucidation for the admirals jointly came in a document signed by all three allied ambassadors in Constantinople, known as the Protocol of 4 September. The protocol first made clear that even neutral vessels bringing 'succours destined for the Turks into Greece' were to be intercepted. It then went on to extend considerably the original instructions. The allied fleet was to protect, in co-operation with the Greeks, all that part of Greece which had 'taken an active and continued part in the insurrection'. This area was defined, generously for the Greeks, as the territory south of a line from Vólos in the east to just north of Mesolongi in the west, including the neighbouring islands; so the whole Peloponnese was covered, plus Athens and Mesolongi, and the islands of Évvia, Hydra and Spétses. The protocol had two more new elements. All Turkish and Egyptian fighting ships were to be 'encouraged' to return to Constantinople or Alexandria, as were transports carrying troops; and any Ottoman ships which persisted in staying at Navarino or Methóni must 'incur all the chances of war'.[13] In two personal letters to Codrington, Stratford Canning was even more explicit. On 19 August he told Codrington 'to keep the peace with your speaking trumpet if possible; but, in case of necessity, with that which is used for the maintenance of a blockade against friends as well as foes; – I mean force.' In the second letter of 1 September he wrote that Codrington's orders were 'ultimately to be enforced, if necessary, and when all other means are exhausted, by cannon shot'.[14] Codrington seemed finally to have been given a fairly clear outline of his task, and a completely clear instruction to use force if he had to in carrying it out.

31

Navarino

The combined Turkish and Egyptian fleet finally anchored in the Bay of Navarino on 7 September 1827, where Ibrahim was already based. Codrington was at Navplion when he heard the news and sailed immediately, taking up station outside the harbour on 12 September. He was joined there ten days later by de Rigny and his fleet, though the Russians were yet to arrive. Codrington found that an Ottoman squadron had already sailed out from Navarino, evidently en route to Hydra, but a firm letter from Codrington and a visit from de Rigny persuaded Ibrahim to recall his ships, and de Rigny arranged that he and Codrington should have a joint interview with Ibrahim a few days later on 25 September.

On that morning, the admirals were rowed ashore to Ibrahim's tent, which was pitched on a little bank rising from the beach just north of the town of Pílos. The admirals were accompanied by some of their senior officers and by the eighteen-year-old Henry Codrington, a midshipman on his father's ship, who left a lively description of the meeting. He describes Ibrahim as seated on his sofa, while Admiral Codrington sat beside him and de Rigny next, so that Codrington was in the centre. The allied officers were ranged in front of the sofa and the Turk and Egyptian leaders behind it, with the exception of Tahir the Turkish naval commander, who was said to be ill. As Henry Codrington described the scene, the tent was open 'and from his sofa [Ibrahim] looked down over the whole harbour, and really the sight was beautiful, covered as it was by the ships, and boats of all sorts continually passing to and fro'. Ibrahim himself, he went on irreverently, 'is not at all good-looking . . . and fat as a porpoise'.[1] After lengthy introductions and an exchange of pleasantries, coffee was brought in with pipes for the three principals, the pipes being enormous and elaborate chibouques studded with precious stones and with stems ten feet long. The admirals thus found that they had been sent abroad to smoke for their countries, and dutifully did so.

Then business began. Admiral Codrington, according to his own account, told Ibrahim that as a consequence of the Treaty of London 'it became [the admirals'] imperative duty to intercept every supply sent by sea of men, arms etc., destined against Greece'. Ibrahim then stated his own position, 'that his orders were to attack Hydra, and that he must put them in execution'. Codrington expressed sympathy, 'aware what must be the feelings of a brave man under such circumstances'. Nevertheless, if Ibrahim put to sea the allies would prevent him, and 'if he resisted by force, the total destruction of his fleet must follow'. Ibrahim acknowledged what he had heard, and therefore undertook to remain at Navarino and 'to suspend all operations of the land and sea forces forming the expedition from Alexandria till he received answers from Constantinople and Alexandria' giving him new instructions.[2]

The formal business was now over, and was followed by what Henry Codrington called a 'joking' conversation, which was not all jokes. At one point Ibrahim was mocking the Greeks, saying that 'there never was a Greek worth anything', but Admiral Codrington brought him up short by answering 'that his Highness ought to abstain from undervaluing those men whom he had been such a time attempting to conquer'.[3]

After three hours the conference ended and the admirals returned to their ships. It was expected to take till about 15 October for Ibrahim to receive his new instructions and Codrington believed Ibrahim had undertaken not to move during those twenty days. Codrington and de Rigny therefore sailed away to reprovision and to patrol other sectors of the coast, leaving only two ships, one from each nation, to watch Navarino. But Ibrahim and his colleagues had, or claimed to have, a different understanding of what had been agreed with the admirals. Ibrahim later recorded two extra points in his favour from the 25 September meeting, points which almost certainly had not been conceded: that the Greeks as well as the Turks should observe a temporary armistice until his new instructions arrived; and that he had permission from the admirals to take provisions to the Turkish garrison of Patras.

However, the Greeks were still fighting, on the ground that while they had accepted the Treaty of London, the Ottoman government had not. In the last days of September Church was leading a Greek force against Patras, and Hastings in the *Kartería* had destroyed a flotilla of seven Turkish ships at Itéa in the Gulf of Corinth. Ibrahim's reaction was to bring forty-eight of his ships out of Navarino to head for Patras, far more of course than would be needed for an agreed supply drop. In the course of three days and nights of appalling weather Codrington's much smaller fleet turned them back with the help of some shots across their bows, and they returned to Navarino.

If Ibrahim could not get away with provocative actions at sea, he could try on land where the admirals had no forces. After the failure of his Patras expedition he renewed his previous campaign of devastation of the Peloponnese. Hamilton of the *Cambrian*, Greece's long-term friend and now part of Codrington's fleet, reported on 15 October that the smoke of burning orchards could be seen from his station off Kalamáta. The three admirals, united at last by the arrival of Heiden and his Russian fleet a few days earlier, sent a joint letter to Ibrahim ordering him to desist, but were told that nobody knew where Ibrahim was and that nobody else could accept a message addressed to him.

Ibrahim was clearly stretching his freedom of action to the limit, and deliberately putting himself out of reach of remonstrances from the admirals. Furthermore, he could anticipate very different answers to his requests for instructions from Constantinople and Alexandria. He could expect, rightly as it turned out, that the reply from Constantinople would be bellicose, on the lines of the Porte's forthright rejection of the ambassadors' attempts to mediate, while the reply from Alexandria would be pacific, based on Mehmed Ali's concern not to lose his prized fleet. What was Ibrahim to say to the admirals when two such contradictory instructions reached him? It was better to stay out of their way.

Kolokotrónis intercepted Ibrahim's orders to burn and destroy the trees – olive, fig and mulberry – of the Kalamáta region, and records the splendidly defiant reply he sent:

This action with which you would terrify us, threatening to cut down and burn up our fruit-bearing trees, is not warfare; the senseless trees cannot oppose themselves to any one . . . but we will not submit – no, not if you cut down every branch, not if you burn all our trees and houses, nor leave one stone upon another. And if you do cut down and burn up all our trees, you cannot dig up and carry off the earth which nourished them; that same earth will still remain ours, and will bear them again. If only one Greek shall be left, we will still go on fighting. Never hope that you will make our earth your own.[4]

It was this spirit which had animated the Greeks at their best through-out the war and the many difficulties, some self-imposed, that they had endured. They might now be dependent upon others for success, but it was their own tenacity which had kept the flame of freedom alight for six years until more powerful allies came to their aid.

The admirals, faced with the evasive and delaying tactics of Ibrahim and his breaches in their view of the 25 September agreement, had to decide what to do. A blockade of the harbour of Navarino would be impossible to maintain during the coming winter storms. Even if a blockade could prevent Ibrahim's fleet leaving Navarino, it could not stop Ibrahim's devastations on land. Privately the admirals were in no doubt that they must drive Ibrahim's fleet out of the Peloponnese. On the evening of 14 October Codrington wrote to Stratford Canning stating that he would confer with de Rigny and Heiden 'as to taking measures for forcing Ibrahim's return to Egypt'.[5] On the same day de Rigny wrote to his government that in his opinion the three squadrons should enter Navarino bay 'and there, match in hand, tell the fleets to disperse and to return, one to Constantinople and the other to Alexandria, and, if they do not, attack them immediately'.[6] Heiden agreed, and the three admirals recorded their intentions in the so-called Protocol of 18 October. It was a cautious document, implying that the allies would not use force, and was designed to forestall the later polit-ical criticism which they already anticipated. The protocol listed Ibrahim's breaches of faith, declared a blockade to be impossible, stated their intention of entering the harbour to 'renew propositions' to Ibrahim, and recorded their unanimous agreement that this approach 'may, without effusion of blood and without hostilities, but simply by the imposing presence of the squadrons, produce a determination leading to the desired object'.[7] The admirals, in short, claimed that they were simply following the military maxim of the Romans: *qui desiderat pacem, praeparet bellum.*

There was a final step needed before the allied fleet went in: the French officers acting as advisers to the Egyptian squadron needed to be withdrawn. There were ten of them, of whom Letellier was the most senior. On 15 October de Rigny sent a letter to Letellier, pointing out that he and his fellow officers were at imminent risk of fighting against their own flag and calling on them to leave their posts. The Egyptian admiral Moharrem Bey understood their position, and even offered them transport to Alexandria. In the event all departed on an Austrian ship in the next few days except Letellier, who stayed on Moharrem Bey's flagship and left only when it actually came under fire. Thus on 20 October the Turco-Egyptian fleet was not only without its overall commander Ibrahim but was also deprived of the services of its most experienced foreign advisers.

Letellier now performed one last service by arranging the disposition of the Turco-Egyptian fleet. The Bay of Navarino stretches a little over three miles north to south and two miles east to west. The west side is formed by the island of Sphaktíria, whose northern tip almost joins the mainland. The only entrance to the bay is therefore through the narrow gap at its southern end, which is partly blocked by some jagged needles of rock. There is a small island in the centre of the bay, to the north of which the bay deteriorates into shallow sandy lagoons. The fleets of October 1827 thus had to operate in the southern half of the bay, and it was there that under Letellier's direction the Turkish and Egyptian ships were positioned at anchor in a triple line of horseshoe formation, presenting their broadsides to the centre, the Egyptians on the east side and the Turks on the west, with the small Tunisian contingent in the rear. The fireships were placed on either side of the entrance, which was also protected by batteries at the town of Pílos on the east and at the tip of Sphaktíria on the west. Letellier's dispositions, which took three days to complete, were thus intimidating in the extreme, a sort of maritime version of the Maori *haka.*

It would have taken more than a threatening posture to deter Codrington and his fellow admirals, and in the late morning of 20 October, in fine weather and under a light wind, the allied fleet began to move through the narrow entrance into the bay. The eleven ships of the English squadron led the way, headed by Codrington in his flagship the *Asia*. The *Asia* with the other two English line-of-battle ships, *Genoa* and *Albion*, took up position at anchor in roughly the centre of the enemy horseshoe while the smaller English vessels stayed on either side of the entrance to keep a watch on the fireships. The seven French ships, led by de Rigny in the *Sirène*, came in next, and were stationed on the east side facing the Egyptians, to ensure that any French officers still with the Egyptian fleet would have to leave on pain of fighting their own countrymen. The eight Russian ships came last, under Heiden in the *Azov*, and formed a group more compact than the English or French opposite the mainly Turkish vessels on the west side of the bay.

At 2 p.m., while most of the allied ships were still manoeuvring into position, a small boat was seen coming from the Egyptian flagship to the *Asia*. It brought a letter from Moharrem Bey to Codrington asking him not to persist in entering, to which Codrington immediately replied that he had come to give orders and not to receive them. The officer who had brought the letter then went directly ashore, where a red flag was raised and an unshotted gun fired, presumably to signal the failure of this final conciliatory move. More threatening was the sight of a small boat from the enemy fleet heading for one of their fireships. When this boat arrived the crew of the fireship started preparing it for attack.

The nearest allied ship was the English frigate *Dartmouth*, whose Captain Fellowes sent a pinnace with a few men under a lieutenant to request the fireship crew either to leave their ship or to tow it further inshore out of the *Dartmouth*'s way. Captain Fellowes' last instruction to the lieutenant as the pinnace left was 'Recollect, Sir, that no act of hostility is to be attempted by us *on any account*.'[8] As the pinnace reached its destination a shot from the fireship killed the English coxswain, and in spite of the lieutenant's continued signals to the Turkish captain that no violence was intended several other shots followed, killing and wounding others of the pinnace's crew. The fireship crew now lit the fuse which would set it ablaze, and when another lieutenant in a second boat from the *Dartmouth* was sent to tow it away the lieutenant too was shot dead. Almost simultaneously a shot from an

Egyptian corvette hit the *Sirène*, the flagship of de Rigny, and in his laconic words 'L'engagement devint bientôt général.' Before long the peace of the bay was shattered, the gentle creaking of ships' timbers was drowned by the thunder of cannon fire, and a pall of smoke blocked out the autumn sunlight.

These shots which triggered the battle of Navarino were almost certainly not planned by the Ottoman commanders. They knew they were facing a superior even if numerically smaller force, and seem like the allied statesmen to have put their trust in a mere display of force, hoping that their intimidating crescent line would persuade the allied fleet to withdraw. However, if the shots were unplanned they were also virtually inevitable, given Tahir's order of the day: 'Admiral Tahir Pasha will never raise the signal for combat, but he lays down that in case of attack each ship should defend itself individually.'[9] But what was to count as a case of attack? In this tense confrontation somebody somewhere in the extended Ottoman fleet was almost bound to interpret an allied move as an attack, and the conflict would begin.

Not only were the initial shots very probably unplanned, but it seems that the Turkish and Egyptian commanders, who had never trusted each other, had formed no joint plan of any kind about reacting to the allied fleet, as Codrington's first encounter with his opponents showed. Codrington in the *Asia* was roughly midway between the Turkish flagship of Tahir Pasha and the Egyptian flagship of Moharrem Bey, the *Guerrière*, where Letellier, the last of the French officers, was still on board. Shots were seen coming from Tahir Pasha's ship, but Moharrem Bey sent a message to the *Asia* to say that he did not intend to open fire, and Codrington replied that he would not fire first. Codrington destroyed Tahir's ship, though Tahir survived, and then sent an officer with a Greek interpreter to Moharrem Bey's *Guerrière* to confirm the truce. But the crew of the *Guerrière* either did not know of their admiral's pacific intention or ignored it. As Codrington's party approached the *Guerrière* a pistol shot killed the interpreter, and the *Asia* responded with a broadside which quickly drove the *Guerrière* ashore in flames. As the *Guerrière* joined the battle, Letellier finally went ashore, and Moharrem Bey, with no stomach for a fight which he had done all he could to avoid, went with him. Thus by an early stage of the battle the Ottoman fleet, from which Ibrahim and the French officers were already absent, was virtually without command: Tahir's ship had been sunk, and Moharrem Bey had left.

Never again was a naval battle fought between fleets all under sail, but never before had a naval battle been fought between fleets at anchor, exchanging broadsides at close quarters. The allies were able to swing their ships by the anchor cables in order to bring their broadsides to bear in different directions. These broadsides were enormously heavy: it was later estimated that the three English line-of-battle ships alone had fired over 120 tons of shot. This exceptional figure was partly due to overshotting, that is loading not just the regulation one or two cannon balls but several extra balls and sometimes a canister of grape-shot as well, a practice disapproved of because it could smash the gun but enthusiastically used for its dramatic effects. This weight of shot required a lot of powder, about a ton for every ten tons of shot. There was constant danger of accidental fire on board from ignited powder dust, and not only as a result of enemy shot; the lanterns in the powder store were naked flames behind glass panels which could easily be smashed during a battle, and even the spark from a snapped flintlock could start a blaze.

The more obvious danger of a conflagration in the allied fleet was from the Turkish fireships. The *Dartmouth* escaped the fireship which had started the battle, but another nearly destroyed the French ship of the line *Scipion*. This fireship was firmly attached to the bow of the *Scipion* and brave efforts by the crew to push it off failed. 'It really seemed as if it were drawn to us by a magnetic force,' wrote the *Scipion*'s captain.[10] The *Scipion* had its head to the wind which was blowing the flames down the length of the ship, so the captain began to attempt a turn to divert the blaze. When all seemed lost a small boat from another French ship managed to haul the fireship away with the help of tow ropes from three of the English ships, one of many examples of allied co-operation that afternoon. This fireship was finally sunk by gunfire, and not one Turkish fireship attack was successful during the whole battle.

Smoke from the cannon fire soon shrouded the bay, and visibility was down to a few yards. Signals could not be seen, and Codrington had to shout orders to the neighbouring ship through a loudhailer. The noise was literally deafening, and some of the men did not recover their hearing for two days. Flying fragments, usually of wood, were as common a danger as a direct hit, and the quarter-deck of the *Genoa* was described as 'so bestrewed with splinters of wood that it presented the appearance of a carpenter's shop'.[11] A flying splinter could break an arm, or cause a horrible wound if it penetrated. Young Henry Codrington was wounded in the leg by a fragment of iron railing, then in the same leg by a musket ball, and had his collarbone badly bruised, though not broken, by a splinter of wood. In a letter to his brother he described going down to the *Asia's* sick bay:

> I found myself almost in the dark and in an atmosphere which was as hot, though not so pure, as many an oven. On the chests, etc. the men's mess tables had been laid, and over them beds; on these lay the wounded, some too bad to speak, others groaning and crying out with the agony they were in. Some (generally the least hurt) calling out lustily for the doctor. I managed to feel my way to an unoccupied berth amidships, alongside a poor fellow who had been severely wounded, and I think we made a pretty quiet pair, except occasional, nay frequent, calls for water, of which, owing to my excessive thirst, I must have drunk a great deal, besides what I poured on the bandage which had just been put on my wound which felt as if it were on fire and devilish uncomfortable.[12]

Henry Codrington's wounds were more serious than he admitted, and he came close to having the leg amputated. The jaunty bravado of his letter was no doubt to spare his family anxiety and showed less than the harsh reality. In the *Genoa* sick bay, as a crew member described it, 'The stifled groans, the figures of the surgeon and his mates, their bare arms and faces smeared with blood, the dead and dying all round, some in the last agonies of death, and others screaming under the amputating knife, formed a horrid scene of misery, and made a hideous contrast to the "pomp, pride, and circumstance of glorious war".'[13] Medical treatment, however rough, was at least fairly quickly available at sea, so that the sailor was better off than the soldier who in that era would too often be left to die where he fell on the battlefield.

By six o'clock, after nearly four hours of intense fighting, the battle was over. Amazingly not a single allied ship had been sunk, and casualties were relatively light: 174 killed and 475 wounded. But the Ottoman fleet had lost sixty of its eighty-nine fighting ships, with appalling losses of men: by Codrington's estimate, some 6,000 killed and 4,000 wounded. Turkish honour required that no ship should strike its flag in surrender, and none did. Honour also required that Turkish ships damaged beyond repair should be blown up, sometimes with men still on board. Codrington tried next day to get Tahir Pasha to desist from this, but without success. The few surviving ships of the Ottoman fleet limped back to their home ports.

It was clear immediately that Navarino had ensured the ultimate independence of Greece, the cause which had seemed almost lost when Athens surrendered to the Turks only a few months earlier. As Howe wrote when he learnt of the battle twelve days later, 'This day has been to me one of the happiest of my existence, and to all Greece one of joy and exultation. For it has brought the confirmation of the news of the destruction of the Turkish fleet at Navarino, and for ever puts at rest the question of the reconquest of Greece by Turkey.'[14] The Russian and French courts were also delighted, and in England the Lord High Admiral, the Duke of Clarence, on his own initiative awarded Codrington the Grand Cross of the Order of the Bath. But then Codrington's troubles began.

After Canning's death in August he had been succeeded as prime minister by the ineffectual Lord Goderich, described as 'firm as a bullrush', while Dudley, no more than a fair-weather friend of Codrington's, remained foreign secretary. A month after the battle it was Dudley who forwarded to Codrington a list of ten queries about his conduct, all clearly designed to show that Codrington had exceeded his instructions. To any unprejudiced eye Codrington's answers were wholly convincing. Then in January 1828 the Goderich administration collapsed and was replaced by a cabinet of ultra Tories under the Duke of Wellington, men who thought it wrong to have destroyed the fleet of a country with which England was not at war in a cause, Greek independence, for which they had little sympathy. The King's Speech at the opening of Parliament at the end of January reflected their views: it described the battle as 'a collision, wholly unexpected by His Majesty', went on to say that 'His Majesty laments that this conflict should have occurred with the naval force of an ancient ally', and characterised Navarino as 'this untoward event'.[15] The King was reported as saying privately of Codrington's Order of the Bath, 'I send him the ribbon but he deserves the rope.'[16]

Dudley's queries had tried unsuccessfully to show that Codrington had done too much. Codrington's enemies now accused him of doing too little. When the last of Ibrahim's ships left Navarino in December they carried, as Codrington himself reported, 'about 600 unfortunate Greek women and children' to be sold as slaves in Alexandria. This may not have been quite right; there is evidence that many were servants of the Turks who chose to go to Egypt. But the accusation smacked of the alleged barbarisation project, and provided another charge against Codrington, that he had carelessly or callously allowed this traffic. Codrington pointed out that he had no orders to intercept or search Egyptian ships returning to Alexandria, and that to do so would have provoked just those hostilities which he had been ordered to avoid. Nevertheless, Codrington's enemies would not let the accusation die, and it rumbled on, with an ever larger number of captives being suggested, until a debate in Parliament in 1830 when both sides had their say but neither it seems convinced the other.

On 21 June 1828 Wellington's cabinet relieved Codrington of his command on the ground that he had misinterpreted his instructions. After his return to England in September Codrington tackled the Duke of Wellington himself, and records that he was told he had been recalled 'Because you seemed to understand your orders differently from myself and my colleagues and I felt that we could not go on.' When Codrington pressed the Duke on what the points of difference were, the Duke, 'with a repelling wave of the hand', only said, 'You must excuse me.' Codrington bowed low and retired, obviously furious, and the Duke followed him, trying to calm matters by saying, 'When you come to town again I shall always be glad to see you.' Codrington, unappeased, replied, 'If Your Grace cannot answer me the only question I ask you, I have no wish to come and see Your Grace again.'[17] Very few people had the nerve to stand up to the Iron Duke like that.

Codrington's last battle was not over his own reputation but about justice for his officers and men. Within weeks of the battle he applied for compensation for their losses of clothing and equipment, which officers and seamen alike had to provide at their own expense. After repeated submissions over the next two and a half years his request was finally refused in May 1830 on the ground that there was no precedent for compensation unless war had been declared. Armed with exactly such precedents Codrington took his campaign to the House of Commons, which he entered as member for Devonport in 1831. In the summer of 1834 he introduced another debate on Navarino, as a result of which the Admiralty at last granted £60,000 as compensation for the men who had served under Codrington. They expressed their gratitude by presenting him with a splendidly elaborate silver bowl which replicated the bows of his flagship the *Asia*, and which is still used by his descendants on festive family occasions.

Codrington emerged with honour from the controversies surrounding the high point of his career. It is regrettably not uncommon for politicians to will the end without willing, or even thinking through, the means. Consequently it also often happens, especially when no formal war has been declared, that commanders are given vague and contradictory instructions. Codrington suffered in both these ways, and his story was unusual only in that such a conscientious servant of his country received from his country's government such deplorably shabby treatment.

32

Kapodhístrias, a Border and a King

By the end of 1827, some two months after Navarino, Kapodhístrias had completed his extensive visits to European capitals, and was at last ready to take up the post of president of Greece which had been offered to him in the previous April. At the beginning of January 1828 he was taken by a British warship from Ancona in Italy to Codrington's head-quarters in Malta, where the two men met for the first time and got on well together. Kapodhístrias asked to be escorted by a ship from each of the three allied navies, to avoid signalling that he favoured one of the powers against the others. Codrington agreed, and so it was in the British *Warspite* accompanied by two veteran ships of Navarino, the Russian *Helena* and the French *Daphne*, that Kapodhístrias reached Navplion on 18 January 1828. He was greeted by a fifteen-gun salute, and stepped ashore to an enthusiastic welcome from all classes, followed by a church service. A week later he reached Éyina, to which the provisional government had moved because of the civil strife in Navplion, and there received an equally warm and universal welcome. 'Never did men look more favourably on their deliverer,' wrote Trikoúpis. 'The soldier, the politician and the private citizen of Greece all celebrated with the same joy, since all perceived the same need.'[1] It was a promising start for Kapodhístrias.

However it was not long before he began to spend some of the capital of goodwill which he had been so generously given. By the end of January he had persuaded the Senate to grant him for the moment full powers and to suspend the constitution established by the Trizíni National Assembly of the previous year. The Senate itself was to be replaced by a twenty-seven-member Panhellenion, which sounded like an all-inclusive body but was not, since all its members were appointed by the president. These twenty-seven members were divided into three groups responsible for finance, internal affairs and war, with a secretary of state presiding over all. Trikoúpis accepted the position of secretary of state, though with serious misgivings. He believed that Kapodhístrias should have immediately summoned a new National Assembly, which alone had the power to suspend or alter the constitution. Furthermore he thought that in the early honeymoon period of Kapodhístrias' presidency an Assembly would have given him all he asked. Kapodhístrias did promise a National Assembly for April 1828, only a month away, but with repeated postponements nearly eighteen months passed before it actually met.

Others condemned this early move by Kapodhístrias more harshly than Trikoúpis, and saw it as an unscrupulous bid for personal power. It was not; it stemmed directly from Kapodhístrias' political views. First, he had a deep distrust of the men who had led the revolution: as he saw it, they had consistently failed to unite in the common cause, and had all too often oppressed the people for their own advantage. It was the common people to whom he was devoted, and who repaid his active concern with unwavering support. But he believed that the people were not yet ready to exercise their power through representative institutions. To grant a constitution now, said Kapodhístrias, would be like giving a child a razor;[2] the child did not need it yet, and might kill himself with it. The people would be fit for their responsibilities as voters only when they had a stake in the country through ownership of property, particularly land, and had been educated, and neither process could happen quickly. Meanwhile the right solution was to give power to a few, and preferably to one man, as Kapodhístrias had urged to the very first National Assembly back in 1821, and for which his service under the benevolently autocratic Tsar Alexander gave him a model.

Unfortunately Kapodhístrias often expressed these cool philosophical ideas in intemperate language. He spoke of simply crushing the revolutionary leaders: 'Il faut éteindre les brandons de la révolution.'[3] More specifically, says Trikoúpis, 'He called the primates, Turks masquerading under Christian names; the military chieftains, brigands; the Phanariots, vessels of Satan; and the intellectuals, fools. Only the peasants and the artisans did he consider worthy of his love and protection, and he openly declared that his administration was conducted solely for their benefit.'⁴ And on one of his many tours of the country he complained, on a despairing note: 'Nobody does his duty. The army, the fleet, the political leaders, they are all corrupt. I get no support, and what can I do on my own? God gave me intelligence, but He did not give me the power to mould men.'⁵

If nobody else could be trusted, Kapodhístrias would have to manage everything himself, and there was much to be done in what he called 'le chaos qui ressemble à la Grèce'. Though the outcome of the war was no longer in doubt – after Navarino Greek independence in some form was certain – the fighting had not ended. Ibrahim's troops were still in the Peloponnese. In Roumeli Greek forces fought to win back territory, to help push Greece's eventual border northwards. The threat from internal strife was as bad as at any time in the war; when Kapodhístrias first stepped ashore at Navplion, rival commanders were still bombarding each other from the town's two fortresses. The only way to stop the captains fighting each other was to embark on the slow process of establishing a regular army, dependent on the government for its pay. In the wasteland of the Peloponnese the people were starving, and Roumeli was no better. 'From Árta to Návpaktos,' wrote a contemporary traveller, 'we did not meet a single human creature. It is a vast desert. Elsewhere a few Greeks came out from the rocks and appeared before us like ghosts, famished ghosts.'⁶ Many Greek refugees were saved from starvation only by provisions sent by charitable Americans and distributed with every attempt at fairness by Howe and his colleagues. On top of other problems there were constant outbreaks of plague.

Against this background Kapodhístrias struggled to lay the foundations of civil society: a currency, a method of taxation, a legal framework, courts of justice, a postal system, and – his special concern – schools and the sorely needed orphanages. Everything required money, and until there was an effective tax system the country depended upon loans from abroad, for which Kapodhístrias' old friend, the Swiss banker Jean-Gabriel Eynard, was his principal agent. Kapodhístrias, working from five in the morning till ten at night, involved himself in every detail of this massive effort of national reconstruction, and regularly toured the country. He wrote to local commanders about the

339

precise building works the troops should undertake and even about the cloth for their uniforms. He sent letters to schools about the equipment they needed, down to the pumps for their wells, and about the priorities for their pupils – cleanliness, health, good conduct and regular prayers.

In spite of Kapodhístrias' intense dedication, his insistence on directing everything himself and his scorn for the contribution of others were bound to make enemies. To bring the Mani under the control of the central government he removed members of the Mavromichális clan from their offices and encouraged the rival Moúrtsinos family, thus making an enemy of Pétrobey. Hydra, led by former president of the Executive Georgios Koundouriótis, resented not only the loss of the autonomy it had previously enjoyed, but also Kapodhístrias' rejection of its claim for huge compensation for wartime losses. Mavrokordhátos, another opponent, took his stand against Kapodhístrias' suspension of the constitution, and those who were against Kapodhístrias were loosely labelled the Constitutionalists. In the background to this opposition was the rumble of suspicion that Kapodhístrias was too closely tied to Russia, and might even make Greece a Russian satellite state.

But Kapodhístrias could not have carried on without support from some of the leaders of the revolutionary years. Trikoúpis, despite misgivings, served as his secretary of state. Makriyánnis was appointed first as head of a force to put down disturbances in the Peloponnese and later as battalion commander in the new regular army, and acted as counsellor and privately outspoken critic of the president. Kolokotrónis was Kapodhístrias' most consistent supporter. This unlikely alliance of rugged guerrilla leader and polished international diplomat was probably based on three things: Kolokotrónis' acceptance of Kapodhístrias as the only man fit to be president, the links of both with the common people, and the determination of both to ignore legal niceties in doing what had to be done. As Kolokotrónis wrote after a successful campaign against plunderers in the Peloponnese: 'Thus terminated this expedition. I made five hundred decisions in the course of it, which, if they had been carried to the lawyers, would have taken them three hundred years to decide upon; and so I put the districts in order and quieted them.'[7]

This campaign of Koloktrónis came in the aftermath of the final departure of Ibrahim's forces from the Peloponnese. After Navarino the surviving crippled ships of the Turco-Egyptian fleet crept back to their home ports, but Ibrahim's troops remained. They were still a formidable force: about 20,000 infantry and 4,000 cavalry, mainly in the fortresses of the south-west Peloponnese at New Navarino, Methóni and Koróni, but with some 1,500 at Patras. There was a series of attempts to persuade Ibrahim to leave. In February 1828 Sir Frederick Adam, the governor of the Ionian islands, on his government's instructions met Ibrahim at Methóni, but Ibrahim said he could not withdraw without direct orders from Mehmed Ali. Colonel Cradock, Canning's emissary to Egypt the previous summer, returned to Alexandria to persuade Mehmed Ali to give these orders, but Mehmed claimed that he could not do so without the Sultan's approval, an approval which at the end of March the Sultan refused. But by now Ibrahim was having great difficulty in supplying his troops, especially as Adam had finally banned Ionian ships from bringing them provisions, and a French force under General Maison designed to drive Ibrahim from the Peloponnese was assembling at Toulon. It was Drovetti, the French consul at Alexandria, who found a way round the impasse. In May he put to Mehmed Ali an intricate proposal that would satisfy all concerned. An Egyptian fleet, carrying the Greek slaves whose capture had caused such an outcry, would be allowed by the allied fleets to sail for the Peloponnese; off Navarino it would be intercepted by the allies and 'compelled' to land the slaves and then embark the bulk of Ibrahim's army. Two concessions sweetened the pill for Mehmed Ali: that he would be given the protection of the three powers once the troops had left, and that Ibrahim should keep possession of his four fortresses.

It fell to Codrington, in the last days before his successor arrived, to implement the agreement with the warm support of his fellow admirals. Codrington reached Egypt on 1 August 1828 and a week later the Convention of Alexandria was signed, ratifying Drovetti's plan. The only modification was that, at Codrington's insistence, the number of Egyptians remaining in the fortresses was limited to an insignificant 1,200. At the end of August the Egyptian ships reached Navarino as planned and on 7 September Ibrahim, succumbing after initial resistance to the forceful arguments of the allied admirals, accepted the Alexandria Convention. When Ibrahim himself left on 4 October 1828 the evacuation was complete, apart from the 1,200 soldiers in the fortresses. But the French forces, anxious for at least a show of victory, had now arrived, and in a final charade the fortress garrisons, who had been ordered by Ibrahim not to fire on the French, surrendered to them after mock attacks. Thus the tragedy of Ibrahim's three-year-long wreckage of lives and livelihoods in the Peloponnese ended in scenes of farce.

Meanwhile real fighting continued north of the Gulf of Corinth; the further north the Greeks could push their military successes, the larger the territory they could claim for an independent Greek state. Cochrane was no longer the supreme naval commander. He had left Greece for England in March 1828 to try to raise money and find crews to replace the Greeks whom he condemned as incompetent, unreliable and cowardly. He had no success, and came back to Greece briefly at the end of the year, where he was coolly received by Kapodhístrias, and finally left the Greek service a few days before Christmas 1828, with relief on both sides. 'Glad shall I be', wrote Cochrane, 'when the tops of these mountains sink beneath the horizon, and when new and agreeable objects shall obliterate the names of Mavrocordato, Tombazi and such double dealing knaves from my recollection.'[8] And of Cochrane's departure Trikoúpis wrote: 'He said goodbye forever to Greece having done nothing worthy of his reputation or of the expectations and the sacrifices of the Greeks and of the philhellenes.'[9]

The main naval effort therefore fell to Hastings, who concentrated on Mesolongi and began the painful process of recapturing the islands in the lagoon which the Greeks had defended so stoutly a year before. Thanks to the powerful guns of the steamship *Kartería* he took Vasiládhi in the last days of 1827, but in the following month an attack on Póros in the lagoon failed, as did a prolonged assault on Anatolikó in May 1828. It was in this attack that Hastings, leading a flotilla of small craft in his own boat, received a wound in the wrist which led to his death from tetanus a few days later. 'No man', wrote Finlay, 'ever served a foreign cause more disinterestedly.'[10] It was another year before Anatolikó and Mesolongi finally fell to the Greeks in the spring of 1829. In the same month the Greeks took Návpaktos, which had been held by the Turks throughout the war, and had not been in Greek hands since the Byzantine era. At least the north shore of the Gulf of Corinth was now firmly under Greek control.

In Roumeli north of the gulf Dhimítrios Ipsilántis returned to prominence as head of the eastern forces, while Church was commander in the west. Though Ipsilántis was unable to capture the prize of Athens, he steadily increased the Greek area of control as far as Thermopylae, capturing Karpenísi, Salóna and Livadhiá, and fought the last battle of the war at Pétra near Thebes on 26 September 1829. In the west Church was even more successful, though at first restrained by Kapodhístrias, who hoped that the French forces from the Peloponnese could be used in Roumeli, hopes that were dashed when in September 1828 the British government opposed and the French government forbade such a move, on the ground that it was not the business of foreign troops to extend the Greeks' area of control. By April 1829 Church was master of both the Gulf of Árta and the Makrinóros mountains to the east of it, whose passes had been the key to troop movements in Western Roumeli in the early years of the war.

Kapodhístrias came close to losing both his commanders in Roumeli by his habit of constant interference and criticism. He visited Ipsilántis' camp and accused him of incompetence, and like a pompous schoolmaster returned a report of Ipsilántis on the state of his army as 'a monstrous and unacceptable communication'.[11] Church was criticised for favouring the local captains against the regular army, inflating his ration strengths and failing to attack vigorously enough. Kapodhístrias' final insult was to bring over from Corfu his arrogant brother Agostino and in February 1829 to appoint him as lieutenant-plenipotentiary of Roumeli, with authority overriding that of Church and Ipsilántis to control pay, rations and military equipment. Church was incensed. 'Let me ask you seriously', he wrote to Kapodhístrias, 'to think of the position of a General in Chief of an Army before the enemy who has not the authority to order a payment of a sou, or the delivery of a ration of bread.'[12]

Another overbearing brother, Viaro, was appointed to overall control of the islands off the east coast of Greece, including Éyina, the seat of government, and Hydra. 'Do not examine the actions of the government,' ran a sinister letter of his to the Hydriots, 'and do not pass judgement on them, because to do so can lead you into error, with harmful consequences to you.'[13]

These two disastrous appointments marked the end of an unfortunate path down which Kapodhístrias' instincts had led him. The first step was innocent enough: he was by nature, as Trikoúpis described him, *átolmos*, that is, un-daring, risk-averse. To avoid risks he tried to control everything. But his insistence on control alienated so many that in time he gave authority only to a few who were close to him and whom he trusted unquestioningly. Thus risk-aversion progressed through control-obsession to cronyism, and Kapodhístrias ended by failing to exercise control over the most essential area of all, that is the behaviour of those who acted in his name.

However, two major aspects of Greece's future could at best be influenced by Kapodhístrias, and were in fact outside his control: the extent of the new country and its status. These were in the hands of the London Conference, established by the Treaty of London, which consisted of the British foreign secretary and the ambassadors to Britain of France and Russia, and which met periodically in London from the time of the battle of Navarino. On the instructions of the London Conference the ambassadors to Constantinople of the three powers met on the island of Póros off the north-east Peloponnese in September 1828 to consider the boundary question. They were given four choices: the most generous to the Greeks was from the Gulf of Vólos running south-west and just including Mesolongi, but which still excluded the area up to Árta which Church was fighting to claim; the least generous, a boundary across the isthmus of Corinth, confined independent Greece to the Peloponnese; and there were two intermediate options. In the event the ambassadors went beyond their brief, largely thanks to Britain's Stratford Canning, and in their report of 12 December 1828 recommended a line due west from Vólos to Árta, plus the inclusion of the islands of Évvia which had a large Greek population, Sámos which had been in revolt throughout the war, and possibly Crete. There were good reasons for their recommendation. The ambassadors all agreed that their proposed line was the only defensible one. Furthermore any line further south would mean the influx of thousands of excluded Greeks into the new state, which was barely able to support its existing population. But the ambassadors' report, which also recommended a monarchy for Greece, was unwelcome to the London Conference, and in particular to the British Tory government. Wellington maintained that the allies' aim 'was not to conquer territory from the Porte but to pacify a country in a state of insurrection',[14] and so argued for the southernmost border limiting Greece to the Peloponnese. The Póros report was accepted by the three governments, but as a basis of negotiation only, and because its recommended frontier was not accepted unequivocally Stratford Canning resigned over the issue in the following February. For the moment the Póros report was shelved.

If the Póros recommendations were to be a basis of negotiation, the Turks had to come to the negotiating table, and this they had consistently refused to do. They had never accepted the armistice and allied mediation proposed by the Treaty of London of July 1827, and stuck to the increasingly unrealistic view that the war could be ended only by the Greeks returning to their allegiance to the Sultan. Intransigence also marked Turkey's attitude to Russia. In November 1827 Turkey repudiated the Convention of Akkermann which had settled her previous differences with Russia, and in June 1828 Russia declared war on Turkey. Russia's initial success soon faltered. The Russian army had little more than half its nominal numbers, unpopular conscription was introduced, plague broke out among the Russian troops, and the Turks resisted more strongly than expected. Once the Russians had taken Adrianople, little more than a hundred miles west of Constantinople, the Russian effort was exhausted, and both sides were ready for peace. As part of the settlement Turkey abandoned her intransigent line on Greece, and the Treaty of Adrianople of September 1829 not only ended the war but also included Turkish acceptance of allied mediation and an armistice in Greece, as proposed by the Treaty of London of 1827, and of the broad outline of the status of Greece, as put forward at Póros in early 1829, but with more limited boundaries. Even more significantly, Turkey agreed to abide by whatever future decision on Greece was taken by the allies at the London Conference. Turkish resistance to an independent Greece was finally broken.

If Greece was to be a monarchy, who was to be the king? Many candidates from the ruling houses of Europe had been proposed over the previous five years, and at one time there were as many as seven being considered. By the time that Turkey had accepted the inevitability of Greek independence, one candidate had emerged who was acceptable to all three allied powers: Prince Leopold of Saxe-Coburg. Leopold was the widower of George IV's daughter Princess Charlotte, who had died in 1817, but he was not in the line of succession to the English throne, which would have disqualified him from the Greek monarchy. On 3 February 1830 the allied powers formally offered Leopold the Greek throne, but with severe limitations on Greece's extent: the boundary was to run from Lamía on the east coast to just above Mesolongi in the west, far short of the line recommended by the Póros conference, and both Crete and Sámos were to be excluded. Leopold, encouraged by Kapodhístrias, insisted on discussing not only the unsatisfactory boundaries but other matters: a guaranteed loan from the allied powers, provision of a body of foreign troops to impose order, and his acceptance by a constitutionally established body representing the Greek people. After three weeks he believed he had made enough progress on these points to accept his nomination formally on 23 February, but the boundary question remained a stumbling block, and eventually proved insurmountable. On 21 May Leopold withdrew his acceptance, explaining that as king he would either have to force the Greeks to accept the frontier imposed or join them in defying the allies who had imposed it, and he was not prepared to do either. Thus by the summer of 1830, nearly three years after Navarino, Greece was still without a settlement, a border and a king.

For the first eighteen months of Kapodhístrias' presidency Greece was also still waiting for a National Assembly to approve or amend the provisional government which Kapodhístrias had introduced. After repeated postponements this new Assembly finally met at Árgos in July 1829. There were 236 delegates, the great majority supporters of Kapodhístrias, who was accused by his opponents of rigging their election. However, pressure on voters was almost certainly the work of his over-zealous agents, and in the single recorded instance of malpractice Kapodhístrias condemned it and ordered new elections. The Assembly heard and approved an account of the acts of the government in a report which Kapodhístrias, pleading exhaustion and ill-health, had read out for him. The report included a recommendation that the Panhellenion of twenty-seven members appointed by the president should be replaced by a Senate of twenty-seven. The only real difference was that the Senate now had a veto on matters of finance and national lands. Six of the Senate members were still to be appointed directly by the president and the remaining twenty-one chosen by him from a list of sixty-three drawn up by the Assembly, in which his supporters were dominant. It was a barely perceptible loosening of Kapodhístrias' control. The most significant resolution passed at Árgos required the final settlement of Greece's status and extent to be approved by a National Assembly, approval on which Leopold too insisted. Greece was demanding at least some element of control over her own future.

In spite of Kapodhístrias' overt success at the Árgos Assembly, his opponents continued to grow in strength. They were supported by the English Resident, Edward Dawkins, who with French and Russian colleagues had been sent to Greece by the Conference of London to co-ordinate allied action on Greece. Kapodhístrias' opponents were also supported by the octogenarian Koraís in Paris, whom age alone can excuse for the pettiness of his venomous attacks on Kapodhístrias. The opposition came to a head on Hydra in May 1831, where with support from Mavrokordhátos a rival seven-man government commission was established, including Georgios Koundouriótis and the widely respected naval commander Miaoúlis. The Hydriots convened their own Assembly, which voted to make Pétrobey Mavromichális president in place of Kapodhístrias. Kapodhístrias ordered the loyal Kanáris, of equal fame to Miaoúlis as a revolutionary hero, to prepare a fleet at nearby Póros to blockade the rebels. At the end of July Miaoúlis responded by entering Póros harbour at night and seizing Kanáris' ships, which included the American-built *Éllas*. Kapodhístrias also had the backing of the Russian admiral Ricord, who also entered Póros harbour on the morning of 13 August and ordered the rebels to retreat. Miaoúlis threatened to sink the ships he had seized unless Ricord withdrew, Ricord refused, and within a few hours Miaoúlis carried out his threat. So the beautiful frigate *Éllas*, one of the few successful fruits of the second English loan, was sent to the bottom by the man whose fleet it had been built to serve.

The other main focus of opposition to Kapodhístrias was the Mani, as the Hydriot rebels' choice of Pétrobey as president indicated. The Mavromichális family had two main grievances. Like the Hydriots, they claimed compensation for war losses, which Kapodhístrias refused because there was no money to pay it; and they resented Kapodhístrias' claim to collect their taxes, which even under the Turks they had collected themselves. At the end of 1830 they set up a virtually independent capital at the port of Liméni, only a mile or so from Areópolis where Pétrobey had proclaimed the revolution nearly ten years before. As at Póros, Kanáris was sent by Kapodhístrias against the rebels, and he brought back to Navplion Pétrobey's brother Konstantínos and son Georgios as sureties for the Mani's good behaviour. Meanwhile Pétrobey, living in Navplion as a senator, tried to get away on Gordon's yacht bound for Zákinthos, but when the yacht put ashore on the west coast of the Peloponnese Pétrobey was arrested, brought back to Navplion and imprisoned. Konstantínos and Georgios however were only under a loose sort of surveillance, and were free to move about the town under escort.

Signs multiplied of the tragedy to come. Konstantínos and Georgios were said to have held whispered conversations with Pétrobey at his cell window, though Pétrobey later denied that he was involved in any plot. The pair reconnoitred the church of Áyios Spirídhon in the side streets of Navplion where Kapodhístrias regularly worshipped, and an agent of Georgios bought pistols. Even Dawkins, the English Resident, no friend of Kapodhístrias, warned him of danger. Nevertheless on Sunday 9 October 1831 Kapodhístrias went to his customary early-morning service with two companions. When he saw Konstantínos and Georgios Mavromichális standing on either side of the church door he hesitated, but then walked forward again. As he passed them Georgios plunged a dagger into Kapodhístrias' chest, and almost simultaneously Konstantínos drew a pistol and shot him in the back of the head. Kapodhístrias died without a sound. Konstantínos was killed on the spot by one of Kapodhístrias' companions, and Georgios fled to the house of the French Resident, who handed him over to the Greek authorities. He was imprisoned in the Palamídhi fortress, court-martialled and condemned, and was executed within two weeks of his crime.

The common people, for whom Kapodhístrias had laboured with such dedication, grieved for their lost president, and feared for them-selves: 'What is to become of us?' they asked Kolokotrónis.[15] For them the arguments over forms of government meant little or nothing. They were only aware of Kapodhístrias' dedication, the visits he had made to them, the more secure lives they were now leading, and the many new schools which Kapodhístrias himself would have wanted to stand as his monument. The affection for his memory has not faded with time. In the 1960s the verger of Áyios Spirídhon would show visitors the spot where Kapodhístrias fell and, conflating the Mavromichális pair with the German occupiers of his own day, condemn the assassins with tears in his eyes and fury in his voice as 'Rausbotte'.

The year 1832 brought more confusion and conflict to Greece than any year since the war began, and widespread devastation which undid much of Kapodhístrias' work of reconstruction. As in the last phase of the civil wars of 1824, the basic conflict was between the Peloponnese led by Kolokotrónis and Roumeli led by Koléttis, and it was the Roumeliot troops brought into the Peloponnese whose uncontrolled plundering did most of the damage. After Kapodhístrias' death the Senate appointed a three-man government commission of Agostino Kapodhístrias as president, Kolokotrónis and Koléttis. Agostino, who foolishly proclaimed his pro-Russian sympathies, was disowned by the allied powers in March and forced to flee to Corfu by Koléttis' advance on Navplion at the head of a Roumeliot army, backed by French troops now operating to bring some order to the country. In July yet another Assembly held near Navplion appointed a new government commission led by Koléttis. As counter to this, in November a group of former Kapodhístrias supporters named Kolokotrónis as head of a military commission to govern Greece. French troops, supporting Koléttis as the only leader with a claim to legitimacy, occupied Navplion, where they were attacked by Kolokotrónis' soldiers.

But while utter confusion reigned within Greece, events elsewhere at last began to move in her favour. Elections in Britain following the death of George IV removed the Tories under Wellington from office and installed a Whig administration led by Lord Grey. The new foreign secretary was Palmerston, long an advocate of a larger Greece. Though the inclusion of Crete and Sámos had by now been dropped, the Árta–Vólos line was revived and Stratford Canning returned as ambassador to Constantinople to negotiate this frontier with the Turkish government, two years after he had resigned because of his support for it. Acceptance of a larger Greece was a bitter pill for the Turks to swallow, but they were now under threat from their nominal dependants in Egypt. Mehmed Ali's long-matured plan to expand his own empire had been put into effect, Ibrahim had seized Acre in modern Israel, and announced his intention of marching on Constantinople. Stratford Canning's guarded

349

promises of support for Turkey against Egypt were crucial to his negoti-ations, and on 21 July 1832, after a discussion lasting sixteen hours, the Turks agreed to the Árta–Vólos frontier.

The question of a king for Greece was also at last settled. King Ludwig I of Bavaria was an enthusiastic classical archaeologist and phil-hellene, and the idea of a Bavarian king for Greece had been floated as far back as 1829. Only days before Kapodhístrias was assassinated Ludwig's emissary arrived in Greece to promote the candidacy of Ludwig's seventeen-year-old son Otto. Until Otto reached twenty-one three Bavarian regents appointed by his father were to rule in his name. In the early months of 1832 the last difficulties melted away. To avoid the possibility of Otto also succeeding to the Bavarian throne, a formula was adopted forbidding the union of the Greek and Bavarian crowns. The allied powers agreed to guarantee a loan to Greece of £2,400,000, larger than either of the two earlier English loans. The Conference of London offered the throne of Greece to Prince Otto in May 1832, he formally accepted in July and, although the London Conference had disdainfully laid down that Greek approval was not necessary, the National Assembly which met in the summer of 1832 ratified the choice.

On the morning of 6 February 1833, in glorious sunshine which her-alded the coming spring, Otto arrived in Navplion Bay escorted by a fleet of twenty-five allied warships, and stepped ashore from an English frigate. 'The scene itself formed a splendid picture . . . ' wrote Finlay.

> Greeks and Albanians, mountaineers and islanders, soldiers, sailors, and peasants, in their varied and picturesque dresses, hailed the young monarch as their deliverer from a state of society as intolerable as Turkish tyranny. Families in bright attire glided in boats over the calm sea amidst the gaily decorated frigates of the Allied squadrons. The music of many bands in the ships and on shore enlivened the scene, and the roar of artil-lery in every direction gave an imposing pomp to the ceremony. The uniforms of many armies and navies, and the sounds of many languages, testified that most civilized nations had sent deputies to inaugurate the festival of the regeneration of Greece.[16]

For the present civil strife was set aside. As Finlay put it in the same passage, 'Anarchy and order shook hands,' but he was perhaps forget-ting that opponents are as likely to shake hands at the beginning of a contest as at the end of it. Over the next century many of the conflicts of the war of independence would be repeated: anarchy against order, high national ambitions without the strength to achieve them, dependence on foreign powers but resentment at those powers' alternating generosity and arrogance. But on the day of Otto's arrival the Greeks could rightly rejoice in what they had achieved. They had opened the first cracks in the structure of the mighty Ottoman empire, and against all the odds had become the first of its domains to win full independence as a nation state.

Notes

CHAPTER I: REVOLUTION AND THE GREAT CHURCH (pp. 1–7)

The legend of Áyia Lávra is in F. C. H. L. Pouqueville, *Histoire de la régénération de la Grèce*, vol. II. The principal sources for the Greek church are: S. Runciman, *The Fall of Constantinople* and *The Great Church in Captivity*, and T. H. Papadopoullos, *The Greek Church and People under Turkish Domination*.

1. Pouqueville II, pp. 325–37
2. R. J. von Hammer-Purgstall, quoted in L. Kelly, ed., *Istanbul: A Travellers' Companion*, p. 166
3. Runciman, *Great Church*, p. 169
4. Runciman, *Great Church*, p. 209
5. Angelomatis-Tsougarakis, *The Eve of the Greek Revival*, p. 83
6. Clogg, *Movement*, pp. 56–64

CHAPTER 2: RESENTMENT AND REGERATION (pp. 8–16)

Ottoman administration, including taxation, is covered in detail by H. Gibb and H. Bowen, *Islamic Society and the West*. H. Angelomatis-Tsougarakis, *The Eve of the Greek Revival* draws together British travellers' reports on Greece in the decades before the revolution. Turkish documents on the devshirme in English translation are in J. K. Vasdravellis, *Kelphts, Armatoles and Pirates*. For education see L. Theocharides, *The Greek National Revival and the French Enlightenment*, and the chapter 'Education and Culture' in Angelomatis-Tsougarakis.

Notes

1. Gibb and Bowen I, p. 256
2. Angelomatis-Tsougarakis, p. 150
3. Gibb and Bowen I, p. 258
4. Vasdravellis, p. 112
5. Vasdravellis, p. 114
6. G. Vláchos, *Politiká Árthra* (Political Articles), Athens, 1965 (1st edn, 1961), pp. 158–60
7. Theocharides, pp. 180–93. Extracts in Clogg, *Movement*, pp. 106–17
8. Clogg, *Movement*, pp. 56–64
9. Clogg, *Movement*, pp. 86–8
10. Theocharides, pp. 229, 242
11. Theocharides, p. 35
12. Angelomatis-Tsougarakis, p. 125
13. Clogg, *Movement*, pp. 79–80
14. Waddington, p. xxxix
15. *Kolokotrones*, tr. Edmonds, p. 127

CHAPTER 3: TWO PROPHETS OF REVOLUTION (pp. 17–25)

For a contemporary's account of Rígas' life see Ch. Perrevós, *Síntomos Viographía tou Aïdhímou Ríga Pheréou* (Short Biography of Rígas Pheréos of Blessed Memory). The most recent work in English is C. M. Woodhouse, *Rhigas Velestinlis*.

A good summary of Koraís' views is in I. Notáras, *O Patriotikós Agónas tou Koraí* (The Patriotic Struggle of Koraís). Both Rígas and Koraís are discussed in chapter 1 of N. Kaltchas, *Introduction to the Constitutional History of Modern Greece*.

1. Perrevós, pp. 319–20
2. Perrevós, pp. 321–2
3. Clogg, *Movement*, p. 157
4. Clogg, *Movement*, p. 151
5. Clogg, *Movement*, p. 156
6. Clogg, *Movement*, p. 154
7. Perrevós, p. 328
8. Hobhouse, quoted in Marchand, *Byron: A Portrait*, p. 75
9. Clogg, *Movement*, p. 122
10. Clogg, *Movement*, p. 126
11. Notáras, pp. 26–7
12. Clogg, *Movement*, p. 127

13. Notáras, p. 11
14. Notáras, p. 18
15. Notáras, p. 18
16. Notáras, pp. 13–14
17. Notáras, p. 22
18. Notáras, p. 16

CHAPTER 4: THE PHILIKI ETERIA (pp. 26–35)

Documents in R. Clogg, *Movement* include translations of Xánthos' own account of his activities, and of the Etería's initiation rituals. Further details of the Etería's systems are in T. Vournas, ed., *Philikí Etería*. For analysis of Etería membership and discussion of its achievement see G. Frangos' essay in R. Clogg, *Struggle* and his contribution to *Istoría tou Ellinikoú Éthnous* (hereafter *IEE*), vol. XI, pp. 424–32. For Kapodhístrias' involvement see C. M. Woodhouse, *Capodistria* and an essay by him in R. Clogg, *Struggle*.

1. Clogg, *Movement*, p. 183
2. Vournas, pp. 48–51
3. Finlay I, p. 100
4. *IEE* XI, p.431
5. Woodhouse, *Capodistria*, p. 163
6. Clogg, *Movement*, p. 192
7. Clogg, *Movement*, p. 192
8. Clogg, *Movement*, p. 193

CHAPTER 5: ALI PASHA (pp. 36–48)

The most comprehensive book on Ali Pasha is K. E. Fleming, *The Muslim Bonaparte*. There are two valuable essays by D. N. Skiotis: 'The Greek Revolution: Ali Pasha's Last Gamble', in N. P. Diamandouros, ed., *Hellenism*, and 'From Bandit to Pasha . . . Ali of Tepelen 1750–1784'. For Ali's relations with foreign powers see J. W. Baggally, *Ali Pasha and Great Britain*. Details of Ali Pasha's Iánnina are in H. Angelomatis-Tsougarakis, *The Eve of the Greek Revival*. See also L. A. Marchand's edition of *Byron's Letters and Journals* (Byron, *L&J*).

1. Skiotis, 'Bandit', p. 222
2. W. M. Leake, *Travels in Northern Greece*, 4 vols, London, 1835, I, pp. 30–1

3. Finlay I, p. 45
4. Clogg, *Movement*, pp. 28–9
5. Byron, *L&J* I, p. 254
6. Byron, *L&J* I, p. 227
7. Quoted in Clogg, *Movement*, p. 143
8. For example, *IEE* XI, p. 402
9. Finlay I, p. 74
10. Skiotis, 'Last Gamble', p. 104

CHAPTER 6: REVOLT ALONG THE DANUBE (pp. 49–61)

For Ipsilántis' expedition as a whole see T. Gordon, *History of the Greek Revolution*; G. Finlay, *History of the Greek Revolution*; and the essay by E. D. Tappe in R. Clogg, *Struggle*. An on-the-spot account by a contemporary is in R. Neroúlos, *Histoire moderne de la Grèce*. Kapodhístrias' part is covered in C. M. Woodhouse, *Capodistria* and Tsar Alexander's in A. Palmer, *Alexander I*.

1. Woodhouse, *Capodistria*, p. 230
2. Kapodhístrias, *Aperçu de ma carrière publique*, p. 94
3. Woodhouse, *Capodistria*, p. 229
4. See *Néa Éstia*, 1 December 1964, pp. 1693–4
5. Neroúlos, p. 235
6. Finlay I, pp. 114–15
7. Gordon I, p. 96
8. Neroúlos, p. 309
9. Clogg, *Movement*, pp. 201–3
10. Woodhouse, *Capodistria*, p. 252
11. Clogg, *Struggle*, p. 145
12. Clogg, *Movement*, pp. 204–5
13. Woodhouse, *Capodistria*, p. 251
14. Woodhouse, *Capodistria*, pp. 246–7
15. Woodhouse, *Capodistria*, pp. 254–5
16. *IEE* XII, p. 55
17. Trikoúpis I, pp. 158–60
18. Gordon I, p. 108
19. Neroúlos, p. 282
20. Finlay I, pp. 134–5
21. *IEE* XII, p. 55

CHAPTER 7: DOUBTS AND DELIBERATIONS IN THE SOUTH (pp. 62–9)

The main sources in English are Gordon and Finlay, and in Greek Photákos, *Víos tou Pápa Phléssa* (Life of Papaphléssas); G. Yermanós, *Apomnimonévmata* (Memoirs); and *IEE* XII, pp. 75–83.

1. Finlay I, p. 140
2. Gordon I, p. 150
3. Saitas, pp. 22–3
4. Finlay I, p. 148; Gordon I, pp. 151–2
5. Finlay I, p. 141
6. Gordon I, p. 222
7. *Kolokotrones*, tr. Edmonds, p. 254
8. Photákos, p. 26
9. Yermanós, p. 81
10. Photákos, pp. 20–1

CHAPTER 8: THE STORM BREAKS (pp. 70–8)

Virtually all histories of the revolution give an account of its outbreak, but see especially Gordon, Finlay, Trikoúpis and Kolokotrónis (tr. Edmonds). For the debate over events at Patras see P. J. and R. L. Green, *Sketches of the War in Greece* and F. C. H. L. Pouqueville, *Histoire*.

1. *Kolokotrones*, tr. Edmonds, p. 131
2. Finlay I, p. 150
3. Trikoúpis I, p. 230; Gordon I, p. 183
4. Raybaud I, p. 365
5. Gordon I, p. 145
6. Green, p. vii
7. Green, p. 5
8. Pouqueville II, pp. 345–6
9. Green, p. 19
10. Green, p. 271
11. Green, p. 23
12. Gordon I, p. 156
13. Green, p. 24
14. Yermanós, p. 96
15. Green, p. 17
16. See for example K. Simópoulos, *Pós Ídhan i Xéni tin Elládha tou '21* (How Foreigners Viewed the Greece of '21), 5 vols, Athens, 1979, I, pp. 183–211

CHAPTER 9: THE LAND WAR (pp. 79–88)

For the battle of Valtétsi and its prelude see *Kolokotrones*, tr. Edmonds. For the history of Monemvasía see A. G. and H. A. Kalligas, *Monemvasia*, and for its siege K. N. Papamichalópoulos, *Poliorkía kai Álosis tis Monemvasías* (Siege and Capture of Monemvasía). For military organisation see A. E. Vakalópoulos, *Ta Ellínika Stratévmata tou 1821* (The Greek Armies of 1821). For the klepht–armátolos symbiosis see the early chapters of J. S. Koliopoulos, *Brigands with a Cause*.

1. *Kolokotrones*, tr. Edmonds, p. 139
2. *Kolokotrones*, tr. Edmonds, p. 144
3. *Kolokotrones*, tr. Edmonds, p. 146
4. A. A. Vasiliev, *History of the Byzantine Empire*, 2 vols, Madison, 1958 (1st edn, 1928), II, p. 465
5. Kalligas, p. 9
6. Kalligas, p. 15
7. Papamichalópoulos, p. 92
8. Gordon I, p. 280
9. Vakalópoulos, p. 140
10. *Makriyannis*, tr. Lidderdale, pp. 38–9
11. Raybaud II, p. 277
12. Gordon I, pp. 262–3

CHAPTER 10: THE WAR AT SEA (pp. 89–99)

For naval warfare in general see J. Keegan, *The Price of Admiralty*, and for the contemporary British navy N. A. M. Rodger, *The Wooden World* and G. E. Manwaring and B. Dobrée, *The Floating Republic*. Details of fireships are in K. A. Alexándhris, *To Návtikon tou ipér Anexartisías Agónos tou 1821–1829* (The Navy in the Fight for Independence of 1821–1829), and contemporary descriptions are in Trikoúpis I, pp. 392–6 and S. G. Howe, *An Historical Sketch of the Greek Revolution*, pp. 65–6.

1. Gordon I, p. 164
2. Gordon I, p. 165
3. Waddington, p. 105
4. Green, p. 64
5. Green, pp. 64–5
6. Green, p. 65

7. Emerson, Pecchio and Humphreys, p. 172
8. Gordon I, p. 253
9. Emerson, Pecchio and Humphreys, p. 127

CHAPTER 11: THE TURKISH REACTION (pp. 100–10)

For the Ottoman Empire in the period before the Greek revolution see B. Lewis, *The Emergence of Modern Turkey*; E. J. Zürcher, *Turkey*; S. J. and E. K. Shaw, *History of the Ottoman Empire and Modern Turkey*, vol. II; and A. Wheatcroft, *The Ottomans*. For the patriarchate see C. A. Frazee, *The Orthodox Church and Independent Greece 1821–1852*.

1. *Makriyannis*, tr. Lidderdale, pp. 17–18
2. Gordon I, p. 191
3. Trikoúpis I, pp. 397–8
4. Wheatcroft, p. 125
5. Frazee, p. 24
6. Clogg, *Movement*, p. 207
7. Waddington, p. 10
8. Woodhouse, *Capodistria*, p. 262
9. St Clair, *Greece*, p. 57
10. Woodhouse, *Capodistria*, p. 264
11. Trikoúpis I, pp. 103–5
12. Frazee, p. 36
13. Frazee, p. 35
14. Finlay I, p. 189

CHAPTER 12: THE CAPTURE OF TRIPOLIS (pp. 111–23)

There are first-hand accounts of the events at Tripolis by Gordon, Kolokotrónis (tr. Edmonds) and Raybaud.

1. *Kolokotrones*, tr. Edmonds, p. 151
2. *Kolokotrones*, tr. Edmonds, p. 155
3. Howe, *Sketch*, p. 83
4. Raybaud I, p. 403
5. Raybaud I, p. 433
6. Raybaud I, p. 461
7. Gordon I, p. 246
8. Gordon I, pp. 241, 247
9. *Kolokotrones*, tr. Edmonds, p. 157

CHAPTER 13: FORMING A GOVERNMENT (pp. 124–34)

The principal sources are J. A. Petropulos, *Politics and Statecraft in the Kingdom of Greece 1833–1843*; N. Kaltchas, *Introduction to the Constitutional History of Modern Greece*; G. D. Dhimakópoulos, *I Dhiikitikí Orgánosis katá tin Ellinikín Epanástasin 1821–1827* (Administrative Organisation during the Greek Revolution 1821–1827); and F. Rosen, *Bentham, Byron and Greece*. The main parts of the Constitution of Epídhavros in English are in S. G. Howe, *Sketch*. The full document in Greek is in A. Svólos, *Ta Elliniká Sintágmata 1822–1952* (The Greek Constitutions 1822–1952).

1. Trikoúpis I, p. 346
2. Petropulos, p. 21
3. Gordon I, p. 322
4. Howe, *Sketch*, pp. 78–9
5. Raybaud II, p. 166
6. Trikoúpis II, p. 149
7. Finlay I, pp. 332–3
8. Finlay I, p. 244
9. Howe, *Sketch*, p. 105
10. Dhimakópoulos, p. 101
11. Rosen, p. 77
12. Dhimakópoulos, p. 84

CHAPTER 14: THE EYES OF THE WORLD ON GREECE (pp. 135–44)

For the politics of post-Napoleonic Europe see H. Nicolson, *The Congress of Vienna* and D. Thomson, *Europe since Napoleon*. The Russian response to the Greek situation is covered in T. C. Prousis, *Russian Society and the Greek Revolution*, and the American in P. C. Pappas, *The United States and the Greek War for Independence 1821–1828*. The most comprehensive book on the philhellenes is W. St Clair, *That Greece Might Still Be Free*.

1. Thomson, p. 96
2. Thomson, p. 96
3. R. Holmes, *Shelley: The Pursuit*, London, 1976 (1st edn, 1974), p. 681
4. Raybaud I, p. 268
5. St Clair, *Greece*, p. 67

6. St Clair, *Greece*, p. 70
7. Rosen, p. 221
8. Woodhouse, *Philhellenes*, p. 77
9. St Clair, *Greece*, p. 59
10. Pappas, p. 142
11. Pappas, p. 42
12. Prousis, p. 60
13. Prousis, p. 59
14. Prousis, p. 60
15. Prousis, p. 62
16. Prousis, p. 63

CHAPTER 15: THE PHILHELLENES IN ACTION (pp. 145–53)

Gordon gives a detailed account of the battle of Péta. For forms of collaboration, see J. Petropulos in N. P. Diamandouros, ed., *Hellenism*.

1. *Kolokotrones*, tr. Edmonds, p. 163.
2. Raybaud II, p. 261
3. Gordon I, p. 389
4. Protopsáltis, p. 66
5. Trikoúpis II, p. 282

CHAPTER 16: CHIOS (pp. 154–67)

The most comprehensive account is P. Argenti, *The Massacres of Chios*. A. M. Vlasto, *A History of the Island of Chios* provides valuable background. All anecdotes of survivors are from S. G. Víos, *I Sphayí tis Chíou* (The Massacre of Chios).

1. Gordon I, p. 351
2. Vlasto, p. 143
3. Finlay I, p. 253
4. Argenti, p. 10
5. Argenti, pp. 6–7
6. Argenti, p. 13
7. Gordon I, p. 358
8. Gordon I, p. 361
9. Argenti, p. 19
10. Argenti, p. xix

11. Argenti, p. 20
12. Argenti, p. 155
13. Argenti, p. 26

CHAPTER 17: THE EXPEDITION OF DRAMALI (pp. 168–80)

1. Finlay I, p. 280
2. Finlay I, p. 162
3. Byron, *L&J* II, p. 37
4. Howe, *Sketch*, p. 128
5. Howe, *Sketch*, p. 131
6. Waddington, pp. 58–9
7. Raybaud II, pp. 344–5
8. Gordon I, pp. 416–17
9. Gordon I, p. 419
10. Gordon I, p. 422
11. *Koloktrones*, tr. Edmonds, p. 178
12. Gordon I, p. 426
13. Gordon I, p. 436
14. Gordon I, p. 438

CHAPTER 18: THE GREEKS DIVIDED (pp. 181–93)

See Gordon and Trikoúpis for the main events, and Dhimakópoulos for the shifting alignments of the Greek government.

1. Trikoúpis III, p. 35
2. Gordon II, p. 5
3. *IEE* XII, p. 300
4. Finlay I, p. 316
5. Gordon II, pp. 13, 59
6. Gordon II, p. 173
7. *Koloktrones*, tr. Edmonds, p. 201
8. Howe, *Sketch*, p. 207

CHAPTER 19: BYRON'S ROAD TO GREECE (pp. 194–203)

The outstanding works on Byron are L. A. Marchand's three-volume *Byron: A Biography* and its one-volume abridgement *Byron: A Portrait*, to which the references here apply. Also invaluable is Marchand's eleven-volume edition of *Byron's Letters and Journals* (Byron, *L&J*). See also I. Origo, *The Last Attachment*; H. Nicolson, *Byron: The Last Journey*; and D. L. Moore, *Lord Byron: Accounts Rendered*.

1. Marchand, p. 80
2. Origo, p. 169
3. Origo, p. 252
4. Marchand, p. 372
5. Marchand, p. 382
6. Byron, *L&J* IX, p. 198
7. Byron, *L&J* X, p. 139
8. Byron, *L&J* X, p. 213
9. Byron, *L&J* X, p. 154
10. St Clair, *Greece*, p. 152
11. Byron, *L&J* X, p. 199
12. Trelawny, p. 135
13. P. Napier, *Revolution and the Napier Brothers*, London, 1973, p. 40; Nicolson, *Byron*, p. 219
14. Woodhouse, *Philhellenes*, p. 114
15. Moore, p. 380
16. Nicolson, *Byron*, p. 160
17. Finlay I, p. 326
18. Byron, *L&J* XI, p. 33
19. Moore, p. 393
20. Nicolson, *Byron*, p. 174
21. Byron, *L&J* XI, p. 68
22. Byron, *L&J* XI, p. 83
23. Byron, *L&J* XI, p. 82
24. Marchand, p. 418
25. Byron, *L&J* XI, p. 73
26. Finlay I, p. 325

CHAPTER 20: BYRON AT MESOLONGI (pp. 204–19)

As well as the sources for Chapter 19, see P. Gamba, *A Narrative of Lord Byron's Last Journey to Greece* and F. Rosen, *Bentham, Byron and Greece*.

1. Byron, *L&J* XI, p. 92
2. Byron, *L&J* V, pp. 119–20
3. Byron, *L&J* XI, p. 22

4. Byron, *L&J* X, p. 12
5. Trelawny, p. 138
6. Rosen, p. 188
7. Rosen, p. 189
8. Rosen, p. 189
9. Rosen, pp. 260–1
10. Byron, *L&J* XI, p. 102
11. Byron, *L&J* XI, p. 108
12. Byron, *L&J* XI, p. 109
13. Green, pp. 169–70
14. Byron, *L&J* XI, pp. 111–12
15. Byron, *L&J* XI, p. 123
16. Gamba, p. 187
17. Byron, *L&J* XI, p. 97
18. Byron, *L&J* XI, p. 134
19. Byron, *L&J* XI, p. 83
20. Byron, *L&J* X, p. 199
21. Dakin, *Philhellenes*, p. 68
22. Dakin, *Philhellenes*, p. 69
23. Byron, *L&J* XI, p. 151
24. Gamba, p. 244
25. Marchand, p. 454

CHAPTER 21: GOLD FROM LONDON (pp. 220–5)

See J. A. Levandis, *The Greek Foreign Debt and the Great Powers 1821–1898*; F. Rosen, *Bentham, Byron and Greece*; and E. Blaquiere's two reports, *The Greek Revolution* and *Narrative of a Second Visit to Greece*.

1. Gordon II, p. 77
2. Levandis, p. 13
3. Levandis, p. 9
4. Blaquiere, *Greek Revolution*, p. 305; Blaquiere, *Second Visit*, pp. 123–8
5. Green, p. 174
6. St Clair, *Greece*, p. 209
7. Rosen, p. 110
8. Rosen, p. 118
9. Gordon II, p. 104

CHAPTER 22: CIVIL WAR IN GREECE (pp. 226–33)

1. Protopsáltis, p. 126
2. Trikoúpis III, pp. 113–14
3. Trikoúpis III, p. 130
4. Gordon II, p. 100
5. Gordon II, p. 174
6. Finlay I, pp. 338, 341
7. *IEE* XII, p. 354
8. Trikoúpis III, p. 181
9. *Kolokotrones*, tr. Edmonds, p. 203
10. Gordon II, p. 180
11. *Makriyannis*, tr. Lidderdale, p. 59
12. *Makriyannis*, tr. Lidderdale, p. 60

CHAPTER 23: IBRAHIM IN THE PELOPONNESE (pp. 234–46)

See G. Douin, *Les Premières Frégates de Mohamed Aly (1824–1827)* for the Egyptian fleet; W. St Clair, *Greece* for philhellene involvement; and K. Andrews, *Castles of the Morea* for fortress details. S. G. Howe's *Letters and Journals* (Howe, *L&J*) are an important source.

1. Gordon II, p. 136
2. Howe, *L&J*, p. 90
3. Green, p. 250
4. Finlay I, p. 358
5. *IEE* XII, p. 377
6. Howe, *L&J*, p. 49
7. Howe, *L&J*, p. 27
8. Howe, *L&J*, p. 51
9. Howe, *L&J*, pp. 67–8
10. Howe, *L&J*, p. 34
11. *Kolokotrones*, tr. Edmonds, p. 207
12. Howe, *L&J*, p. 101
13. Gordon II, pp. 215–16
14. Temperley, p. 350

CHAPTER 24: THE INVOLVEMENT OF THE POWERS (pp. 247–57)

The classic and very readable account of British foreign policy in this period is H. Temperley, *The Foreign Policy of Canning 1822–1827*, which also has much to say about the policies of the other powers. Further details are in C. W. Crawley, *The Question of Greek Independence*. The death of Tsar Alexander I, the Decembrist revolt and the accession of Nicholas I are covered in A. Palmer, *Alexander I*.

1. Howe, *L&J*, p. 91
2. Gordon II, p. 283
3. Temperley, p. 342
4. *Encyclopaedia Britannica* (1929), The Eastern Question
5. Temperley, p. 335
6. J. W. Croker, quoted in H. M. Hyde, *The Strange Death of Lord Castlereagh*, London, 1967 (1st edn, London, 1959), p. 141
7. Temperley, p. 329
8. Temperley, pp. 333–4
9. Temperley, p. 454
10. Temperley, p. 339
11. Temperley, p. 339
12. Temperley, pp. 346–7
13. Temperley, p. 349
14. Temperley, p. 353
15. Palmer, p. 411
16. Crawley, p. 58
17. Temperley, pp. 586–7
18. Temperley, p. 361

CHAPTER 25: ODYSSEUS AND TRELAWNY (pp. 258–68)

The main documents about the death of Odysseus are in K. Papadhópoulos, *Odysseus Andhroútsos*, and most are in B. Ánninos, *I Apoloyía tou Odhysséos Andhroútsou* (The Defence of Odysseus Andhroútsos). Contemporary accounts of the assassination attempt in the cave are in E. J. Trelawny, *Recollections of the Last Days of Shelley and Byron*, S. G. Howe, *Letters and Journals* and G. Jarvis, *Journal*. The story is told in W. St Clair, *Trelawny: The Incurable Romancer*, and the central section of D. Crane, *Lord Byron's Jackal* has a detailed discussion of the involvement of the different participants.

1. Papadhópoulos, p. 74
2. Papadhópoulos, p. 75
3. Papadhópoulos, pp. 75–7

4. Gordon II, pp. 186–7
5. Finlay I, p. 380
6. St Clair, *Trelawny*, p. 113
7. Trelawny, p. 167
8. Humphreys, quoted in Crane, pp. 146–7
9. Trelawny, p. 173
10. Quoted in Crane, p. 180
11. Howe, *L&J*, p. 42
12. Trelawny, pp. 181–2
13. Howe, *L&J*, p. 104
14. Trelawny, p. 180
15. Trelawny, p. 178
16. Quoted in Crane, p. 226
17. Jarvis, p. 248
18. Jarvis, p. 241
19. Jarvis, p. 245
20. Jarvis, pp. 247–8
21. Jarvis, p. 248
22. Howe, *L&J*, p. 42

CHAPTER 26: THE FALL OF MESOLONGI (pp. 269–88)

The memoirs of the siege, mentioned in the text, are by Spiromílios, Kasamoúlis in vol. II, Míchos and Mákris, and a reproduction of Kokkínis' detailed map of the bastions is in Stasinópoulos I, p. 144; for full titles see the Select Bibliography. For the impact of Mesolongi on western Europe see S. A. Kanínias, *Elevtheria* (Freedom) and N. M. Athanassoglou-Kallmyer, *French Images from the Greek War of Independence 1821–1830*.

1. Mákris, p. 15
2. Mákris, p. 37
3. Spiromílios, p. 221
4. Trikoúpis III, p. 279
5. Trikoúpis III, p. 280
6. Gordon II, p. 233
7. Kasomoúlis, p. 116
8. Kasomoúlis, p. 108
9. Kasomoúlis, p. 102
10. Finlay I, p. 385

11. Mákris, pp. 44–5
12. Trikoúpis III, pp. 320–1
13. Trikoúpis III, p. 401
14. Gordon II, p. 258
15. Kasomoúlis, p. 237
16. Spiromílios, pp. 191–2
17. Kasomoúlis, p. 275
18. Kasomoúlis, pp. 289–90
19. *Kolokotrones*, tr. Edmonds, pp. 230–1
20. Howe, *L&J*, p. 170
21. Kanínias, pp. 92–3
22. Athanassouglou-Kallmyer, p. 107

CHAPTER 27: THE SECOND ENGLISH LOAN (pp. 289–96)

The main sources are J. A. Levandis, *The Greek Foreign Debt and the Great Powers 1821–1898*; D. Dakin, *British and American Philhellenes*; and P. C. Pappas, *The United States and the Greek War for Independence 1821–1828*. C. Lloyd, *Lord Cochrane* is a useful biography, and F. Rosen, *Bentham, Byron and Greece* is good on the controversy over the loans.

1. Lloyd, p. 40
2. Lloyd, p. 169
3. Lloyd, p. 171
4. Finlay II, p. 337
5. Finlay II, p. 338
6. Lloyd, p. 171
7. Finlay II, p. 343
8. Dakin, *Philhellenes*, p. 36
9. Pappas, p. 104
10. Gordon II, p. 299
11. Pappas, p. 115
12. Rosen, p. 276
13. T. Lignádhis in *IEE* XII, p. 611

CHAPTER 28: DESPERATE REMEDIES (pp. 297–305)

Gordon and Finlay were in Greece during the events of this chapter, and Trikoúpis was closely involved in them, so the accounts of all three have a particular immediacy. For constitutional matters see Petropulos,

Dhimakópoulos, Svólos and Kaltchas, as for Chapter 13. C. M Woodhouse, *Capodistria* is indispensable for the life of Greece's first president.

1. Trikoúpis IV, pp. 10–11
2. Trikoúpis IV, p. 21
3. Gordon II, p. 305
4. Gordon II, p. 303
5. *Koloktrones*, tr. Edmonds, p. 243
6. Gordon II, p. 361
7. Finlay I, pp. 418–19
8. Gordon II, p. 362
9. Gordon II, p. 362
10. Woodhouse, *Capodistria*, p. 295
11. Woodhouse, *Capodistria*, pp. 309–10
12. Woodhouse, *Capodistria*, p. 345
13. Gordon II, p. 366
14. Gordon II, p. 410
15. Howe, *L&J*, pp. 193–5
16. Kaltchas, p. 53

CHAPTER 29: ATHENS, THE LAST OTTOMAN SUCCESS (pp. 306–15)

For the reform of the janissaries see Lewis, Zürcher, Shaw and Wheatcroft. The battle for Athens is covered at length in Gordon and Trikoúpis, and there are memoirs of participants by Makriyánnis, Howe, Thomas Whitcombe (whose brother shot Trelawny) and others. The introduction to Whitcombe's book by C. W. J. Eliot, its editor, gives an excellent outline of the events at Athens.

1. Crawley, p. 57
2. Wheatcroft, p. 92
3. Shaw, p. 19
4. Wheatcroft, p. 126
5. Gordon II, p. 339
6. *Makriyannis*, tr. Lidderdale, p. 113
7. Gordon II, p. 378
8. Gordon II, p. 391
9. Trikoúpis IV, p. 147
10. Trikoúpis IV, p. 148

11. Gordon II, p. 395
12. Whitcombe, p. 21
13. *Makriyannis*, tr. Lidderdale, p. 125

CHAPTER 30: THE TREATY OF LONDON AND THE ADMIRALS' INSTRUCTIONS
(pp. 316–24)

For the political and diplomatic background see Temperley, Crawley and E. Halévy, *The Liberal Awakening 1815–1830*. Egypt is covered in Douin, and the admirals and their instructions in C. M. Woodhouse, *The Battle of Navarino*. More information can be found in the Codrington papers, in the possession of the family.

1. Crawley, p. 75
2. Halévy, p. 248
3. Temperley, p. 605
4. Crawley, p. 79
5. Crawley, p. 63
6. Crawley, p. 71
7. Temperley, p. 402
8. Temperley, p. 403
9. Crawley, p. 82
10. Douin, p. 96
11. Codrington papers for comments on de Rigny and Heiden
12. Woodhouse, *Navarino*, pp. 46–7
13. Woodhouse, *Navarino*, p. 62
14. Woodhouse, *Navarino*, pp. 53–4

CHAPTER 31: NAVARINO (pp. 325–36)

The indispensable work is C. M. Woodhouse, *The Battle of Navarino*, which quotes at length from the major sources. Codrington published three documents in one volume: a compressed narrative of his actions, Dudley's queries and his answers, and papers relating to his recall. Further details are in the Codrington papers, in Henry Codrington's *Letters*, and in the anonymous *Précis de la bataille navale de Navarin*.

1. Henry Codrington, pp. 19–20
2. Woodhouse, *Navarino*, pp. 78–9
3. Henry Codrington, p. 22

4. *Kolokotrones*, tr. Edmonds, p. 270
5. Woodhouse, *Navarino*, p. 93
6. Woodhouse, *Navarino*, p. 93
7. Woodhouse, *Navarino*, p. 106
8. Woodhouse, *Navarino*, p. 115
9. *Précis*, p. 15
10. Woodhouse, *Navarino*, p. 117
11. Woodhouse, *Navarino*, p. 130
12. Henry Codrington, pp. 33–4
13. Woodhouse, *Navarino*, p. 129
14. Howe, *L&J*, p. 270
15. Woodhouse, *Navarino*, p. 163
16. E. Longford, *Wellington: Pillar of State*, London, 1975 (1st edn, 1972), p. 189
17. Codrington papers

CHAPTER 32: KAPODHISTRIAS, A BORDER AND A KING (pp. 337–51)

The main sources are C. M. Woodhouse, *Capodistria*; D. C. Fleming, *John Capodistrias and the Conference of London (1828–1831)*; C. W. Crawley, *The Question of Greek Independence*; and D. N. Dontas, *The Last Phase of the War of Independence in Western Greece*.

1. Trikoúpis IV, p. 242
2. Woodhouse, *Capodistria*, p. 443
3. Woodhouse, *Capodistria*, p. 372
4. Trikoúpis IV, p. 285
5. Trikoúpis IV, p. 303
6. Dontas, p. 68
7. *Kolokotrones*, tr. Edmonds, p. 288
8. Lloyd, p. 183
9. Trikoúpis IV, p. 229
10. Finlay II, p. 24
11. Woodhouse, *Capodistria*, p. 374
12. Dontas, p. 156
13. Trikoúpis IV, p. 294
14. Crawley, p. 120
15. *Kolokotrones*, tr. Edmonds, p. 294
16. Finlay II, p. 108

Select Bibliography

On this journey through the often tortuous paths of the Greek struggle we have had the company of a number of guides who were there at the time and speak from immediate experience, though each had to a certain extent his own agenda. Gordon is perhaps the surest of them, though he was not always completely open about the part he himself played. Finlay was a true friend of Greece, and spent most of the rest of his life in the country whose birth he had attended, but in his writings was always judgemental, often caustic and sometimes prejudiced; he aptly described himself as a disappointed enthusiast. Trikoúpis, though naturally seeing the conflict through Greek eyes and particularly those of his own primate class, was not blind to Greek faults, and provides detailed information going well beyond what he borrowed from Gordon. One warms to Makriyánnis, patriotic and conscientious, angry and compassionate, even if he sometimes placed himself nearer centre stage than was strictly justified. The bigoted François Pouqueville may not tell us the truth about what happened, but he does tell us what many would like to have happened. The sometimes gossipy detail of Kasomoúlis is in sharp contrast to the laconic style of Kolokotrónis, through which his feelings just occasionally blaze out. Raybaud always had an eye for the dramatic scene, while Howe was meticulous and sympathetic, a truly good man who could express his concerns in a telling phrase. And perhaps the most delightful companion of all was Byron.

Invaluable as these contemporary witnesses are, the story could not take shape without the many later works of analysis and interpretation, and the bibliography which follows includes those to which this book is most indebted. It is not a full bibliography, which would almost be a book in itself. For an excellent survey of relevant writings up to 1976 see the bibliographical essay in N. P. Diamandouros, ed., *Hellenism and the First Greek War of Liberation.*

Alexándris, K. A., *To Návtikon tou ipér Anexartisías Agónos tou 1821–1829* (The Navy in the Fight for Independence of 1821–1829), Athens, 1968.

Andrews, K., *Castles of the Morea*, Princeton, 1953.

Angelomatis-Tsougarakis, H., *The Eve of the Greek Revival*, London, 1990.

Ánninos, B., *I Apoloyía tou Odhysséos Andhroútsou* (The Defence of Odysseus Andhroútsos), Athens, 1925.

Anon., *Précis de la bataille navale de Navarin*, Paris, 1829.

Apomnimonévmata ton Agonistón tou '21 (Memoirs of the Fighters of '21), 20 vols, Athens, 1956–9.

Argenti, P., *The Massacres of Chios*, London, 1932.

Athanassoglou-Kallmyer, N. M., *French Images from the Greek War of Independence 1821–1830*, New Haven, 1989.

Baggally, J. W., *Ali Pasha and Great Britain*, Oxford, 1938.

Blaquiere, E., *The Greek Revolution*, London, 1824.

——, *Narrative of a Second Visit to Greece*, London, 1825.

Byron, Lord, ed. Marchand, L. A., *Byron's Letters and Journals* (Byron, *L&J*), 12 vols, London, 1973–81.

Capodistrias, see Kapodhístrias.

Clogg, R., ed., *The Struggle for Greek Independence*, London, 1973.

——, *The Movement for Greek Independence 1770–1821*, London, 1976.

Codrington, Sir E., *Compressed Narrative of the Proceedings of Vice-Admiral Sir Edward Codrington*, London, 1832.

——, *Queries and Answers*, London, undated.

——, *Documents relating to the Recall of Vice-Admiral Sir Edward Codrington*, London, undated.

Codrington, Sir H., ed. Lady Bourchier, *Selections from the Letters*, London, 1880.

Crane, D., *Lord Byron's Jackal*, London, 1998.

Crawley, C. W., *The Question of Greek Independence*, New York, 1973 (1st edn, Cambridge, 1930).

Dakin, D., *British and American Phihellenes*, Thessalonika, 1955.

——, *British Intelligence of Events in Greece 1824–1827*, Athens, 1959.

Diamandouros, N. P., ed., *Hellenism and the First Greek War of Liberation (1821–1830)*, Thessalonika, 1976.

Dhimakópoulos, G. D., *I Dhiikitikí Orgánosis katá tin Ellinikín Epanástasin 1821–1827* (Administrative Organisation during the Greek Revolution 1821–1827), Athens, 1966.

Dontas, D. N., *The Last Phase of the War of Independence in Western Greece*, Thessalonika, 1966.

Douin, G., *Les Premières Frégates de Mohamed Aly (1824–1827)*, Cairo, 1926.

Emerson, J., Pecchio, G., and Humphreys, W. H., *A Picture of Greece in 1825*, London, 1826.

Finlay, G., *History of the Greek Revolution*, 2 vols, London, 1971 (1st edn, Oxford, 1877).

Fleming, D. C., *John Capodistrias and the Conference of London (1828–1831)*, Thessalonika, 1970.

Fleming, K. E., *The Muslim Bonaparte: Diplomacy and Orientalism in Ali Pasha's Greece*, Princeton, 1999.

Frazee, C. A., *The Orthodox Church and Independent Greece 1821–1852*, Cambridge, 1969.

Gamba, P., *A Narrative of Lord Byron's Last Journey to Greece*, Paris, 1825.

Germanos, see Yermanós.

Gibb, H., and Bowen, H., *Islamic Society and the West*, 2 vols, London, 1957.

Gordon, T., *History of the Greek Revolution*, 2 vols, London, 1844.

Green, P. J. and R. L., *Sketches of the War in Greece*, London, 1827.

Halévy, E., *The Liberal Awakening 1815–1830*, London, 1926.

Howe, S. G., *An Historical Sketch of the Greek Revolution*, New York, 1828 (parts 1–4 of 7, Austin, Texas, 1966).

——, ed. Richards, L. E., *Letters and Journals* (Howe, *L&J*), London, 1907.

Humphreys, W. H., see Emerson.

Istoría tou Ellinikoú Éthnous (*IEE*) (*History of the Greek Nation*), vols XI and XII, Athens 1975.

Jarvis, G., ed., Arnakis, G. G., *George Jarvis: His Journals and Related Documents*, Thessalonika, 1965.

Kalligas, A. G. and H. A., *Monemvasia*, Athens, 1986 (in English).

Kaltchas, N., *Introduction to the Constitutional History of Modern Greece*, New York, 1940.

Kanínias, S. A., *Elevthería* (Freedom), Athens, 1997 (in Greek and English).

Kapodhístrias, I., *Aperçu de ma carrière publique*, St Petersburg, 1868 (in English, *Letters to the Tsar Nicholas I*, Athens, 1977).

Kasomoúlis, N. K., *Enthimímata Stratiotiká* (Military Reminiscences), 3 vols, Athens, 1940.

Keegan, J., *The Price of Admiralty*, London, 1988.

Koliopoulos, J. S., *Brigands with a Cause*, Oxford, 1987.

Kolokotrónis, Th., *Apomnimonévmata* (Memoirs), Athens, 1852.

———, tr. Edmonds, E. M., *Kolokotrones, the Klepht and the Warrior*, London, 1892.

Larrabee, S. A., *Hellas Observed*, New York, 1957.

Levandis, J. A., *The Greek Foreign Debt and the Great Powers 1821–1898*, New York, 1944.

Lewis, B., *The Emergence of Modern Turkey*, Oxford, 1961.

Lloyd, C., *Lord Cochrane*, New York, 1998 (1st edn, London, 1947).

Long, H., *Greek Fire: The Massacres of Chios*, Bristol, 1992.

Mákris, N. D., *Istoría tou Mesolongíou* (History of Mesolongi), vol. XIX of *Apomnimonévmata ton Agonistón tou '21* (Memoirs of the Fighters of '21), see above.

Makriyánnis, *Apomnimonévmata* (Memoirs), Athens, 1964.

———, tr. Lidderdale, H. A., *Makriyannis: The Memoirs of General Makriyannis 1797–1864*, Oxford, 1966.

Manwaring, G. E., and Dobrée, B., *The Floating Republic*, London, 1935.

Marchand, L. A., *Byron: A Biography*, 3 vols, London, 1957.

———, *Byron: A Portrait*, London, 1971.

Míchos, A. N., *Apomnimonévmata tis Dhévteras Poliorkías tou Mesolongíou 1825–1826* (Memoirs of the Second Siege of Mesolongi 1825–1826), Athens, 1883.

Moore, D. L., *Lord Byron: Accounts Rendered*, London, 1974.

Neroúlos, R., *Histoire moderne de la Grèce*, Geneva, 1928.

Nicolson, H., *Byron: The Last Journey*, London, 1924.

———, *The Congress of Vienna*, London, 1946.

Notáras, I., *O Patriotikós Agónas tou Koraí* (The Patriotic Struggle of Koraís), Thessalonika, 1976.

Origo, I., *The Last Attachment*, London, 1949.

Palmer, A., *Alexander I*, London, 1974.

Papadhópoulos, K., *Odysseus Andhroútsos* (in Greek), vol. XII of *Apomnimonévmata ton Agonistón tou '21* (Memoirs of the Fighters of '21), see above.

Papadopoullos, T. H., *The Greek Church and People under Turkish Domination*, rev. edn Aldershot, 1990 (1st edn, Brussels, 1952).

Papamichalópoulos, K. N., *Poliorkía kai Álosis tis Monemvasías* (Siege and Capture of Monemvasía), Athens, 1874.

Pappas, P. C., *The United States and the Greek War for Independence 1821–1828*, New York, 1985.

Pecchio, G., see Emerson.

Perrevós, Ch., *Síntomos Viographía tou Aidhímou Ríga Pheréou* (Short Biography of Rígas Pheréos of Blessed Memory), Athens, 1971 (1st edn, Athens, 1860).

Petropulos, J. A., *Politics and Statecraft in the Kingdom of Greece 1833–1843*, Princeton, 1968.

Photákos, *Víos tou Pápa Phléssa* (Life of Papaphléssas), Athens, 1868.

Pouqueville, F. C. H. L., *Histoire de la régénération de la Grèce*, 4 vols, Paris, 1825.

Protopsáltis, E. G., *Alexándhros Mavrokordhátos*, Athens, 1982.

Prousis, T. C., *Russian Society and the Greek Revolution*, DeKalb, Illinois, 1994.

Rádhos, K., *O Ástinx kai to Érgon tou en Elládhi* (Hastings and his Work in Greece), Athens, 1928.

Raybaud, M., *Mémoires sur la Grèce*, 2 vols, Paris, 1824.

Rodger, N. A. M., *The Wooden World*, London, 1986.

Rosen F., *Bentham, Byron and Greece*, Oxford, 1992.

Roússos-Milidhónis, M., *To Mnimío Philellínon sto Návplio* (The Philhellene Memorial in Navplion), Athens, 1991.

Runciman, S., *The Fall of Constantinople*, Cambridge, 1965.

——, *The Great Church in Captivity*, Cambridge, 1968.

St Clair, W., *That Greece Might Still Be Free*, Oxford, 1972.

——, *Trelawny: The Incurable Romancer*, London, 1977.

Saitas, I., *Mani*, Athens, 1990 (in English).

Shaw, S. J. and E. K., *History of the Ottoman Empire and Modern Turkey*, 2 vols, Cambridge, 1977.

Skiotis, D. N., 'From Bandit to Pasha: First Steps in the Rise to Power of Ali of Tepelen 1750–1784', *Int. J. Middle East Stud.* 2 (1971), 219–44.

Spiromílios, *Chronikó tou Mesolongíou 1825–1826* (Chronicle of Mesolongi 1825–1826), Athens, 1969 (1st edn, Athens, 1926).

Stasinópoulos, K. A., *To Mesolóngi*, 3 vols, Athens, 1925.

Svólos, A., *Ta Elliniká Sintágmata 1822–1952* (The Greek Constitutions 1822–1952), Athens, 1972.

Temperley, H., *The Foreign Policy of Canning 1822–1827*, London, 1925.

Theocharides, L., *The Greek National Revival and the French Enlightenment*, Ann Arbor, Michigan, 1975.

Thomson, D., *Europe since Napoleon*, London, 1966 (1st edn, London, 1957).

Trelawny, E. J., *Recollections of the Last Days of Shelley and Byron*, London, 1931 (1st edn, London, 1906).

Trikoúpis, S., *Istoría tis Ellinikís Epanastáseos* (History of the Greek Revolution), 4 vols, Athens, 1996 (1st edn, London, 1853–7).

Vakalópoulos, A. E., *Ta Elliniká Stratévmata tou 1821* (The Greek Armies of 1821), Thessalonika, 1991.

Vasdravellis, J. K., *Klephts, Armatoles and Pirates in Macedonia*, Thessalonika, 1975.

Vikélas, D., *Loukís Láras*, Athens, 1879 (in Greek).

Víos, S. G., *I Sphayí tis Chíou* (The Massacre of Chios), Chios, 1989.

Vizántios, Ch. S., *O Táktikos Strátos 1821–1833* (The Regular Army 1821–1833), Athens, 1874.

Vlasto, A. M., *A History of the Island of Chios*, London, 1913.

Voúrnas, T., ed., *Philikí Etería*, Athens, undated (in Greek).

Waddington, G., *A Visit to Greece in 1823 and 1824*, London, 1825.

Wheatcroft, A., *The Ottomans*, London, 1993.

Whitcombe, T. D., ed. Eliot, C. W. J., *Campaign of the Falieri and Piraeus in the Year 1827*, Princeton, 1992.

Woodhouse, C. M., *The Greek War of Independence*, London, 1952.

——, *The Battle of Navarino*, London, 1965.

——, *The Philhellenes*, London, 1969.

——, *Capodistria*, Oxford, 1973.

——, *Rhigas Velestinlis*, Limni, 1995.

Yermanós, G., *Apomnimonévmata* (Memoirs), vol, III of *Apomnimonévmata ton Agonistón tou '21* (*Memoirs of the Fighters of '21*), see above.

Zürcher, E. J., *Turkey*, London, 1993.

INDEX

Index